FROM THE COUNTRY OF EIGHT ISLANDS

WITHDRAWN

10/90 $16.00

HIROAKI SATO was born in Japan and has lived in New York City since March 1968. Among the Japanese poets he has translated are Hagiwara Sakutarō, Miyazawa Kenji, and Takamura Kōtarō. He is the sole translator for the Floating World Modern Poets Series of Chicago Review Press, in which four volumes have been published so far.

BURTON WATSON received his education in Chinese and Japanese literature from Columbia University and Kyoto University (as a Ford Foundation Overseas Fellow). He has taught Chinese and Japanese language and literature at Columbia, Stanford, and Kyoto universities, and has published over twenty volumes of translation from and studies of Chinese and Japanese literature. In 1979, Mr. Watson received the Gold Medal Award of the Translation Center at Columbia University. He currently resides in Japan.

From the Country
of Eight Islands

An Anthology of Japanese Poetry

Edited and Translated by

HIROAKI SATO and BURTON WATSON

with an Introduction by Thomas Rimer

Associate Editor: Robert Fagan

COLUMBIA UNIVERSITY PRESS   *New York*
1986

Copyright © 1981 by Hiroaki Sato and Burton Watson
Published by arrangement with Doubleday & Company, Inc.
Printed in the United States of America

Library of Congress Cataloging-in-Publication Data

From the country of eight islands.

Bibliography: p.
Includes index.
1. Japanese poetry—Translations into English.
2. English poetry—Translations from Japanese.
I. Sato, Hiroaki, 1942– . II. Watson, Burton, 1925–
[PL782.E3F74 1986]   895.6'1'008   86-7881
ISBN 0-231-06395-4

Columbia University Press Morningside Edition 1986
Columbia University Press, New York

ACKNOWLEDGMENTS

Acknowledgment is made to Grove Press, Inc., for permission to reprint "To Comfort My Little Son and Daughter" and Sesson Yūbai's poem ("In heaven and earth") from *Anthology of Japanese Literature* by Donald Keene, © 1955 by Grove Press; to Chicago Review Press for permission to reprint "Spring & Asura," "Bamboo & Oak," "The Last Farewell," "Okhotsk Elegy," "The Prefectural Engineer's Statement Regarding Clouds," and "The Breeze Comes Filling the Valley" from *Spring & Asura: Poems of Kenji Miyazawa*, translated by Hiroaki Sato, © 1973 by Chicago Review Press; "Sleeping Wrestler," "Dream of Barcelona: My Ancient World," "Winter: 1955," and "Forecome and Come" from *Mutsuo Takahashi: Poems of a Penisist*, translated by Hiroaki Sato, © 1975 by Chicago Review Press; "Pastorale," "Still Life," "The Past," "Confession," "Coolie," "Ode to an Old Man," "Diarrhea," "Negative," "Quiet House," and "Lilac Garden" from *Lilac Garden: Poems of Minoru Yoshioka*, translated by Hiroaki Sato, © 1976 by Chicago Review Press; and "Between—," "Let Me Tell You about Myself," "Just the Two of Us," "Please Say Something," "see you soon," "There's Nothing to Do in New York," and "Age" from *See You Soon: Poems of Taeko Tomioka*, translated by Hiroaki Sato, © 1979 by Chicago Review Press; to the University of Tokyo Press for permission to reprint "Bamboo," "Sickly Face at the Bottom of the Ground," "Spring Night," "Sunny Spring," "Lover of Love," "White Public Benches," "The Hand Is a Cake," "Twilight Room," "The Army," and "In the Horse Carriage" from *Howling at the Moon: Poems of Hagiwara Sakutarō*, translated by Hiroaki Sato, © 1978 by University of Tokyo Press; and to The University Press of Hawaii for permission to reprint "To Someone," "In Adoration of Love," "Cathedral in the Thrashing Rain," "Comic Verse," "Knife Whetter," "Lemon Elegy," "Beautiful Dead Leaf," "Shōan Temple," "Sculpting in the Imperial Presence," "Cooperative Council," and "The Day of Pearl Harbor" from *Chieko and Other Poems of Takamura Kōtarō*, translated by Hiroaki Sato, © 1980 by The University Press of Hawaii.

Acknowledgment is also made to the editors and publishers of the following, in which some of the other translations first appeared: *Assassin, Chicago Review, Cicada, Evergreen Magazine, Footprint Magazine, Frogpond, Gay Sunshine, Granite, Hawaii Review, Japanese Literature in Chinese, Montemora, New Directions, Partisan Review, Pequod, Plum, Ryōkan: Zen Monk-Poet of Japan, Ten Japanese Poets, World,* and *Zero.*

TRANSLATORS' NOTE

In compiling an anthology, one can include a few works by a great many writers, or limit the number of writers and give a larger selection from each. We chose the latter course here because we thought it would convey a clearer and more effective picture of the nature and worth of Japanese poetry.

In general, Sato did the planning and Watson the editing. We checked each other's work, but each is responsible for his selections and translations as they appear here. Sato translates "traditional" tanka, hokku, and haiku into one-line form except when, as in the case of Ishikawa Takuboku, the lineation is specified by the poet; elsewhere he more often than not translates the combination of 5–7 or 7–5 syllable units as one line. Watson generally translates 5-syllable and 7-syllable units as single lines. In *Man'yōshū* or *Man'yōshū* style poems, Watson sometimes leaves *makura kotoba*, or pillow words, untranslated, a practice Sato deplores.

Most titles or headings to poems have been translated in full, though in a few cases they have for the sake of convenience been abbreviated or somewhat adapted in translation. Titles supplied by the translator are enclosed in quotation marks, and explanations preceding the poems not in the original appear in brackets.

Because the selections have been drawn from such a wide variety of works, and because no standard texts exist for many of the poems translated, it has not been feasible to include identification of the sources of the originals. At some future date, we hope it may be possible to publish an accompanying volume containing the original texts of the poems.

All Japanese names except that of the translator Sato are given in Japanese fashion: family name first, given name second.

After their initial appearance, Japanese poets are sometimes referred to by their given name alone, according to Japanese custom—for example, Matsuo Bashō at the first occurrence; thereafter, simply Bashō.

In poetry written before the beginning of the modern period in 1868, the months referred to are those of the lunar calendar, in which the first month began sometime between January 21 and February 19 by the Western calendar and was counted as the first month of spring. Thus, for example, the seventh month is regarded as the first month of autumn and corresponds roughly to August and early September. This should be kept in mind when attempting to understand the nature imagery of the poems.

Among the many persons Sato wishes to thank for helping him in translation—with patience, goodwill, and love of the English language—are Robert Fagan, Michael O'Brien, Thomas Rimer, Nancy Rossiter, Kyoko Selden, and Eleanor Wolff. Watson thanks Barbara Stoler Miller and Eliot Weinberger for their much-appreciated interest and encouragement.

Hiroaki Sato and Burton Watson

CONTENTS

THE AGE OF TANKA

THE AGE OF RENGA

THE MODERN AGE

A GUIDE TO THE PRONUNCIATION OF JAPANESE

There are five vowels in Japanese. Each vowel can be long or short. Long vowels are indicated by macrons when in romanized form; for example, ō or ū. Rough equivalents with English pronunciation are as follows:

a as in *father*
i as in *machine*
u as in *rhubarb*
e as in *get*
o as in *horse*

The consonants are pronounced as in English.

AN OUTLINE OF MAJOR PERIODS IN JAPANESE HISTORY

NAME	APPROXIMATE DATES	IMPORTANT COLLECTIONS MENTIONED IN THE ANTHOLOGY	
Nara	710–794	712	Kojiki
		760?	Man'yōshū
Heian	794–1185	905?	Kokinshū
		1180?	Ryōjin hishō
Kamakura	1185–1392	1188	Senzaishū
		1206?	Shinkokinshū
		1370?	Tsukubashū
Muromachi	1392–1568	1530?	Inutsukubashū
Momoyama	1568–1600		
Tokugawa/Edo	1600–1868		
Modern Period	1868–present		
Meiji	1868–1912	1882	Shintaishishō
Taishō	1912–1926		
Shōwa	1926–present		

INTRODUCTION

I

The history of Japanese poetry is long and rich; poetic possibilities first explored in the earliest examples recorded continue to unfold today. The earliest fragments of Japanese poetry are preserved in ancient historical works such as the *Kojiki* (Record of Ancient Matters), compiled early in the eighth century, and those poems doubtless represent an oral literature that extends back many centuries. They are short, quite free in form, and simple in utterance, seemingly spontaneous outbursts inspired by the beauties of nature, the passions of love, or the power of the ruler and his court.

The *Man'yōshū* (Collection of Myriad Leaves), a vast anthology containing over four thousand poems composed, according to traditional attributions, over a period of several centuries, was compiled late in the eighth century. The *Man'yōshū* marks the real beginning of the tradition of Japanese poetry and contains poems so powerful in artistic and emotional appeal that they have seldom if ever been surpassed in later periods. Although the anthology was compiled by court officials, the authors of the poems range from emperors and priests to anonymous soldiers and peasants. From the evidence provided by the poems themselves, the art of poetry at this period was neither a hereditary calling nor the function of a particular social class. Nor was the composition of poetry reserved to particular gifted individuals. Rather, poetry was a part of daily life, a means of expression for anyone who felt the need to manifest emotion through ordered language. The underlying tone of the *Man'yōshū* was true to the national character; its virtues were those of openness, directness of expression, and intensity of feeling. (In later periods, when poetic tastes came to be dominated by members of the court aristocracy, these qualities were overlaid with an emphasis on artifice and indirection. In such an atmosphere, displays of wit and verbal cleverness were much admired, but genuine sensibility and sincerity of feeling, or *makoto*, remained the ultimate virtues.) Subjects first treated in the *Man'yōshū* have continued to find powerful expression down to the present century. The beauty and awesomeness of nature, love and separation, laments for the dead and the impermanence of life, affairs of the common people, and the loneliness of soldiers far away from home and family all echo through poetry composed in generation after generation.

The *Man'yōshū* employs two major poetic forms: the tanka (short poem), which consists of 31 syllables arranged in units of 5, 7, 5, 7, and 7 syllables, and the chōka (long poem), which uses the same basic units of 5 and 7 syllables but is unlimited in length, although it seldom exceeds a hundred units or lines. Nothing comparable to an epic form of poetry developed in Japan. (For additional information on these and other terms used in the anthology, see the Glossary, pp. 627–29.)

The precise identity of the compiler or compilers of the *Man'yōshū* is uncertain. In succeeding centuries, the court took an increasingly active role in encouraging poetry and defining canons of taste, and for some reason not yet fully understood, tanka verse of 31 syllables became the standard form of court poetry. Poetry contests were held, and a series of anthologies were compiled on imperial command to preserve the best works of the time. For a man or woman of the aristocracy, poetry became an undertaking of intense seriousness, a means of attracting notice or advancing a career, and to have a work included in an imperial anthology might well represent the crowning achievement of a lifetime. The conception of poetry as a group activity, rather than as a solitary pursuit—a principle so important in the composition of renga or linked verse—had its beginnings in the court tradition.

In addition to the imperial anthologies, works of individual poets were compiled, and schools of poetry appeared to teach those who aspired to write poetry, often espousing rival esthetic ideals and handing down carefully guarded secrets of the art. Poetry of the kind recognized in court circles thus became less a form of spontaneous expression than the product of long practice and careful study of the works of the past, an art that only the upper classes had the leisure to pursue. In addition, the court, as the repository for the highest cultural ideals and accomplishments, was also responsible for the development of literary works in prose and poetry written directly in Chinese. As early as the *Man'yōshū*, influences from Chinese poetry and culture can be found in Japanese poetry. At that time, China was enjoying one of its greatest periods of artistic, political, and cultural maturity during the T'ang Dynasty (618–907), and Japan learned an enormous amount in the spheres of linguistic and poetic modes of expression from its continental neighbor. Court officials and other highly educated persons expressed their thoughts and feelings in Chinese in somewhat the same fashion that medieval clerics in Europe used Latin. The tradition of kanshi or poems written in classical Chinese has continued on and off until the present century.

The development of these sophisticated traditions did not mean, however, that poetry ceased to play a part in the lives of the common people. Examples translated in this book begin with selections of poems by border guards and other anonymous figures in the *Man'yōshū*, followed by Shinto dance songs, then by excerpts from the *Ryōjin hishō* (Secret Selection of Songs) and other collections from the Heian period, some love songs from the *Kanginshū* (Collection of Leisure Songs), compiled in 1518, and a selection of folksongs of the Tokugawa period. The kind of popular sentiment expressed in this poetry remains just as genuine, and is just as effective in its own way, as much that was written in the high literary forms.

The tanka became the dominant form of poetry in the Heian and medieval periods, and because of this the supposition has sometimes been made—incorrectly—that Japanese poetry is invariably brief. At the time of the *Man'yōshū*, Japanese poetry included long poems, and the tradition produced a resurgence of extended forms in the twentieth century. The preference for tanka and later for the 5–7–5 syllable hokku popular in the Tokugawa period has often been explained, or explained away, through linguistic configurations and limitations. Nevertheless, there has always existed a tension in the tradition between the self-contained brevity of a single poetic unit and the larger scope of a more general poetic conception. Even in the *Man'yōshū*, headnotes were sometimes provided in order to give the setting of a poem as a proper background to the lyrical impulse (see, for example, the various poems by Ōtomo no Yakamochi). In imperial and other anthologies, more systematic designs were imposed by the editors, who selected and arranged poems by different authors in seasonal or other sequences in order to suggest, by means of juxtaposition, association, and progression, a composite image larger than, and sometimes slightly at variance with, any one of its particular aspects. Fujiwara no Teika's compilation of one hundred three tanka is translated here in its entirety to show this technique (p. 202).

Toward the end of the Heian period, poets composing in the tanka form began to follow a tendency to divide the 31-syllable form and organize images into two smaller parts of 5–7–5 and 7–7 syllables. By the fourteenth century, such a division had made dominant the poetic form of renga, in which usually two or more poets wrote alternating 5–7–5 and 7–7 syllable parts. Although any two consecutive parts—but not more—of a renga were to relate directly, such linking did permit the development of longer poetic structures. The rules for the composition of these verses became exceedingly complex and required extensive training and practice on the part of the participants. The amount of concentration and cooperation required for successful renga composition might be compared with the challenge of playing chamber music: in both cases, each participant must listen carefully to his companions as well as to himself in order to keep the momentum going. The pleasure of "performing" poetry in a group, already an important element in the tanka contests of the imperial court, flowered in the cooperative esthetic of the renga.

In content, there were two kinds of renga: the formal, serious kind that stressed elegance in the court poetry tradition, and the light, humorous kind that stressed earthiness and realism. The latter, known as haikai no renga or simply haikai, often overwhelmed the serious renga in sheer popularity in the fourteenth and fifteenth centuries and became predominant thereafter. In the Edo period Matsuo Bashō elevated haikai no renga to high art, giving it a spirit that, while still lyrical, was playful and contemporary in feeling, vocabulary, and theme.

In renga, the opening part, or hokku, made up of 5–7–5 syllables, was intended to set the general tone of the links that followed. By tradition, and because renga composition was essentially a group activity, a sequence was usually required to begin in a propitious, congratulatory, lofty, or otherwise affirmative tone. Often, the principal guest would use the hokku to compliment the host, who in turn would write the following part, the wakiku, deprecating himself or returning the compliment. Mainly because of this practice, hokku remained positive in outlook long after they came to be written independently as they did early in the development of renga. In the modern period, independent hokku were given the designation of haiku and are so referred to today.

The general principle of adding short, self-contained poetic units together to illustrate a larger conception continues to show vitality in the modern period: Saitō Mokichi in his tanka sequence *Mother Dies* (p. 456) uses his particular psychological insights to create a remarkably personal vision of reality while remaining well within the scope of the traditional forms. His fifty-nine poems are each complete and perfect in themselves, yet each contributes to a larger "poem" the author has in mind.

While the Japanese tradition gained newer forms, such as haikai no renga, poets also continued writing in the older forms. In the Tokugawa period there were distinguished practitioners of Chinese verse and of tanka as well. These forms managed to serve as vehicles for the expression of poetic sentiments until the middle of the nineteenth century, when the coming of the West and the opening of Japan brought profound changes to every aspect of Japanese life. Many poets found it difficult to express their emotions in forms as restricted as tanka, renga, hokku, and kanshi, and eventually sought to derive inspiration from the longer, freer forms of European poetry. The *Shintaishishō* (A Selection of New Style Verse), published in 1882, introduced British and American poetry in translation, plus a few original poems in the same style by Japanese authors. Other anthologies of translations brought French and German poetry to Japanese readers. There was an intense period of experimentation from the 1890s to the period of World War I. With the publication of Hagiwara Sakutarō's anthology *Tsuki ni hoeru* (Howling at the Moon) in 1917, many Japanese felt that modern poetry in their own language had come of age. Poets since that time have continued to extend their interests into politics, philosophy, and psychology, just as poets have done in the West. The longer forms these subjects require have become the accepted vehicle for contemporary verse, although the tanka and the haiku in particular continue to attract certain of the younger poets.

This anthology, then, is designed to show something of the complexity and richness of well over a thousand years of poetry. The preface to the tenth-century anthology, *Kokinshū* (Collection of Waka of Ancient and Modern Times), states that poetry should "move heaven and earth, stir the feelings of the unseen gods and spirits, soften the relations between man and woman, and soothe the heart of the fierce warrior." In transmuted terms, that prescript remains a strong one today: the poetry of every period represented in the anthology shows a fruitful mingling of new and traditional ways to manifest that ancient yet timeless intent.

II

In order to give some idea of the musical and esthetic effect of Japanese poetry, a simple description of the language in which it is written may be useful. Although Japanese has gone through many changes since the time of the *Man'yōshū*, particularly in the writing system, certain general principles apply to much of the poetic tradition. Japanese is an agglutinative language that strings together short semantic elements to create long and often very complex word formations. Japanese verbs in particular are often highly inflected through the addition of suffixes expressing variations of mood and probability concerning the action. A single verb form may thus occupy an entire 5- or 7-syllable unit of a poem. In addition, the language employs a variety of emotive particles used to vary the tone and to add to the exclamatory force of an utterance. The result is a flowing syntax that, although often imprecise in meaning, is capable of expressing subtle shades of emotion.

The sound system of Japanese is quite simple, although it was evidently slightly more complex in the early periods. Nearly all the syllables in the language, when represented in a Western alphabet, consist of a consonant followed by a vowel. There is no stress accent, each syllable being pronounced with more or less equal emphasis. Meters based on stress, familiar to readers of English poetry, become virtually impossible. Since nearly every syllable ends in a vowel, of which there are only five, rhyming becomes so simple that it is pointless, so end rhyme has never become an important technique in Japanese poetry. And while pitch accent may serve as a factor in poetic diction, there seems little general agreement among scholars as to what its effect might be on the prosody or other aspects of Japanese poetry.

As noted above, the basic form employed in traditional poetry is distinguished by its use of units of 5 and 7 syllables, and nearly all its poetic forms are of a fixed length. Tanka is restricted to 31 syllables, and what is now called haiku in 17 syllables is constructed of a pattern of 5, 7, and 5 syllables. Other literary devices include parallelism, conventional epithets prefixed to certain nouns, and particularly in later poetry, double entendres, word associations, and allusive variations on phrases from earlier poetry.

Burton Watson has supplied the following example by way of illustrating some of these characteristics:

> Here is a well-known work by a semi-legendary poet of the Heian period named Semimaru. It is in tanka form and describes a famous barrier or checkpoint near Kyoto on the road connecting the capital with eastern Japan. Friends or relatives of persons journeying east frequently accompanied the travelers as far as the barrier before taking leave of them. The barrier was located at a place named Ausaka (Ōsaka in modern pronunciation), which means "meeting slope."

> *Kore ya kono*
> *yuku mo kaeru mo*
> *wakaretsutsu*
> *shiru mo shiranu mo*
> *Ausaka no seki*

> This is the spot—
> where those going, those returning
> take their leave,
> those who know each other, those who don't,
> the barrier at Meeting Slope

The poem plays on the meaning of the place name Ausaka (meeting slope, contrary to its name, is really a place of parting), and through its rapid succession of verbs suggests the bustling activity of the barrier and the bitterness of the leave-takings conducted there. But the real beauty of the poem lies in the repetition of the *mo* particle and the wonderful interweaving of "k" and "s" sounds. It is euphonies and musical resonances of this type, and the intrinsic flowing quality of the language, rather than elaborate prosodic devices, that in most cases account for the particular appeal of Japanese poetry in the original.

III

Within the Japanese tradition, there exists a remarkable variety of thematic and artistic concerns, yet there remains some suggestion of an implicit unity as well. What gives this sense of cohesion? An examination—and reexamination—of the various poems included here will reveal a resonance of forms, images, and ideas which may help define the special sense of the world that hovers unseen behind the different texts.

The first and most obvious source of unity has to do with the close relationship poets in all periods show for the manifestations and processes of nature. Some aspect or phenomenon of the natural world, as witnessed by the poet, often serves as a kernel for individual insight. Even when such personal observation seems to lie well within the canons of precedent and taste so important in court poetry, it is the presence of this close and genuinely felt observation that invariably gives a good poem both its emotional center and its sharpness of focus. True, the subject matter of much nature poetry seems, superficially, to be restricted, but the natural images themselves possess a history of their own. Bamboo is as important in the *Kojiki* of the eighth century as it is in the poetry of Hagiwara Sakutarō (1886–1942), and the image of dew is as moving for Saigyō (1118–1190) ("Drops of dew," p. 178) as it is for Kobayashi Issa (1763–1827) ("The world of dew," p. 399).

Tradition and the individual talent of the poet are meant to come together to produce a poem that, while within the boundaries of literary taste and possibility, also gives sufficient scope to the poet to observe and comment both on what he has personally felt and on how he responds to what he has read and learned of earlier literary reactions to the same sort of natural stimulus. A new poem on, say, cherry blossoms can thus serve not only as a record of the poet's own observations on nature, but also as his personal commentary on the way in which others before him have responded to a similar scene. A contemporary English-language reader will doubtless grasp the beauty of the individual observation quickly, but may quite understandably find difficulty in placing that observation in the larger scheme of literary precedent. This anthology helps document the growth of the tradition and provides some record of how the central natural images in Japanese poetry grew and changed over the centuries.

The literary purposes behind a close observation of nature changed and expanded as the tradition grew more sophisticated. The assumptions about nature and its purposes revealed in the *Man'yōshū* are rather artless and certainly less self-conscious than they were to become in the work of later poets. Still, even in that earliest collection, the first stirrings of an esthetic that makes use of nature as a metaphor for the transcendental can easily be seen. In a beautiful tanka by an eighth century priest, Mansei, the mechanism for creating a linguistic and spiritual bridge from observation to abstraction is constructed with consummate art:

> To what shall I compare this world? A boat that rows off with morning, leaving no trace behind.

As such methods grew in sophistication in the later Heian and Kamakura periods, they came to be defined as an artistic quality or virtue called *yūgen*, the representation of the ineffable or the unseen, a summoning up of what lies beneath the surface of perceived nature. Yūgen, as described by the poet and critic Kamo no Chōmei (1153–1216), became a central principle in a metaphysical concept of the poetic art:

> [T]hose who have attained the state say it is in essence an overtone that does not appear in words, a feeling that is not visible in form. . . . For example, the evening sky in autumn has no color, no voice. And yet, though there seems to be no

reason why this should happen, you find tears welling up in your eyes. But those without heart think nothing of such a sight, appreciating only the blossoms and crimson leaves that are so obvious to the eye. . . . Again, when you look at the autumn hills through rifts in the mist, what you can see is vague, but what lies beyond enchants you, making you wonder endlessly how interesting the whole spread of crimson leaves must be; such a view is superior to seeing it all too clearly. (TR. SATO)

In such an esthetic scheme, a poem was intended to remain grounded on one level in a directly felt observation of nature, behind or beyond which some intimation of the existence of a different or higher reality was suggested. Poems fully given over to abstraction, such as the following by Minamoto Sanetomo (1192–1219), the Third Kamakura shogun and a student of Fujiwara no Teika (1162–1241), did not challenge the dominant esthetic:

This world—
call it an image
caught in a mirror—
real it is not,
nor unreal either.

Rather, the stress was on a mystic closeness with nature on the part of the poet, a closeness that, allied to an exacting craft, was considered the best means to achieve genuine poetic insight. Matsuo Bashō (1644–1694) understood this principle to its fullest, as his disciple Hattori Tohō (1657–1730) recorded in his *Sanzōshi*, three notebooks in which he took down his master's various teachings:

"Learn about the pine from the pine, learn about the bamboo from the bamboo"—this dictum of our teacher means that you must forgo your subjectivity. If you interpret "learn" in your own way, you will end up not learning. To "learn" here means to enter the object; then if its essence reveals itself and moves you, you may come up with a verse. Even if you seem to have described the object, unless [your description] has an emotion that comes out of it naturally, the object and your self will remain separated, and the emotion you have described will not have attained sincerity, because it will be something made up by your subjectivity. (TR. SATO)

The means to achieve a mystic union of personal emotion and literary craft was given its first classic statement in the opening lines of Fujiwara no Teika's advice to other tanka poets in the *Eiga Taigai* (An Outline for Composing Tanka) written about 1222 and translated here. Teika, generally considered the greatest critic in the tradition of court poetry, laid down principles that were influential for his contemporaries and for all those who followed:

> In emotion, newness is foremost: look for sentiments others have yet to sing, and sing them. In diction, use the old: don't go further back than the Three Anthologies, but use the diction of the masters. . . . (p. 202)

Such sentiments, and the examples of suitable poems Teika provided, helped solidify the tradition that still remains visible in the work of such important modern poets as Masaoka Shiki (1867–1902) or even in the work of Ozaki Hōsai (1885–1926), who strove to create a free-form style of haiku. In more subtle ways, the same concerns are expressed in a writer of modern poetry like Miyazawa Kenji (1896–1933), whose poems seem often to represent a final affirmation of the poetic self as defined through an identification with the great natural forces in the world.

Then too, as the anthology shows, the tradition of Japanese poetry, like others, possesses figures who serve as models to be emulated, despaired over, or frowned upon, depending on the poet, his period, and his own sense of vocation. In a sense, most of the poets included here have served as models at one time or another, but among them are those who tower over the others and who cast long shadows, even today.

The earliest of such poets is Kakinomoto no Hitomaro (c. 700), whose moving elegies in the *Man'yōshū* are among the most treasured older poems in the language. A contemporary poet such as Anzai Hitoshi (born 1919) can conjure up, with the full emotional support of his Japanese readers, his own vision of that archaic world in a poem called "Hitomaro" (see p. 578). For Anzai and his audience, Hitomaro's name serves not as an archaic reference, but rather as some vital chord that, when struck, still produces strong overtones. In the early Heian period, Ki no Tsurayuki (c. 868–c. 916), the chief editor of the *Kokinshū* and the author of the *Tosa nikki* (Tosa Diary), became the first of the great poet-critics whose taste set the directions for tanka poetry. Two hundred fifty years later, the Buddhist priest and recluse Saigyō deepened Tsurayuki's concepts and provided possibilities for a more profound pathos, yet Saigyō's own poems on death (see p. 180) owe much in style and mood to models he found in the *Tosa Diary*.

Tsurayuki's role as a poet-critic was taken over in turn by Fujiwara no Teika. The Nō play *Teika*, written about one hundred fifty years after his death and attributed to one of the great poets of the medieval theater, Komparu Zenchiku (1405–1468), indicates Teika's importance for the history of Japanese poetry. His mistress in the play, Princess Shikishi (died 1201), was also an accomplished poet, and translations of her work appear in this anthology. The play shows the importance of tanka as a source of quotation and inspiration in this high dramatic art. Teika and Saigyō both became important models for the poets who followed them. For a haikai poet like Bashō, Saigyō was still, five hundred years later, the supreme master of tanka poetry, since he was one "who in art follows nature and makes friends with the four seasons" (see p. 283). Bashō paid Saigyō the compliment of incorporating references to the older poet's work in his own haikai not as an attempt at imitation, but as an act of respect to an absolute master.

Bashō himself was deified as the great master of haikai poetry by his colleagues and by later generations of poets who continued to pay homage to him. Thus Bashō's most famous hokku:

An old pond: a frog jumps in—the sound of water

is followed by one of Yosa Buson (1716–1783) with a preface, "After the venerable Bashō's hokku":

In an old pond a frog ages while leaves fall.

Buson's poem is an elegant variation, an act of respect to an older master of the sort that we find familiar in musical terms (Mozart on Bach, Tchaikovsky on Mozart, Stravinsky on Tchaikovsky, and so on), but that we meet less often in our poetic tradition. Buson himself became an influential model whose work was studied into this century. Masaoka Shiki, the modern haiku poet mentioned above, ranked Buson higher than Bashō, and Hagiwara Sakutarō wrote an important book on him as well.

The traditions of Japanese poetry continue to provide individual inspiration that modern writers value. Kawabata Yasunari (1899–1972), in his 1968 Nobel Prize acceptance speech, chose citations from the poetry of the Buddhist priest Myōe (1173–1232) to exemplify the deeper significance of his own art:

Watching the Moon Go Down

Set now,
and I too will go below
the rim of the hill—
so night after night
let us keep company.

For Kawabata, such a poem showed a warm, delicate compassion, the deep quiet of the Japanese spirit. Even today, the past can inform the present through an act of homage.

Still another source of unity in the tradition can be observed in what might be termed a consistent desire for the cosmopolitan, a penchant for using images and ideas from other civilizations to enrich and enlarge the native tradition. This attitude goes back to before the time of the *Man'yōshū*, when an influx of Chinese culture sanctioned the influence of foreign models. At its least effective, such openness may seem to produce a sort of mindless eclecticism, but in the best Japanese poetry this artistic point of view can ground a poem in a more complex view of reality by extending the literary frame of reference. A comparison with the Chinese tradition is particularly striking, since that tradition is remarkably self-contained and has allowed little to enter that lies outside its linguistic and cultural boundaries. For the Japanese, Chinese art and poetry (perfectly or imperfectly understood, depending to some extent on the historical period in question) provided a set of additional points of reference, and of departure, for more than a thousand years. Bashō occasionally paraphrased some of the great Chinese poets because his spirit reached out in sympathy toward the esthetic values they upheld, and his own poetry became richer for this cross-cultural underpinning.

In the modern period, the field of attraction shifted from China to Europe. In the early years of this century, the growing sense in Japanese artistic circles of the power of European culture provided in its way as profound a stimulus to Japanese poetry as the discovery of Buddhism and Chinese literature had a millennium before. Few Japanese artists and poets had actually managed to visit China, but many Japanese writers now went to Europe, and the reaction was often one of high excitement. Writing of Notre Dame in Paris, Takamura Kōtarō (1883–1956) spoke in hyperbole:

> O Cathedral, you who at such a moment keep ever more silent and soar,
> Cathedral, you who watch motionless the houses of Paris suffering the storm,
> please do not think me rude,
> who, hands on your cornerstone,
> has his hot cheek pressed on your skin,
> it's me, the drunken one.
> It's that Japanese.

With exposure, knowledge followed, and by the 1930s a poet like Nishiwaki Junzaburō (born 1894) could casually mention Rilke or Pascal in one of his poems and expect the reference to be understood by his readers.

Some poets came to imitate what they took to be the European style so closely that their work might be viewed as a new kind of kanshi (albeit in Japanese) which attempts to reproduce not only European ideas, but even Western syntax. The work of Takiguchi Shūzō (1903–1979) included here provides perhaps the most extreme example in this vein, but many poets work in a larger cultural context, from Nishiwaki, with his love of Baudelaire and Anglo-Saxon poetry, to Tamura Ryūichi (born 1923) and his fascination with T. S. Eliot. Again, such Western models are not chosen for imitation, but are rather regarded as sources that can lend extra resonance to ideas, emotions, and attitudes held by the Japanese poets themselves. At its best, modern Japanese poetry is cosmopolitan, not imitative, just like the best poetry in earlier centuries. Nevertheless, Japanese poets have always felt that, however complex the allusions, the original poetic impulse must always spring from *makoto* (sincerity), that oldest and most durable of the Japanese literary virtues. If modern poets such as Hagiwara Sakutarō and Takahashi Mutsuo (born 1937) occasionally write poems that seem eccentric or even awkward, such poems are likely to be the results of their efforts to be sincere, their attempts to reflect in their poetry the kind of world they know.

One particular feature of modern poetry involves the ability, doubtless gained because of the resurgence of longer poetic forms, to introduce the personality of the poet directly back into the poem. There have been striking personalities throughout the history of Japanese poetry, but the brevity of tanka and the intricate restrictions on renga circumscribed the space available for the direct expression of personal emotional states. Of course, a number of important poets resisted such a tendency toward circumspection, notably women poets such as Ono no Komachi (mid-ninth century) or Lady Izumi (born c. 976), but in general, direct personal statements were not usually made in tanka and renga. The personalities of the poets come through vividly, but refracted through the natural images that often provide the ostensible subject matter for the poems. By the turn of this century, however, the attitudes of the poet were being expressed more extensively, even in the brief traditional forms. It would be hard to imagine either of the following tanka being written before the arrival of Western poetic influences:

> Who shall I tell of the color rouge? my blood wavers, thoughts
>   of spring, life in its prime
>
> (Yosano Akiko)

> I look at my dirty hands—
> it's just like
> coming face to face with my mind these days.
>
> (Ishikawa Takuboku)

The vast difference in the means available to express the poet's personality can be seen in the following comparison of a hokku and a section of a modern poem. Bashō wrote, "A cuckoo fades away, and in its direction, a single island" (p. 284). In "Island," a poem by Ishigaki Rin (born 1920), a single island also appears, ". . . a dot,/a small island./Separate from everyone" (p. 574). Yet the reader of the modern poem is not required to read back, as it were, from the natural image in order to determine the human connection, for that connection now forms the subject of the text:

> I live
> on my island.
> Cultivate it and build it up.
> And yet
> I can't know
> all of this island.
> Can't settle on it forever.
>
> In the looking glass I gaze
> at myself—a far-off island.

In Bashō's hokku, brevity requires that the poet himself be hidden. In Ishigaki's "Island," the persona *is* the poem.

The emergence of the poet's personality came about in part because of the enormous changes in poetic diction since the late nineteenth century. From the 1880s onward, the increasing presence of the colloquial language in the rapidly expanding poetic vocabulary produced genuinely revolutionary results. But such changes did not come about easily. Efforts to create a truly contemporary poetry, inspired by Western examples, took nearly half a century of experiments. Many of the changes in language must remain invisible in translation; yet we hope enough have survived the sea change to show both the vitality of poetry in contemporary Japan and the profound debt the new poetry owes to the tradition of which it is the newest part—that ancient trunk, to paraphrase Bashō, of which it is the youngest flower.

Thomas Rimer

Songs from the Kojiki

"Susano-o's Song"

When this great deity [Prince Susano-o] first built the palace of Suga, clouds rose from there. So he sang a song. The song:

Eightfold fence of Izumo where eight clouds rise,
I make an eightfold fence to surround my wife,
that eightfold fence!

"Songs Exchanged between Prince Ōkuninushi and
Princess Nunakawa, and Songs Exchanged between
Prince Ōkuninushi and his Wife"

When he, the deity of eight thousand spears [Prince Ōkuni-
nushi], went to pay court to Princess Nunakawa in the
country of Koshi, he sang as he reached her house:

The divine prince of eight thousand spears,
finding no wife to pillow in the country of eight islands,[1]
hearing that there was a wise woman,
hearing that there was a fair woman
far away, in the country of Koshi,
set out to pay court to her,
came here to pay court.
My sword thongs still untied,
my mantle still untied,
at the wooden door where the maiden sleeps
I stand, pushing and shaking,
I stand, pulling and shoving.
On the green hills thrushes are calling;
birds of the field, pheasants echo;
birds of the garden, roosters call.
Damn them all, those calling birds!
Won't someone hit those birds and shut them up?
This is the way the story's told
by the low-running fisherman messenger.

Princess Nunakawa, not yet opening the door, sang from
within:

Divine prince of eight thousand spears,
because I am a woman, a pliant grass blade,
my heart is a bird on the shore.
Now I am my own bird,
but later I will be your bird.

---

[1] An old name for Japan.

Live on—do not ever die!
This is the way the story's told
by the low-running fisherman messenger.
When the sun hides behind the green hills,
night will come, black as leopard-flower seeds.
Then, like the morning sun, come, smiling, blooming!
These arms white as mulberry rope,
breasts youthful as soft snow—
hold them with your bare hands, caress them;
your hand and my hand for a pillow,
we'll sleep, thighs outstretched.
So do not speak with too much love,
divine prince of eight thousand spears.
This is the way the story's told.

Accordingly, they did not meet that night but came together on the night of the following day.
Then the deity's chief wife, the divine princess Suseri, became extremely concubine-jealous. Her husband deity, at a
loss, was about to leave Izumo for Yamato. When he had
dressed and stood ready, he put one hand on the saddle of
his horse, one foot in the stirrup, and sang:

When, having carefully put on
a garment black as leopard-flower seeds,
I look down at my chest like a bird of the offing
and flap my wings—it won't do.
Like a shore wave, roll it back and toss it away!
When, having carefully put on
a garment in kingfisher-green,
I look down at my chest like a bird of the offing
and flap my wings—it too won't do.
Like a shore wave, roll it back and toss it away!
When, having carefully put on
a garment dyed with juice of the dye-tree,
indigo grown on the hill and pounded,
I look down at my chest like a bird of the offing
and flap my wings—it is good.
My dear love, my princess,
though I flock away like a flock of birds,
though I retreat like birds retreating,

you won't cry, you say,
but like a pampas grass stalk on the hill,
head drooping, that's how you'll cry,
like morning rain that rises in mist,
my young-grass wife, my princess.
This is the way the story's told.

Here his wife fetched the great wine cup and, approaching,
offered it to him, singing:

Divine prince of eight thousand spears,
    great ruler of our land,
because you are a man,
at every island point you row around,
at each and every shore point you row around
you must have a young-grass wife.
But look, because I am a woman,
I have no man besides you,
I have no husband besides you.
Under fluffy painted curtains,
under downy silken covers,
under rustling mulberry covers,
breasts youthful as soft snow,
arms white as mulberry rope—
hold them with your bare hands, caress them;
and, your hand and my hand for a pillow,
let us sleep, thighs outstretched.
Drink this superb wine.

She sang; then they were united through the cup and em-
braced each other around the neck. They remain so until
today.

"Emperor Ōjin's Song"

When [Emperor Ōjin] reached the village of Kohata, he met a beautiful maiden at the fork of the road. The emperor asked her, "Whose daughter are you?" In reply, she said: "I am the daughter of Lord Hifure of Wani and my name is Princess Miyanushi Yakawae." The emperor said to her, "When I return tomorrow, I'll come into your house." Princess Yakawae told her father of this in detail. In response, her father said: "He is the emperor! This is awesome! My child, serve him." Then he adorned and decorated his house and waited. The next day the emperor came in. When [Lord Hifure] held a great feast for him, he had his daughter, Princess Yakawae, take the great wine cup and present it to him. The emperor, as he accepted it, sang this song:

This crab, where is it from?
A crab from Tsunuga, a hundred relays away.
Crawling sideways, where is it going?
It arrives at Ichijishima, Mishima,
like a grebe, diving, panting,
slowed by the slope, along the road to Sasanami—
but I, how briskly I walked,
and met you, maiden on the Kohata road.
Seen from behind, you are a shield,
your teeth are pasania nuts, water chestnuts.
The clay near Wani in Ichihii—
not the top-clay, which is flesh-red,
nor the bottom-clay, which is soil-dark,
but the middle-clay, like the middle chestnut in a batch of three,
baked not in the strong fire that strikes the forehead—
with it you've drawn your eyebrows, drawing them thick and arched,
    woman whom I met,

child, when I saw you, I thought, "I'd like to do this,"
child, when I saw you, I thought, "I'd like to do that,"
unexpectedly I am with you, face to face,
I am with you, close to you.

Thus they were united, and the child she bore was the
young prince Uji.

"Song of a Lady from Mie"

When the emperor [Yūryaku] held a banquet under a hundred-branch zelkova tree at Hatsuse, a lady from Mie of the land of Ise took up a great wine cup to present to him. At that moment, a leaf fell from the zelkova tree and floated in the cup. The lady, unaware of the leaf, presented the wine. The emperor saw the leaf floating in the cup, struck her down, put a sword to her neck and was about to kill her, when she said to him, "Don't kill me, I have something to say," and sang:

The palace of Sun-White at Makimuku
is a palace on which the morning sun shines,
a palace on which the evening sun casts light,
a palace where bamboo roots grow full,
a palace where roots of trees crawl,
a palace built by firming the good earth with pestles,
a gate of wood of flourishing cypress trees—
growing by the hall of the first fruits,
this zelkova tree has a full hundred branches:
the upper branches cover the heavens,
the middle branches cover the east,
the lower branches cover the villages;
a leaf at the tip of an upper branch
falls and touches a middle branch,
a leaf at the tip of a middle branch
falls and touches a lower branch,
a leaf at the tip of a lower branch
falls and settles like floating oil[2]
in this beautiful cup, which I,
a child of the silk-cloth Mie, present.
The water rolls and rolls,[3]

2,3 Allusion to the creation of the land as described at the opening of the *Kojiki*.

all this, so awesome,
child of the high-shining sun!
This is the way the story's told.

Because she presented this song, he forgave her for her offense.

Poems from the Man'yōshū

EMPEROR YŪRYAKU

(418–479)

Song

With a basket, a lovely basket,
with a trowel, a lovely trowel,
you pick herbs on this hill, child,
I ask you about your house, tell me.
This sky-filling land of Yamato,
I am the one who rules it all,
seated, I govern it all.
I will tell you
my house and my name.

EMPEROR JOMEI

(593–641)

Climbing Mount Kagu and Surveying the Land

Yamato has clusters of mountains
but closest to the city is heavenly Mount Kagu.[1]
I climb, I stand and survey the land:
smoke rises in the countryside,
gulls rise over the lake.
A good land, this, the island of the dragonfly,
the land of Yamato.

TANKA

The stag that calls on Mount Ogura when the evening comes does
not call tonight. He must have gone to sleep

---

[1] So called because it was believed to have come down from the sky.

FUJIWARA NO KAMATARI

(614–669)

Upon Marrying Yasumiko, a Palace Attendant

I've won Yasumiko! I've won Yasumiko who everyone said was hard
to win!

EMPEROR TENJI

(died 671)

TANKA

I saw the sun set in clouds like the sea god's banners: may the moon
tonight clearly shine

PRINCE ARIMA

(640–658)

Pitying Himself as He Was Taken to the Execution Place

At Iwashiro I tie together branches of a beach pine; if I'm lucky, I'll
return and see them again

At home I pile rice in a bowl; but now on a grass-pillow journey, I
pile it on pasania leaves

PRINCE IKUSA

(dates uncertain)

On the Occasion of the Imperial Visit to Aya District in Sanuki Province, Prince Ikusa Wrote This as He Viewed the Mountains

The long spring day,
its mists rising,
before I know it
has turned to twilight
and the heart that crowds my chest
hurts me so
I moan
like the mountain thrushes.
And then from the mountains
where our great lord,
a god aloof,
is pleased to wander,
a wind comes blowing,
and as I stand alone,
morning and night
it turns back my sleeve
and I think how auspicious
is that one word "back"!
I call myself
a man of spirit,
but on this journey,
grass for a pillow,
my thoughts keep going back—
no way to stop them—
and like the fires that burn
when fishergirls of Ami Bay
boil down their salt,
these memories burn
deep within my heart!

ENVOY

Because the winds across the mountain
blow without cease,
each night in sleep unfailingly
I think with longing
of my love back home

PRINCESS NUKADA

(seventh century)

TANKA

At Nikitatsu, before boarding our ships we wait for the moon. The tide has become right—now let us row out!

"When Emperor Tenji"

When Emperor Tenji commanded the minister of the center, Fujiwara no Kamatari, to debate the merits of the fragrance of thousands of flowers on a spring hill as opposed to the color of hundreds of leaves on an autumn hill, Princess Nukada settled the question with this poem:

When, after holing up for winter, the spring comes,
birds that weren't singing come and sing,
flowers that weren't blooming bloom;
but the hills are so dense with growth I can't go in and pick the flowers,
the grass so thick I can't pick and look at them.
When I look at the leaves of trees on an autumn hill,
I take the yellow leaves and admire them.
I leave the green ones, and I'm sorry,
that's something I regret.
But for me, the autumn hill!

Remembering Emperor Tenji

Waiting for you, I am filled with longing, when, stirring the blind of my house, the autumn wind blows

ANONYMOUS LADY

Upon Emperor Tenji's Death

Because I am human and unable to be near a god,
separated, I sorrow for you in the morning,
separated, I long for you.
Were you a jewel I would keep you strung around my hand,
were you a garment I would at no time take you off.
You, whom I long for, last night
appeared in my dream.

EMPEROR TEMMU

(645–686)

To Lady Fujiwara

Tons of snow have fallen in my village. Your antiquated village of Ōhara will, if ever, have such snow only much later!

Lady Fujiwara Replies

I told the water god on my hill to let the snow fall. It scattered, and some must have fallen over your way!

EMPRESS JITŌ

(645–702)

TANKA

Spring has passed
and summer come, it seems—
white cloth robes
are spread to dry
on the heavenly hill of Kagu

To Old Lady Shii

"Enough!" I say,
but Shii *will* force
her stories on me.
Lately, though, not hearing them,
I miss them.

Old Lady Shii Replies

"Enough!" I say,
but "Go on! go on!"
is all I hear—
and now she claims
that Shii forces stories on her!

PRINCE ŌTSU

(663–686)

To Lady Ishikawa

In the dripping dew of the foot-wearying mountain I stood waiting
for you, getting wet in the dripping dew of the mountain

Lady Ishikawa Replies

The dripping dew of the foot-wearying mountain where you waited
for me, getting wet, that's what I'd like to have been

PRINCE SHIKI

(668–716)

*When Emperor Mommu Visited the Palace of Naniwa
in 706*

The ducks along the reedy shore—frost has fallen on their wings; this
evening is so cold I think of Yamato

In Joy

Above the cascade running down the rocks, bracken sprouts; the
spring has come

PRINCESS TAJIMA

(died 708)

Thinking of Prince Hozumi While at Prince Takechi's Palace

As in the autumn paddies rice stalks lean only one way, so would I lean to you, though the rumor pains me

When Her Secret Affair with Prince Hozumi Was Revealed

Because people's words are rampant and the rumor pains me, I cross the morning river that I've never crossed in my life

PRINCE NIU

(dates uncertain)

Upon Prince Iwata's Death

Our prince, pliant as the soft bamboo,
our sovereign with ruddy cheeks,
like a god has been enshrined
on looming Mount Hatsuse,
so said a person bearing the catalpa branch.
Was it a deceiver's rumor I heard?
Was it a madman's word I heard?
What I regret most in heaven and earth,
what I regret most in this world—
as far as the heavenly clouds, to the end of all distances,
to the place where heaven and earth meet
I should have walked with my stick or without it,
consulted words at evening, divined with stones;
I should have built a sacred seat in my house,
put a holy jar near my pillow,
strung bamboo rings uninterruptedly and hung them,
put a robe-tucking sash of hemp on my upper arms,
and in my hands a seven-jointed sedge
from the Field of Sasara that's in heaven,
I should have gone out and purified myself
on the Riverbed of Eternal Heaven.
But on the crag of a high mountain
he has seated himself.

ENVOYS

Is it a deceiver's rumor, a madman's word? —that on the crag of a
high mountain you lay yourself

Unlike the stand of cedars on Mount Furu at Isonokami, you are not
one I'll let pass from my mind

KAKINOMOTO NO HITOMARO

(active c. 700)

Passing by the Wasted Capital in Ōmi

Since the reign of Kashihara's sun-ruler
under Mount Unebi of the robe-tucking sash,
all the gods who were born
ruled all-under-heaven
one after another like hemlock trees
in Yamato that fills the sky.
                              But the emperor,[1]
the divine prince, left it,
crossed the hills of Nara where the clay is good,
and, we don't know what he thought,
ruled all-under-heaven
from the palace at Ōtsu in Sasanami
in the land of rock-rushing Ōmi,
though it was a heaven-remote village.
I heard his great palace was here,
they say his great hall was here,
but spring grass grows rank,
haze rising, the spring sun is blurred.
This place, where the hundred-acre palace stood—
looking at it fills me with sorrow.

ENVOYS

Karasaki of Shiga in Sasanami remains unchanged, but waits in vain
    for the courtiers' boats

Though the broad cove of Shiga in Sasanami may lie calm, will it
    ever meet again the people of the past?

[1] Emperor Tenji. He moved the capital from Yamato to Ōmi on Lake
Biwa in 667. After the Jinshin rebellion in 672, Emperor Temmu moved it
back to the original area.

When Empress Jitō Visited the Palace in Yoshino

In all-under-heaven where our sovereign,
familiar with the eight corners, is heard,
the provinces are many,
but she feels close to the province of Yoshino
where the mountain river meanders, sparkling,
and in the field of Akizu where cherry blossoms fall,
she has built herself a thick-pillared palace.
Here the courtiers of the hundred-acre palace
cross the morning river, their boats side by side,
cross the evening river, their boats racing.
Uninterrupted as this river,
as lofty as these mountains, she rules.
This capital of boiling waterfalls
never tires my eyes.

ENVOY

Like the constant moss of Yoshino River that never tires my eyes,
uninterrupted will I return to look at the palace

When Prince Karu Camped in the Field of Aki

Our sovereign familiar with the eight corners,
the prince of the high-shining sun,
being a god, acting as a god acts,
leaves the capital built with thick pillars.
Through looming Mount Hatsuse,
the wild mountain path with tall trees,
he pushes down the deep-rooted rocks and blocking trees
as he crosses over with morning, a rising bird.
When evening comes, gleaming like a gem,
in the spacious field of Aki where the snow falls,
he pushes down the bannerlike pampas grass and short bamboo,
takes up his lodging on the grass-pillow journey,
and thinks of the past.

ENVOYS

Travelers lodging in the field of Aki lie down to sleep, but cannot
sleep because they think of the past

To this grass-mown wild field, because you,[2] who passed like a
yellow leaf, are remembered here, we have come

In the east, over the field, I see the dawn glow rise; I look back—the
moon has declined

The prince, the child equal to the sun,[3] set out hunting, horses bridle
to bridle—that time has come!

On Parting with His Wife, as He Set Out from the Province of Iwami for the Capital

In vine-trailing Iwami's sea,
at uncertain Cape Kara,
deep-sea fleece grows on hidden rocks,
lovely seaweeds grow on the wild shore.
Like those lovely seaweeds, yielding, you slept with me,
deeply as deep-sea fleece I think of you,
but the nights we slept together were not many,
I came away, parting with you as trailing vines do.
My heart aches, center of my vitals,
longing, I turn around to look,
but on Mount Ferry of large ships
yellow leaves scatter, flutter so
I cannot see your sleeves clearly.
Like the moon sailing through a cloud rift
above wife-secluding Mount Yakami,
though longed for, you hide from sight
when, after coursing heaven, the setting sun casts its glow.
I, who thought myself a strong man—
my white-cloth sleeves
have become wet through and through.

ENVOYS

My blue steed gallops so swiftly, the place of my love that I passed,
now as distant as a cloud

Yellow leaves falling on the autumn hill—don't scatter or flutter for a
while, I'd like to see the place of my love

[2,3] Crown Prince Kusakabe, father of Prince Karu.

During Prince Takechi's Temporary Enshrinement[4] at Kinohe

Fearsome even to allow in mind,
ineffable and awesome even to put in words,
our sovereign familiar with the eight corners
who made the awesome decision
and set up his heavenly imperial gate
in Makami Field of Asuka,
but who now, god that he is, hides under the rock,[5]
crossed Mount Fuwa of tall trees
in the province to the north where he was heard,
descended and was seated in the temporary palace
in Wazami Field of the Korean sword.
There to govern all-under-heaven
and determine the domain to be ruled,
he summoned imperial warriors
from Azuma Province where roosters call
and commissioned our prince, his child though he was,[6]
to soften the storm-like people
and sway the disobedient provinces.
Thereupon the prince armed his body with a sword,
grasped a bow in his hand,
and called the warriors to order.
The drums that line men up
sounded like thunder,
the lesser horns they blew resounded
till people thought in terror
tigers roared, sighting an enemy.
The sway of the banners they held lifted
was like the sway in wind
of the flames left burning on every field
when, after holing up for winter, the spring comes.
The commotion of the bowstrings they made
was awesome to hear, making men think
of a whirlwind swooping
through the snow-falling winter wood.
The arrows they shot were so thick,

[4] Some members of the imperial household were laid in a shrine after death, until tombs were ready.

[5,7] Emperor Temmu, Takechi's father. "To hide under the rock" means to be buried after death.

[6,8] Prince Takechi, appointed commander of the imperial army during the Jinshin rebellion, became prime minister in 689 and died in 696.

coming as turbulent as great snow,
even the unsubmissive rising to fight
did not mind perishing, if they must, like dew or frost
as they vied like darting birds. At that moment,
from the holy shrine at Watarai
the prince unleashed a divine wind, confounding them,
and by not showing the sun's eye in heaven's clouds
and shrouding all in utter darkness
brought peace to this rice-rich country.
Being a god, building thick pillars,
our sovereign familiar with the eight corners[7]—
his realm it was that our sovereign[8]
accepted.
         So, we thought his rule, as it was,
would remain for thousands of ages,
and it did prosper like a blossom of mulberry cloth.
                              But then the prince's gate
was adorned as a shrine for a god.[9]
The gate people he employed
wore white-cloth hempen robes
and through the madder-bright days
crawled, prostrated themselves, looking like deer
in the field before the gate at Haniyasu.
When evening came, black as leopard-flower seeds,
looking back at the great hall,
they crawled and lingered like quail.
Unable to serve him as they wished,
they moaned and cried like spring birds.
But before their grief had passed,
before their thoughts had run dry,
through the uncertain Kudara Plain
he went for burial, for divine burial
and they exalted as an eternal shrine
the shrine at Kinohe of the good hempen robes,
where, being a god, he settled in peace.
For all this, our sovereign
built the palace on Mount Kagu,
meaning it to last for thousands of ages—
how can I think it will pass away in thousands of years?
Looking back at it as at heaven,
I'll keep it bound in my thoughts like a robe-tucking sash,
awesome though it is.

[9] That is, he died.

ENVOYS

Though you have come to rule eternal heaven, I keep longing for
you, not knowing the days and months

Like the hidden marsh near the bank of Haniyasu Pond, not knowing
where to go, your servants are lost

During Princess Asuka's Temporary Enshrinement[10] at Kinohe

Across the river of Asuka where the birds fly,
a stone bridge spans the upper shallows,
a log bridge spans the lower shallows.
The lovely waterweed that grows and wavers
from the stone bridge, ceases to be but grows again,
the river weed that grows and flourishes
from the log bridge, withers but sprouts again.
Why then, my sovereign,[11]
have you forgotten the morning palace,
have you turned away from the evening palace
of your good lord, with whom you wavered,
resembling the lovely waterweed, when standing,
like the river weed, when lying?
While you thought you were in this world,
in springtime you would break off and sport a twig of blossoms,
when autumn came you would sport yellow leaves,
white-cloth sleeve to sleeve with him,
never tiring of looking at him, like a mirror,
thinking you admired him, a full moon,
more and more, as when, from time to time,
you came out to play with him
here at the Kinohe palace where the diners sit face to face.
Now you have decided to make it your permanent palace
and stopped eyeing him like a duck or talking.
That may be why, saddened beyond words,
a thrush, a husband in one-sided love,
a morning bird, your lord frequents this place,
wilted like summer grass by thoughts,
coming and going like the evening star,

[10] See note 4 above.
[11] Princess Asuka (died 700).

hesitating like a great ship. When I see him like this,
I do not have the heart to console him.
And so I do not know what to do.
But the sound, your name, if nothing else, will not cease to be.
As far and everlasting as heaven and earth
I will go on longing for it. May Asuka River
of your name last for thousands of generations.
I feel close, my sovereign,
to your keepsake here.

ENVOYS

If we had spanned Asuka River with a weir to dam it, the flowing
water would be full of peace

Asuka River: would I ever think I'd see her tomorrow?[12] Still I do
not forget my sovereign's name

Seeing a Man Lying Dead among the Rocks on Samine Island in Sanuki

The province of Sanuki, renowned for lovely seaweed—
perhaps for the character of the province I never tire of looking at it,
perhaps for the character of its deity it is noble in many ways,
and with heaven and earth, with sun and moon,
it will remain replete. There, handed down
as the face of the deity,[13] is the port of Naka.
As we came away from it by boat, rowing,
the regular wind was blowing where the clouds are,
and when we looked at the offing, choppy waves were rising,
when we looked toward the coast, white waves were churning.
Awestruck by the sea where whales are caught,
we pulled up the oars of the moving boat
and though there are many islands near and far,

---

[12] Play on "Asuka," in which *asu* is homonymous to "tomorrow."

[13] The *Kojiki* describes the creation of the four-sided island Shikoku, or Iyo, of which Sanuki is one of the four provinces: "Next [the two deities] bore the two-name island of Iyo. This island has one body but four faces. Each face has a name."

we have sheltered on the rough beach
of Samine, the island with a fine name.
Here, making a white-cloth pillow
of the shore where noises of waves are frequent,
you lay yourself on the rough bed.
If I knew your home I would go and speak.
If your wife knew, she would come and ask.
But not even knowing of the spear-adorned road,
she must be anxious, waiting, missing you—
the wife you love.

ENVOYS

With your wife, you would have picked and eaten those starworts.
On Mount Sami, near its slopes, is not their season past?

Offshore waves roll in onto the rough beach where, making a white-
cloth pillow of it, you lie asleep

In Grief after His Wife's Death

When she was alive, now a memory,
the two of us used to see, hand in hand,
the hundred-branch zelkova tree standing on the bank near us.
In as many ways as it sticks out its branches,
as luxuriantly as its leaves grow in spring,
I thought of my wife,
I depended upon her.
But because one cannot go against the way of the world,
in the wild field where heat haze flares
she hid herself with white-cloth scarves of heaven,
she rose and left with morning like a bird
and hid herself as the sun does, setting.
Each time the infant my lover left
as a keepsake for me cries, begging,
because I have nothing to give, nothing to leave with him,
though a man I lift him by his armpits.
In the bedroom with pillows
where my lover and I used to sleep,
I spend days, lonely, desolate till dark,

I spend nights, sighing till dawn.
I grieve but don't know what else to do,
I long for her but have no way of seeing her.
"Your wife you long for is seated
on Mount Wing of the great birds,"
someone says, so I come climbing over rocks
with difficulty. But there is nothing fortunate here,
with my wife who I thought was alive
lying in ashes.

ENVOYS

The autumn moon we saw last year crosses the sky, but my wife
whom I saw it with has grown apart one year

Leaving my wife on Mount Hikide of the sliding path, I think of the
mountain path and no longer feel alive

I come home and look at our room; facing away from me on our bed
lies my wife's wooden pillow

On Seeing a Corpse on Mount Kagu

With grass for a pillow, on a journey, whose husband is it, forgetting
his country? His house must be waiting for him

When the Maiden of Hijikata Was Cremated on Mount Hatsuse

On looming Mount Hatsuse—at the edge of the mountain a cloud
lingers. Can that be my love?

On Coming to the Capital from Ōmi Province

In the Uji, the river of eighty clans of officials—the waves that linger
around the weirs do not know where to go

TANKA

Plovers over the evening waves of Lake Ōmi, when you call, my
heart stirs and I think of the past

When He Was in Iwami Province and Was about to Die

I make a pillow of a rock-root on Mount Kamo—but not knowing
this my wife must be waiting for me

YOSAMI

(dates uncertain)[1]

On Hitomaro's Death

Thinking "Today! Today!" I wait for you—but don't they say you are among the shells in Stone River?

To meet face to face, to meet so is impossible. Over Stone River, clouds, rise, so I may see and remember!

---

[1] Said to have been Kakinomoto no Hitomaro's second wife.

TAKECHI NO KUROHITO

(dates uncertain)

When the Ex-Empress Jitō Went to Mikawa Province in 702
Where will it find harbor, the boat that rowed round Cape Are—that small deckless boat?

On Traveling

On a journey and lonesome, I see below a hill a boat painted with red clay rowing toward the offing

Toward Sakura paddies cranes fly, calling. Over the Ayuchi marsh the tide, it seems, has gone out. Cranes fly, calling

Having come over Mount Shihatsu, I look: a small deckless boat rows out of sight behind Kasanui Island

As we travel, rowing round the shore points, in many inlets of Lake Ōmi cranes in flocks call

Row our boat and tie up in the inlet of Hira. Don't go toward the middle of the lake—the night is late

Where shall I stay if, in Takashima, in the fields of Kachino, the day grows dark?

Perhaps because you and I are one, on Double-View Road that lies in
Three Rivers, I can't part with you

I should have come more quickly to see them: in Taka in Yamashiro
the zelkova trees have shed their leaves

MIKATA NO SAMI

(dates uncertain)

To His Wife, When He Fell Ill Shortly after Marrying Her

Your hair comes undone when you put it up, it's long when you don't; I haven't seen it lately—have you done it up?

In Reply

Everyone says "It's so long—put it up!"—but I'll leave my hair as you saw it, though it may become disheveled

PRINCE AKI

(dates uncertain)

Song[1]

My wife is far away,
not here beside me,
and because the road
is such a long one,
my heart is restless
with feelings of desire,
my heart has no rest
from these feelings of pain,
and I wish I were the cloud
that crosses the sky,
I wish I were the bird
flying high above—
I would go tomorrow
and speak with my love,
and because of me
my love would be at ease,
and because of her
I too would be at ease—
if only I could see her
and be with her now!

ENVOY

So long since
we stretched out our arms
for a pillow—
to think we've gone
a whole year without meeting!

---

[1] A note appended to the poem says that he married a lady-in-waiting
at court, a violation of court regulations, and was punished by being forced
to separate from her.

ONO NO OYU

(died 738)

TANKA

The city of Nara of good blue clay glows like a blooming flower,
now at its prime

YAMANOUE NO OKURA

(?660–?733)

Upon Excusing Himself from a Banquet

I, Okura, must excuse myself now: my child must be crying, the
mother, carrying it on her back, must be waiting for me

A Dialogue on Poverty

On nights when, wind mixing in, the rain falls,
on nights when, rain mixing in, the snow falls,
I'm utterly lost, it's so cold
I take out a piece of black salt and nibble it,
I sip hot water with sake dregs.
Coughing, nose snuffling,
scratching my skimpy beard,
I boast to myself, "I'm the only one
who's worthy." But it's so cold
I pull the hempen quilt over myself,
put on all the cloth vests
I have. On such a cold night,
someone poorer than I am—
his father and mother must be starved, freezing,
his wife and children must be feebly weeping.
At a time like this, what are you doing
to live through it all?

Heaven and earth are wide, they say,
but for me they have grown narrow.
The sun and the moon are bright, they say,
but for me they do not shine.
Is this so for everyone, or for me alone?
I happened to be born a human
but am no worse than others.
Yet vests with no cotton,
mere rags tattered and dangling

like sea-fleece, are hung on my shoulders.
In this flattened hut, this leaning hut,
on straw spread on the bare ground
father and mother by my pillow,
wife and children by my feet
surround me, whimpering.
From the stove no steam spurts up,
in the steamer a spider weaves its web,
and rice-cooking forgotten,
we moan like thrushes—
when, as they say, "to cut the ends
of what's too short already,"
with stick in hand the village chief shouts,
he comes to our sleeping-place and yells at us.
Is it as helpless as this,
the way of the world?

ENVOY

I find this world sad and wearying, but cannot fly away because I am
    not a bird

Longing for His Son, Furuhi

The seven types of treasures
people prize and desire—
        what do I have to do with them?
Born of us two,
our son, Furuhi, a pearl,
when the day broke with the morning star
wouldn't leave his bed of white cloth
but, standing or sitting,
        he would play with us.
When the evening of the evening star came,
"Let's sleep," he would say, taking our hands.
"Father, mother, stay near me, don't go away.
Like a marigold I'll sleep in the middle."
He'd say this so lovingly
that we looked forward to the time we'd see him
an adult, for better or worse,
trusting in him as in a great ship.

But unexpectedly a crosswind
swept down and overwhelmed him.
Not knowing what to do, what could be done,
I tucked up my sleeves with a white-cloth sash,
held a clear mirror in my hand
and looked up, begged, prayed to the gods of heaven,
prostrated myself, forehead on the ground, before the gods of earth.
"Whether it is this way or is not,
    is up to the gods,"
I said, pacing up and down, as I begged and prayed.
But he never got better even for a moment;
bit by bit his face lost color,
morning by morning he spoke less,
till his precious life came to an end.
I jumped to my feet, stamped, shouted;
I prostrated myself, looked up, beat my chest, grieved.
My son, who I held in my hands, I've let fly away—
the way of this world!

ENVOY

So young he wouldn't know his way. I offer you gifts, messenger of
the underworld—carry him on your back

On Tanabata[1]

Seventh of the Seventh Month, 722

You, for whom I have longed standing across the River of Heaven,
are coming. Let me untie my sash and be ready

Seventh of the Seventh Month, 724

Putting a boat in the River of Eternal Heaven, tonight you'll be
coming to my place

[1] Tanabata: A legend of Chinese origin about two lovers, the Princess
Weaver (the star Vega) and the Oxherd (the star Altair), who are fated
to meet only once a year, on the seventh of the seventh month. Here, the
boat is the vehicle for crossing the River of Heaven (the Milky Way),
which separates them, but in one variation of the story compassionate mag-
pies form a bridge for them.

Seventh of the Seventh Month, 729

The Cowherd, since parting with the Princess Weaver
as heaven did with earth,
has stood facing the straw mat, the river,
thinking, and becoming upset,
grieving, and becoming upset,
his hopes gone in the blue waves,
his tears dried in the white clouds—
how could he be just sighing like that?
How could he be just longing like that?
He wants a clay-coated boat,
he wants gem-studded oars.
Then he would paddle across in morning calm,
he would row across at evening tide,
spread on the Riverbed of Eternal Heaven
her heaven-flying scarf,
and her gemlike arm, his gemlike arm for a pillow,
sleep many a night,
though it may not be autumn.

ENVOYS

Though winds and clouds pass between the two banks, never do the
 words of my distant wife

Only a stone's throw away it seems, but the River of Heaven sets us
 apart—there aren't many things I can do

ŌTOMO NO TABITO

(665–731)

In Praise of Sake

Don't think about useless things—you should be drinking, it seems to me, a bowl of raw sake

Choosing "sage" as a name for sake—how good the words of those great sages of the past![1]

Those seven wise men of the past—what they too wanted, it seems, was sake[2]

Better than to say things like a wise fellow, it seems, is to drink sake, get drunk, and weep

I don't know how to say it, what to do about it—the noblest of all, it seems, is sake

Rather than be a so-so human being, I'd like to be a sake jar and get steeped in sake[3]

[1] When the Wei dynasty outlawed drinking in third-century China, secret drinkers referred to raw or unrefined sake as "the worthy" and refined sake as "the sage."

[2] The so-called Seven Sages of the Bamboo Grove, a group of philosopher-poets of third-century China who often met to drink and make music.

[3] Cheng Ch'üan, a Chinese who loved wine, asked his son to bury him beside a pottery kiln so that, after his bones had turned to clay, someone might perhaps mold him into a wine jar.

How ugly—take a good look at a man who acts wise and doesn't drink—just like a monkey!

A priceless treasure it may be, but how can it be better than a bowl of raw sake?

A gem that gleams at night it may be, but how can it compare to drinking sake and opening your heart?

When you're unfilled in ways of worldly entertainment, you should, it seems, get drunk and weep

If I enjoy myself in this world, in the world to come I won't mind being an insect or a bird

Since all living things die in the end, while I'm in this world I'll enjoy myself

To keep silent and act wise—still not as good as drinking sake, getting drunk, and weeping

In 728, Longing for His Deceased Wife

My arm, the pillow of hemp cloth my dear one used to sleep on—is there anyone to sleep on it now?

It is time to return. In the capital, whose arm will be my pillow?

Sleeping alone in the untended house in the capital—that will be far more bitter than this journey

TAKAHASHI MUSHIMARO

(dates uncertain)

From the *Mushimaro Collection*

The Boy Urashima of Mizunoe

Seasons when the spring sun
is misted over
and I go out on the shore
of Suminoe
and see the fishing boats
bobbing there,
I think of things
that happened long ago.
That boy Urashima
of Mizunoe,
proud of his bonito catch,
his catch of sea bream,
for seven whole days
never came home
but rowed on and on
beyond the slope of the sea,
rowed until
by chance
he met the
sea god's daughter.
And when they'd spoken friendly words,
showed themselves of one mind,
they exchanged their vows,
journeying all the way
to the Timeless Land,
and there in the sea god's palace,
in a wonderful chamber
within the inmost wall,
hand in hand,
they went in and lived together.

There, never growing old,
never dying,
they might have remained
for ages on end.
But this fellow,
a fool in the world's ways,
spoke up
and said to his wife:
"I must go home
for a little while
and tell my father and mother
what's happened—
I'll be back again
the very next day!"
When he'd said this,
his wife replied:
"If you want to return
to the Timeless Land
and see me once more
as I am now,
never open this comb box,
whatever may come!"—
how many times
she warned him of it.
When he'd come home
to Suminoe
he looked for his house
but could see no house,
looked for his village
but could see no village.
Strange! he thought,
when only three years
have gone by
since I left my home—
could the house have vanished
fence and all?
Perhaps if I try
opening this box,
the house will be there
as it was before—
He opened the jeweled comb box
just a crack

and a white cloud
came out of the box
and went trailing away
toward the Timeless Land.
He jumped up, ran after it,
shouting, waving his sleeve.
He rolled on the ground,
stamped his foot in anger.
And then in a moment,
his wits deserted him,
his boyish skin
grew wrinkled all over,
his black hair
turned utterly white.
Before long
even his breathing ceased
and in the end
all life went out of him.
That boy Urashima
of Mizunoe—
I see the place where his house once stood.

ENVOY

He could have lived forever
in the Timeless Land—
what a fool,
that fellow—
and he did it all himself

*Watching a Young Girl Going Alone over the Big Bridge
of Kawachi*

Over the big
red-painted bridge
she crosses the
Katashiwa River,
trailing
her crimson skirts,
wearing a cloak dyed
with mountain indigo,

all by herself
passing over—
Has she a husband
young as grass?
does she sleep alone
like an acorn from an oak?
I don't know where
that young girl's house is,
and how I'd like to ask!

ENVOY

If I had a house
by the side of the bridge
I'd give her lodging,
that girl who looks so sad,
going all alone!

The Cuckoo

A lone cuckoo
that hatched out
among the
bush warbler's eggs,
you do not cry
with a voice like your father's,
you do not cry
with a voice like your mother's,
but over the fields
where the deutzia blooms
you fly round and round,
crying till the echoes ring,
scattering the blossoms
of the orange tree.
But though you cry all day
your song is good to hear—
I'll give you gifts, my bird—
don't fly too far away
but go on living
in the orange tree
that flowers by my house

ENVOY

When skies darken
and rain falls in the night,
cuckoo,
you go on crying,
my admirable bird

Written When I Climbed the Peak of Tsukuba for the Song Meet[1]

On Tsukuba mountain
where the eagles nest,
above the ford
of Mohakitsu,
hand in hand
the young men and women
come crowding round
to sing in the song meet.
And I will sleep
with other men's wives
and others will make
proposals to mine—
for years past
this is a custom
the gods who rule the mountain
have not condemned,
so for today alone
don't look at me reproachfully,
don't speak words of blame!

ENVOY

On Man God peak
the clouds rise up
and showers fall,
but though I'm wet through and through
I've no wish to go home

[1] *Kagai:* A festival in which young people gathered to sing, dance, and make love.

Tegona of Mama

In the land of Azuma
where the cocks crow,
it took place
far in the past,
though they tell
of it still—
Tegona of Mama
in Katsushika
dressed herself in hemp cloth,
trimmed it with a blue collar,
wove herself a skirt to wear
out of pure hemp,
no comb
for her hair,
no shoes on her feet
when she went abroad,
but what pampered daughter
done up in
patterns and brocades
could compare to her?
Her face
perfect as the full moon,
when she stood there
smiling like a flower,
men swarmed around her
like summer insects
drawn to a flame,
like ships rowing
for the harbor mouth.
But then,
as though life weren't
short enough already,
what did she do
but take herself off,
laid herself down
where the noise
of the waves is loudest,
in the deepest part of the harbor!
Though this happened
in an age long ago,
I think of it

as if I had seen it
only yesterday

ENVOY

When I look at the well
at Mama in Katsushika,
I think of Tegona
who used to stand here
drawing water

KASA NO KANAMURA

(dates uncertain)

*On the Fifteenth of the Ninth Month in 726, When the
Emperor [Shōmu] Went to Visit Inamino in the Province
of Harima*

In the bay of Matsuho of Awaji Island
visible from the breakwater of Nakizumi,
there is, I hear, a girl of the sea
who in the morning calm reaps lovely seaweed,
in the evening calm burns seaweed for salt;
but because I have no means of going to see her,
manliness gone out of my heart,
thoughts pent up like a weak-armed woman's,
going back and forth, I keep longing for her,
without boat or oar.

ENVOYS

If only I had a boat and oar to go look at the girls reaping seaweed,
high though the waves may be!

I walk about and look, but never tire of the white waves rolling in on
Nakizumi's breakwater beach

YAMABE NO AKAHITO

(active beginning of the eighth century)

Looking at Mount Fuji in the Distance

Since heaven and earth parted,
godlike, lofty, and noble
in Suruga, Fuji the lofty peak—
as I turn and look at the Plain of Heaven,
the light of the coursing sun is hidden behind it,
the shining moon's rays can't be seen,
white clouds can't move, blocked,
and regardless of time, the snow's falling.
We'll tell, we'll go on talking
about Fuji, this lofty peak.

ENVOY

Coming out on the beach of Tago, I look: pure white—on Fuji the
lofty peak, the snow's falling

Climbing Kasuga Field

On Mount Kasuga of the spring days,
on Mount Mikasa of the high platform,
every morning clouds lie,
cuckoos call, ceaseless and incessant.
Like the clouds my heart lingers,
like those birds I'm in one-sided love,
in the day, all through the day,

in the night, all through the night,
standing or sitting, I brood,
though I cannot meet her.

ENVOY

Like the birds that call on Mount Mikasa of the high platform, my
thoughts of love start up as soon as they cease

*Composed on the Fifth of the Tenth Month, 724, While
the Emperor Shōmu Was Visiting the Province of Ki*

Our sovereign familiar with the eight corners—
his eternal palace where we serve
in Saika Field—visible from its back
is an island in the offing. There on its clean shore
when the wind blows, white waves churn,
when the tide ebbs, lovely seaweed is harvested.
So noble since the age of gods,
that island mountain of Tamatsu!

ENVOYS

On the rocky shore of the island in the offing, the lovely seaweed—I
will miss it when it goes under the flowing tide

As the tide comes flowing into Waka Bay and the marshes vanish,
toward the reedy shore cranes fly, calling

Song

The palace of Yoshino where our sovereign,
familiar with the eight corners, rules on high
is surrounded by layer on layer of green fences
and circled by a river of clear waves.

In spring, blossoms open and flourish,
when autumn comes, mists rise and trail.
Greater in number than these mountains,
uninterrupted as this river,
the courtiers of the hundred-acre palace
will come to this place.

ENVOYS

In Yoshino, on treetops in a Kisayama vale, a great many birds make
a commotion as they call

As the night deepens, black as leopard-flower seeds, on the clear river
beach where everlasting trees grow, plovers call ceaselessly

Song

Our sovereign familiar with the eight corners,
being a god, rules on high
in Ōmi Field of Inamino.
There, in coarse-fabric Wisteria Bay,
fishing boats make a commotion, angling for tuna,
many people work, burning seaweed for salt.
Because the bay is good, they fish, yes,
because the shore is good, they burn seaweed for salt, yes.
Clear to the eye why he frequents this place—
this clean, white shore!

ENVOYS

Because waves in the offing and waves near the shore are calm, they
fish in Wisteria Bay, boats making a commotion

Having pushed down the short reeds in Inamino and slept so many
nights, I miss my home

Through the Akashi marsh, along the tide-bare path, I won't be able
to help smiling tomorrow, for my home will be near

TWO TANKA

I came to this spring field to pick violets. But I loved the field so much I've slept here all night

In the field I've roped off, thinking to pick spring herbs from tomorrow, it's been snowing yesterday and today

LADY ŌTOMO NO SAKANOUE

(active beginning of the eighth century)

For a Religious Service to a God

Divine prince, born and descended
from the Plain of Eternal Heaven,
I attach a white tuft and mulberry fibers
to longan branches from the depth of a mountain,
dig the earth and set in the holy jar,
string numberless bamboo rings and hang them,
bend my knees like a deer and prostrate myself,
and put on a gentlewoman's robe—
like this I pray,
but can I not meet you?

ENVOY

A fold of mulberry fibers in my hands, like this I pray, but can I not
meet you?

Grieving over the Death of the Nun Rigan, in 735

From the mulberry-rope country of Silla,
hearing people say that it was good
you came to this country where you had no
family or relatives to turn to.
In this country where our sovereign rules,
crowding the sun-shining capital
streets and houses are many,
but, I don't know what you thought,
here close to these strange hills of Saho
you came, yearning like a weeping child,
built yourself a house with furnishings and all,
and dwelled in it and lived
long through a string of years.

But all living things die, they say,
and no one's exempted from it.
While everyone you counted on
was traveling, with grass for a pillow,
you crossed Saho River in the morning,
and seeing Saho Field behind you
you walked toward the foot-wearying hills,
forlorn, and hid yourself.
Not knowing what to say, what to do,
I go back and forth, all alone,
my white-hemp sleeves never dry,
in grief I weep, shedding tears.
On Mount Arima clouds linger,
Have they fallen in rain?

ENVOY

Because life can't be made to stay, you left your house, furnishings
and all, and hid among the clouds

Love's Complaint

Those sedges in light-flooded Naniwa—
you spoke as intimately as their clinging roots,
you said it would run deep into years, it would last long,
so I gave you my heart, as spotless
as a clear mirror.   From that day,
unlike the seaweed that sways with the waves,
I did not have a heart that goes this way and that,
I trusted as one trusts a great ship.
But has a god, a rock-smasher, put us apart?
Or someone of this world interfered?
You used to come but you no longer do,
and no messenger bearing the catalpa branch appears.
Because of this there's nothing I can do.
All through the night black as leopard-flower seeds,
through the day till the red-rayed sun sets,
I grieve, but there's no sign,
I brood, but I don't know what to do.

They speak of "weak women"—I am just that,
weeping loudly like a child,
I go back and forth, waiting for your messenger—
will all this be in vain?

ENVOY

If at the outset you hadn't said "It would last long," and made me
trust you, would I have thoughts like this?

TANKA

A bell lily blooming under a shrub in the summer field—love so
unrecognized is painful indeed!

LADY KASA

(mid-eighth century)

Eighteen tanka written to Ōtomo no Yakamochi:

My keepsake—
look at it and think of me,
and I will love you
through the long years
strung like beads on a string

Like the crane whose cry
I hear in the dark night,
I hear of you only
as someone far away—
we never so much as meet

I love you,
it's utterly hopeless—
on the Nara hills,
under the little pines
I stand and weep

At my home
the bright dew fades
from evening grasses—
I too will fade away,
so helpless my love for you!

As long as I live
can I forget you?
Each passing day
my love
grows stronger

Eight hundred days
journeying along the shore—
can its sands
outweigh my love,
guardian of the outer island?

The world has so many eyes—
though we're close
as steppingstones in a brook,
I must live with my love unspoken

A person can die of love—
like a hidden stream,
unseen I waste away
each month, each day that passes

Though I only
saw you dimly
as in a morning mist,
I now live with a love
that will cost me my life

I go on loving him—
a man awesome as the waves
of the sea of Ise
that thunder in
upon the shore

When evening comes
I long for you more than ever,
before my eyes
I see you as you looked
when you spoke

If one can die of love,
then a thousand times
I must have died,
died and come alive again

I dreamt
I clasped a sword
to my body—
what sign is this?
does it mean I'll meet you?

If the gods
of heaven and earth
lacked all reason,
they'd let me die
without seeing you

I love you—
do not forget me!
Like winds blowing
over the bay,
never let us cease!

I hear the bell striking,
saying "All to bed!"
but I think of you so,
I could never hope to sleep

Loving someone
who doesn't love you—
it's like kowtowing to the back
of the hungry demon
at the great temple![1]

I can bear
not seeing you
so long as you're near,
but how will I endure it
when you're far away?

---

[1] According to Buddhist belief, one who does evil risks being reborn as a hungry demon (*gaki*). Statues of hungry demons were apparently displayed in Nara period temples as a warning, but to pray to such statues was of course pointless and ineffectual.

SAMI MANSEI

(dates uncertain)

TANKA

To what shall I compare this world? A boat that rows off with morning, leaving no trace behind

THREE ANONYMOUS POEMS WITH STORIES

It is reported that there was once a young woman who, without letting her parents know, began an affair in secret with a young man. The man, fearful of being scolded by her parents, was somewhat hesitant about the matter. The young woman thereupon composed this poem and gave it to him:

Should you hide in the rock tomb
of Mount Hatsuse,
should it come to that
I'd join you there—
do not doubt me, love!

Legend relates that long ago there was a young woman who separated from her husband. She continued to love him and yearn for him over the years, but the husband took another wife and never went to see the young woman. All he did was send her presents. The young woman replied with the following poem of resentment:

I put good rice in water
and brewed wine
and waited,
and all for nothing—
you never even came

According to report, there was once a lady-in-waiting in the personal service of Prince Sai. Nights she was on duty in the prince's palace and had little free time, so it was very difficult for her to meet her husband. But her thoughts turned constantly toward him, for her love for him was very deep. One evening when she was on night duty, she saw her husband in a dream, but when she awoke and reached out to embrace him, her arms encountered only emptiness. Weeping and sobbing, she thereupon intoned this poem in a loud voice. The prince, hearing it, was moved to pity and saw to it that thereafter she would be permanently excused from night duty:

I eat my food
but it has no flavor,
I sleep
but I know no rest—
your love,
my madder-cheeked,
is so hard to forget!

THIRTEEN ANONYMOUS SEDŌKA

Don't cut the shrub on Idemi Beach in Sumiyoshi.
I'd like to see the young women walk, wetting the hems of their red
  skirts.

.

Don't cut the bamboo grass under the elm by the pond.
If nothing else, I'd look on it as your keepsake and remember.

.

On the way to the lustrous shrine, my skirt was torn.
Thoughts disturbed like unstrung beads, I should have stayed home.

.

This is the cloth I've woven for you, tiring my arms.
Come spring, what color do you want me to dye it?

.

Even on spring days you work the fields and tire yourself, my love.
With no wife like young grass you work the fields and tire yourself.

.

Who has broken the tops of the reeds in the port?
To see my husband wave, I have broken them.

.

My wife whom I hid under the holy elm in Hatsuse—
has anyone seen her in the moonlight, shining madder-red?

.

One of your cords of Koguryo brocade was lying on the floor.
Say you'll come tomorrow night, and I'll keep it for you.

.

With morning you leave and wet your leggings in the dewy field.
I'd like to get up as early and wet the hem of my skirt.

·

You are to me my breath, my life. But so many people watch us.
If only you were a blowing wind, I could see you so often!

·

May no one take the path around the tip of the hill,
so it will remain the path you take unobserved.

·

Come to see me through the spaces of the beautifully hanging shade.
If mother with sagging breasts asks, I'll tell her, "It's just a wind."

·

I'd like to see you as in a clear mirror, I'd like to meet you—
my love for you, snapped once like a string of beads, lush again these
    days.

EIGHT ANONYMOUS EXCHANGES

Scratching your eyebrows, sneezing, sash undone, were you waiting
for me? Wondering when I could see you, longing, I've come

Today I know: I sneezed and sneezed and thought how itchy my eyebrows were—it was because of you!

.

Longing for you, my love, but not knowing what to do, I had my
white-cloth sleeve turned. Have I appeared in your dreams?[1]

It was a dream on the night you had your sleeve turned, I'm sure: I
met you as if in reality

.

No way of consoling myself for this love; for days on end you didn't
appear in my dreams, and the year has passed

Even if for days on end you don't appear in my dreams, and you die,
my one-sided love will never cease

.

Don't wilt and brood on things. My heart, when I think of you, never
shifts like a cloud

[1] It was believed that if you slept with your sleeve turned, you would
appear in your lover's dreams.

I won't wilt and brood on things; even the Waterless River, as time
passes, they say, will have water flowing in it

.

The sedge of the marsh where irises bloom—as I've waited for the day
to sew it into a hat and wear it, years have passed

The sedge hat of light-flooded Naniwa—it's not the kind of hat someone wears after it's been left unworn for long

.

Like this I'll wait for you, my love—till the moon, that appears when
night deepens, has gone down

Admiring the moon drifting from tree to tree, I walked to and fro,
and now the night is old

.

You are like those scarves, those white beach waves—I can't go near
you, you're cold, my love, yet I long for you

Just the reverse—it's you who have no time to come near me, as if I
were those scarves, those white beach waves

.

If I'd known you were coming, love, I'd have spread gems in my
weed-covered garden

What would I do with a gem-filled house? A weed-covered hut is
fine, if I can be with you

SIX ANONYMOUS CHŌKA

On Travel

How marvelous a fellow
is the sea god!
He sets Awaji Island
squarely in the middle,
sends his white waves
circling round Iyo,
and from the Akashi narrows
where we await the moon,
when evening comes,
he floods the tides to their fullest,
and with the dawn
draws them down again.
And we in terror
at the wresting of the waves
shelter in the lee
of Awaji's shores,
not sleeping
but watching
to see
when this night will end.
But now above the waterfall
the pheasants of Asano
are crying out, it seems,
that dawn has come.
So up, men,
and let's be rowing—
the sea lies calm and still!

ENVOY

We rowed from island to island,
but when we rounded
Minume point

I thought in longing of Yamato,
so many the cranes that cried there

Composed by a Mother When She Saw Her Son off from Naniwa on an Embassy to China in 733

The deer that weds
the autumn bush clover,
they say,
sires a single fawn,[1]
and this fawn of mine,
this lone boy
sets off on a journey,
grass for his pillow.
I thread strands
till they're thick with bamboo beads,
deck the sacred wine jar
with streamers of mulberry paper,
begging the gods that this
child of mine I love so
may go unharmed.

ENVOY

If frost should fall
on fields
where the traveler sleeps,
you flocks of cranes in the sky,
shelter my boy with your wings!

On Love

In that little ugly hut
I'd like to burn down,
on a spread of rotten bedding
fit for the trash,
entwined in those
ugliest of ugly arms—
may they break!—

[1] A folk belief of the time.

you're sleeping, I suppose—
and because of you every hour
of the madder-red day,
all through the night
black as leopard-flower seeds,
till the floor beneath me
creaks and groans,
I lie here tormented!

ENVOY

It is I, poor thing,
who burn up
my own heart—
this same heart that makes me
long for you so!

On Love

This is what
the villagers told me:
"Your beloved husband
that you long for so,
from this mountainside
of Kamunabi
where the yellow leaves
scatter in confusion,
riding a horse
black as leopard-flower seeds,
crossed over the river shoals,
seven shoals in all—
We saw your husband
and he looked so sad!"—
that's what they told me.

ENVOY

I shouldn't have asked,
I should have kept still—
why did they have to tell me
the way you looked!

On the Roads of Yamashiro

On the roads of Yamashiro
where the chloranthus grows,
other women's husbands
ride on horseback,
but my husband
plods along on foot,
and each time I see it
all I do is cry,
whenever I think of it
my heart pains me.
This precious mirror of mine,
a keepsake
from my mother
of the sagging breasts,
this scarf thin as dragonfly wing—
take them, husband,
and buy yourself a horse!

ENVOYS

At the Izumi River crossing
the shoals are so deep,
my husband's traveling clothes
get soaked right through!

This precious mirror I own
means nothing to me
when I see you
struggling
to make your way on foot

"The Husband Replies"

If I buy a horse,
you must go on foot, love—
Let it be!
Though we walk on stones,
you and I will go together!

Beggar Song[2]

Beloved one, my lord,
here in your home, in your home,
but should you go abroad, Korean tigers,
the godly ones, you'd seize alive,
eight head you'd take, and of their pelts
make folded mats, eight-folded mats
like the folded hills of Heguri
where in the fourth and fifth months
I serve in the medicine hunt.
On those foot-wearying mountain slopes,
where two yew trees stand,
clasping in my hand eight bows of catalpa,
clasping in my hand eight turnip-tip arrows,
I lay in wait for the deer.
And as I waited a stag came and stood
and spoke in sorrow:
"In a moment I must die—
now I will serve my great lord,
my horns trim his headgear,
my ears fashion inkwells,
my eyes be clear mirrors,
my hoofs tip the bow ends,
my hairs make writing brushes,
my hide the hide of boxes,
my flesh for mincemeat,
my liver too for mincemeat,
my guts to be pickled.
Old toiler, my one body
will have a sevenfold flowering,
an eightfold flowering—
praise me, sing my praise!"

---

[2] Sung by beggar minstrels who went from house to house. The "medicine hunt" was held in early summer to catch deer, whose newly grown horns were used in medicine.

TWENTY-THREE ANONYMOUS TANKA ON LOVE

By the light of the flares
of the fishermen
who fish the sea of Noto
make your way along
while you wait for moonlight

I didn't take
a good look at him
when he left at dawn,
and so for a whole day
all I do is pine

When I love her
so much,
can I watch her pass by
like any other person,
not take her in my arms?

Let me die now,
love,
for in love
not one night, not one day
of peace is mine!

I dusted the bed
with my sleeves
and sat waiting for you,
and while that was going on
the moon went down[1]

Flocks of birds are singing
all round my door—
get up! get up!
my husband for a night—
no one must know of this!

Here I thought I was
a big man,
hardly smaller than
earth and heaven—
and yet in love my courage fails

So that no one will see
or blame me,
tonight I'll come to you in dreams—
just be sure you leave
the door unlatched

Like a little boat pushing through reeds
to make the harbor,
so many things block my way—
but I try to reach you—
never think I don't!

[1] Once the moon has set, she knows there is little possibility that her lover will come to her.

As far as sleeping goes
I could sleep with anyone—
but you, who've bent to me
like seaweed in the surge—
it's your word I wait for

I'll not die of love
but go on living, it seems,
a grain of sand
floating on the foam
when the tide comes in

The mere echo
of a horse's hoof
and I go out to see—
in the shadow of the pines,
wondering, could it be you?

If I go
when she's not expecting me,
she'll grin with delight—
I can just picture
how her eyebrows will look!

Straw matting
to sleep on
only one layer thick—
but when I sleep with you
I'm not the least bit cold

Pay no mind to my mother
with the sagging breasts—
if you do
you and I
will never get together

The day I go
to pick arrowhead
in the mountain pond—
let's meet then at least,
whatever my mother may say!

Is he here? Is he here?
But when I went out
to look for him,
light snow was falling
softly over the courtyard

Don't go!
now with the night so far gone,
tonight when
by the roadside
frost falls on the thick bamboo

"A woman angrily rejects her lover's excuses":
Could a little spring rain
get your clothes so very wet?
And if it rained seven days,
then seven nights
you wouldn't come?

"For a dead lover":
"My love?" I said,
"he'd never leave me!"
So we slept back to back
like two sticks of bamboo—
now how I regret it!

Like the huts
of the men of Naniwa,
sooty from the reeds they burn,
my wife too is gray with age—
but to me forever new

Though I'm old now,
my strength waning,
how I think of you
who were as close to me
as these white sleeves of mine!

Absurd!
at my age
to mouth such nonsense—
speaking the words of youth,
and I an old man

TWENTY-FIVE AZUMA UTA AND SAKIMORI NO UTA

At the post station
where bells of swift horses
jangle,
give me water from the boxed well
dipped up with your own hands

The maples
of Mount Komochi—
till their green leaves turn red
I'd like to sleep with you—
what do you think of that?

On Tsukuba peak
is that a snowfall
perhaps
or only my dear girl
spreading hemp cloth to dry?

Though the hemp you've spun
barely fills
a basket,
there's always tomorrow—
come with me to bed!

Was it only last night
I slept with her?
The crane that flies
crying over the clouds—
that far away it seems!

Till they see it
plain as the rainbow
arced over the eight-foot dam
of Ikaho
I want to sleep and sleep with you!

That girl
lovely as the little oaks
of Mount Mikamo
in Shimotsukeno—
whose supper will she be fixing?

Over Shimotsuke fields,
across the streambed of Aso,
not stepping on stones
but through the sky I've come—
tell me what's in your heart!

These hands all chapped
from pounding rice—
will the young lord of the hall
tonight again
sigh in pity as he holds them?

In Katsushika of the grebes
I make offerings of new rice,
but that dear boy—
I can't leave him
standing outside

I wish I had a pony
with hoofs that make no noise—
I'd never stop going to you
by the linked bridge
of Mama in Katsushika

In the twilight
that day he crossed
Mount Usuhi
my husband—I saw him clearly—
waved with his sleeve

The road to Shinano
is a new-cut trail—
you'll be walking on hacked-up stubs,
husband,
wear your shoes!

When evening mist
rises from reed leaves,
in the chill dusk
when the wild duck cries,
I'll think of you

On frost-filled nights
when bamboo leaves rustle,
better than a robe
of seven layers
is the body of my wife

How awesome
the imperial command—
from tomorrow
I sleep among the grasses,
no more with my wife

"Whose husband this time,
off to frontier duty?"
How I eye with envy
that woman who asks,
not a worry in her head

The children
who cried,
dragging on my robe—
I've gone away and left them,
and they with no mother

If only I had time
to paint a picture of my wife—
from now on
on my journeys
I'd look at it and remember

At the corner of the reed fence
she stood and cried
till her sleeve was sopping,
my wife—
I remember

That morning I set off
for border duty,
out the door,
my wife in tears,
how she hated to part hands

The husband speaks:

If I leave her and go away,
my wife will grieve—
if only I could make her
the grip of the catalpa bow
I bear with me!

The wife replies:

If I am left behind and long for you
I will suffer—
I wish I could be
the bow that goes with you
on your morning hunts!

Father and mother
patting my head,
saying, "Luck go with you!"—
how hard
to forget those words

We've traveled a road
with a hundred turnings
and now we set out
past eighty islets,
going ever farther from home

ŌTOMO NO YAKAMOCHI

(716–?785)

Sorrowing at the Death of His Mistress

In my garden
the blossoms have opened,
but when I look at them
my heart is unmoved.
I loved her so—
if she were only here
we'd be like ducks in the water,
the two of us side by side,
I'd break off sprays
and show them to her—
But in this life
all we have are borrowed bodies
that vanish
like dew or frost.
You headed for the road
to the foot-wearying mountains,
you were the setting sun
that hides itself away.
When I think of it
my chest aches,
I can barely speak,
not knowing what words to use,
but while we live in a world
that fades without a trace,
there's nothing we can do.

ENVOYS

The time—
sooner or later it would have come,
but how it pained her
to have to go
and leave the newborn child

If I'd known
what road she would go by,
I'd have gotten there first,
built a barrier
to block the way

In the garden she knew,
blossoms have opened,
seasons pass
but the tears I shed
never run dry

Still Sorrowing

And this
is all there is—
when my love and I
counted on a thousand years

My love left the house,
I couldn't stop her,
and I let her hide
in the mountain—
I have no spirit now

The world is never
any more than just this—
I knew it all along,
but an aching heart
is still hard to bear

Each time I see the mist
drifting over the hills of Saho,
I remember my love—
there's no day when I don't weep

In the past I saw them as strangers,
but now when I think
my love is buried there,
I feel close to those Saho hills

Sent to a Young Woman

That fording place in the Saho
where the plovers cry,
when will my horse
splash through its clear stream,
going to you?

Day and night
without distinction
my heart longs for you—
haven't you seen me
in your dreams?

When I least expected,
in dreams I saw
my darling's smile—
now it keeps
burning in my heart

Sent to Lady Sakanoue's Elder Daughter

These dream meetings
are too painful—
when I wake up
I reach out,
but my hands touch nothing

Poking Fun at a Lean Man

Iwamaro, these words
I address to you:
They say it's just the thing
for summer leanness—
try some eels!

Lean, lean you may be,
but be sure to stay alive!
Take care, take care,
when you catch those eels,
don't wash away in the river!

Longing for my Stray Hawk, I Dreamed about Him and Wrote These in my Joy

In this distant outpost
of our sovereign,
this place called Koshi
where the snows fall,
so far away
it's under a separate sky,
mountains are tall,
rivers magnificent,
plains so broad
the grass grows thick on them.
When sweetfish run
in the peak of summer,
the men who fish with cormorants,
those island birds,
shine their torches
on every clear shoal
of the running river,
pushing upstream through the waters.[1]
And when fall comes
with dew and frost,
and birds in great number

---

[1] The cormorants swallow the fish attracted by the torches; the fishermen then force the cormorants to disgorge them.

flock in the fields,
I call out
my hardy men,
and of all the many hawks
in the world,
none like my arrow-tailed,
my Big Black,
decked out with
his silver-coated bells!
In the morning hunt
he flushes five hundred birds,
at the twilight hunt
downs a thousand.
Whatever he chases
never gets away,
and though he leaves my arm,
he returns with no trouble—
you'd look long to find
another like him!
No other hawk
could be his equal,
I thought in my heart,
and proud
and smiling
I passed my days,
when that fool,
that idiot old man,
not even telling me
what he was up to,
on a rainy day
when skies were overcast,
said simply
that he was going hawking—
And then he came back
and reported between coughs
that my hawk had turned tail
on the Mishima fields,
"soared away
over Mount Futagami,
flying on and on
till he was lost in clouds. . . ."
I had no way
to call him back,

couldn't even think
what to say,
a fire burning
in my brain,
pondering, longing,
with sighs that had no end.
And on the chance
I might meet him,
on this side and that side
of the foot-wearying mountain
I spread nets
and posted watchers.
At the shrine
of the awesome gods
I offered a shining mirror,
with woven goods besides,
praying, entreating.
And while I waited,
in a dream
a young girl announced to me:
"That fine hawk
you dote on—
he circles till evening
above the beach at Matsudae,
crosses the Himi River
where they catch the shad,
sails back and forth
over Tako Island.
In Furue
where the reed ducks gather—
he was there yesterday
and the day before.
As soon perhaps
as the next two days,
at the latest
no longer than seven days—
before that time has passed
he'll come back to you—
don't grieve your heart
any longer!"—
so the dream told me.

ENVOYS

With my arrow-tailed hawk
perched on my arm,
so many days since I've hunted
in Mishima fields—
it's been a month now!

Spreading nets
on this side and that side
of Mount Futagami,
that hawk I waited for—
a dream brought word of him!

TWELVE TANKA WRITTEN IN EARLY 750

Written on viewing peach and damson blossoms in my garden at twilight on the first day of the third month:

The spring garden
shimmers in crimson—
peach blossoms shed
their red glow over paths
where young girls idle

In my garden,
are they petals of the damson,
or the last of the light snow
that fell
in the courtyard?

Spring comes
and the night sadly wanes away.
The snipe that beats its wings
and cries—in whose field
does it make its home?

Second day: I picked a willow catkin and thought of the capital:

On a spring day,
the trailing willows—
I take them in my hand
and remember
the broad streets of the capital

Plucking a blossom of the dogtooth violet:

Like a throng of warriors,
young girls crowd around
to draw water—
a temple well, and beside it,
flowers of dogtooth violet

Watching wild geese returning north:

The season has come
for swallows to appear—
hidden in clouds
the wild geese cry,
recalling their old home

Because spring's here,
they return to their old home,
but on autumn winds
they'll come again,
crossing the red-leafed mountains

Hearing plovers cry in the night:

Night far gone,
and when I woke,
plovers crying,
circling the river shoals
with a heart-breaking sound

River plovers crying
in the waning night—
the men of old,
how right they were
to find it moving

Hearing pheasants call at dawn:

Darting over the cedar brakes,
the pheasants cry so loud,
like incautious lovers
that give themselves away

Echoing with the cries
of pheasants among
the eightfold peaks,
the mists of daybreak
are mournful to look at

Hearing the song of a boatman rowing up the river in the distance:

In my morning bed
I hear him far off—
the boatman at dawn
singing as he ascends
the Imizu River

Sorrowing at the Impermanence of Life

Since that time far off
when heaven and earth began,
the world has been a place
where nothing goes unchanged—
so it has been told
over the ages.
And when I look up

to scan the fields of heaven
I see the bright moon
waxing and waning,
and those treetops there
on the foot-wearying mountain—
when spring comes
their blossoms open and shine,
but with autumn
dew and frost will blanket them,
the winds worry them
till their yellow leaves have scattered.
And we of this world
are the same, it seems—
the glow of red faces
fading away,
hair black as leopard-flower seeds
that loses its color,
the morning smile
vanished by evening—
like the buffeting wind
that no eye can see,
like flowing water
that never rests,
nothing is constant,
everything changes,
and seeing it, my tears
fall in sudden showers
and I cannot make them stop.

ENVOYS

Even the trees that speak no word
flower in spring
and when fall comes
scatter their yellow leaves—
for nothing goes unchanged

When I see how in this life
nothing remains constant,
I hold my heart
apart from the world
and spend many days in thought

SEVEN TANKA WRITTEN IN EARLY 753

On the eleventh day of the first month a heavy snow fell,
piling up a foot and two inches:

In the palace and beyond,
the wonder
of this huge fall of snow—
don't trample it,
don't spoil it!

From bamboo groves
in my garden
already the bush warbler
now and again calls—
and here it is, snowing!

Plums already blooming
in the fence yard
where bush warblers call—
in this snow
will their petals scatter?

Twelfth day: serving in the palace, I heard the plovers cry:

On river flats, too,
the snow must have fallen:
in the palace,
plovers crying—
they have no place to go

Second month, twenty-third day, two poems written on the spur of the moment:

Mists trailing over them,
the spring fields
are sad—
in the evening shadows
a bush warbler calls

Breezes blowing
through the little clump
of bamboo by my house—
how soft their sound
this evening

On the twenty-fifth day:

Through the bright gleaming
rays of spring sun
the lark ascends—
alone, pondering it,
my heart is sad

Expressing My Humble Thoughts

In the reign of
that far-off ancestor too,[2]
all under heaven
was ruled from
this light-swept land
of Naniwa—
even today
they go on telling of it.
And now our great lord—[3]
it awes me
to speak of her,
god that she is—

[2] Emperor Nintoku (313–399), who had his palace at the seaside in Naniwa in present-day Osaka.
[3] Empress Kōken (718–770).

in the start of spring
with its bending limbs,
when a thousand different blossoms
unfold and shine
and mountains when you look at them
are the rarest sights,
and rivers when you look at them
flow fresh and clear,
now when all things
are in their splendor,
she surveyed the land,
observed it with care,
and here raised up
these halls of
the Naniwa palace.
From lands of the four directions
the boats bearing
tribute for her
thread their way
through the canals,
in the morning calm
plying oars as they go upstream,
with the evening tide
dipping their poles, moving seaward.
Pushing and crowding
like flocks of mallards,
we go out to the beach
and look over the sea,
and beyond the white waves
that break in fold on fold,
the little boats of the fishermen
are bobbing here and there,
near and far
fishing with flares
to provide food
for the royal table.
A setting wonderful
in its spaciousness,
so superb,
so vast—
seeing it, I know
why rulers have dwelt here
since the age of the gods.

ENVOYS

Cherry flowers
at their finest now,
when in the light-swept palace
by the sea of Naniwa
our sovereign reigns

I think how I'd like to spend
a year in Naniwa
where the reed leaves blow,
looking out at the vastness
of these stretching seas

The Age of Tanka

Preface to the KOKINSHŪ[1]

Japanese poetry has its seeds in the human heart, and takes form in the countless leaves that are words. So much happens to us while we live in this world that we must voice the thoughts that are in our hearts, conveying them through the things we see and the things we hear. We hear the bush warbler singing in the flowers or the voice of the frogs that live in the water and know that among all living creatures there is not one that does not have its song. It is poetry that, without exerting force, can move heaven and earth, wake the feelings of the unseen gods and spirits, soften the relations between man and woman, and soothe the heart of the fierce warrior.

[1] The opening paragraph is translated. The five poets that follow are among the major figures in the anthology and its period, even though one of them, Sugawara no Michizane, is represented here only by his kanshi.

ARIWARA NO NARIHIRA

(825–880)

EIGHTEEN TANKA

Though winds blow,
coloring the
autumn bush clover,
my heart is no grass or leaf
that changes hue

On Nunobiki Waterfall:

Someone must be
unstringing them wildly—
white beads shower down
without pause,
my sleeve too narrow to catch them

Before we've had our fill,
must the moon so quickly
hide itself?
If only the rim of the hill
would flee and refuse it shelter!

If there were no such thing
as cherry blossoms
in this world,
in springtime how untroubled
our hearts would be!

On a birthday:

Cherry blossoms,
scatter and hide it,
that road they say
old age comes by—
make him lose his way!

In the end I find
I take no pleasure in the moon—
these very moons,
when they pile up,
are what bring us to old age!

To a lady glimpsed in her carriage:

Seen, and yet not seen—
that such a one could be
so longed for—
today I spend the whole day
hopelessly gazing

Neither waking or sleeping,
I saw the night out,
and now spend
all day in thought,
staring at these long spring rains

Pushing home at dawn
through autumn fields of bamboo grass,
my sleeve is wet—
wetter still on those nights
when I return without seeing you

So fleeting,
that dream of a night
we spent together—
and when I doze off it seems
more insubstantial than ever

When Narihira went to the province of Ise, he met in secret
with one of the priestesses of the Ise Shrine. The following
morning he was fretting because he had no way to send her
a message, when this poem came from her:

Did you come here?
Did I go to you?
I don't even know—
Was it a dream? a reality?
Were we sleeping? were we awake?

Reply:

I lost my way
in a darkness
that blinds my heart—
dream or reality—
let the people of the world decide

Written for a woman in Narihira's household to send to a
suitor [Fujiwara no Toshiyuki] who complained he was
wetting his sleeve with a "river of tears":

A shallow river of tears
if it only wets your sleeve!
When I hear you've washed away
body and all,
then perhaps I'll trust you

Fujiwara no Toshiyuki sent the same woman a letter saying,
"I wish I could go to you at once, but since it's raining, I'm

afraid that would be difficult." When Narihira heard of this,
he wrote the following poem for her to send as her reply:

So much to ask,
so hard to ask it—
do you still care or don't you—
the rain knows my dilemma,
falling in greater torrents than ever

Narihira had been carrying on an affair in secret with a
woman who lived in the west annex of the palace of the
Gojō Empress, but after the tenth day of the first month,
she went into hiding somewhere else. He learned where she
was living, but was unable even to send her a letter. In the
spring of the following year, on a beautiful moonlit night
when the plum blossoms were at their height, he recalled
the events of the previous year and went to the west annex,
where he lay all night on the rough floorboards and composed this poem:

Surely this is the moon,
surely this spring
is the spring of years past—
or am I the only one
the same as before?

When Narihira's mother was living in Nagaoka [south of
the capital], Narihira was often unable to visit her because
of his duties at the palace. Once, in the closing month of the
year, a message arrived from her marked "urgent." When
Narihira opened it, he found no letter, but this poem:

I'm getting older,
and there's that parting
that won't be put off—
more and more
it makes me want to see you!

Reply:

In this world
there should be an end to
partings that won't be put off!—
for the sake of a son
who'd have you live a thousand years

Written when ill:

In the end
that's the road I'll travel—
I've known that all along—
but I didn't think I'd have to start
this very day

ONO NO KOMACHI

(mid-ninth century)

NINETEEN TANKA

Submit to you—
could that be what you're saying?
the way ripples on the water
submit to an idling wind?

No seaweed in this bay—
and no seeing me either—
doesn't he know that?
forever coming here,
wearing out his fisherman feet

I've gone to him
by dream paths,
my feet never resting—
but it can never match
one glimpse of him in real life

Because I fell asleep
thinking of him—
was that why he appeared?
If I'd known it was a dream
I'd never have waked up

Ever since I dozed off
and met the one I long for,
I've begun to count on
these things called dreams

My thoughts of you are endless,
and now that night has come
I'll visit you by dream paths—
they can't blame me for that

Sheer fiction,
that autumn nights are longer—
we've hardly met
and before we know it
dawn's breaking through!

In waking hours
natural perhaps,
but even in dreams—
how miserable, to be forever hiding
from the eyes of others

When longings
press too fiercely,
in the night,
black as leopard-flower seeds,
I wear my robe turned inside out[1]

No way to meet him,
no moon to light his way,
I wake up with longing,
my chest a raging fire,
my heart in flames

[1] See note to the second anonymous exchange, p. 74.

What do you tell me now,
I who grow old
in this rain of tears?
Your words, like the leaves,
have changed their hue

They change,
though you can't see it
in the color of their faces—
these blossoms that are the hearts
of the people of this world

A time comes when
leaves yellow in the blustering wind,
pile up before you know it
like heaps of gloomy words—
is it that time now?

I pity those rice stalks
blasted by the autumn wind,
fruitless as this love of mine
you've grown tired of

Forgotten by the one
I was so sure
would come asking about me—
since then all I do
is wonder if I even exist

When Fun'ya no Yasuhide was made a third-rank provincial
official in Mikawa, he sent a message asking if she wouldn't
like to do some country sightseeing. She sent this answer:

I've grown so wretched,
I'd break this sad body
off from its roots,
drift away like a floating weed
if the current were to beckon

The beauty of the flowers faded—
no one cared—
and I watched myself
grow old in the world
as the long rains were falling

Those who were here are gone,
and the gone grow in number—
in this world I sorrow,
wondering how long
I myself can go on sighing

"Imagining her death and cremation":
Sad—the end that waits me—
to think at last
I'll be a mere haze
pale green over the fields

TWENTY-ONE ANONYMOUS TANKA FROM THE *KOKINSHŪ*

Now that I've built my house
near the meadows,
morning after morning
I hear the sound
of the warbler singing

Cherry flowers,
the image of
our fleeting world—
no sooner have they opened
than they begin to fall

Orange blossoms that came
with the fifth month—
breathing their scent,
I catch the fragrance of the sleeve
of someone from long ago

That cuckoo who sang
on and on last summer—
is it he now,
or another,
calling in a voice unchanged?

When I see the moonlight pouring
through gaps in the trees,
I know that autumn
with its heartaches
has come

On autumn nights
the dew is
colder than ever—
in every clump of grasses
the insects weep

Even before they fall
I think how I'll miss
these autumn leaves—
they're the last bit
of color we'll see

Autumn mists,
don't rise up this morning!
give me at least a far-off glimpse
of oak leaves reddening
on the Saho hills

Through autumn fields of bush clover
where the wasps drone,
at dawn the traveler
sets out—
when can I look for his return?

We part,
I go beyond the
endless clouds,
but would I ever let you
out of my heart?

How I think of it!
that boat in the morning mist
of Akashi Bay,
moving dimly dimly
out of sight beyond the islands

Even in the roaring torrent
there are quiet spots,
they say—
why has my love
no stretches of calm water?

Now summer's come,
smoky torches at every house
drive away mosquitoes—
and I—how long will I go on
smoldering with love?

If a seed is there
the pine will sprout
even among boulders;
if I love and keep on loving,
can we fail to meet?

If love could be bought
at the price of a life,
how willingly
would I die

Because I loved someone
who didn't love back,
I wail till the
mountain echoes answer

Like the light snow
that piles up
until it crumbles,
how often my thoughts crumble
under the weight of love

If I'd known
it was old age calling,
I'd have locked the door,
said "No one home!"
and refused to see him

What is constant
in this world of ours?
Yesterday's deeps
in the Asuka River
today have turned to shallows[1]

My hut is at the foot
of Mount Miwa—
if you miss me,
come look for me
at the gate where cedars stand

In this world
what can I point to
and call my home?
Home is wherever
I rest my feet

[1] The Asuka River was noted for its varying depths.

SUGAWARA NO MICHIZANE

(845–903)

I Give up Trying to Learn to Play the Lute[1]

I was certain that lute and calligraphy would help my studies,
idle seasons beside the window, seven stretched strings—
but no concentration of mind brings improvement—I squint in vain
    at the score,
fingering so confused I keep having to ask the teacher.
My choppy "Rapids" never has an autumn river sound,
my frigid "Raven" no sadness of a nighttime cry.
Music experts all inform me I'm merely wasting time—
better stick to the family tradition, writing poems!

Dreaming of Amaro

Since Amaro died I cannot sleep at night;
if I do, I meet him in dreams and tears come coursing down.
Last summer he was over three feet tall;
this year he would have been seven years old.
He was diligent and wanted to know how to be a good son,
read his books and recited by heart the "Poem on the Capital."[2]
Medicine stayed the bitter pain, but only for ten days;
then the wind took his wandering soul off to the Nine Springs.
Since then, I hate the gods and buddhas;
better if they had never made heaven and earth!
I stare at my knees, often laugh in bitterness,
grieve for your little brother, too, buried in an infant's grave. . . .[3]

---

1 The *koto* or horizontal lute, called in Chinese *ch'in*. A Chinese gentleman was expected to be accomplished at lute and calligraphy.

2 A long poem on the city of Ch'ang-an by the seventh-century T'ang poet Lo Pin-wang; according to contemporary sources, it was used in Japan as a text for little boys learning to read Chinese.

3 A note by the poet says that Amaro's little brother died shortly after. Two lines of very uncertain meaning have been omitted at this point; they are philosophical in purport and apparently refer to the transitory nature of human life.

How can I bear to hear your sisters call your name, searching;
to see your mother waste away her life in grief!
For a while I thought the ache in my bowels had mended;
now suddenly it comes boiling up again.
Your mulberry bow over the door, the mugwort arrows;
your stilts by the hedge top, the riding whip of vine;
in the garden the flower seeds we planted in fun;
on the wall, words you'd learned, your scribblings beside them—
each time I recall your voice, your laugh, you are here again;
then I hardly see you day or night and all becomes a daze.
A million missteps in this realm of Sumeru,
three thousand darknesses in this world of life—
O Bodhisattva of Mercy,
watch over my child, seat him on the great lotus!

On Vacation: A Poem to Record My Thoughts

[Written in 892 in Kyoto, when the poet was a high government official. Officials were given every sixth day off from work, but those of upper rank could request a special five-day leave.]

I put in for a five-day leave,
a little vacation from early duty at the office.
And during my leave where do I stay?
At my home in the Sempū Ward.
Gates bolted, no one comes to call;
the bridge broken, no horses pass by.[4]
Up early, I call the boy
to prop up the last of the chrysanthemums.
As the sun climbs higher, I urge the old groom
to sweep and tidy the sand in the garden.
At twilight I take a turn by the eastern fence,
try to wash and dust it, but the bamboo topples over.
When evening comes, I begin thinking of my books,
in rue-scented silk covers, five cartloads.[5]

---

[4] His house in the Sempū Ward faced west on a small stream called the Horikawa.

[5] The rue was to protect the books from insects. In the fifth month of this year, Michizane had presented his work on Japanese history, entitled *Ruijū kokushi*, to Emperor Uda and was probably preparing additions or corrections to it.

Spotting the volumes I need, I take them down,
making notes to add on items overlooked.
The cold sound of fallen leaves by the stairs;
in dawn breath, flowers of frost on the flagstones:
at cockcrow I lie down, arm for a pillow,
quietly thinking, grieving for friends far away.
My girls are in the inner rooms helping their mother;
the little boy tags around after Grandpa;[6]
but I have duties that cannot be shirked,
I must leave and set out on the long road to the palace.
One sigh brings a sinking feeling in my stomach,
a second sigh and tears begin to flow.
The east already light and still I haven't slept;
glumly I sip a cup of tea.
Heaven is indifferent to my longings for leisure;
even at home I'm busy all the time.
Karma piled up from long ages past
keeps us coming and going in these bitter lives.

To Comfort My Little Son and Daughter

[Written in 901, in Kyushu, where the poet had been
banished after being stripped of his titles and offices. All of
Michizane's older daughters remained in Kyoto, while his
older sons were exiled to other provinces. Only his two
youngest children were allowed to accompany their father
to his place of exile in Kyushu.]

Your sisters all must stay at home,
your brothers are sent away.
Just we three together, my little children,
shall chat as we go along.
Each day we have our meals before us,
at night we sleep all together.
We have lamps and tapers to peer in the dark,
and warm clothes for the cold.
In past years you saw how the Counselor's son
fell out of favor in the capital;

---

[6] In a poem written in Sanuki, Michizane mentions that one of his
daughters had given birth to a son in the seventh month of 889, presumably
this boy.

now people say he's a ragged gambler,
and call him names on the street.[7]
You've seen the barefoot wandering musician
the townspeople call the Justice's Miss—
her father, too, was a great official;
they were all in their day exceedingly rich.
Once their gold was like sand in the sea;
now they have barely enough to eat.
When you look, my children, at other people,
you can see how kind Heaven has been!

Reading a Letter from Home
[Written in 902 in Kyushu]

Three lonely months and more without news—
now a favorable wind blows me a letter.
"Someone made off with the tree by the western gate.
Strangers have set up camp in that lot in the north garden."
Ginger wrapped in a paper marked MEDICINE,
a bamboo packet of seaweed "for fasting days."
Not a word of the hunger and cold my wife and children must be
    suffering—
she didn't mean it that way, but I worry all the more.

On a Snowy Night Thinking of the Bamboos at Home
[Written in 902]

Since I was suddenly sent away
I had to leave you far behind;
between this western outpost and the eastern hedge at home
barriers and mountains cut off all word.
Not only does the earth yawn between us,
but we must face the sharp chills of heaven.
Unable to sleep, I fret in silence
at the flurry and tumble of an all-night snow.
Nearby I watch white-thatched roofs being buried;
far away I know your jade-sleek stalks must be breaking.

---

[7] Yoshiomi, son of the Dainagon Nambuchi no Toshina; he lost his
post as an official sometime after 887 and drifted into the life of a gambler.

The old family servant ran off long ago—
who will brave the cold to sweep your branches clean?
Upright by nature, you bend in confusion;
holding firm, you are mercilessly cracked and broken.
Your tall stalks would have made fine fishing poles—
I'm sorry I didn't cut them sooner;
short ones were just right for writing slips—
a pity I didn't long ago whittle them into shape.
With writing slips to fondle, fishing poles to dip,
how unbearably happy life might have been!
No matter how many times I say it, it's useless now,
and only brings more tears and sighs.
Though I cannot be there to prop them up,
I know my bamboos will never forsake their constant green.

Rainy Night

[Written in 902, in exile. As may be seen, the poet was
suffering seriously from the effects of malnutrition.]

The hours of the spring night are not many,
the breath of spring rain should be warm,
but a man with many sorrows
finds himself at odds with the season.
When the heart is cold, the rain too is cold;
nights when you can't sleep are never short.
The gloss is gone from my skin, my bones dry up;
tears keep coming to sting my eyes;
boils and rash, beriberi in my legs—
shadows of sickness darken my whole body.
Not only does my body fail me—
the roof leaks, no boards to fix it,
dampening the clothes draped on the rack,
ruining the books and letters in their boxes.
And what of the plaints of the cook,
tending a stove where no smoke rises?
Rain may bring excess of joy to farmers;
for a stranger in exile it only means more grief.
The grief and worry form a knot in my chest;
I get up and drink a cup of tea,
drink it all, but feel no relief.
I heat a stone, try to warm the cramps in my stomach,

but this too has no effect,
and I force myself to down half a cup of wine.
I must think of the Emerald Radiance,[8]
think! think! put my whole heart in it!
Heaven's ways of dealing out fortune—
how can they be so unfair!

The Lamp Goes Out

[Written late in 902, a few months before the poet's death]

It was not the wind—the oil is gone;
I hate the lamp that will not see me through the night.
How hard—to make ashes of the mind, to still the body!
I rise and move into the moonlight by the cold window.

[8] The Pure Land of the Emerald Radiance, presided over by the Buddha of Healing, Yakushi Nyorai.

LADY ISE

(died 939)

ELEVEN TANKA

On a plum tree blooming by a stream:
This stream that
through the years
has played mirror to the blossoms—
will they cloud it,
scattering their dust of petals?

Now when spring mists rise,
the wild geese
turn and fly away!
They must be used to living in villages
where no cherries bloom

Spring rains weaving
eccentric brocades
across the face of the water—
will they dye all the hills green?

Sleeping with someone who came in secret:
Speak of this to no one,
not even in dreams—
and in case the pillow
should be too wise,
we'll have no pillow but our arms

My love is as endless
as the waves of the Sea of Ariso
that, driven by fierce winds,
never cease their breaking

I want to see him
but even in dreams I don't dare—
morning after morning
I'm more ashamed to see
how love has changed my looks

Written when, troubled with thoughts of love, she went
along the road and saw the fields being burned off:

If only my body
were these winter-seared fields—
though I burned,
I could look forward
to the spring to come

Well matched, well matched to mine—
the moon's teary face
lodging in the tears
on my sleeve
when I think of the one I love

Wishing someone long life:

Whether winds from the mountain
blow over them or not,
the cliffs the white waves break on
endure forever

On selling her house:

Though the Asuka River[1]
is not my home,
my deeps, it seems,
have given way to shallows,
my house become a trickle of coins

In a humorous vein:

Even the old Nagara Bridge in Naniwa
I hear has been rebuilt—
now what's left
that's ancient enough
to compare to me?

[1] See note to the tanka on p. 120, "What Is Constant."

KI NO TSURAYUKI

(c. 868–c. 946)

THIRTY-FIVE TANKA

Waters we dipped from,
wetting our sleeves,
are frozen now—
will the breezes of this
first day of spring unbind them?

Mists rise, tree buds swell,
and when the spring snow falls,
even in villages with no blossoms
blossoms come whirling down

Whenever I visited Hatsuse, I stayed at a certain person's home. One time when I went there after a long absence, the host said (with some sarcasm), "Your house is right here where it's always been!" I broke a spray from a flowering plum that stood nearby and recited this:

As for people—well,
I don't know how they feel,
but in my old home
these flowers still bloom
with the same scent as before

In springtime
when the plum trees bloom,
though I cross Mount Kurabu
after dark,
I know for sure they're there

When night fell, when day broke
I never took my eyes off you,
plum blossoms—
in what moment of my absence
did you fade?

Blossoms, at least wait
until the breezes
scatter you—
it's too sad to see you
wither of your own

It's spring!
when threads of the green willow
twine together,
or tangle among blossoms
that are bursting their seams

Have the spring mists
so completely hidden Mount Miwa?
Flowers must be blooming there
that no one knows of

Written when visiting a mountain temple:

I found lodging
on the spring mountainside
and slept the night—
and in my dreams, too,
blossoms were falling

Kerria roses on the banks
of Yoshino River—
even their shadows in the river bottom
have been carried away
by the blowing winds

On the impermanence of life:
Autumn chrysanthemums—
while they're at their best
I'll make them my ornament—
for all I know
I may be gone before the flowers

On summer nights
just when I'm about to lie down,
a cuckoo sings out his one note
in the breaking dawn

That hill where
the twilight cicadas sing—
it's so close
I hear their voices
as the last sun rays shine

As autumn mists
rise up to veil them,
the red leaves
seem to drift down
in the dimness

The rays of the autumn moon
shine so clear,
you can even see
the shapes of
the red leaves as they fall

We've hardly parted
when I long
to see you again,
like white waves
that keep returning to the shore

Seeing someone off:

This thing called parting
has no color,
yet it seeps into our hearts
and stains them with loneliness

That's how life is—
someone I've never set eyes on,
faceless as the blowing wind,
and yet I love her

Like a wild cherry
glimpsed dimly
through a break in the mist—
that's the kind can
stir you to desire

Fifth-month hills,
treetops so tall
the cuckoo seems to sing
from the empty air—
and I cry in this empty love of mine

Along the Yodo
where they cut wild rice,
when it rains the marsh waters overflow,
like my love,
growing deeper than ever

On the death of his nephew Ki no Tomonori:

For all I know, I myself
may never see tomorrow,
but while today lasts
I'll grieve for another

On viewing plum flowers at a house where the master had
died:

You bloom
with a color and fragrance
as rich as in the past,
but I long for the sight
of the one who planted you

My longings unbearable,
I went to see my love—
the winter night's river wind
so cold the plovers cried

My heart, so entranced
by the springtime hills,
today again has passed
the long long day there

Stalks of rice,
reaped and drying
in the mountain paddy—
hard to see them as the little seedlings
we wet our sleeves planting

Kudzu vines clinging to
the hedges in the shrine
of the awesome gods—
they too, when fall comes,
must put on a different hue

Foot-wearying mountain
with white clouds
trailing over it—
is this the day I cross
by its pathway of jutting planks?

Sixth month, cormorant fishing:

When torches cast their light,
in the depths of the night river
black as leopard-flower seeds,
the water bursts into flame

At the Yamagoe pass in Shiga I talked with a certain person
by a rocky spring. When we parted, I wrote this:

I dip with my hands
but drops muddy the mountain spring
before I've quenched my thirst—
still thirsty for your company,
I must move on

"Written in the year before his death":

Though I know in time
it will come again,
I'm the one
who can't be trusted—
that's why I hate to see spring go

"On a dead child, from the *Tosa Diary*":

She's dead—but in my grief
I forget,
and as though she were still alive,
I keep asking,
"Where's she gotten to!"

In this world
there are many kinds of longing,
but no longing to match
the longing for one's child

Some, childless when they left,
return now with children—
and one who *had* a child
comes home in sorrow alone

Born here, you never lived
to come home again—
it hurts to see
this little pine
that grows by my house

ŌE NO ASATSUNA

(886–957)

Rhyme-prose on the Marriage of Man and Woman

[The rhymes used in this *fu* or poem in rhyme-prose form
spell out a sentence reading: "Love and emotion bring mutual response, and afterward the body becomes pregnant
(full)."]

Most virile of beings—man;
Gentlest creature—woman:
Their love and affection will find a way to mingle,
No matter how parents may prohibit and protect.
First he solicits the matchmaker,
Skilled in all the art a glib tongue can command,
Then plies her with Japanese poems,
Bit by bit tangling the strings of her heart.
He seeks a glimpse of her face, so hard to see,
Listens for a voice as yet unheard.
As his yearning grows more fervid, he smiles in secret;
As the talks grow more intimate, he feels his heart break.
"Like the jeweled tree in my garden,
Like the faithful pine," he gestures, "I vow to flourish!
Like the felicitous herbs in my room,
Like the golden orchid," he points, "I promise to be pure!"
And now bodies grow subtly mild,
Their wills little by little aroused,
She dwelling in loveliness,
In charms a match for Ono no Komachi,
He speaking with a quiet elegance
That would shame Ariwara no Narihira.[1]
Their longings begin to race forth wildly;
True passion now is born.
Her form resplendent, replete with all beauty,

---

[1] Ono no Komachi was famous for her beauty, Ariwara no Narihira
for his handsome looks and finesse as a lover.

Her posture tall and stately, with power to topple cities;[2]
She dyes her crimson sleeve in a hundred scents
Till he has fallen slave to their fragrance;
Wraps her white fingers tight about his hand
And already he is lost in mazes of emotion.
A woman values her chastity,
The completion that comes with the marriage rite;
But when they've vowed to be true for a thousand years,
She finds joy in the first night's union.
When the dew of dawn gathers,
It wets her fresh new garments;
Where night's pale moonlight falls,
It lights her soft shining form.
Her eyebrows painted in willows of Wei,
Lips touched with rouge of Yen,
Where once she hung silk curtains about her,
Bashful lest even her kin catch a glimpse,
Now she turns the gauze lamp to the wall
And suddenly snuggles up to a stranger.
What at first she only endures
Later becomes most familiar.
Unbinding the sash of her single robe,
Knowing she cannot tie it again,
Baring flesh white as snow,
Forgetting for once to be ashamed:
"He's the one I'm to be buried with,
The mate I will share through all my life!"
When the form is lovely, love will be deep,
When passion penetrates, the body will grow full:
Not the union of husband and wife alone that counts,
But the thought of sons and grandsons to rely upon!
He broaches the gate where moisture abounds,
And fluids overflow to stain their undergarments;
They look about, but there's no one at the door:
Moans grow louder, impossible to still.
Love's raptures are hard to forbear—
Who among us is a saint or sage?

[2] A reference to the lines in the poem attributed to Li Yen-nien of the
Former Han:

> "Beautiful lady in a northern land,
>   standing alone, none in the world like her,
>   a single glance and she upsets a city,
>   a second glance, she upsets the state!"

The mutual response of yin and yang,
This is the Creator's natural way.
And when hearts have subsided and rest in stillness,
They linger by Peachflower Paradise banks, forgetting to return;
After juices have freely flowed,
They lie wrapped in dreams of a Heaven of Perfect Peace.
But thoughts once roused know no end,
And longings may leave one sleepless and distraught;
Should widows and young boys hear of such things,
None but would be stirred to desire!

MINAMOTO NO SHITAGŌ

(911–983)

Song of the Tailless Ox

I have an ox but its tail is missing;
everyone pokes fun at my tailless ox.
Born a wild calf, it was chewed by a wolf,
but I well understand why it escaped the wolf's jaws:
it's so wise you'd take it for an old pine spirit,[1]
far plumper and bigger than those grazers under the fruit trees.
And though it lacks a tail, it has five virtues;
with your leave, I'll rap its horn and count them one by one.
  (first virtue)
First, when it eats tender grass and turds come flopping down,
it has no tail to swish about and dirty up the shafts.
  (second virtue)
Should it stray into a garden and rouse the owner's ire,
there's nothing he can tie a dead ox skull to.[2]
  (third virtue)
Again if it mingles with herds of cows in the broad meadow,
the herdboy can spot it far off without searching about.
  (fourth virtue)
Black ox with dots of white hair on its back—
a wise man of old examined it and caught the thief.[3]
But in your case, to seize the scoundrel, determine the thief,
what need to scrutinize and report on hair?
Even a short tail might omen long life for the culprit,
but with you he's certain to end up in chains.

[1] Reference to a Chinese legend concerning the spirit of an ancient pine tree that turned into a gray-green ox.
[2] A note by the poet explains that if an ox wanders into a garden, the owner of the garden will tie an ox skull to its tail and make it run several miles.
[3] According to a Chinese work, a man had a black ox with white markings on its back which was stolen. The magistrate thereupon offered to pay double the regular price for ox hides, and when one of that description was brought to him and identified by the owner of the ox, the thief was arrested.

(fifth virtue)
Other people's sons and daughters race about in carts,
off on long trips to mountain temples, short ones to market taverns,
sometimes not returning till dusk or even the following day,
wearying the ox, wearing down the wheels, worrying the owner.
But because my ox has no tail, no one wants to borrow it—
though others laugh in scorn, I have no cares.
Tailless, tailless, hark to what I say!
Never have I used you to plow paddy or field,
nor driven you east and west, fetching and hauling,
and the rare times you hauled a load, I charged no fee.
It's not that I can't bear to see you put to work;
poor, I've forgotten how to make a living at farming or trade.
Old now, I stick to my post, though the stipend's skimpy,
and number in my household no lackey or groom.
In grass-green spring I have no sleek horse to straddle,
in snow-white winter I've trouble patching together a proper cloak.
True, you're here to pull me, but is that such a comfort?
Tailless, tailless, do you know what I mean?
While we serve a wise sovereign, we live for loyalty, not wealth!
That's why I get up early, rest but little at night.
And if my worthless loyalty should win some paltry return,
tailless, I'll surely pay you for your years of hard work!

LADY IZUMI

(born c. 976)

Love

Unaware of my black hair in disorder, I lay face down, till he first lifted it—it's him I miss

•

Tonight, as hail falls on bamboo leaves, rustling, rustling, I don't feel like sleeping alone

•

Loving you, my heart may shatter into a thousand pieces, but not one piece will be lost

•

Someone who did not come to visit for a long time finally did, but again stopped coming:
If you'd left me unhappy and hadn't come, by this time I might have forgotten all about you

•

Waiting for my two lovers stationed in distant places:
Having waited for this one for this, that one for that, I can no longer tell which is who

•

In the ninth month, to someone who went home at dawn:
You left, the mist lingered by the hedge, and yes, I had nothing to do but gaze at the sky

•

Even my pillow, not knowing, won't talk. Don't tell of your dream
of this spring night, my love, as you have seen it

.

Don't tell people how it was, pillow of white cloth; what you think
of me is troubling enough

.

I want to see and be seen by you—if only you were the mirror I face
when I wake each morning!

.

To someone, when I was distressed:
To remember you in the next world, where I will be soon, I'd like to
meet you just one more time!

.

Sometime in the third month a man spent a whole night talking with me and went home. The next morning he sent
word that he felt frustrated:
No wonder you're grieved this morning; you didn't even try to dream
one spring night through

.

To a man I met only briefly:
White dew, a dream, this life, an illusion—all these, by comparison,
last long indeed

.

There's no color called love in this world, yet how thoroughly it has
dyed my heart!

.

In the eighth month a man came to see me and left behind a
fan with a painting of dew on bamboo leaves. In returning it
a while later:
You rose with eastern clouds and left—the dew on bamboo leaves has
stayed longer with me

.

If I should forget you because of this unhappiness, I would not consider my heart my own

.

While both he and I had to keep our affair secret, he demurred, "This is not my heart's desire." Finding it hard that he should be so resentful:

Aware that your body cannot follow what your heart desires, you should show me more understanding

.

To a man who said, "You've forgotten me":

Have I not forgotten you! If I hadn't, I certainly would, if I looked into your heart again!

.

A man who used to write to me didn't get in touch with me for a long time:

Less troublesome than unforgettable: an affair that simply ended without any acrimony

.

To a man who left me early in my life:

Whether or not I am as I was—I'd like to ask the one I used to see, for I can't tell

.

Down the mountain into the path of darkness I've come, so as to see you just one more time

.

From Prince Atsumichi:

If I speak of love you'll think I am like everyone else, but my heart this morning is incomparable

In reply:

I don't think you are like everyone else; for the first time I find myself in troubled thought

From Prince Atsumichi:

I tell myself not to doubt you, never to resent you, but my heart
doesn't follow my heart

In reply:

Don't keep your heart from resenting me; I too doubt you, you rely
on me boundlessly

*Elegies for Prince Atsumichi, Who Died on the Second
Day of the Tenth Month, 1007*

On the night of the last day of the year:

Dead people come to visit tonight, I'm told, but you aren't with me;
the village I live in is without souls

·

On the seventh day of the first month, when it snowed heavily:

I wish I could see you like this snow: last year it faded—it is falling
again!

·

As I began to think of becoming a nun:

Discard myself—just the thought is bitter: this body, after all, once
so intimate with you!

·

You are gone, and I have nothing unhappy to remember—this or that,
which would make me forget you

·

I miss your voice as you talked to me—your face is before me as it
was, but it does not say a word

·

One body, but heart shattered into a thousand pieces, a great many
things grieve me

·

Because I do not know where you are, I cannot direct my thoughts, saddened as they are by things

·

Though my heart isn't a summer field, luxuriantly my love for you goes on growing

·

Clearly he would notice: in my eyes, clouded by tears, the moon at dusk

·

It would console me to see you—even between flashes of lightning at dusk, seen, not seen

·

No dreams through the night, and the day breaks—yearnings then go as far as yearnings can

Elegies for Her Daughter, Ko-Shikibu, Who Died in the Eleventh Month, 1025:

Donating for sutra-chanting a box she used to carry with her:

That she may know I love her and miss her—clinking a bell, thinking of her, without a moment's interval

·

The retired empress Jōtōmon sent word, "Have [Ko-Shikibu's] Chinese robe with a dew design sent to me; I'd like to use it for the cover of my sutra." In having the robe sent to her, I tied the following to it:

The dew that formed remains; to what shall I compare that transient one who faded?

Jōtōmon's reply:

Had we expected this—that the dew that formed transiently on the sleeve would be a keepsake?

The retired empress Jōtōmon sent a roll of fabric as she used to do before Ko-Shikibu's death. Seeing "For Lady-in-Waiting Ko-Shikibu" written on it:

Bitter—that I should not have decayed under the moss with you, but found your unburied name!

•

Looking at my grandchildren:

Having left us, which of us does she care for? I think more of my child, she, surely, of her children

Seasons and Other Subjects

On spring fields there was only snow, I thought, but they're sprouting—those young herbs!

•

Plum fragrance startles me again and again—darkness of this spring night makes me yearn for my love

•

No soothing time for someone who thinks of blossoms, though in the heart no wind blows

•

Breaking off rock azaleas, I look at them; they're like the vermilion clothes my love wore

•

Today again, quietly and leisurely I make my ablutions, as dew from hemp leaves falls on my cicada-wing robe

•

Harbor plovers calling to their friends, voices sharp—clear above the ice, a daybreak moon

•

I look around: because charcoal firing warms the air, the snow on the Ōhara hills has faded in places

•

Lost in thought—even the firefly from the marsh seems to rise out of my body, like my soul

•

"Among the tanka written for screen paintings": Three people passing on horseback, looking at wild flowers:
We retain the flowers in mind as we pass, leaving ourselves to the unconcerned horses

•

"Matters I want settled": three tanka:
Which should I think shouldn't exist in this world, those who neglect or those who are neglected?

Which is worse, to miss someone dead or to be unable to meet someone alive?

Which is worse, to love someone far away or to see often someone you don't love?

•

The moon above the clouds doesn't look like the moon; I feel as if I were facing a dustless mirror

•

To a sage in Harima:
From darkness into the path of darkness I'm bound to enter. Shine on me in the distance, moon at the rim of the hill

KAGURA

Sakaki, or a Sacred Tree

FIRST HALF

Because of the fragrance
of sakaki leaves I came;
here a great many people have gathered,
   many people have gathered.

SECOND HALF

The sakaki leaves
on the divinely fenced hill of the gods' chambers
grow in front of the gods luxuriantly,
   luxuriantly.

Bamboo Grass

FIRST HALF

On the bamboo grass
snow falls and piles up this winter night;
what a delight to dance!

SECOND HALF

Since the age of freshly made fences and the gods,
we've held the leaves of bamboo grass
and danced!

Sword

FIRST HALF

Sporting a sword
with clasp ornaments made of silver,
whose son is it, sauntering through Nara,
   whose son is it, sauntering?

SECOND HALF

I wish I had the sword
of that man of Furuya in Isonokami!
Flaunting a braided cord I'd walk the road to the palace,
walk the road to the palace!

Ina Field

FIRST HALF

In the brushwood field of Ina
known for grebes, snipes come flying,
the sound of their wingbeats exciting,
the sound of their wingbeats!

SECOND HALF

In the brushwood field of Ina
known for grebes, my husband spread a net.
How many has he caught?
How many has he caught?

Ripples

FIRST HALF

Ripples! Karasaki in Shiga!
You women pounding rice are good!
You here, you there,
let me be your loving husband,
your loving husband!

SECOND HALF

Rice-pounding crab in the paddies by the reed plain!
Is it that you haven't got a bride?
Raising your arms, lowering them,
lowering them and raising them,
doing an exercise like that!

Cricket

FIRST HALF

The cricket's angry, furious!
He came to the royal garden,
    dug and ate the roots of a tree,
and broke his feelers, broke his feelers!

SECOND HALF

He's angry, furious!
He came to the royal garden,
    dug and ate the roots of a tree,
and broke his feelers!

Kehi Shrine

FIRST HALF

Like the leaves of kudzu vines
on Mount Kumasaka near the capital,
I'm restless, but you tell me to sleep alone at night,
dear god, you tell me to sleep alone at night!

SECOND HALF

Like the leaves of kudzu vines
I'm restless, but you tell me to sleep alone at night,
dear god, you tell me to sleep alone at night!

SAIBARA

Summer Spinning

"I have seven measures of white thread
I spun in the summer.
I'll make a jacket from it for you.
      Come, leave your wife!"
"You talk silly, that's what you do.
Your hemp clothes—you aren't my wife,
you can't make the sleeves well, the shoulders easy to wear,
the collar comfortable, or can you?"

House

"At your house, at the end of your roof,
the rain pours, and I have stood, getting drenched.
      Open the door of your room!"
"There's neither clamp nor lock
on that door. Why should I lock it?
Open it and come in. Am I someone's wife?"

What Can I Do?

What can I do? What?
To be like ducks, wood ducks,
I go out, and father grumbles that I loiter.
But has he picked a wife for me?

The Cock Crows

The cock crows.
May Sakuramaro keep coming,
thrusting his thing forward, and doing it,
till you bear a child!

Yamashiro

In Yamashiro, near Koma,
lives a melon grower, a melon grower,
    a melon grower.
The melon grower says he wants me.
What will I do? What will I do?
    What will I do?
What will I do? It'll work out all right
by the time his melons grow ripe, grow ripe,
    by the time his melons grow ripe.

My Wife and I

Here on the hill where my wife and I live,
don't touch the magnolia,
it will look better if you don't, look better faster!

Two Kids

Two kids slept separately,
arm's length apart, but they rolled toward each other,
    and ended up together.

Powerless Frog

Powerless frog, powerless frog,
boneless earthworm, boneless earthworm.

Deep in the Mountain

Deep in the mountain, are you cutting trees, grandpa?
Are you carving trees, are you carving those trees,
    carving trees, grandpa?

AZUMA ASOBI UTA

Suruga Dance

On Udo Beach,
on Udo Beach in Suruga, waves roll in and break;
my love like seven grasses says things that please me,
    says things that please me;
my love like seven grasses says things that please me;
when she comes to me, yes, we'll go to bed!
my love like seven grasses says things that please me!

FŪZOKU UTA

Koyorogi

"Stepping about on the beach of Koyorogi,
on that beach,
  the girl is gathering plants.
Don't wet her, don't wet her,
stay in the offing, stay, waves!"
"I won't mind getting wet, if I can gather plants
for you to eat, plants for you to eat."

Wood Ducks

Wood ducks, teals, even mallards come and stay
in Hara Pond. Don't reap the plants in it, roots and all,
  so they can grow again,
  so they can grow again!

In the Distance

"In the distance, way over there,
in Adachi Field, a trunk stands,
a trunk stands, a trunk grows,
and he thinks he's like that,
  when I won't even sleep with him."
"If he wants to think he's like that, let him.
Though he thinks he's like that, I don't think he's bad."

Brocaded Sash

"I'll untie my sash brocaded with a wheel design.
When you come in the evening, be quiet, my love."
"Let me in quietly, my darling, let me in quietly.
They've all gone to sleep."
"Like the cloud crossing the face of the moon,
I see you clearly, I see you clearly."

THIRTY-TWO SONGS FROM
THE *RYŌJIN HISHŌ*

Lord Buddha is present everywhere,
but it's a pity he's not incarnate.
When there's no human sound, at daybreak,
he shows himself faintly in my dreams.

.

Lying awake quietly at daybreak,
I can't hold back my tears at various thoughts.
Having spent my life in vain,
when can I expect to reach the Pure Land?

.

Things that dance well, exquisitely:
vestals, oak leaves, hubs of wheels,
thousand-tops, midget dancers, puppeteers,
and in the flower garden, butterflies and birds.

.

Even if I had to sleep alone
        for a hundred days, a hundred nights,
why in the world should I want
        someone's husband for the night?
From evening till midnight would be good,
but at daybreak, when the rooster calls,
        my bed would be desolate.

.

Here at the row of shacks on the hunting ground,
I'll make him stand outside my room a while,
I'll punish him early tonight;
last night and the night before, he didn't come.
He said sorry, yes, he did,
        but I must teach him a lesson.

.

You, a man who made me wait but didn't come,
may you turn into a devil who sprouts three horns,
may people hate you!
Turn into a bird in water paddies
     where frost, snow, hailstones fall,
and get your feet frozen!
Turn into a floating weed on the pond
and waver and wobble, this way and that!

.

Four Songs

The young man came to make you his wife,
posing, he slept with you two nights;
on the third night, around midnight,
     before the break of day,
he picked up his pants and ran away!

You have no heart.
If you said I was nothing
     or that you wouldn't live with me,
I might hate you.
We were torn apart by my father and mother—
they can cut me up or slice me, I won't live without you!

Looking at you, my beauty,
I wish I could be a single-root vine
that I could twine around you from root to tip!
They can cut me up or slice me, I won't separate from you,
     that's my fate.

The brocade and rush hat you loved—
it dropped, it dropped
into the Kamo River, into midstream!
I've been looking for it, asking for it,
and now the day has come, the day has come
after a rustling, clear autumn night!

.

Was I born to play?
Was I born to frolic?
Hearing the voices of children playing,
I feel my body stir.

.

The bamboo grass in front of the Ōji Shrine
thrives, though horses eat it.
Though you don't come to my night-room,
I thrive because I'm young.

.

My daughter must be past ten by now,
must be going places, a wandering vestal.
When she carries salt water in Tago Bay,
many workers will gather.
        Saying, "She's too young,"
asking her questions or not asking, they'll abuse her.
        Poor child!

.

My son must be twenty by now,
must be going places, a wandering gambler.
Facing gambler-bosses in various provinces—
he's my son after all, I certainly don't hate him.
You Ōji gods of Sumiyoshi and Nishinomiya,
don't let him lose!

.

Things lately fashionable in the capital:
painted eyebrows, hairdos, hairpieces,
saltwater bathrobes, Ōmi ladies, women in men's clothes,
and not a nun who doesn't have her halberd!

.

Things exceedingly swift:
goshawk, falcon, hawk on the hand,
        waterfall,
bundles of brushwood rolling down the hillside,
prayers said at the Three Places, Five Places.[1]

.

1 Shrines in Kumano.

The potter at Mimaki in Kusuha—
he makes pots, but his daughter's good-looking.
Ah, she's so beautiful!
If I could put her on a love cart
in a procession of three carts, four carts,
and have her called "the governor's lady"!

.

Things a prostitute likes:
songs, a drum, a boat,
a bearer of a large umbrella, a woman sculler,
a Hyakudayū to pray to for a man's love.[2]

.

Things hilariously bent:
shrimps, traps, cows' horns, they say,
tips of old-fashioned caps, they say,
hips of the old men leaning on their sticks, they say!

.

Women are at their best
when fourteen, fifteen, twenty-three, or twenty-four;
when they get to be thirty-four or thirty-five,
they're no different from the lower leaves on a maple.

.

Dance, dance, snail!
If you don't,
I'll make a colt, a calf, kick you!
I'll make them stomp on you and crush you!
If you dance truly prettily,
I'll let you go and play in the flower garden!

.

---

[2] Emperor Goshirakawa (1127–1192), who compiled the *Ryōjin hishō*, had an *asobi* or prostitute for his teacher of songs. Singing was a prostitute's chief means of entertainment, and the drum the sole instrument for accompaniment. Many prostitutes lived in port towns, and having a boat was important for welcoming and sending off a customer. Two retired prostitutes helped the active one on her boat, one holding a large umbrella over her head, the other sculling. The Hyakudayū was probably a phallic object of worship.

When my mirror clouds up,
I look worn to a shadow;
when I look worn to a shadow,
my man turns away from me.

.

Head-lice make merry on my head,
always eat the hollow of my nape,
descend from heaven on the teeth of my comb,
end their lives on the lid of my fiber box!

.

Things a sage likes:
just go to visit Mount Hira—
        he sends his acolyte to gather
honey mushrooms, meadow mushrooms, sulfur shelves,
even the roots of lotus lodging in the pond,
        parsley roots, water shields,
burdocks, spatterdocks, asparagus, fiddleheads, horsetails.

.

Things a terrifying exorcist likes:
distasteful!—frozen wild potatoes,
mustard, rice washed with water, raindrops,
and from the marshes, parsley roots.

.

Things that pierce the heart:
night travel, boat travel, being on the road,
        a roadside inn,
a voice reciting sutras from a mountain temple
        in a dark wood,
a lover who leaves you before you're tired of him.

.

Stay, stay, dragonfly!
I'll give you lump salt, so stay,
        don't move!
I'll twist a horsetail hair
        on a bamboo-blind slat,
tie you to it,
and let a child, a boy, pull it,
        play with you!

.

If I could only trust a letter to the blowing wind!
    that's what I think,
but then it might drop in some damnable field!

.

Listen, waves, tell of this, beach,
    witness, pine trees:
if a wind blows from someone
    who says I'm the only one for him,
I'll yield to whichever bay!

.

"Much, much in love, you see her by chance,
    then go to bed; that night,
what kind of dream will you have?"
"Thrusting, thrusting, then
holding her tight—that's what I'll dream!"

.

It's raining, but you say, "Go away!"
    I have no hat,
I'm not even carrying a straw coat with me.
How disgusting, you village people,
    that you won't put me up!

.

Let's make love. The night has turned
    to daybreak. Bells are ringing.
We've made love since evening
but I'm not tired.
            What shall I do?

FUJIWARA NO SHUNZEI

(1114–1204)

THIRTY TANKA

We hearing them
are the ones who shed tears—
wild geese bound for home,
crying as they make their way
across the dawn sky

.

The glowing moon
keeps circling on its course
above the clouds—
but cherries are what light
this world of ours

.

Spring night,
and even the moonbeams
filtering through the plum
by the eaves
seem to be scented

.

In my grass hut
in night rain,
thinking of the past—
cuckoo of the mountain,
don't add to my tears!

.

Cuckoo, what are you
doing to my heart?
in the moonlight from
a rift in the clouds,
singing away

.

Showers wet
the orange blossoms,
winds blow over them,
a mountain cuckoo
is singing in the clouds

.

Will someone,
at the scent of orange blossom,
think of me
when I too
am a person of long ago?

.

Where the water
tumbles over the rocks,
each white bead can be counted—
moonlight shining
on Clear Cascade River

.

On the Fushimi hills
as I look out
from the shade of the pines,
over paddies where dawn is breaking,
fall wind blows

.

Kibune River—
the rocky waves of its rapids
tossing beads of spray,
like ice shattered in the
moonlight of an autumn night

.

As evening comes,
autumn wind from the meadows
strikes with a chill—
quails cry
in the village of Fukakusa

.

The mountain stream,
half frozen, half thawed—
its voice at daybreak
sobbing among the boulders

.

   Congratulations:
Our lord's reign—
I would not have it
be a thousand years,
but endless as the moon and sun
coming out from heaven's door

.

Sailing close to shore,
sheltering in a rush hut
on the beach,
I hear beside my pillow
the unaccustomed sound of waves

.

This world—
no road that takes us out of it.
I thought there was,
and pushed deep into the mountains,
but even here the lone deer cries

.

In this world,
so many moments of pain—
journeying through
plains of bamboo grass,
I met my loved one in a dream

.

Sent to a woman on a rainy day:

When longings are too great
and I stare
at the sky in your direction,
spring rains come down,
breaking through the mist

•

One-sided love:

Even *I* hate
this sorry self of mine—
so hate me,
and I'll know we share
at least that emotion

•

Sent to a woman:

Very well—
but at least let me
hope for favor
in some life to come,
I who now suffer beyond enduring

•

The journey is a short one,
this separation I can bear,
but the old have no power
to hold back their tears

•

Written in autumn when spending the night near the grave
of his wife, the mother of Teika:

So seldom I come at night—
there beneath the moss
does she hear forever
this mournful wind in the pines?

•

Written around the middle of the ninth month, when the
moon was shining brightly. In the late fall of the previous
year, he had fallen ill and taken Buddhist vows:

Who'd have thought it?
that the autumn I said goodby to
would come round again
and I'd be here
to see its moon once more

•

When spring comes,
this world once more
calls to me—
in what other world
could I see such blossoms?

•

Dawn:

On my boxwood pillow
I strain to catch it—
the sad note of the temple bell
telling us it's dawn

•

"Written when the poet was seventy-six; his mother died
when he was twenty-five":

Even years ago
I thought of her
as one from years ago—
how useless!—
to be still longing for my mother

•

Old though I am
I still offer gifts—
these jewel tears—
to the year that greets me
and the year that departs

•

"Written when he was well over eighty":

I've picked a grave site,
assuming the time is near—
on autumn hills,
among the mugwort roots,
pine crickets sing

Tangled in neglect,
the autumn garden is mournful—
more so at evening
with the dew about to fade

.

Looking over poems by persons of long ago when compiling
the anthology *Senzaishū:*

Years to come
will there be those
who wish they'd known me too?—
like me, letting their mind
dwell on the past

.

While I gaze far off,
thinking on and on
about this world of ours,
a white cloud vanishes
in the empty sky

SAIGYŌ

(1118–1190)

SIXTY-FOUR TANKA

"A woman forsaken in love":
Why should I resent
a person's growing cold?
Time was
when he didn't know me
and I didn't know him either

Does the moon say "Grieve!"
does it force
these thoughts on me?
And yet the tears come
to my reproving eyes

"A perilous love affair":
Keen to the danger,
constantly I shun
the eyes of others,
treading like one on a plank trail
rigged across the face of the cliff

Now I understand—
when you said, "Remember!"
and swore to do the same,
already you had it
in mind to forget

Why does no one say, "Pitiful!"
or come to comfort me?
In the house
where I long for my love
the wind blows over the rushes

"I know
how you must feel!"
And with those words
she grows more hateful
than if she'd never spoken at all

In some far-off
cleft of the rock
let me live alone,
thinking no longer of outsiders' eyes,
thinking only of my love

Why regret to leave
a world that merits
no regrets?
You save yourself only
when you cast yourself away

"After entering religious life":
I have cast off the world
but there are thoughts
I cannot cast away—
I who have yet
to part from the capital

Let me take a good look:
the old cherry,
even its blossoms are sad—
how many more times
will they see the spring?

Cherry petals,
like the tears
of someone who's lonely,
showering down
when the wind blows cold

Why should my heart
still harbor
this passion for cherry flowers,
I who thought
I had put all that behind me?

Gazing at them,
these blossoms have grown
so much a part of me,
to part with them when they fall
seems bitter indeed!

The deep snow that
fell and piled up on the high peaks
has melted:
white waves on the waters
of Clear Cascade River

Ice wedged fast
in the crevice of the rock
this morning begins to melt—
under the moss the water
will be feeling out a channel

Cuckoo—
I've yet to hear him
but I'll wait for him here
in this stand of dense cedars
on Yamada moor

Across the face of the field
ragged grasses
darken:
the chill clouding-over
of a sudden storm sky

Moon-viewings in the capital
when I thought
such sad thoughts—
now I know they were no more
than idle pastimes

Even a person free of passion
would understand
this sadness:
autumn evening
in a marsh where snipes fly up

In a hailstorm
you can hear
they're there all right—
the dried leaves fallen
from the twigs of the oaks

In Akishino
is it raining
in the foothill villages?
Clouds hang over
Ikoma's peak

On the road with not a soul
to keep me company,
as evening falls
katydids lift their voices
and cheer me along

In willow shade
where clear water flows
by the wayside—
"Just a while" I said
as I stopped to rest

With blooms of pampas grass
for markers
I push my way along,
no trace of the trail
I vaguely remembered

Was it a dream,
that spring in Naniwa
in the land of Tsu?
Now the wind blows over
the dead leaves of the reeds

As banked clouds
are swept apart by the wind,
at dawn the cry
of the first wild geese
winging across the mountains

Little boat with no treadboard
crossing the straits,
take care!
The hail pelts wildly
and the swift wind sweeps in

Pearls plucked,
the oyster shells
lie heaped in mounds,
showing us
the aftermath of treasure

In a channel
where the turban shells live,
the sight of divers busily
hunting them
in the hollows of the rock

Side by side
the bonito boats approach
the cape of Irako,
bobbing on the waves
of the northwest wind

The float-rigged strands
of the nets
that catch little bream
seem to be moving shoreward—
sad work in Shiozaki Bay[1]

[1] Here and elsewhere Saigyō deplores occupations such as hunting or fishing that involve the taking of life.

Neglectful, we've yet
to fix the towrope
to the sled—
and here they're piled up already,
the white snows of Koshi!

Mount Arachi so steep,
no ravine to descend by,
but the white snow
offers us
a snowshoe trail

Clear waters unchanged
in a meadow
I saw once long ago,
will you remember
this face of mine?

The leaves have fallen
in this village at
the foot of Mount Ogura
and I can see the moon
shining in the tops of the trees

How lonely, the light of the moon
shining into my hut,
the only sound, the clackers
that shoo away birds
in the mountain paddies

Today again
I'll go to the hill
where pine winds blow—
perhaps to meet my friend
who was cooling himself there yesterday

Shut in by spring showers
that pour from the eaves,
idle, idle,
unknown to others—
this is the place he lives

The twilight cuckoo
quite at home in our village—
I pretend not to hear,
hoping to make him
speak his name again

The wild geese departing,
their wings in white clouds,
call longingly to their friends
in the paddies
before my gate

In the little weeds
that sprout in my wall
a cricket wails—
he must be peeved at the dew
that soaks my garden

Crickets—
as the cold of night
deepens into autumn
are you weakening? your voices
grow farther and farther away

Who lives here
must know what sadness means—
mountain village,
rain drenching down
from the evening sky

A garden that recalls the past,
but in it I stack
driftwood for fuel—
hardly the kind of year-end
I used to know

If only there were
someone else
willing to bear this loneliness—
side by side we'd build our huts
for winter in a mountain village

In a mountain village
at autumn's end—
that's when you learn
what sadness means
in the blast of the wintry wind

In the shade of a remote mountain
where I live alone,
will you be my companion
now the storm has passed,
moon of the winter night?

As I look at the moon
my mind goes roaming,
till I live again
the autumns that I
knew long ago

Butterflies darting
so familiarly among the flowers
that bloom by the fence—
I envy them, yet know
how little time they have left

Trailing on the wind,
the smoke of Mount Fuji
fades in the sky,
moving like my thoughts
toward some unknown end

One lone pine tree
growing in the hollow—
and I thought
I was the only one
without a friend

On the impermanence of life:

Drops of dew
strung on strands
of spider web—
such are the trappings
that deck out this world

Since I no longer think
of reality
as reality,
what reason would I have
to think of dreams as dreams?

[Saigyō's statement on poetics: Look to the past, for only
then can your work serve as a model for the future.]

Let us seek the past,
be an age
that cherishes the old—
then our "today" one day
will be someone's "long ago"

Did I ever think
in old age
I would cross it again?
So long I've lived,
Saya-between-the-Hills[2]

Who lies here
I do not know:
Mount Toribe at sundown,[3]
one after another
the terrible graves

[One of a series on scenes depicted in paintings of Hell]

Did I hear you ask
what the fires of Hell
are burning for?
They burn away evil
and the firewood is you!

[From a series of thirteen poems written "in a light vein"]

Startled by the sound
of children wildly blowing
on straw whistles,
I wake from my summer
noonday nap

Drawing his
sparrow-hunting bow
of bent bamboo,
the little boy seems to be wishing
for a guardsman's black hat

---

[2] A long winding road over the mountains in present-day Shizuoka.
[3] Mount Toribe is a hill east of Kyoto used as a crematorium and graveyard.

Just to play
hide and seek
the way I did long ago—
crouched down in a corner,
squeezing in so tight

"Observing children":
I too
grew up the same way,
playing games
like them
in the garden sand

To the dead
make offerings
of cherry flowers—
so I would say if someone
were to mourn me when I'm gone

Let me die in spring
beneath the blossoming trees,
let it be around
the full moon
of Kisaragi month

When you consider,
all in this world
are blossoms that fall—
and this body of mine,
where will I lay it down?

PRINCESS SHIKISHI

(died 1201)

SEVENTY-EIGHT TANKA

Spring

In spring too, what first stands out is Mount Otowa:[1] from the snow
at its peak the sunrays appear

Deep in the mountains, the pine door isn't aware of spring—on it,
intermittently dripping, beads of melting snow

The rim of a foot-wearying mountain hazy at dawn—from the valley
rises the call of a bird

I look far to the end of the haze—mountains with shelves of white
clouds against the dawning sky

With spring manifest on moss-grown, decaying eaves, the plum tree
of my house, unaged, emits its fragrance

With plum blossoms from the fence visiting my sleeves, dreams while
I doze fade on my pillow

Opening on plum twigs in the unfaded snow—cloth dyed with those
first blossoms brings back the past

---

[1] A mountain east of Kyoto, famous for its maple trees.

Allured outside by someone's plum branches in bloom—the wind is
fragrant in the darkness of the spring evening

Which peak do these blossoms come from?—cascading into my garden
as if released from a dam

Would there were other means of consolation than blossoms! Coldly
they fall, coldly I watch

As I sleep somewhere near a mountain away from home, spring is
fragrant in reality and in dreams

Only intermittent beads of water from the eaves calling; it's hard to
console myself in a village where spring has aged

Layers of eightfold kerria roses in such a glow, when what is left of
spring is counted in days

The wild geese leave no trace in the citadel of water, as they disappear over the waves into the clouds

As I look, there's no place for my thoughts to go, with spring ending
in the evening sky

Summer

Did the cuckoo pity me in the sky and speak to me? As sleepless
nights continue, a single call at midnight

Calls of a clapper rail far into the night—moss-grown gate closed to
all but the moon

As I gaze, the moon dims; on the face of the garden only a few fireflies are left

Summer night—little time to see the crescent moon decline, before the
day breaks at the rim of the hill

Water fragrant in my hands, I traced it upstream, where I found its
source under an orange in bloom[2]

The clouds of May rain have closed into one—water beads from the
roof, unstrung, chaotic

Without a trace it has cleared on this side of the clouds—the shower
toward evening drenching the mountain slope

A short night—outside the window bamboo rustles, faintly hinting
autumn, while I sleep

Leaves of bamboo near my window stirring with the wind, ever
shorter my sleep, and my dreams

Sleeping, wanting to have the past that does not return—to the pillow
in my dream a fragrance of orange

The night deepens, the sound of water trickling among the rocks becomes clear, and it becomes cool in the bed where I lie

Though the shining sun is clearly of the summer sky, among the
winds under the pine leaves, that season has passed

Passing the cedar grove at Osaka Barrier, I cup my hands together
and scoop water from the mountain well

Autumn

The first day starts, and "All's changed," I think, but my autumn-
dyed heart may be the first to turn color

Since a wind over the rushes told me that autumn came, things I think
about have become unusual at dusk

The clear-toned cicadas have exhausted their voices on the hillside
when, again, the evening bell startles

In the garden where no one comes, wrapped in short reeds, in the
depth of the dew, a pine cricket chirps

Away from home: over the dewdrops fragile on my pillow, lightning
at dusk gleams intermittently

The voices of insects and a stag by the fence, as one, disturb me to
tears this autumn evening

Evening mists in the depths of my heart, while I grieve; the autumn,
as it wanes, is mine alone[3]

Through the autumn night, quiet and dark, rain beats on the window,
I in grief, until the air grows white

Oppressing all, sunken in autumn sorrows: a village at the foot of the
mountain in the depth of evening mists

---

[3] Allusion to Ōe no Chisato's tanka on p. 208, "Looking at the moon."

Watching, I have grown lonely. If only I had a lodging outside the autumn! The moon lives in the field and on the hills

The autumn night grows late; on a flower the moon and the beads become more polished

Dream broken by the sound of a mallet beating a thousand times, my thoughts, dewdrops on my sleeves, shatter

I've grown used to the pine door unclosed, leaving it to the light of the moon that nightly crosses the River of Heaven

The moonlight is and is not as of old; more and more my thoughts turn round the same thing, like a *shizu* spool[4]

Winter

October: as a storm sweeps down Mount Mimuro, Tatsuta River tie-dyes itself in crimson[5]

The brocades left at the treetops ceased to be; from the garden the autumn colors have departed

Over the shingled roof the shower has passed, but still falling, unceasing—it must be the leaves

As winter comes, the sound from the valley stream stops, and a wind from the mountain visits my window

---

4 Allusion to the tanka in Chapter 32, *The Tales of Ise:* "Turning the old *shizu* spool round and round, if only I could turn the past into the present!" *Shizu* is an old type of fabric.

5 Allusion to Ariwara no Narihira's tanka on p. 211, "Unheard of."

As I looked, winter came: along the edge of a cove with wild ducks, thin ice formed

In the cold winds, leaves are cleared from the trees night by night, baring the garden in the moonlight

A winter night: the moon, clear beyond a leafless tree, clouds suddenly as the first shower comes

Frost that will not fall from the grebe's wings, no matter how he flaps them—can't you see it's moonlight?

Tumultuous winter sky all day—now it suddenly turns cloudy, sleet slashes aslant, winds competing

An Uji River boat piled with brushwood, unable to pull up to shore— one after another the drops from the pole turn to ice

Away from home, in Fushimi village, the day breaks; across the frost of harvested fields a crane calls

Piercing to the marrow: beyond a garden fire, a frosty star, clear, rising into the daybreak sky

Wind of heaven, the maidens cross the ice this winter night, as the moonlight glistens on their sleeves[6]

Days accumulate; the more snow falls, the more smoke from charcoal kilns, desolate in Ōhara village

---

[6]Allusion to Yoshimine no Munesada's tanka (*Kokinshˆu*, no. 872), "On seeing Gosechi dancing princesses": "Wind of heaven, blow shut the path to the clouds, so the figures of the maidens may stay a while."

Love

Be a guide—this is a boat rowing in the traceless waves, not knowing
where to go, eightfold ocean wind

Faintly as a fisherman's bonfire way in the offing, I saw him and since
have been in love

Not even for a moment have we joined—gossip already as rank as the
grass in a summer field

Does he not know how, like a cloud on Mount Katsuragi, I rise and
sit, and how I feel each time?

For a moment we lay in the village of Fushimi, until the evening dew
lodged in our sleeves and we have returned

"I'm much in love, but look at me, I'll survive all this"—that isn't what
I said, and you know it

String of beads, if you must break, break. If you last longer, my endurance is sure to weaken[7]

Forgetting, I grieve this evening—these months and days I've lived,
when only I have known

Waiting for you, I have not entered my bedroom. Do not stop shining
on its cypress door, moon at the rim of the hill

[7] A "string of beads" is a metaphor for life.

"And still," I say, and wait, but months and days pass, all reliant on his heart, the blossom, the color[8]

Shallow of me: I have grieved over this uncertain life, when our vow was destined to turn out this way

Yet to be reconciled with the reality of the dark for a moment, I go on wandering from dream to dream

Miscellany

As I grow used to the mattress of moss and the pillow of rock, the sound of mountain water cleanses my heart[9]

No one to lose his way among the heaped up leaves, even the birds do not step into the garden of my house

Deep in the mountains, through the pine door closed soon after dark, only moonlight leaked in at daybreak

Every day, throwing my heart down into the valley a thousand times, I am and I am not, while I live

Counting the dewdrops that vie in falling off, I still rely on those at the tips of short reeds

[8] Allusion to Ono no Komachi's tanka on p. 115. "They change."
[9] Allusion to a tanka in vol. 4 of *Sagoromo monogatari:* "These days, with a mattress of moss laid out for himself, he must be fond of sleeping with a pillow of rock."

How could I possibly have lived until today, while saying of someone, "If only he were alive"?[10]

On the evening when, alone, I leave my village, I know the moon at
least will see me off

Things I have seen, the future I have yet to see, all in the illusion that
forms a moment over my pillow

When I look around in the quiet before dawn, the night is still deep,
troubled with dreams

Not knowing the dream without beginning has been a dream, will I
wake when this one ends?

[10] Allusion to Fujiwara no Tameyori's tanka (*Shūishū*, no. 1299): "The
people who I wish were alive in this world have grown so many!"

MYŌE

(1173–1232)

TEN TANKA

How they sting!
my single-layered
summer robe
can't shield me from
the feet of the rain

Night deepening,
and in this mountain temple
where winds are chill,
over my robe I wear
a layer of autumn mist

Because fog engulfs
the grass hut
where I am,
I feel as though
I've melted into the sky

A shining moon,
the mind is cleared
from clouds of darkness,
and in the gate of deliverance
pine winds blow

Winter moon
emerging from the clouds

to keep me company,
the wind—how it stings!
the snow—how cold it is!

Watching the moon go down:
Set now,
and I too will go below
the rim of the hill—
so night after night
let us keep company

A floating cloud
has no fixed place
it stays—
why should I hate
the buffeting winds?

Under the pines,
on the cliff top,
sleet on my
black-dyed sleeves—
strings of white jewels

While I, with no guide,
am left to stray
in darkness;
where has the clear moon
wandered to?

Bright bright!
bright bright bright!
bright bright!
bright bright bright!
bright bright, the moon!

FUJIWARA NO TEIKA

(1162–1241)

EIGHTY-FOUR TANKA[1]

The rising sun casts the same light over the sea in all directions, but among the waves today, spring stirs

In May rains the water, the waves, rise around the water oats, as short the summer night before the day breaks

The Plain of Heaven, think of it, is no different in color, but autumn has that light of the moon

Only one or two nights since winter came, but each blade of bamboo grass is crowded with frost

Look, this must be love that fills the sky! As soon as the thought rises, smoke smolders

Somehow my heart settles on the hill's rim, where this year, I first see the crescent moon[2]

Away from the direction of falling blossoms, spring passes on the other side of the haze

---

[1] Arranged in rough chronological order.
[2] Recalls Ōtomo no Yakamochi's tanka (*Man'yōshū*, no. 994): "As I turn round and see the crescent moon, I think of the eyebrow of someone I had a glimpse of."

Cicada voices rising continually, far away, I beneath an oak I cannot see the top of

Here again, another useless sign of the floating world: in an autumn field, on a flower, a dewdrop

As I look out, there are neither blossoms nor crimson leaves: by a cove, a thatched hut, this autumn evening[3]

Coming to an end and leaving the moon as a keepsake, autumn adds even to it some strange light

The light of the moon that crosses the Plain of Heaven: almost touchable, yet beyond the clouds

Thinking of the past I wake, mind empty—the moonlight gone, I do not know where

Under the lower leaves of hydrangea fireflies cluster—another set of petals, I first thought

If only I had my phantom to send to you, passing through people's eyes meshed as tightly as a reed fence

In my birthplace, the garden and the hedges are overgrown with moss, the flowers, flowering orange flowers, scattering

[3] Allusion to a passage in the "Akashi" chapter of *The Tale of Genji:* "The sound of an instrument that is not especially remarkable can be marvelous, depending on the occasion. Here, there was the sea, stretching far into the distance with nothing interfering, and though there were no blossoms or crimson leaves of spring or autumn at their best, the shadows of plants simply growing here and there looked all the more elegant."

The sound of pine winds and their color are one, the valley river water falling green

Dozing, thoughts interminable in paths of dream—then into reality, when first geese call

Loneliness is more intense with frost than with snow, trees at the hilltop against the dawning sky

On his way home, he may be watching this—the moon at daybreak after I waited throughout the night

Dew, scatter if you will: I part you through bushclover, becoming wet to remember the blossoms

With no more fragrance, the *sakaki*, its voice, and the night has deepened, till the sky with the morning star pierces me

For the one I await the path must have ended at the hill's base; the snow weighs on the cedar near my eaves

In the past too, hearts have separated from hearts—so is the water for seedling beds drawn separate ways

Against the cherries on the hazy hilltop the dawn breaks, the waves of the River of Heaven tie-dyed scarlet[4]

Retaining the colors of snow and moon that I yearn for, the treetops are fragrant in a mountain wind of spring

---

[4] Allusion to Ariwara no Narihira's tanka on p. 211, "Unheard of."

Straw mattress: the Bridge Princess of Uji waits through the night,
autumn wind deepening, moon laid out, alone[5]

As I look, the moon has moved west of the pine tree, its light grown
distant toward daybreak

In the sixth month of the second year of Kenkyū [1191], as
the night with the moon shining bright deepened, the major
captain[6] sent a request that I compose forty-seven tanka incorporating i-ro-ha[7] and have his messenger deliver them to
him. At once I wrote the following:[8]

TEN SUMMER TANKA

Lush emerald the summer color becomes, as pond water reflects the
green of hills

Woods again holing up for winter, under snow—my thought as I part
deutzia along a narrow valley path

Wakeful for last year's call that I loved—still, it's as fresh as ever
when the cuckoo comes

---

[5] Allusion to an anonymous tanka (Kokinshū, no. 689), "Alone with
your clothes laid out on a straw mattress, are you waiting for me tonight
again, Bridge Princess of Uji?" The Bridge Princess of Uji is the guardian
goddess of the bridge; here, a prostitute or a mistress may be referred to.

[6] Fujiwara no Yoshitsune (1169–1206), poet, calligrapher, and prime
minister.

[7] The classical Japanese syllabary, consisting of forty-seven syllables. It
is also a poem, which may be translated: "Their luster remains, but the
blossoms have fallen;/in our world, who goes on forever?/Crossing the
deep mountain of Being today,/I saw no shallow dreams, nor was I drunk."
"Incorporating i-ro-ha" means beginning each tanka with one of the forty-
seven syllables.

[8] Here, only the ten tanka on summer (nos. 11–20) and one tanka on love
(no. 41) are translated acrostically.

Carried overhead and wished upon, hollyhock, under this shining sun
how long shall I last?

You, weary of the waves rolling into autumn—you don't come in the
summer, pine wind of the shore

Take it as a pledge: a dewdrop on a lotus leaf—after it disappears my
soul will be that jewel

Relished as cooler than usual tonight, this wind—as we wait for
autumn by the water of this mountain well

So light the sleeves of this cicada-wing robe I've grown used to—
what if the first wind of autumn comes up and cuts it apart?

Turning and turning, these summer days, to my regret—think of it,
half the year is already gone

Negligently the day opens before I have time to sleep—today this will
end as June comes to a close

ONE LOVE TANKA

Missives, fleeting, my lover's only trace, today my sleeve, the weir,
cannot hold

Suddenly darkening, the sky beyond my eaves shows a number of
them, and before I know it, snowflakes fall

Through a rift in evening rainclouds the sun shines out; across this
side of the mountain a white heron flies

Well into the distance young leaves of grass undulate, skylarks calling
above the fields this spring evening

Troubled throughout the year, I step out this morning: light snow
frozen at the end of loneliness

Even her heart again a stranger's—why then am I unable to give up,
staying on a path of dreams?

In autumn, on the day when there was a storm, I went to
Gojō. As I took my leave:[9]

Like tinkling gems, neither dewdrops nor tears stay—at the house
where I long for the one who's dead, or in the autumn wind

While we bring to dawn the flower and the moon of deep night, the
lamp of spring fades elsewhere

A wind passes, the mirror of blossoms clouds, and I count the spring
days on the garden stone bridge

A stalling ox, shuffling, swirls up dust—hot, even the wind, the summer cart

At the rising, climbing, southern limit there are clouds, but the glaring
sun is spotless these days in the great sky

A traveler's sleeves fluttered by an autumn wind, the evening sun
desolate across the suspended mountain bridge

9 The heading of this tanka in the *Shinkokinshū* (no. 788) says, in part,
"In the autumn of the year when my mother died." Teika's mother, Lady
Kaga, died on the thirteenth day of the second month in 1193. For the
tanka on the same subject by his father, Shunzei, see "So seldom I come at
night," p. 166.

Drawn by the memory of your face I turn to look: above the mountains of the city, the moon, slender

The great sky hazy with scents of plum blossoms, the clouds never leave the moon this spring night

The floating bridge of dreams this spring night comes to an end; on the mountaintop a layer of cloud parts in the sky

Like some ailing leaf, they used to visit me long ago; then the footprints in my garden ceased to be

On the sea god's plain the waves and the sky merge, without a hilltop to receive the setting sun

Not like an ordinary cloud, those mountain cherries, reminding me this morning of an old dream

The scent of plum blossoms touches my sleeve, vying with the moonlight that filters through the eaves

Yearning for the moon hazy with the fragrance of blossoms, I no longer see clear dreams

No shade for halting the horse to shake my sleeves, here near Sano this snowy evening

Autumn gone, the past distant in the great sky, I alone the moonlight as it used to be[10]

---

[10] Allusion to Ariwara no Narihira's tanka on p. 111, "Surely this is the moon."

Above a clear, penetrating wind, the evening moon—on the light it casts, frost falls

How many autumns have I passed shattered in a thousand ways, troubling myself alone with the moon?[11]

Fading, desolate: at the autumn coloring of someone who is changing, I am seared like dew on the forest ground

How can I forget?—spring hazes lost among the blossoms, with only a hint of dawn breaking

Rippling, a wind from the Bay of Grebes interrupts my dreams: under the moon crossing the night, an autumn fisherman[12]

Izumi River: like the bubbles on a pole cleanly plied in the river waves, the summer effaces itself

My thoughts, useless dreams in midair—even if you break, do not break, painful string of beads[13]

When there's love as unrecognized as a lily, a firefly goes about, revealing it himself[14]

The snow falling in quantities and the valley deep, there must be an unknown pine tree buried in it

11 Allusion to Ōe no Chisato's tanka on p. 208, "Looking at the moon."
12 The Bay of Grebes is Lake Biwa.
13 Allusion to Princess Shikishi's tanka on p. 187, "String of beads."
14 Allusion to Lady Ōtomo's tanka on p. 64, "A bell lily."

He does not come, but I wait—by the inlet in the evening calm, my body seared like the seaweed I burn for salt[15]

A hint at the hilltop of the moon I wait for, and I take the spring lamp away from the blossoms

Neglectful, I have not died of love—another year gone, counting on meeting you by living on

The evening voices of cicadas have not dyed them—the lower parts of the trees still with green leaves

Under the lamplight that grows feeble toward daybreak, my troubling thoughts alone do not fade

Above the wind the starlight is clear, as I listen to the random spattering of the hailstones

Regarding my infants as friends from old days, grown used to them, still I feel troubled under this evening sky

Orange flowers scatter in a village against the evening moon, leaving in the sky invisible traces

A lamplight in the window at slow dawn, I have no one who comes to see how I am

On my way home at dusk, the wind blows northward, splashing waves over deutzia flowers along the bank

---

[15] Allusion to Kasa no Kanamura's poem on p. 57.

More melancholy than the bright moon at daybreak is to part at dusk
and lose you among the stars[16]

I lifted her black hair strand by strand—the way she lay face down
rises in my mind[17]

They become fragrant, and the spring ends; the kerria flowers, of all
flowers, must feel the pain

Unable to settle: through the long unending night, your black hair
on our sleeves, spilling, the dew in disorder

Mists above the crimson leaves cleanly swept aside, the peak of Storm
Mountain becomes clear-cut

[16] Allusion to Mibu no Tadamine's tanka on p. 217, "Since our parting."
[17] Allusion to Lady Izumi's tanka on p. 142, "Unaware."

An Outline for Composing Tanka[1]

In emotion, newness is foremost: look for sentiments others have yet to sing, and sing them. In diction, use the old: don't go further back than the Three Anthologies,[2] but use the diction of the masters, including those ancient poets in the *Shinkokinshū*.[3] In style, learn the good tanka of gifted masters: don't ask if they're ancient or modern, but look at appropriate tanka and learn their style. As for the sentiments and diction of the poets of recent times, respectfully ignore them: try hard not to adopt the diction of the poets of the last seventy to eighty years. To use much of the same diction as that of ancient poets is an old practice; but if you borrow from an ancient tanka, you must compose a new one. To borrow as many as three units out of the five[4] is quite excessive and results in a lack of novelty; to borrow two units plus three or four syllables is admissible. Considering this further, it is quite mindless to borrow from an ancient tanka when composing on the same subject: flower alluded to and flower sung of, moon alluded to and moon sung of. When you allude to a tanka on one of the four seasons and sing of love or a miscellaneous subject, or allude to a tanka on love or a miscellaneous subject and sing of one of the four seasons, then no one would criticize your borrowing from an ancient tanka.

---

[1] Believed to have been prepared for Prince Kajii no Miya Sonkai-hō in 1222. A passage of instruction followed by an anthology of exemplary tanka, *Eiga taigai* (An Outline for Composing Tanka), is similar to *Kindai shūka* (Good Tanka of Modern Times), which Teika prepared for the shogun and poet Minamoto no Sanetomo in 1209.

[2] First three of the tanka anthologies compiled by imperial order: the *Kokinshū*, the *Gosenshū* (951), and the *Shūishū* (c. 1005).

[3] Eighth imperial anthology of tanka (1205), of which Fujiwara no Teika was one of the six editors. It includes tanka from the *Man'yōshū*; hence, "ancient poets."

[4] A tanka consists of five syllabic units: 5, 7, 5, 7, 7. Allusion in tanka, a practice not at all discouraged, most often took the form of direct borrowing of words and phrases, and duplication of up to three of the five units was not uncommon.

cuckoo on the foot-wearying mountain[5]

Mount Yoshino on Miyoshi Plain[6]

katsura *tree on the eternal moon*[7]

cuckoos call in May[8]

someone who walks along the spear-adorned road[9]

Things like these [the five phrases cited above] may be used frequently with impunity.

spring has come before the year's end[10]

surely this is the moon, surely this spring[11]

wind under cherry trees as petals scatter[12]

faintly, on the bay of Akashi[13]

5 Five tanka begin with the phrase in the Three Anthologies alone; none of Teika's does.

6 An anonymous tanka in the *Gosenshū* (no. 117) begins with the phrase; none of Teika's does.

7 A tanka by Mibu no Tadamine in the *Kokinshū* (no. 194) and another by Sugawara no Michizane's mother in the *Shūishū* (no. 473) begin with the phrase; Teika has left one beginning with the phrase (*Shūi gusō*, no. 2209). *Katsura* is a tree, *cercidiphyllum japonicum*.

8 An anonymous tanka in the *Kokinshū* (no. 469) and another anonymous one in the *Shūishū* (no. 125) begin with the phrase; so do at least two pieces by Teika (nos. 1855 and 1888).

9 A tanka in the *Shinkokinshū* (no. 232) begins with the phrase; it is by Teika.

10 The opening tanka of the *Kokinshū*, by Ariwara no Motokata, begins with the phrase.

11 See Ariwara no Narihira's tanka beginning with the phrase on p. 111. It is among the more famous pieces by the poet, and tops the fifth volume on love of the *Kokinshū*.

12 A tanka by Ki no Tsurayuki in the *Shūishū* (no. 64) begins with the phrase. The tanka is often quoted as exemplary.

13 A tanka attributed to Kakinomoto no Hitomaro in the *Kokinshū* (no. 409) begins with the phrase. The tanka is often quoted as exemplary.

Things of this sort [the four phrases cited above], though of only two units, may never be used.

Always keep in mind the tones of ancient tanka and steep your mind in them. The ones you should especially follow are the especially skillful tanka in the *Kokinshū, The Tales of Ise,*[14] the *Gosenshū,* the *Shūishū,* and the collections of the Thirty-Six Poets:[15] poets such as Hitomaro, Tsurayuki, Tadamine,[16] Ise, and Komachi. Though he was not a tanka poet, grasp and play lovingly with the first and second books of Po Chü-yi's *Collected Writings*[17] so as to know the truth of the matter, such as the feel of the season and the ups and downs of society; he is deeply empathetic to the heart of tanka.

In tanka, there are no teachers. Simply make old tanka your teachers. Those who steep their minds in the old style and learn their diction from the masters—who of them will fail to sing?

[14] A collection of episodes, each incorporating one to several tanka, which is believed to have taken its present form around 900.

[15] Those chosen as preeminent by Fujiwara no Kintō (966–1041).

[16] Mibu no Tadamine (c. 860–c. 920).

[17] The Chinese poet Po Chü-yi (772–846) greatly influenced the Japanese poets of the time. The first two books consist of poems.

A Compendium of Good Tanka:

> *"I've listed the following as I
> remember them in my senility.
> A mixture of ancient and modern, it
> must be as disorderly as it can be."*

It's the start of spring, they say—is that why the mountains of Yoshino look hazy this morning?[1]

As I pick young herbs for you out in a spring field, snow falls on the sleeves of my robe[2]

As a warbler flits from one plum twig to another, singing, turning its wings cloth-white, soft snow falls[3]

Plum blossoms are hard to make out, because snow is falling everywhere from the endless heavens[4]

About people, no, I don't know how they feel. In my home village the blossoms are as fragrant as they used to be[5]

Cherry blossoms must have opened: in the space between the foot-wearying hills I see a white cloud[6]

---

[1] Mibu no Tadamine. The opening piece of the *Shūishū*.

[2] Emperor Kōkō (830–887). Allusion to Yamabe no Akahito's tanka on p. 61, "In the field."

[3] Anonymous (*Shinkokinshū*, no. 30).

[4] Attributed to Kakinomoto no Hitomaro.

[5] Ki no Tsurayuki. For the heading and Watson's translation, see "As for people," p. 130.

[6] Ki no Tsurayuki.

Since the mountain cherries began to bloom, cascades, white threads, visible where boundless clouds gather[7]

Cherries blossom on distant hills—through a long day, long as the drooping tail of a pheasant, that is the color we never tire of[8]

Throughout the land, blossoms are in their prime: on every ridge a white cloud lingers[9]

The people of the hundred-acre palace must have leisure; sporting cherry blossoms, they have played all day[10]

Now, today, I'll lose myself on a spring hill; if evening falls, won't there be cherry blossoms to rest under?[11]

As I searched for cherry blossoms the rain began to fall; since I'll get wet in any case, I'll hide in the shade of the blossoms[12]

The flower's color has passed, I gazed on it in vain, while I was trying to live my life[13]

Will I see it again—hunting for cherry blossoms in Katano Field, the spring dawn with the flowers falling like snow?[14]

---

[7] Minamoto no Toshiyori (died 1125).

[8] Retired Emperor Gotoba (1180–1239): "When [Fujiwara no] Shunzei celebrated his ninetieth birthday at the Tanka Office, [I wrote the following] on screens, on blooming mountain cherries." Allusion to the ninety-seventh tanka in this compendium.

[9] Saigyō.

[10] Yamabe no Akahito.

[11] Sosei (early Heian).

[12] Anonymous (Shūishū, no. 50).

[13] Ono no Komachi. For Watson's translation, see "The beauty of the flowers faded," p. 116.

[14] Fujiwara no Shunzei.

On a spring day when boundless light is soothing, the blossoms fall so restlessly[15]

From tomorrow, who will visit, if only rarely, the flower garden of Shiga, the old city that spring has left?[16]

Spring passed, and summer it seems has come: they spread cloth-white robes to dry on heavenly Mount Kagu[17]

As I look around, I see a weir of waves built in the village of Tama River, with deutzia in bloom[18]

In May rain, the smoke from the seaweed he burns grows damper, he, more soaked with brine, the cove man of Suma[19]

Under a willow by the road where clear water flows, I stood, thinking, Just for a while[20]

Unexpectedly cool, in summer clothes, when the day turns to evening and the rain has come[21]

The years and months, reluctantly parted with at any other time, are cast away in ablutions this summer evening[22]

[15] Ki no Tomonori (early Heian).
[16] Fujiwara no Yoshitsune (1169–1206).
[17] Empress Jitō. For Watson's translation, see "Spring has passed," p. 23.
[18] Lady Sagami (mid-Heian). Blooming deutzia looks like a weir made of white waves.
[19] Fujiwara no Shunzei.
[20] Saigyō. For Watson's translation, see "In willow shade," on p. 173.
[21] Fujiwara no Kiyosuke (1104–1177).
[22] Fujiwara no Shunzei: "When I respectfully submitted one hundred tanka, I wrote on the ablutions of the sixth month." The sixth month is the last month of summer.

Not many days have passed since autumn began, yet as I lie at day-break, the wind is cool to my sleeves[23]

To my hut overgrown with burdocks, and lonely, no one comes, but autumn has[24]

"Autumn's come"—"The year's half gone"—is the wind saying so, blowing over the reeds, surprising us?[25]

Pity, how the dew must spill from grass leaves—autumn winds have risen on the Miyagino Plain[26]

Looking at the moon, I feel sad in a thousand ways, though the autumn isn't mine alone[27]

Since the sparse bush clover began to flower in my home village, the garden moon changes night by night[28]

Tomorrow I'll come again to this wild path by the Tama River, where, beyond bush clover, in the colorful waves, the moon lodges[29]

[23] Prince Aki (eighth century).
[24] Egyō (mid-Heian). Allusion to an anonymous tanka (*Gosenshū*, no. 194): "My hut where burdocks grow has the voices of summer insects, but not one person comes to visit."
[25] Jakuren (died 1202).
[26] Saigyō. Allusion to an anonymous tanka (*Kokinshū*, no. 1091): "Servants, tell your masters to put on their hats—the dew from the trees here in Miyagino is worse than rain."
[27] Ōe no Chisato (early Heian).
[28] Fujiwara no Yoshitsune. Allusion to an anonymous tanka (*Kokinshū*, no. 694): "Just as the sparse bush clover in Miyagino, laden with dew, waits for a wind, so do I wait for you."
[29] Minamoto no Toshiyori.

Looking at it, just thinking about it, makes me lonely: the sky at daybreak over the eternal Moon Palace[30]

Is it because autumn dew has collected heavily on my sleeves that the moon stays through the long night, never tiring?[31]

The tears of wild geese crying across the sky must have fallen: by the hut where I live, troubled, dew on the bush clover[32]

Bush clovers must have shed their flowers in the field; getting wet with dew I will go, though the night is deep[33]

In the autumn paddies, the roof mats for the makeshift hut are so coarse, my sleeves become wet with dew[34]

As winds blow over white dewdrops in the autumn fields, the unstrung beads scatter away[35]

Princess Tatsuta's headband loosened, disturbing the beads—that's the way they look, these white dewdrops[36]

The wild geese departing, their wings in white clouds, must long for their friends in the paddies by my gate[37]

[30] Fujiwara no Ietaka (1158–1237). It was believed that a kingdom existed on the moon, complete with a palace.
[31] Retired Emperor Gotoba. Allusion to a tanka in the "Kiritsubo" chapter in *The Tale of Genji:* "Even though bell crickets cry as much as they can, through the long night, never tiring, my tears fall."
[32] Anonymous (*Kokinshū*, no. 221).
[33] Anonymous (*Kokinshū*, no. 224).
[34] Emperor Tenji.
[35] Fun'ya no Asayasu (early Heian).
[36] Fujiwara no Kiyosuke. Princess Tatsuta is the goddess of autumn.
[37] Saigyō. Alludes to an anonymous tanka (*Kokinshū*, no. 191): "Wild geese beating their wings in white clouds—even their number can be counted in this autumn moon."

Wild geese lured by the autumn wind and passing over: may they stay away from the hut where someone's deep in thought[38]

Dream broken by the sound of a mallet beating a thousand times, my thoughts, dewdrops on my sleeves, shatter[39]

As far away as distant China is the mind that wakes from a sleep in the midst of autumn[40]

When evening falls, the autumn wind rustles the rice stalks in front of my gate and then comes to my reed-thatched hut[41]

Loneliness has no special color: mountain with stands of black pine in the autumn evening[42]

The autumn wind is and is not as of old. More and more my thoughts turn around the same thing, like a *shizu* spool[43]

As soon as it blows, autumn grass and trees wither—that must be why they call the mountain wind "storm"[44]

Those early-rice paddies by the hill where the stag calls to his wife—I won't harvest them, even if frost forms[45]

---

[38] Anonymous (*Gosenshū*, no. 360).
[39] Princess Shikishi.
[40] Daini no Sammi (Heian).
[41] Minamoto no Tsunenobu (1016–1097).
[42] Jakuren.
[43] Princess Shikishi. For notes, see a variant of the tanka, "The moonlight," on p. 185.
[44] Fun'ya no Yasuhide (ninth century). An ideographic pun: Ideographs for "mountain" and "wind," combined, make an ideograph for "storm."
[45] Kakinomoto no Hitomaro.

When I hear deep in the mountains the call of a deer picking its way through crimson leaves, the autumn makes me full of sorrow[46]

White chrysanthemums they've set up at Fukiage in the autumn wind —aren't they flowers, are they waves breaking?[47]

If I must, I'll have to pick them haphazardly; the first frost obscures the white chrysanthemums[48]

On Mount Moru where both white dew and showers come down heavily, even the lower leaves have all changed their color[49]

Crimson leaves flow in Tatsuta River: showers must have fallen on Mount Mimuro where the gods dwell[50]

Autumn has come; crimson leaves have fallen around my hut: there's no one who picks his way through to visit me[51]

Unheard of even in the age of mighty gods: tie-dyeing the waters of Tatsuta River in Korean crimson![52]

The weir that winds have made in a mountain stream, it's crimson leaves, stuck and unable to flow[53]

[46] Anonymous (*Kokinshū*, no. 215).
[47] Sugawara no Michizane: "A tanka I contributed when a sand beach was made and flowers were planted for a chrysanthemum-matching contest during the same reign [of Emperor Uda]. I wrote of the chrysanthemums planted toward the beach of Fukiage."
[48] Ōshikōchi no Mitsune (early Heian).
[49] Ki no Tsurayuki.
[50] Anonymous (*Kokinshū*, no. 284).
[51] Anonymous (*Kokinshū*, no. 287).
[52] Ariwara no Narihira.
[53] Harumichi no Tsuraki (died 920).

Faintly, in the dawn moonlight, a wind sweeps crimson leaves down the mountainside[54]

Its dark green—what if it should be unable to resist? Ceaselessly showers fall on the divine cedar[55]

In Akishino is it raining on the villages among the outer mountains? Clouds hang over Ikoma's peak[56]

In a winter-seared forest, on decayed leaves, on the frost, the moonlight lies so cold[57]

If you do not come, must I sleep alone, the bamboo-grass on the hill soughing, rustling, through the frosty night?[58]

The ice on my laid-out sleeve still frozen, unmelted, I cannot sleep; dreams tonight are short[59]

In Yatano Field the reeds have turned color; on Mount Arachi the soft snow at the peak must be cold[60]

[54] Minamoto no Saneakira (910–970).
[55] Retired Emperor Gotoba. Allusion to an anonymous tanka (Man'yōshū, no. 2196): "Because showers, rains, ceaselessly fall, the evergreen leaves, unable to resist, have changed their color."
[56] Saigyō. For Watson's translation, see "In Akishino" on p. 173.
[57] Fujiwara no Kiyosuke.
[58] Fujiwara no Kiyosuke. Allusion to a tanka (envoy) by Kakinomoto no Hitomaro (Man'yōshū, no. 133): "Though the bamboo grass, disturbed, rustles the hills, I think of my wife because I parted and came away."
[59] Fujiwara no Yoshitsune. Allusion to a tanka in the "Asagao" chapter in The Tale of Genji: "A winter's night, I wake, lonely, from unmelting sleep; how short are the frozen dreams!"
[60] Kakinomoto no Hitomaro.

Because my home village is close to Mount Yoshino, not one day
passes without snow falling[61]

From now on may it go on falling—the white snow that falls, tossing
the pampas grass near my hut[62]

As it begins to dawn, I almost take for daybreak moonlight the white
snow fallen in the village of Yoshino[63]

Frost has touched the bamboo grass in the Furu Plain of Isonokami
—only one night is left this year[64]

Your Majesty's reign will never end, I think, as long as Mimosuso,
river of the Divine Wind, runs clear[65]

Dew at the tip of a leaf and the drop on the stalk—evidence that
sooner or later everyone in this world will die[66]

Everyone else has changed to a flowery robe. My moss-grown sleeves,
if only they would become dry![67]

[61] Anonymous (*Kokinshū*, no. 321).
[62] Anonymous (*Kokinshū*, no. 318). Allusion to Takechi no Kurohito's
tanka (*Man'yōshū*, no. 4016): "Because of the snow that falls, tossing the
pampas grass on Mehi Plain, I ask for shelter today, I feel sad."
[63] Sakanoue no Koremori (early Heian).
[64] Fujiwara no Yoshitsune.
[65] Minamoto no Tsunenobu.
[66] Henjō (816–890).
[67] Henjō: "During the reign of the Emperor of Fukakusa [Nimmyō,
810–850] I was serving His Majesty in close attendance, day and night, as
chief chamberlain; but when the anniversary of his parent's death came, I
stopped even going to my office, climbed Mount Hiei, and shaved my
head. The following year, hearing that the people shed their mourning
clothes and that some were promoted and were joyful, I wrote this." "Moss-
grown sleeves" here symbolizes priesthood.

Bitter—that I should not have decayed under the moss with you, but found your unburied name![68]

Because limits are set, today I have taken off my mourning robe, but there's no end to my tears[69]

I remember, I burn brushwood, smoke rises in the evening—happy to cry in, it reminds me of you[70]

The cloud, a reminder of my lover who passed away, must have faded, though its color is not visible in the evening rain[71]

Parting from you, I go to Inaba, but if I hear you're pining at the hilltop, waiting, I will return at once[72]

Even in a remote place eightfold heaps of white clouds away, do not feel distant from someone who will think of you[73]

---

[68] Lady Izumi. For the heading, see the same tanka on p. 147.

[69] Fujiwara no Michinobu (early Heian).

[70] Retired Emperor Gotoba: "In the tenth month, when I was in Minase, I sent to the former abbot Jien 'wetting, a shower' and other words; among the many tanka on transience that I wrote and sent to him the following tenth month [was this one]." The incident that prompted Gotoba to write the tanka was the death of his mistress, Lady Owari. The tanka referred to reads in full: "What, again, I forget, it passes; on my sleeves, wetting, a shower seems to take me by surprise."

[71] Retired Emperor Gotoba. Allusion to a tanka in the "Yūgao" chapter in *The Tale of Genji*: "When I regard as a cloud the smoke the one I knew turned into, the evening sky too feels friendly."

[72] Ariwara no Yukihira (818–893).

[73] Ki no Tsurayuki. Allusion to Nakatomi no Yakamori's tanka (*Man'yōshū*, no. 3764): "Even if we are far apart, with mountains and rivers in between, keep your heart close and think of me, my love."

If by chance someone asks, say I am in a cove in Suma, drenched with
seaweed brine, suffering[74]

On this trip I couldn't come with offerings. Accept the brocade of
crimson leaves on Mount Tamuke, as willed by the goddess[75]

Lodging in a hut where the Naniwa men burn reeds, for no reason
brine begins to drip from my sleeves[76]

I will return and look on Matsushima once again. Do not let the
waves ravage the hut on the islet of Oshima[77]

When day breaks, must I go over the mountain ridge again, there
beyond the sky-coursing moon, where the white clouds are?[78]

A lovely rock buried under the seaweed of Naniwa Bay, I wish I
could be openly in love with you![79]

Do not let it be known, first shower on the ridge where clouds are,
even if the lower leaves of trees change their color[80]

Building a Sano boat-bridge like the one on the Eastern Road, my
thoughts have crossed over to you, but you never even notice[81]

[74] Ariwara no Yukihira: "During the reign of the Emperor Tamura
[Montoku, 827–858], because of some incident I confined myself in the
place called Suma in the province of Tsu, from where I sent the following
to someone in the palace."
[75] Sugawara Michizane: "When the Suzakuin [Retired Emperor Uda]
went to Nara, I wrote at Mount Tamuke."
[76] Fujiwara no Shunzei. Allusion to the anonymous tanka on p. 85,
"Like the huts."
[77] Fujiwara no Shunzei.
[78] Fujiwara no Ietaka.
[79] Minamoto no Toshiyori.
[80] Fujiwara no Yoshitsune. "It" refers to a secret love affair.
[81] Minamoto no Hitoshi (880–951).

Rampant rank reed, to repress it I try, but why do I long for you so very much?[82]

What should I do? If only I had a hut on Muro no Yashima, so I might raise the smoke of my love into the sky![83]

In the evening my thoughts go toward the end of the clouds, being in love with someone in the far-off sky[84]

Though the space may be short as the joint of a reed on Naniwa shore, are you saying I must endure this world, not seeing you?[85]

The one who's unkind is like you, wind blowing down Mount Hatsuse, though I never prayed she be fierce[86]

Like a mountain stream whose rapids are blocked by boulders, though we broke up, in the end we'd meet again, I know[87]

Like the foam on the ever-flowing Thinking River, how can I possibly fade without seeing you?[88]

Though false rumors pop up as at a fair, people hubbubbing, still I've no way of getting my lover[89]

---

[82] Minamoto no Hitoshi. Allusion to an anonymous tanka in the *Kokinshū* (no. 505): "Rampant rank reed, to repress it I try, but does he know, with no one telling him?"

[83] Fujiwara no Shunzei.

[84] Anonymous (*Kokinshū*, 484).

[85] Lady Ise.

[86] Minamoto no Toshiyori.

[87] Emperor Sutoku (1119–1164).

[88] Lady Ise: "During the days when I kept secret where I was, a man with whom I had renewed friendship got these words to me: 'As I was unable to visit you for days, I feel as if you'd vanished.' And so."

[89] Kakinomoto no Hitomaro.

If I can't twist my thread with yours, if I can't meet you, how can I make a string of beads?[90]

Like the white dewdrop that forms at the leaf-tip of a "thinking-grass," you come only rarely, and then slip from my hand[91]

Had I expected this?—to end up marking tallies on the cart stool and sleeping a hundred nights in my clothes?[92]

Since our parting when the moon at dawn looked unfriendly, nothing so melancholy as the break of day[93]

Like trees buried in the shallows of Natori River, if exposed, what would we do? Wondering, we've begun to meet[94]

Just because you said, "I'll come right away," I've waited until the September moon, at daybreak, has come out[95]

So far apart our meetings, each time I put on the hunting robe with the Far-off Mountain pattern, I can only weep in vain[96]

[90] Anonymous (*Kokinshū*, no. 483). "Make a string of beads" here means "to live."
[91] Minamoto no Toshiyori.
[92] Fujiwara no Shunzei. Allusion to an old story about a man who fell in love with a woman he saw on an oxcart. Told of his avowed love, the woman asked him to prove it by coming to the cart and sleeping beside it in his clothes one hundred consecutive nights, wind or rain; on the last night, she would sleep with him. He did what he was told for ninety-nine nights, but on the hundredth day his parent suddenly died, and he could not make it to the place that night.
[93] Mibu no Tadamine.
[94] Anonymous (*Kokinshū*, no. 650).
[95] Sosei.
[96] Prince Motoyoshi (890–943): "A woman I was seeing in secrecy sent me a hunting outfit: since there was a hunting robe in it [I wrote the following]."

Long as the foot-wearying mountain pheasant's tail, its drooping tail,
through this long night, must I sleep alone?[97]

I suffer enough, now it would all be the same: I'll stand up like a
Naniwa channel marker and meet you at all cost[98]

My love affair is like the clumps of bush clover in the garden:
withering, both my lover and I in the autumn dusk[99]

The dew on my sleeves turned a strange color, fading, while I
grieved about passing, about changing[100]

My thought grows like rock azaleas on Timeless Hill, and like the
rocks, though I do not speak, I love all the more[101]

Didn't we make a vow, wringing each other's sleeves, that "waves
wouldn't swallow up the Pine Hill of Sue"?[102]

Would the moon ever tell us to grieve, make us brood on things?
Tears come to my reproving eyes[103]

---

[97] Kakinomoto no Hitomaro.
[98] Prince Motoyoshi.
[99] Former Abbot Jien (1155–1225).
[100] Retired Emperor Gotoba. Allusion to the thirteenth tanka in this
compendium.
[101] Anonymous (Kokinshū, no. 495).
[102] Kiyowara no Motosuke (908–990): "In the role of someone
addressing a woman who has changed her mind." Allusion to an azuma uta
in the Kokinshū (no. 1093): "Should I ever become fickle and think of
someone other than you, the waves would swallow up the Pine Hill of
Sue!"
[103] Saigyō: "On the subject of 'being in love under the moon.'" For
Watson's translation, see "Does the moon say 'Grieve!'" on p. 169.

MINAMOTO NO SANETOMO

(1192–1219)

TWENTY-FOUR TANKA

Grown over with straggly saw grass,
the garden of a house
where no one lives—
how many nights has the moon
dwelt in brightness here?

Fabrics swirled in a thousand
baths of crimson,
spreading the sky
as the sun sinks
under the rim of the hill

The long-drawn-out autumn
has come, stretching
like the float-borne strands
of the fishnets
of Cape Yura in the land of Ki

The leaves of the small oaks
of Mount Saho
turn a thousand colors—
it's autumn
and the cold rain comes down

So cold the night,
the foam drifting
on the river rapids
is frozen before
it can melt away

As the warrior reaches up
to straighten his quivered arrows,
hail glances
from his gauntlet—
Nasu's plain of bamboo grass

Sleet rattles on the leaves
of the bamboo grass,
and from the peaks
of deep mountains the winter gale
blows unceasingly

I open the pine door
on streamers of dawn cloud,
the wind of the mountain storm
dashing snow
over my sleeve

Bird hunting at a place called Tokami Plain, I saw a clump
of boneset blossoming in front of a deserted hut:

Boneset, why are you blooming
in the autumn wind?
Your master's in his
old house now—
didn't you know?

By Hakone Road
I cross over—and come
to Izu Bay!
On the little island offshore
I see the waves breaking

As evening comes
the sea wind blows cold;
on the little islands
in sight beyond the waves,
snow goes on falling

The waves of the great sea,
rending, toppling,
splitting, scattering,
thunder in
upon the rocky shore

Is it always so bleak a sight?
By reed shacks
the fierce-burning
fires of fishermen
boiling down their salt

If only the world
could stay this way always:
how fine—the towlines
of the little fishing boats
being towed along the shore!

Gull-haunted,
the windblown shore of Susaki
recedes from sight as the tide sweeps in—
you too have gone
but my love grows only stronger

In the rockbound pool
deep in the mountains,
leaves fall and sink:
so my heart sinks—
could she possibly understand?

When a lady-in-waiting with whom he was intimate asked
permission to go to a distant province:

When the wild goose
has flown far off
beyond the mountain,
its companion, left alone,
will surely cry

On seeing a child crying by the road and learning that its
parents had died:

Bitter sight—
I watch and my tears
will not stop—
the orphaned child
searching for its mother

I didn't mean
to recall the past,
but in my old village
in twilight rain,
that scent of orange blossoms—

Written in the seventh month of 1211, when the farmers
were much troubled by floods:

Too much
at one time
is a grief to the people—
O Eight Great Dragon Kings,
stop the rain!

[Believed to be addressed to Retired Emperor Gotoba]

Though a time come
when mountains crack
and seas go dry,
never to my lord
will I be found double-hearted!

The bamboo frond
the shamaness dipped
in boiling water
gently bends, bobbing and recovering—
so bobs the world—let it

You erect pagodas,
build Buddha halls,
but far more merit lies
in repenting
the ill you do others

This world—
call it an image
caught in a mirror—
real it is not,
nor unreal either

KYŌGOKU TAMEKANE

(1254–1332)

TWENTY-THREE TANKA

Bird voices gently calling,
and as morning breaks
on the hills,
in the color of the mist,
a feel of spring

Plum flowers
blooming crimson
in the twilight,
willows swaying
as the spring rain falls

So few rays
of morning sun
filter through the branches,
how cool it is
deep within the bamboo!

Weighed down with dew,
sprays of bush clover
bend to the ground,
their flowers in the wind that sways them
brighter-colored than ever

In the snow piled
on the bedroom roof
the hail makes no sound,
but as it slants down,
it raps at the window

Though the glow
of the evening sun
shines over the waves,
the little island in the distance
has grayed into darkness

The mountain wind
has finished tossing
the bamboos in the hedge,
but now from summit pines
it comes echoing down again

The warbler's voice
softly resounds,
and the sunlight,
veiled in haze,
gives no sign of fading

Late at night
looking out from the Uji landing,
the river runs
with a clear sound,
the moon hazes over

The wind
that for a time blew so wildly
has died down—
what blossoms it left,
fall softly

The cuckoo,
repeating his cry,
now right here singing—
how clear and cool
the color of his voice!

Wind that tossed the pines
subsides in the grass
of the foothill plain,
rain races the clouds
of the rising storm

A rainy night
when insects in the garden
have stopped their singing—
and now from the wall,
a cricket's voice!

From peaks in the morning storm
fog drifts down,
floats over the Ōi River,
and then flows away

On the storm's freezing blast,
the sound of two tollings—
then I hear no more
from the morning bell

While day lasted,
the wind now and then
blew the bamboo leaves clean,
but it's died away now
and snow piles up on them

Drawn on by moonlight,
he passes up the inn
where he meant to stay,
a traveler in the night
walking tomorrow's road

Takase Mountain:
I push along
a trail under the pines,
an evening storm blowing up,
not meeting a soul

The white dew,
come from no óne knows where—
when evening falls,
here it is on the grass

A traveler's pillow,
bundled up, undone,
changing night by night—
the dreams of these brief naps
are gone without a trace

In the path of the late sun,
almost set now,
they come forth—
those farthermost peaks
of the mist-locked mountains

Where the bright moon comes up,
the sky has cleared,
though drifting clouds
linger far off
by the rim of the mountain

On love:

So great the pain,
I've passed the days
without speaking of sorrow,
till my thoughts are worn out
and I no longer hate you

GOZAN POETRY

[Gozan, or "Five Mountains," is a term used to designate the major Rinzai Zen temples of Kyoto and Kamakura during the Kamakura and Muromachi periods, when Zen was at its height in Japan. At that time, many Japanese monks journeyed to China to study the doctrines of the Zen sect, and Chinese Zen masters came to Japan to teach. These men wrote large numbers of poems in Chinese, some of a doctrinal nature, others recording the experiences and daily lives of the writers. Such works are known as Gozan poetry.]

KOKAN SHIREN
(1278–1346)

Earthquake

Still things moving,
    firm become unfirm,
land like ocean waves,
    house like a boat—
a time to be fearful,
    but to delight as well:
no wind, yet the wind-bells
    keep on ringing.

SESSON YŪBAI

(1290–1346)

[When the Chinese Zen monk Wu-hsüeh Tsu-yüan (1226–1286) was threatened by invading Mongol (Yüan) troops, he composed a four-line poem to express his indifference. Years later, in 1313, when the Japanese Zen monk Sesson Yūbai, who was studying in China, was imprisoned by the Mongols and faced with possible death, he took Tsu-yüan's poem and, using each line as the opening verse of a new poem, composed the following.]

In heaven and earth, no ground to plant my single staff,
but I can hide this body where no trace will be found.
At midnight the wooden man mounts his horse of stone,
crashing through a hundred, a thousand folds of encircling iron.

I delight that man is nothing, all things nothing,
a thousand worlds complete in my one cage.
Blame forgotten, mind demolished, a three-Zen joy—
who says Devadatta is in hell?[1]

Wonderful, this three-foot sword of the Great Yüan,
sparkling with cold frost over ten thousand miles.
Though the skull go dry, these eyes will see again.
My white gem worth a string of cities has never had a flaw.

Like lightning it flashes through the shadows, severing the spring wind.
The god of nothingness bleeds crimson, streaming.
Mount Sumeru to my amazement turns upside down.[2]
I will dive, disappear into the stem of the lotus.

---

[1] Devadatta, who attempted to kill the Buddha, represents the epitome of evil.
[2] Sumeru is the central mountain in the Buddhist universe.

CHŪGAN ENGETSU
(1300–1375)

Atami

[A rare view of the famous hot spring resort near Kamakura as it was in the fourteenth century, with a glimpse of the island of Hatsushima in the distance.]

Midnight dreams broken by the hissing roar—
hot water boiling from the roots of the cliff;
pipes this way and that lead the water, houses wreathed in steam,
every inn fitted with a bath, rooms let out to travelers.
By the sea's border land is warm—winter it never snows,
though cold days on mountain paths, one treads through frost at
    dawn.
A far-off island in fine rain, black with clouds and fog;
over red tides I watch the moon sink dimly out of sight.

RYŪSHŪ SHŪTAKU
(1308–1388)

Sweeping Leaves

No coins to buy my firewood,
I sweep up leaves, sell them in the temple town,
leaf on leaf precious as yellow gold,
pile on pile with a beauty of red brocade.
I chide myself for dreaming of warm knees,
long for their beauty to cheer my cold heart.
Back from town I light the stove, sit by it,
listening to drops of rain on the stairs.

ZEKKAI CHŪSHIN

(1336–1405)

Impromptu Poem in Yün-chien
[Written when Zekkai was studying Zen in China; Yün-chien is the present-day region of Sung-chiang in Kiangsu.]

Coming and going, no fixed lodging,
over rivers and seas, wherever wind and mist take me.
Nights I stay in a temple among the peaks,
mornings make for the Mao Lake boat.
Green hills—and as I turn my head,
white birds in front of the sail winging away.
Ten years a traveler in a foreign land—
wordless, I stand lost in thought.

IKKYŪ SŌJUN

(1394–1481)

I

Ten years in the brothels—hard to wear out desire;
I force myself to live in empty hills, a dark ravine.
Those pleasant places—countless miles of clouds shut them from me
     now;
tall pines—harsh in my ear, winds above the roof.

2

Who is the true transmitter of Rinzai's line?
These elegant ones with their pretty boys attending?
One bowl of muddy wine, three thousand poems—
I laugh at Zen monks who don't know their Zen.

3

Contemplating the Law, reading sutras, trying to be a real master;
yellow robes, the stick, the shouts, till my wooden seat's all crooked;
but it seems my real business was always in the muck,
with my great passion for women, and for boys as well.

4

Blind Mori[3] night after night tends my singing;
under the quilts, two mandarin ducks, we whisper our love once
    more,
once more her vow, "till the dawn of Maitreya's preaching,"
for an old buddha who's been here all along, ten thousand springs!

5

The tree had withered, leaves fallen, then spring came round again;
the green grew out, blossoms were born, old vows made anew—
oh Mori, if I forget the great debt I owe you,
for endless kalpas let me be born a beast!

---

[3] A blind woman Ikkyū fell in love with at the age of seventy-three;
she became his attendant.

TAIKYOKU ZŌSU

(born 1421)

Improvised While Living in the Outskirts of the Capital
[Written in 1468, in the midst of the Ōnin civil war. The writer was a monk of Shōkoku-ji, but it and other temples in Kyoto were at this time occupied by the contending armies, and were eventually destroyed in the fighting.]

Ancient temples with their thousand pines, taken over for army camps;
one shack of bundled grass where my thoughts are cut off from the world:
coarse bedding here in the mist—it serves as a chilly seat;
pair of clogs caked with snow—they do for idle strolling.
Morning after morning priestesses offer music to the gods;
night after night the old men nearby chant the Buddha's name;
forty years and more, nothing but this—
in the dark I clap my hands, laugh at the life I lead.

KEIJO SHŪRIN

(1440–1518)

Torn Windows, No Paper

I'd mend them but there's not half a sheet of paper in my bag.
All my windows torn, I don't have to bother opening them.
Wind comes to my bedside, blows out the lamp for me,
rain from beyond the eaves wets down my inkstone.

KISHUN RYŪKI

(born 1511)

At Shōraku-ji in Ōmi, First Poem of the Year [*1568*]

Over the lake, the wind and snow of a New Year's sky;
in my short straw cape and battered hat I've come through another
    year.
A country monk, ignorant of what goes on in the world,
beside the stove, roasting potatoes, I stretch my legs and doze.

First Poem of the Year [*1591*]

Eighty years, and I've added another,
a drifting traveler, leaving things up to Heaven.
Who understands that a poor monk too can boast of riches—
yellow leaves are his gold, the mosses his copper coins.

The Age of Renga

RENGA

"Highly Renowned" (partial)

[Composed in 1355 by Monk Gusai (1282–1376) and ten other poets[1]]

Highly renowned, the cuckoo's voice cannot be topped	*Gusai*
lush trees—all of them are pines in a wind	*Yoshimoto*
by the mountain there's a cool water flow	*Eiun*
the moon is best when at the ridge	*Shūa*
the autumn sun was just out of the clouds	*Soa*
after a shower morning mists remain in the sky	*Gyōa*
the dew at evening does not settle on my sleeves	*Mokuchin*
in any village there's that sound of beating cloth	*Shigekazu*

1 The most prominent among the ten other participants is Nijō Yoshimoto (1320–1388), a high government official, scholar, and poet. A student of Gusai's in renga, Yoshimoto, with Gusai's help, set rules on renga composition and compiled *Tsukuba shū*, a renga anthology. This is the first of the ten hundred-part sequences composed in Yoshimoto's mansion in the fourth and fifth months of 1355 by five monks led by Gusai, and four aristocrat friends led by Yoshimoto. Of the eleven poets, one— Sugawara Nagatsuna—does not appear in the first twenty-two parts translated here.

back from my travels—is her time of waiting long past?   *Gusai*

from today on I won't count on any blossoms   *Yoshimoto*

though hazy, the winds still blow over the tree tops   *Chikanaga*

the white snow remains in the shaded parts of the mountain   *Gyōa*

the moon upstream must freeze the water   *Gusai*

as waves roll in, the cove grows cold   *Shūa*

the voices of plovers flying away are distant   *Ietada*

friendless, yes, but evening still comes to a traveler   *Gusai*

though I've abandoned the world, let alone myself   *Yoshimoto*

the melancholy of autumn lingers in this mountain village   *Eiun*

if you are dew, be mindful of my tearful sleeves   *Soa*

wait, and the night you count on someone feels so long   *Gyōa*

though the wind stirring over rice stalks may reach the pines   *Gusai*

the shore reeds by the waves have put out ears   *Soa*

TEIKA, a Nō play

[Believed to have been written by Komparu Zenchiku (1405–1468), the play is based on the love affair that is supposed to have existed between Fujiwara no Teika, here called Sadaie at times, and Princess Shikishi, here called Shokushi. Sadaie and Shokushi are different but legitimate readings of the same ideographs.]

PERSONS

Traveling Priest
His Two Companions, also Priests·
"Woman of the Place"
Chorus
"Man of the Place"
Ghost of Princess Shokushi

TIME AND PLACE

Act I, first half: near the Hut of Intermittent Showers in Sembon, Kyoto, one early winter evening with intermittent showers; second half: in front of Princess Shokushi's grave, later the same evening.
Act II: in front of the same grave, late at night with the moon shining.

ACT I

(*The stage assistants bring out a large construction representing a grave mound and place it upstage, in front of the musicians. As the music begins, the* TRAVELING PRIEST *and his* COMPANIONS *enter quietly and stand side by side near front apron. Then they face one another.*)

PRIEST & COMPANIONS

The northern showers come out of the mountains,
the northern showers come out of the mountains,
but seem to have no place to settle.

PRIEST

(*He faces front.*) I'm from a northern province, and I am a priest.
Since I've never seen the capital, I have now decided to go there.

PRIEST & COMPANIONS

(*They face one another.*)
                    When the winter began,
in traveling robes, early in the morning,
in traveling robes, early in the morning
we left, and came away over mountain after mountain,
far and near, with clouds coming and going
      (*The* PRIEST *indicates he is walking*)
                                        till
we came to the flowering capital,
we came to the flowering capital
where the last crimson leaves hold our eyes.
(*He indicates arrival.*)

PRIEST

(*He faces front.*) Hurrying along I've reached a place called Upper
Capital. (*Saying, "Let me look around," he goes to stage center and
stands there. In the meantime, his* COMPANIONS *have taken their seats
at front left corner. The* PRIEST *faces front.*)
                                        Curious:
it's around the tenth of the tenth month,
and the treetops are all seared by winter;
but the crimson leaves remaining on the branches,
though only here and there, the way they look—
the scenery moves me more in the capital,
the view is different this evening.
A shower has started! I think I'll stand by this hut until it clears up.
(*He starts toward front left corner.*)

WOMAN OF THE PLACE

(*Calling to the* PRIEST *from offstage, she enters quietly.*) Tell me—tell
me, why are you standing by that hut?

PRIEST

(*He turns to face the* WOMAN *at front left corner.*) I'm standing here because of the shower that just started. What do you call this place?

WOMAN

(*As she walks on the bridgeway leading to the stage.*) It's known as the Hut of Intermittent Showers, a place with a history. I thought you were standing there because you knew the story—that's why I asked the question.

PRIEST

Indeed, I see a plaque up there, and it has "Hut of Intermittent Showers" written on it. A coincidence, perhaps, but an interesting one. Would you tell me what kind of person built it?

WOMAN

Lord Fujiwara no Sadaie. Though it's within the capital, this place is so desolate, and the showers so moving, that he built this hut and every year wrote tanka on the subject, they say. (*She stops walking and faces front.*) Such is the history of the place, and by coincidence you've happened by, so you might preach the Law and pray for the peace of his soul—
    I thought I'd make that request,
    and gave you a full explanation.
(*She resumes walking and comes onstage.*)

PRIEST

I see, Lord Sadaie built it.
    Well, now, I wonder
    which tanka of his
    caused this hut
    to commemorate the "showers."

WOMAN

    I must say that's hard to settle.
    In the season of showers
    every year, he wrote about them,
    and I can't say with conviction, "This is it."
Nevertheless, on the topic, "Intermittent showers know their time," he wrote:

"No falsity
in this world: another tenth month—
whose sincere heart has caused
the showers to begin again?"[1]
Considering that he wrote "At my house" in the headnote to it, it
may be the tanka in question.

PRIEST

How those words
affect me!
True, with intermittent showers, no falsity
in this world where they stay on,

WOMAN

but the one who's no more! We speak
such words now, in this transient world,

PRIEST

because our ties from another life have not decayed.
We "shelter under the same tree,"

WOMAN

"drink from the flow of the same river."[2]

PRIEST

As if to urge us to realize it,

WOMAN

just then,
(*During the* CHORUS *chanting that follows, the* MAN OF THE PLACE
enters inconspicuously and takes his seat near right corner upstage.)

CHORUS

here a shower starts
on the old house, the shower of the past,
on the old house, the shower of the past,
and we know how the one with a clear heart
must have felt. The world of dreams
never settles. On Sadaie's[3]
eaves,

---

[1] No. 2305 in Teika's anthology of his own poems, *Shūi gusō*.
[2] The two last phrases are believed to be popular sayings of the time.
[3] Pun on the name Sadaie, which means "settled house" or "settling the
house."

the shower falls at dusk—
thoughts of old move me to tears.
The garden and the hedges, no longer separate,
grass bushes, grown ever wilder,
are all seared, dew seldom forming on them.
How desolate this evening,
  how desolate this evening!
(*While looking off into the distance, the* WOMAN *steps backward to rear right corner and turns to face the* PRIEST.)

WOMAN

This happens to be the day I offer prayers for someone who is dead, and I am going to her grave. Would you mind coming with me?

PRIEST

Not at all. I'll be glad to come with you. (*The* WOMAN *moves a few steps forward and turns to the grave mound; the* PRIEST *does the same.*)

WOMAN

Look at the grave mound here.

PRIEST

It's strange. The marker looks very old, but the way kudzu vines crawl all over it and cling to it—I can't even tell its shape. Whose marker is it?

WOMAN

It's Princess Shokushi's grave. Those kudzu vines are called "Teika vines."

PRIEST

How odd. Why are they called "Teika vines"?

WOMAN

Princess Shokushi was, at first, vestal of the Kamo Shrine, but soon left that position.[4] Then Lord Teika fell in love with her, and their love for each other, though secret, was deep. Soon afterward, Princess Shokushi died. Teika's attachment then turned into vines and crawled over her grave, clung to it. So, in their suffering, unable to separate,
  they lust for each other, a delusion,

---

[4] Shikishi was made *saiin* (vestal, priestess) of the Kamo Shrine in 1159, but because of illness she left the position in 1169.

of which I will tell you more, if you are kind enough to offer prayers for them. (*She goes to stage center and takes her seat; the* PRIEST *returns to his seat.*)

CHORUS

Unforgettable, though it was long ago;
"the depth of her heart, Mount Secret
I went over to visit in secrecy"[5]—the dew on the grass
by the path—my telling you this is as purposeless.

WOMAN

Now, "string of beads,
if you must break, break. If you last longer,

CHORUS

my resolve to keep it secret"[6] will weaken,
she felt, and as pampas grass shows its tufts in fall,
began to betray her affair,
when it was cut short and fell apart.

WOMAN

"I did not feel at all before then,"

CHORUS

and "my heart since"[7] has remained astray.
"Know the grief
of the sleeve dyed mountain indigo
that decayed from frost to frost throughout
its life"[8]—full of tears, those past days;
to do without the distress of longing she made ablutions,
she became vestal of the Kamo Shrine,
that was what she became,
but the god did not accept it.[9]

[5] Allusion to the tanka in section 15 of *The Tales of Ise:* "If only there were a path on Mount Secret by which to visit in secrecy, so I might see the depth of her heart."
[6] Shikishi's tanka (*Shinkokinshū,* no. 1034), quoted with the last part slightly changed. For a different translation, see "String of beads," p. 187.
[7] Allusion to Fujiwara no Atsutada's tanka (*Shūishū,* no. 710): "Compared with my heart since meeting you, I did not feel at all before then."
[8] *Shūi gusō,* no. 2579, "Thoughts near the Kamo Shrine," written in 1210.
[9] Allusion to an anonymous tanka (*Kokinshū,* no. 501): "To stop longing I made ablutions in the Mitarashi River, but the god has not accepted them."

Her vow with someone
betrayed its colors[10]—that's what saddens us.
She tried to hide it, in vain in this world
of vanity; her affair came to light,
the rumors grew as vast
as the sky with its terrifying sun,
so that the path to the clouds was cut
and the figure of the maiden could not be kept,[11]
a painful thing for both of them.

WOMAN

Indeed, "I grieve,
I long for you, but there's no way of meeting you:

CHORUS

you are a cloud on Katsuragi peak"[12]—
the feeling that moved him to write it,
we understand, because of that attachment
his body turned into the Teika vines,
and here, where her remains are, from long ago
he's stayed inseparable, vines with crimson leaves,
color scorching,
clinging,
a tangle of hair, bound, binding.
This delusion
that faded and has returned
like frost or dew—
please save me from it.
As we listened to the story of long ago,
soon it's the end of another day, darkening;
mysterious—would you tell us who you are?

WOMAN

Who am I, you ask.
The remains of my dead body have decayed
under miscanthus and frost, only my name
staying on, all to no avail.
(*She turns to the* PRIEST.)

---

[10] Allusion to Taira no Kanemori's tanka (*Shūishū*, no. 622): "I kept
my longing secret, but it betrayed its colors, till someone asked if I was
brooding."
[11] Allusion to Yoshimine no Munesada's tanka quoted in note 6, p. 186.
[12] *Shūi gusō*, no. 2483, quoted with the last part slightly changed.

CHORUS

Placed under grass though you may be,
show your colors, your name.

WOMAN

I would hide it

CHORUS

no longer now:
I am no other than Princess Shokushi.
(*She rises to her feet and, with her eyes fixed on the* PRIEST, *walks toward him slowly, firmly.*)
I have been visible to you till now,
but my true figure is like heat haze,
    (*She faces front*)
and even my form left in stone
    (*She retreats backward to the grave mound*)
is invisible under the kudzu vines.
(*She walks toward the* PRIEST.) Please help me out of this suffering.
(*She circles back to the grave mound and disappears into it.*)
As soon as she said it, she disappeared,
as soon as she said it, she disappeared.

INTERLUDE

(*The* MAN OF THE PLACE *leaves his seat, announces himself, indicates that he has come across the* PRIEST, *and takes his seat at stage center. In response to the* PRIEST'*s questions, he tells the story of the affair between* FUJIWARA NO TEIKA *and* PRINCESS SHOKUSHI *in some detail. He says, among other things, that the kudzu vines that started growing on* SHOKUSHI'*s grave mound soon after* TEIKA'*s death used to be cut and removed, but they would immediately grow back; the cutting was continued until some holy person said that the vines were a manifestation of* TEIKA'*s attachment to the* PRINCESS *and therefore should be left alone. When the* MAN *learns about the woman the* PRIEST *has just met, he says she must be* SHOKUSHI'*s apparition, urges the* PRIEST *to offer prayers to lay her troubled soul to rest, and returns to his original seat. He exits inconspicuously after the* GHOST OF PRINCESS SHOKUSHI *enters in Act II.*)

ACT II

PRIEST & COMPANIONS

The evening passed, and now the moon is out.
The evening passed, and now the moon is out.
This late, when winds blow through pines, under desolate
clumps of grass she lies, a drop of dew.
Although our thoughts are many as our rosary beads,
how fortunate this chance to pray for her,
how fortunate this chance to pray for her.
(*Gloomy, foreboding music is played.*)

GHOST OF PRINCESS SHOKUSHI

(*In the grave mound, in a low voice*)
                          Is this a dream?
In this dark reality, on Mount Real,
I trace by the moonlight
the path buried under the vines.
(*In a high, painful tone*)
                          Once in the past,
a pine wind or the moon through vines
moved us to exchange words;
pillows laid side by side
in green curtains, on a scarlet bed,

PRIEST

we loved each other
in many ways. But in the end,

GHOST

the blossoms and crimson leaves[13] scatter away;

PRIEST

a cloud in the morning,

GHOST

rain in the evening,[14]

---

[13] Echoes Teika's "As I look out," p. 193.
[14] An old Chinese legend tells of an amorous encounter between a mortal ruler and a mountain goddess; as the goddess took her leave, she said, "At dawn I am the morning clouds, at evening I am the passing rain."

CHORUS

that is an old story, yes,
but my body now,
(*Quietly, with emotion*)
and dreams, reality, illusions,
all have become part of the transient world,
leaving not a trace.
(*In a different tone, reflectively*)
Yet, here I am, under the grass—
not in a hut covered with burdock,[15]
but with the Teika vines over me.
Look at this, look at me, holy priest.
(*The stage assistants remove the cloth covering the grave mound, revealing the emaciated* GHOST OF PRINCESS SHOKUSHI. *She is seated on a chair, stiff, looking down, indicating that she is under the spell of Teika's passion.*)

PRIEST

How painful it is to look at you, the way you are. How painful it is.
(*He joins his hands in prayer.*)
"The Buddha's undifferentiated preaching
Is like the rain, all of one flavor;
But beings, according to their nature,
Receive it differently."[16]

GHOST

Look at me.
(*She turns her face to the* PRIEST.)
I stand and sit, uselessly as waves.
Suffering as I am even after death,
I'm bound by the Teika vines;
suffering as I am
without a break—
I'm grateful to you.
What you have kindly recited now is from the "Parable of the Herbs," is it not?

PRIEST

Indeed, you are right.
The wonderful Law overlooks no grass or tree.

---

[15] Such a hut was a traditional abode for a hermit.
[16] From Chapter 5, "The Parable of the Herbs," of the Lotus Sutra.

Sever yourself from the vines of attachment,
and become a buddha.

GHOST

Oh, how grateful I am,
yes, indeed, indeed!
This is the heart
of the wonderful Law!

PRIEST

(*He turns to face front.*)
We receive the blessings
of the universal dew.

GHOST

"Not a second

PRIEST

not a third,"[17]

CHORUS

(*Somewhat forcefully*)
the one rain, the one Law,
sprinkles,
and all turn moist,
grasses, trees, the land,
becoming buddhas.
Having that opportunity
(*Growing quieter*)
the Teika vines,
tears shed on them
in large drops,
unbind themselves, spread
(*The* GHOST *indicates she is being freed*)
and I, tottering,
like a cart with feeble wheels, leave the burning house.[18] (*Rising to her feet, she steps out of the mound.*) How grateful I am. (*She turns toward the* PRIEST *and joins her hands in prayer.*)

---

17 From the passage, "In the buddha-lands of the ten directions/There is only the One-vehicle Law,/Not a second, not a third,/Except the expedient teachings of the Buddha," in Chapter 2, "Expedient Devices," of the Lotus Sutra.

18 The "burning house" is a Buddhist metaphor for "this world." See Chapter 3, "A Parable," of the Lotus Sutra.

In gratitude, may I then
flutter the flowery sleeves, which I once had
above the clouds,[19] and bring back the past,
a dancing princess in the Omi robe?[20]

GHOST

How embarrassing I look,

CHORUS

dancing.
(*She dances a slow, quiet dance.*)

GHOST

How embarrassing I look, dancing.

CHORUS

How embarrassing. I am embarrassed.

GHOST

The way I was,

CHORUS

my face was like the moon,

GHOST

but it began to cloud often,

CHORUS

and my eyebrows painted crescent-shape

GHOST

lost their beauty, in tears.

CHORUS

Even after I faded like dew,
(*She circles back to the rear right corner, then goes to stage center.*)
I was pitilessly covered with vine leaves, and am now like the goddess

---

[19] "Above the clouds" is a metaphor for the imperial court.
[20] The "Omi robe" is official festival attire, used also by dancer-princesses.

of Kazuraki.[21] I'm ashamed of it, but can't help it. (*She sees the* PRIEST *and hides her face with her fan.*) Because we can meet only at night, before this dream ends, so saying, she returned to the place where she had been. (*She walks to the grave.*) Then the vine leaves crawled over her, clung to her, as they used to, those Teika vines. They crawled over her, clung to her, those Teika vines. (*She settles in the grave mound.*) And before we knew it, she was buried, she was gone. (*She covers her face with her fan and lowers her body.*)

[21] The ugly goddess of Kazuraki was so ashamed of her looks that when ordered by an exorcist to build a stone bridge, she would work only during the night when no one was around. As a result, she could not finish the bridge in time, and the angry exorcist bound her with vines.

RENGA

Three Poets at Yuyama

[Composed at the hot spring Arima on the twentieth of the tenth month, 1491, by Botange Shōhaku, Saiokuken Sōchō, and Iio Sōgi]

Thinly covered with snow, the leaves look brighter along this mountain path[1] — *Shōhaku*

the pampas grass by the boulders will be more enjoyable in winter — *Sōchō*

lured by tree crickets I left my home early — *Sōgi*

must be late at night—on my sleeves an autumn wind — *Shōhaku*

dew so cold the moon seems to change its light — *Sōchō*

as you walk through unfamiliar fields — *Sōgi*

someone you talk to—not for long your companion under the sky when you're traveling — *Shōhaku*

the clouds the marker, the ridges so distant — *Sōchō*

---

[1] A renga usually begins in a propitious, congratulatory, or lofty tone; here the beginning is "natural," describing more or less faithfully what was observed.

depressing that I should envy birds—those are blossoms[2]   *Sōgi*

if only I could turn myself into spring, mornings and   *Shōhaku*
evenings

having seen in my village the last of the snow fade   *Sōchō*

I hope there appears a road for the world   *Sōgi*

why should I resent anyone, now that I have moss-grown   *Shōhaku*
sleeves[3]

the way I live, I'm a rustic. Don't come to visit   *Sōchō*

I don't know the names of plants and trees, here where   *Sōgi*
I've settled

my feelings go out more to the moon   *Shōhaku*

this autumn night, while we share a pillow and talk, will   *Sōchō*
turn to dawn

how annoying that I've given a drop of my heart   *Sōgi*

counting desperately on the useless vow that no one made   *Shōhaku*

this hermit is depressed, waiting for a message   *Sōchō*

so far from things, now my place is in the clouds   *Sōgi*

[2] Literary affectation of confusing clouds with cherry blossoms; see some of the opening tanka in Teika's Compendium, pp. 205–6.
[3] "Moss-grown sleeves" is a metaphor for priesthood.

I've taken shelter in the mountains, why should I be lonely?   *Shōhaku*

no distinct color is visible of the wind through the pines   *Sōchō*

listen to the wellspring, the voice of autumn   *Sōgi*

fireflies trail in the sky; till late I stay up on the veranda   *Shōhaku*

lost in thought—there's no place for my soul to rest[4]   *Sōchō*

pretend not to know, my heart, that the pillow knows[5]   *Sōgi*

even tears will be my solace   *Shōhaku*

today I took off my mourning clothes, with much regret   *Sōchō*

sadly in the midst of autumn I leave the mountain temple   *Sōgi*

a stag calling behind me, the mountain ridges in the evening dusk   *Shōhaku*

there was a storm today—how moving the mists!   *Sōchō*

as a bell rings quietly, I see a village waiting for the moon   *Sōgi*

it's depressing to go now and disturb her heart   *Shōhaku*

not just me, but someone else must visit secretly   *Sōchō*

[4] Uses the preceding part to allude to Lady Izumi's tanka on p. 148, "Lost in thought."

[5] See Lady Ise's tanka on p. 127, "Speak of this," for example.

this ancient road to the abandoned capital	*Sōgi*
won't those blooming flowers also think this is just a spring dream?	*Shōhaku*
because they are cherry blossoms, the mountain wind blows	*Sōchō*
when morning dew remains peaceful in the hazy field	*Sōgi*
look closely at it, how merciless this world!	*Shōhaku*
until this late I couldn't turn away from the depressing moon[6]	*Sōchō*
even now I hate to think of the long night's darkness[7]	*Sōgi*
the sight of torches on those offshore boats makes me shiver[8]	*Shōhaku*
choppy evening waves, loud on the rocky beach	*Sōchō*
a cuckoo's call engulfed, who can tell it called?	*Sōgi*
I'll return from this trip—people, don't forget me[9]	*Shōhaku*
I'm just seeing if I tire of living in this mountain village	*Sōchō*

[6] A bright moon is supposed to remind one of unhappy things of the past; hence, "depressing."

[7] "Long night's darkness" is the state in which someone finds himself who cannot attain buddhahood immediately after death.

[8] The offshore boats are fishing; in Buddhism killing any sentient being is a crime.

[9] In an old Chinese story, a cuckoo is associated with a journey of no return.

once used, I won't mind withering, but the storm is   *Sōgi*
depressing

cruel: the frost has killed the fields, but not my seed of   *Shōhaku*
love

has such pining of a heart ever been known?   *Sōchō*

on Waka Bay I've hidden in a cove, indecisive   *Sōgi*

the tide comes in—as if longing for someone   *Shōhaku*

an abandoned, broken boat, but not wholly rotten   *Sōchō*

red leaves under the trees, with no one to visit them   *Sōgi*

dew now hardly forms in my garden; the autumn ends   *Shōhaku*

insects chirp reedily, any day there'll be frost   *Sōchō*

not caring how I feel this sleepless night, the moon is   *Sōgi*
clear

nothing happens in my way; if only I could stop   *Shōhaku*
thinking

with these expectations, this world is all the more de-   *Sōchō*
pressing

once in old age, things should be easier   *Sōgi*

try not to overstep it, and the norm becomes a painful   *Shōhaku*
road[10]

---

[10] Allusion to 2:4 in the Confucian Analects: "At seventy I followed
my heart's desire without overstepping the norm." The pronouncement is
given an ironic twist here.

my stallion, treading in the snow, wearies his legs on   *Sōchō*
this mountain

sleeves felt cold, with showers last night; I left home in   *Sōgi*
the morning

how could I resent them!—those winds through the   *Shōhaku*
pines

while I admired the blossoms, the moon turned hazy   *Sōchō*

in the sky at dusk—time for wisteria to bloom   *Sōgi*

spring goes; how can I not leave my heart here?   *Shōhaku*

deep in the mountain, warbler calls linger   *Sōchō*

the moment autumn comes, lonely mists rise   *Sōgi*

this morning how piercing the wind from the River of   *Shōhaku*
Heaven[11]

I've come away from an inn where they fulled cloth as   *Sōchō*
I lay

no trace of dreams is left in these dewy fields   *Sōgi*

white moonlight for a pillow, in the pampas grass   *Shōhaku*

when will I see my love all the time?   *Sōchō*

---

11 For the "River of Heaven"; see Okura's poems on the subject on pp.
46–47. In the following part, Sōchō takes Shōhaku to be referring to an
actual river by that name, rather than to the legendary one in the sky.

scattering this way and that—the evening smoke from Asama[12]	Sōgi
after fading, who'll know which cloud?	Shōhaku
how insecure to be in a hut, worried about Nirvana![13]	Sōchō
before becoming old, what did I ever think?	Sōgi
pleasures to the eye and ear have grown remote	Shōhaku
in the winter forest, the sound of water freezing	Sōchō
evening crows fly to sleep on the mountain, where the snow has stopped	Sōgi
above the tiled roofs, a cold moon	Shōhaku
who is it making noise under cover of the bell this late at night?	Sōchō
must be someone old—coughing inside[14]	Sōgi
in the mugwort lot, seizing on a visitor she's complaining	Shōhaku
of late, increasingly more of it—the grass on the path[15]	Sōchō
the hot sunbeams weaken in dewy autumn winds	Sōgi

[12] Asama is an active volcano; the smoke here comes out of smoldering passion. The following part assumes that smoke turns into a cloud.

[13] The cloud in the preceding part is taken to mean the one on which the delegation of welcoming angels from Nirvana is supposed to come. The speaker is worried that the delegation may not recognize him because his abode is miserable.

[14] This and the following parts allude to the chapter "Yomogyū" in the Tale of Genji.

[15] The grass grows over because no one comes to visit.

sleeves have become light; evening cicadas chirp	*Shōhaku*
across the coloring mountains white clouds trail	*Sōchō*
the pines on the ridges show their pride	*Sōgi*
though living in a grass hut, I still count on the one who made the vow	*Shōhaku*
how can someone aloof be attractive?	*Sōchō*
irrational—to have come to the front of the "Come-Not" Barrier!	*Sōgi*
calling someone, a cuckoo flies past[16]	*Shōhaku*
making up their minds, the geese rise to the cloudpath hazy in heaven[17]	*Sōchō*
naturally: blossoms are left behind, this side of the mountain	*Sōgi*
still rather attached to it, he renounces the world	*Shōhaku*
about to leave it—home doesn't look that "temporary"	*Sōchō*
as lasting as the dew—don't think your village depressing	*Sōgi*
a shower, and the moon hesitates[18]	*Shōhaku*

[16] The Japanese name given here to the cuckoo is *yobukodori*, "bird that calls"; hence the linkage to the preceding part.

[17] The call of a goose is supposed to sound as if it were announcing its name. Sōchō therefore suggests that what was thought to be a cuckoo was in fact a flock of departing geese.

[18] A formal renga usually ends with a happier observation.

TEN KOUTA FROM THE *KANGINSHŪ*

Wait for me
in the shadow of the willows—
if anyone asks you,
say you're cutting twigs
for toothpicks

.

I'm on his mind
even though he won't let on—
when they look the coolest
they're feeling it most

.

Behind your fan,
staring like that
when you know I have a husband,
saying, shall we try something?
shall we? shall we?

.

Just so a person has heart—
among these dreams of dreams of dreams,
yesterday is today's antiquity,
today is tomorrow's long ago

.

Hey, crazy!
when you know I have a husband—
You're choking me!
you're biting!
I may fool around,
but every girl at seventeen—
If you bite, bite gently—
tooth marks would give us away!

.

It was just one night,
but when he left I missed him so,
I went out to look—
there offshore, how fast the boat,
how thick the fog!

.

Because for one night you don't come,
I take my innocent pillow,
fling it sideways,
fling it in the air—
pillow! you pillow you!

.

Even the little minnows under the bridge
decline to sleep alone,
cruising upstream,
cruising down

.

I just had to start a conversation
somehow—
Look there! how fast those clouds
are moving across the sky!

.

I wanted so to see you,
I slipped away and came running—
First let me go,
let me go and let me speak—
funny—I love you so
I can't think what to do

THIRTY-SIX TSUKEAI FROM THE *INUTSUKUBASHŪ*

[*Tsukeai*, linking, is basic to the renga, and links in the minimum combination of two parts were frequently composed for practice or just for fun. The following sampling of two-part links is from the *Inutsukubashū*, an anthology of links and hokku, believed to have been compiled by Yamazaki Sōkan (died ?1534) in the early sixteenth century. In all the links selected here, the first part is in 7–7 syllables, and the second part in 5–7–5 syllables. The translations are somewhat freer than elsewhere in this anthology, because *tsukeai*, by nature, often depends on punning.]

Spring

A robe of haze is wet at its hem:
Princess Sao of spring pissed as she started[1]

.

A gasp, and it was gone!
morning haze hit by a spring storm

.

Wind, blow, and don't blow!
we hoist sail to hurry to see the cherries in bloom

.

[1] Princess Sao is the goddess of spring.

Looks as if about to snatch the blossoms:
a fiddlehead raising its fist under the azaleas

·

Down the ass-tuft the dew drips, drips:
ice on the water bird's tail melts in the morning

Summer

He lights a lamp at such an awkward spot!
how come a firefly has an ass that glows?

·

It's so hot it makes him squat:
a shrimp lying in the shallows of a summer stream

·

Dammit, they get pulled up all the time:
my bamboo shoots grow in a neighbor's yard

·

They sucked me to their satisfaction:
I slept one whole night in a tattered mosquito net

Autumn

Too beautiful for me, but I have to cleave in:
the moon reflects in a tub for washing my feet

·

The autumn evening is for whisperers:
the crescent moon is there to listen to all sorts of things

Love

Red inside, coal-black outside:
don't know, but it sounds like something a woman has

.

He cranes his neck against the dawning sky:
to kiss a tall young man farewell

.

Married, but they seem to wait for the night:
truth is, they've made up but really haven't

.

We have parents who peep through a hole:
nights we make love they bother us as if they weren't grownups

Miscellany

I think I'll wash my testicles with care:
the old saying says, "If you don't polish a ball, it won't shine"

.

He learns by groping if there's hair or there isn't:
a monk without a disciple has shaved his head himself

.

I want and don't want to slash him:
the burglar I caught turns out to be my son

.

I want and don't want to cut it down:
what hides the clear moon is a branch of cherry blossoms

•

I'm mortified and yet delighted:
someone has run away with the old woman I couldn't leave

•

Thirsty—that's how Mount Fuji makes you feel:
coming out on the beach of Tago, I look, and there isn't even a tea-
shop[2]

•

Squeezing it slender, I slip it in quickly:
the tea bag's too large for the tea jar's small mouth

•

Worthy and not worthy of our respect:
the monk downed a bird with prayer, then devoured it!

•

Lonely and not quite lonely:
turning against the world, he lives in a hut but he's got money

•

Our prime minister made a fast move!
he jumped across the stream beside his gate

•

He wants and doesn't want to roast them:
the poor monk has only a handful of beans

•

2 Allusion to Yamabe no Akahito's tanka on p. 58, "Coming out."

It was so cold she let in the wind:
the beggar woman tore the board off the wall and burned it

.

Each time they meet, they make squishy noises:
sharpening my razor on a stone, a puddle underneath

.

Wetting his head, he slips in:
a man with a coat but no umbrella shelters from the rain

.

Dangerous, yet felicitous:
here comes our bridegroom, crossing the bridge of a single log

.

Each time he gives a thrust, the juice squishes:
the wooden bell hammer is sodden at the mountain temple

.

Getting relaxed, getting tense:
look at the spectators at the archery contest

.

Thinking it sinful, he doesn't dip it:
the shallow well has fish living in it

.

He wonders if he ought to wash his clothes:
having lived with them for a while he now loves the lice

.

Even the young ones are stooping:
baby shrimp are born to look like their parents

.

I made her wet, and myself
folding umbrellas to bow to each other in the rain

RENGA

"Pine Resin" (partial)

[Composed in 1530 by Arakida Moritake (1473–1549)[1]]

The pine resin is just an unguent on the year's first day of the rat[2]

I have a cold, though when the plums are fragrant

spring still freezing, my runny nose with icicles again this morning!

paper sleeves as thin as the haze

he learns calligraphy in the light snow[3]

the bamboo, bent now, will rise up sometime

---

[1] Renga were most frequently composed by two or more persons, but solo compositions, such as this one, were not rare. The first twenty-two parts of this typical haikai or humorous hundred-part sequence are translated here.

[2] On the year's first day of the rat, young pine trees were dug up by the roots as a sign of the wish for a long imperial reign ("long as the pine roots"). Here, to be humorous the poet speaks of the resin rather than the formally accepted poetic image of roots.

[3] Allusion to a legendary Chinese scholar who, too poor to buy oil, read by the light of the snow and eventually became a high government official.

don't know why—it's in front of the window at the end of the guest
room

to see the moon, he says, but he must want to wash his hands

a willow with its lower leaves gone, a brush, now the autumn's here[4]

teeth unclean—when was it? now morning mists in the sky[5]

keep coming back—I mean, those geese, I don't want them[6]

it's set: crows are crows[7]

each time I look at you, my love, you're darker

don't get so suntanned

"My dear, I'll send you a black parasol along with this"

my tears afterward will simply be greasy[8]

---

[4] Willow twigs were made into toothbrushes. Here, the willow itself
looks like one.
[5,6,7] The puns here are *hagasumi* (unclean teeth, to be robbed),
karigane (geese, borrowed money), and *karasu* (crow, to borrow).
[8] Twist on the saying that if you cry too much, tears of blood will
come out. The letter in the preceding part is taken to mean one from
someone whose love is unrequited.

you're a stone letter in a pot[9] with its mouth shut—that's why I'm lost

"It's Ōshū[10] and I can't say a word"

it's going to be tough for the Lord Lieutenant[11] from now on

the way Shizuka[12] feels—what can I compare it to?

viewing the blossoms she can't help pondering the baby in her womb

yes, throughout the long day, long as an umbilical cord

[9] The "stone letter in a pot" (*tsubo no ishibumi*) is the stele Sakanoue no Tamuramaro (758–811), subjugator of the north, built to mark what he believed to be the center of Japan. In poetry it is used to mean someone who does not or is unable to say what is on his mind.

[10] Ōshū, the northern region of Honshū, where the stele was, was considered an almost alien country, its people speaking a different language.

[11] The Lord Lieutenant is Minamoto no Yoshitsune (1156–1189), who went to Ōshū to escape his brother's persecution.

[12] Shizuka is Yoshitsune's mistress, who was forced to part with him. The place of their last meeting was Mount Yoshino, famous for cherry blossoms.

RENGA

I'm a Flower (partial)

[Composed by Nishiyama Sōin (1605–1682) and published in 1671[1]]

"I'm a flower, I won't tell you my name—stop pulling my sleeve!"[2]

"Lasts as long as a dream—your youth, your spring"

they exchange cups, get hazy, warm up

no time to use their arms for pillows[3]

moon daylight-bright, you can't sneak in

that lover, face hidden, getting wet with dew

---

[1] Unlike a regular renga in which the topic keeps changing from part to part, this one deals exclusively with love—though in various manifestations. The first twenty-two parts of the hundred-part sequence are translated here.

[2] Set phrase of a young Kabuki actor.

[3] Suggests that the lovers did not need time for foreplay; coupled with the next part, it suggests they cannot even have that time, let alone time for love-making.

in deep mist he hangs around the front lattice and the gate[4]

the samisen player[5] pulls his face close and looks at him

unable to part, they toy with the mooring rope

as deep as the river, the way they feel

"If I could be with you I wouldn't mind downing this barrel of sake"

"Let it be known to all—even a minute from now!"

after a not-at-all shallow love-talk, she cut her finger off[6]

though a daughter of joy, her resolve is strong

the memento left in Ōiso—the "strength rock"[7]

only a passer-by yet shedding tears[8]

he leaves the inn, his heart's fire smoldering

[4] Suggests a brothel district.
[5] The samisen player is a prostitute.
[6] To show the sincerity of her word, a prostitute often cut off her little finger and gave it to her lover.
[7] Tora, a prostitute and mistress of Soga Sukenari (1172–1193), is said to have turned after her death into a "strength rock" (chikara ishi), which only a most handsome man could lift. Sukenari and his brother, Tokimune (1174–1193), are famous for avenging their father's murder.
[8] Tears for Tora's devotion to Sukenari.

in a thatched hut,[9] still agitated

with the moon out, the amorist uses tea as a pretext

sending just one line this autumn night

he repeats his long stories to the go-between

making her his wife before he knows it

---

[9] A "thatched hut" prompts the association of a man of refinement—
hence, tea. Such a man is called *suki*, which also means someone who
delights in winning female favors.

KONISHI RAIZAN

(1654–1716)

THIRTEEN HOKKU

Green, green, the young herbs are green in the snowy field

White fish graphically move in the water's color

Spring rain: I put my foot out of the footwarmer

Spring rain falls, unknown to the cow's eyes

Spring wind: over the river bank comes a bull's voice

I turn to look: cold in the evening dusk, mountain cherries

Blossoms bloom, I don't wanna die, but this illness

I pluck, I pluck and throw away spring grasses

Both have whiskers—I mean, the cat's wife, too

My son Jōshun died in early spring:
A spring dream—that I don't go mad is what I resent

Mosquitoes came in, and while the two were shaking the mosquito
net, daybreak came

How many autumns? unable to soothe myself, alone with my mother

Living alone:
I hug myself and again it's hard to breathe in the cold of night

MATSUO BASHŌ

(1644–1694)

SEVENTY-SIX HOKKU[1]

1663
The moon as your guide, come in this way to stay, traveler

1666
The iris looks exactly like the one in the water

1667
Plum blossoms at their best—if only the wind blew empty-handed!

1676
At Saya-between-the-Hills:
Alive—under my narrow hat I enjoy the coolness[2]

1677
A scudding cloud: a trotting dog's pisses, these showers!

1680
Ah, spring, spring! Great is the spring, and so forth!

---

[1] The chronological order roughly follows that of Yamamoto Kenkichi in his *Bashō zen hokku* (Complete Hokku by Bashō).
[2] See Saigyō's tanka, "Did I ever think," p. 179.

At night secretly a worm bores a chestnut under the moon

On dead branches crows remain perched at autumn's end[3]

Having been given some kindling by Jokushi's wife while
holing up for the winter:
I'll make a fire tonight to melt the frost on my roof

The rich eat meat, the strong have vegetable roots, but I am
poor:
This snowy morning, alone, I've managed to chew some dried salmon

1681
White fish clustering in seaweed, if caught, will surely melt

Rika gave me a plantain:[4]
Having planted a plantain, at once I hate two stalks of reed

Sentiment on a winter night at Fukagawa:
Sound of paddles slapping the waves, my bowels freeze tonight, and
the tears

[3] This hokku is usually interpreted as describing a single crow on a single branch. The interpretation here is based on one of the paintings Bashō
did to illustrate the hokku, which shows several crows in a treetop and a
flock of others in the air. In 1687, when Bashō revised the hokku somewhat,
Sodō composed a wakiku: "a man with a hoe on his shoulder in a misty
far-off village."
[4] This plantain, or bashō, grew well and the poet became so fond of it
that first his house, then he himself, came to be known by its name. In the
hokku, Bashō says he is worried about the powerful reed overtaking his
plantain—a twist on the traditional sentiment on the reed, a plant favored
by tanka poets.

1682

In response to Kikaku's hokku on smartweed/firefly:[5]

With the morning-glories I eat my meal, I'm that kind of man

1684

In my hut, square light cast by the window moon

In the eighth month, in the autumn of the first year of Jōkyō [1684], as I left my dilapidated hut by the river, the sound of the wind was somewhat chilly:

Skull exposed in a field in my mind—the wind pierces my body[6]

On the day when we passed the Barrier [Hakone], the entire mountain [Fuji] was hidden in clouds:

In mists and rains, the day I do not see Fuji is fun

Made on horseback:

The roadside marsh mallow has been eaten by my horse

As evening came, I went to the outer shrine [of Ise]. Under the first torii, it was dusky, and with holy lanterns visible here and there, and unsurpassing pine winds from the peaks almost piercing my body, I was deeply moved:

The month's last day, no moon—a storm hugs the cedars of a thousand years

---

[5] Kikaku's hokku, "At a grass hut I eat smartweed, I'm that kind of firefly," typifies a literary affectation, the suggestion being that the speaker prefers what ordinary people reject and has fun at night when they are asleep. In response, Bashō says he is one of those ordinary people.

[6] The opening hokku in *Nozarashi kikō*, the first of Bashō's five *kikō*, travel diaries incorporating hokku.

Early in the ninth month I went back to my birthplace; the day lilies of the north hall had died off in the frost,[7] now with no trace left. Everything had changed from the past; my siblings had white hair on their temples, wrinkles on their brows. We could say no more than, "We are alive." My brother opened his amulet and said, "Look at mother's white hair. Urashima's comb box[8]—your eyebrows have grown old, too." He wept for a while:

If taken in hand, autumn frost will melt—the tears are hot

Tired of sleeping on a grass pillow, I went out on the beach while it was still dark:

Daybreak: a white fish is white, just an inch

Spending a day by the sea till dark:

The sea darkens, and the voices of ducks faintly white

1685
On the road to Nara:

It's spring! nameless mountains in morning haze

A view of the lake water:

The pines of Karasaki, more blurred than the blossoms[9]

To have a noontime rest I sat in a shop for travelers:

Azaleas arranged, and by them a woman slivers dried cod

7 An old Chinese expression, meaning that his mother died.
8 See poem on Urashima, p. 50.
9 Alludes to, among others, Hitomaro's poem, "Passing by the Wasted Capital in Ōmi," p. 28, and Taira Tadanori's tanka (Senzaishū, no. 66): "Sazanami—the capital of Shiga lies in ruins, but the mountain cherries remain as in the past."

On a tour to compose hokku:
In a rape field sparrows look as if out to view the flowers

On a road that leads to Ōtsu, as I came over the mountain
path:
Coming by a mountain path—elegant somehow, violets

Only butterflies fly in the field in the sun

Toward the end of the fourth month I returned to my hut
and tried to dispel my weariness from the trip:
Summer clothes: I have yet to pick all the lice

1686
An old pond: a frog jumps in—the sound of water

To Rika:
Lightning in my hand—in the dark, this rushlight

Bright moon: strolling around the pond all night long

Mistaken for a blind man[10] while enjoying the moon

Wanting to see the "first snow" at my grass hut, whenever I
was elsewhere and the sky became cloudy, I would hurry
home—I did it so many times. But one twelfth month, on

---

[10] Bashō chose to look like a monk, head shaven and wearing special
clothes. A blind man traditionally shaved his head, and that also made him
look like a monk.

the eighth, for the first time it snowed [while I was home],
and I was overjoyed:

First snow: luckily I find myself residing in my own hut

1687

Through the long day the skylarks have not sung enough

In the middle of a plain, utterly unconcerned a skylark sings

Of myself:

Hair grown and face pale in this May rain

A pea crab crawls up my leg from the clear water

Take Saigyō's waka, Sōgi's renga, Sesshū's paintings,[11]
Rikyū's tea,[12]—what runs through them is one and the same
thing. Those in art follow nature and make friends with the
four seasons. Whatever they see can only be a flower; whatever they think can only be the moon. Those who see no
flower in anything are no better than barbarians; those who
feel no flower[13] in their hearts are akin to birds and beasts.
Get out from among barbarians, take yourselves away from
birds and beasts. Follow nature and return to nature, that's
what I say.

Early in the tenth month the sky looks uncertain and I
feel like a leaf in the wind, not knowing where I'm going:

I'd like to be called a traveler in the first showers[14]

11 Sesshū (1420–1506) excelled in ink painting.
12 Sen Rikyū (1520–1591) perfected the art of drinking tea.
13 Bashō probably had "moon" in mind here.
14 Followed by Yoshiyuki's wakiku, "again lodging under sasanqua
from place to place."

In Amatsu there was a narrow road through the paddies, and the wind blowing up from the sea was very cold:

A winter day: frozen on horseback, a shadow

1688
Hozo Pass:

In the sky above the skylarks I rest at a mountaintop pass

Nijikō:

Fluttering, kerria roses scatter at the sound of a waterfall

In coming to Japan, Monk Ganjin[15] of Shōdai Temple more than seventy times endured difficulties on his ship, and because the salty winds blew into his eyes he finally became blind. I looked at his holy statue:

With a young leaf may I wipe the dew from your eyes?

The sky in the middle of the fourth month was still hazy, and the moon of the fleeting short night quite alluring, the mountains dark with young leaves. It was time for cuckoos to appear, calling, when the eastern clouds began to turn white beyond the sea:

Fishermen's faces were seen first, then the poppy flowers

A cuckoo fades away, and in its direction, a single island[16]

Staying overnight at Akashi:

Octopus traps: fleeting dreams—the summer moon

[15] Ganjin (688–763), a Chinese Buddhist monk, came to Japan in 754 and in Nara founded the temple Bashō mentions, more correctly called Tōshōdai-ji.

[16] Allusion to Fujiwara Sanesada's tanka (*Senzaishū*, no. 161): "A cuckoo called, and I looked in that direction: there only the daybreak moon was left."

Congratulations on a new house:

A good house: sparrows delight in the millet behind the back door

Cold night:

A pot splits, and the night ice wakes me

1689

As I climbed out of the boat at the place called Senju I was overwhelmed by the thought of the three thousand *li* lying before me and shed tears of parting in the illusory world:[17]

Departing spring: birds cry and in the eyes of fish, tears

Stopping by Saigyō's willow:[18]

One paddy planted, I walk away from the willow

At Takadachi in Ōshū:

Summer grass: where the warriors used to dream

For three days winds and rain raged and we stayed on the miserable mountain:

Fleas, lice—a horse pisses right by my pillow

Quietness: piercing the rocks, the cicadas' voice

Gathering the May rains, and swift, the Mogami River[19]

17 Toward the end of the third month, 1689, Bashō set out on a journey that was to last six months. His famous travel diary, *Oku no hosomichi*, is about that journey. The passage here describes his parting with his friends in Edo. *Li* is a Chinese measure, equivalent to about a third of a mile, and "three thousand *li*" is a set phrase for a long way.

18 Willow famous for Saigyō's tanka, "In willow shade," p. 173.

19 The original version, "Gathering the May rains, and cool, the Mogami River," was followed by Ichi'ei's wakiku, "the pole for boats moors fireflies to the bank."

The Mogami River has poured the hot sun into the sea[20]

In the place called Komatsu in Kaga, the shrine of Tada holds
as its treasure Sanemori's helmet[21] with a chrysanthemum
design, and a brocaded cloth of his. Though it was a matter
of long ago, I could visualize it and was moved:
Cruel: under a helmet, a cricket

Whiter than the stones on Stone Mountain—the autumn wind

Dragonfly—unable to get hold of a grass blade

First shower[22]—even a monkey seems to want a small coat

I usually hate crows, but this snowy morning!

1690
At my house small mosquitoes are the best I can offer

I pluck my gray hair, and under my pillow, a cricket[23]

In a fisherman's hut crickets mingle with small shrimp

[20] The original version, "Coolness: the Mogami River pours into the
sea," was followed by Sendō's wakiku, "floating seaweed among waves
sways the moon."
[21] Saitō Sanemori (1111–1183) was a warrior who first served the Genji
clan, then the opposing Heike clan. After he was killed in a battle with the
Genji forces, his helmet was dedicated to the Tada Shrine by the victorious
general. There is a Nō play based on his life.
[22] First shower of winter.
[23] Followed by Shidō's wakiku, "persimmons in the garden, turn into
bagworms."

By the roadside in my birthplace:
Raining so much it's blackened fresh stubs of rice

1691
Enfeebled: I've bitten on the sand in seaweed

Rakushisha:[24]
May rain: marks on each wall of poetry cards taken down

Scallions just washed white in this cold

Staying at Hōrai Temple:
Blustered by icy winds the boulders grow pointed among the cedar trees

1692
Mottoes:
    Don't mention others' shortcomings;
    Don't dwell on your virtues.
Speak, and your lips feel cold in the autumn wind

Salted breams' gums are cold on a fish-shop shelf

1693
A cuckoo's voice lays itself over the water

In Hatchōbori:
Chrysanthemums bloom among masons' stones

---

[24] Mukai Kyorai's retreat in Saga, Kyoto, where Bashō stayed and wrote *Saga Diary*. The hokku here is the last entry in the diary.

The chrysanthemum didn't spill a dewdrop, now frozen

Alive, sea cucumbers frozen in one lump

1694
As if touching a boil a willow bends

In morning dew, dirty and cool, the mud on the melon

> On the twenty-first of the seventh month of the seventh
> year of Genroku [1694], at Bokusetsu's hut in Ōtsu:

Near autumn our hearts are close in this small room[25]

> Later, spending some time at Bokusetsu's hut in Ōtsu:

Putting my feet on the cool, cool wall, I take a nap

Lightning: going in the dark side, a night heron calls

In the old village, no house without a persimmon tree

This road: no one taking it as autumn ends

People's voices: returning by this road as autumn ends

> Sentiment on a journey:

This autumn, why do I get old? In clouds a bird

---

[25] Followed by Bokusetsu's wakiku, "the pinks with dew lie untidily."

This white chrysanthemum doesn't have a speck of dust that hits the eye[26]

The autumn's deep—my neighbor, what does he do?

Composed while ill:

Falling ill on a journey, my dreams run round a withered field

---

[26] Followed by Sonome's wakiku, "the morning moon lets water flow over crimson leaves."

HAIBUN

Snowball

Sora so-and-so[1] has set up residence near here temporarily, and mornings and evenings we visit each other. When I fix food, he helps me by adding kindling, and on nights when I boil tea, he knocks on my door. He's a man who by nature prefers seclusion and quiet, and our relationship doesn't involve money. One night he visited me in the snow:

You, make a fire. I'll show you something nice—a snowball

Warning on Solitary Living

Here I am, a lazy old man. Normally I find it so bothersome to have people coming to see me that I often vow in my heart, "I'll never meet or invite people." But what can I do?—on a moonlit night or in the snowy morning I long for my friends. At such a time, quietly I drink sake alone, talking in my mind. I push open the door of my hut and look at the snow. I take up my cup again, dip my brush and put it away. Here I am, a demented old man:

I drink sake and find it harder to sleep this snowy night

Visiting the Ise Shrine

Toward the end of the second month in the fifth year of Jōkyō [1688], I went to Ise. This was the fifth time I trod the ground in front of the sanctuary. As I had grown old by still another year, I felt its awesome light and venerableness all the more strongly. Recalling fondly that it was the place

---

[1] Kaai Sora (1649–1710). To call one's friend in this manner was a literary convention.

where Saigyō shed tears and wrote of his "gratitude,"[2] I spread my fan on the ground and put my forehead on it:

From the blossoms of what tree I don't know—but this fragrance!

Matsushima

Matsushima is said to have the best scenery in Japan. People with an elegant turn of mind, past and present, have thought hard and employed skill [in writing poems] about the islands. In the sea area about three square *li*, various islands of unusual shape look as if wonderfully carved by a heavenly artist. Each with pine trees flourishing on it, the islands are beautiful and attractive beyond description:

Islands: shattered into thousands of pieces in the summer sea

Ode to the Galaxy

From the place called Izumozaki in the province of Echigo, Sado Island, it's said, is eighteen *li* away on the sea. With the cragginess of its valleys and peaks distinctly in sight, it lies on its side in the sea, thirty-odd *li* from east to west. Light mists of early fall not rising yet, and the waves not high, I feel as if I could touch it with my hands as I look at it. On the island great quantities of gold well up and in that regard it's a most auspicious island. But from past to present a place of exile for felons and traitors, it has become a distressing name. The thought terrifies me. As the evening moon sets, the surface of the sea becomes quite dark. The shapes of the mountains are still visible through the clouds, and the sound of waves is saddening as I listen:

The rough sea: lying toward Sado Island, the River of Heaven

---

2 Saigyō's tanka: "Though I do not know what it is that resides in it, tears of gratitude well up in my eyes." "It" refers to the Ise Shrine.

The Hut of the Phantom Dwelling[3]

Beyond Ishiyama, with its back to Mount Iwama, is a hill called Kokubuyama—the name I think derives from a *kokubunji* or government temple of long ago. If you cross the narrow stream that runs at the foot and climb the slope for three turnings of the road, some two hundred paces each, you come to a shrine of the god Hachiman. The object of worship is a statue of the Buddha Amida. This is the sort of thing that is greatly abhorred by the Yuiitsu school, though I regard it as admirable that, as the Ryōbu assert, the Buddhas should dim their light and mingle with the dust in order to benefit the world.[4] Ordinarily, few worshippers visit the shrine and it's very solemn and still. Beside it is an abandoned hut with a rush door. Brambles and bamboo grass overgrow the eaves, the roof leaks, the plaster has fallen from the walls, and foxes and badgers make their den there. It is called the Genjūan or Hut of the Phantom Dwelling. The owner was a monk, an uncle of the warrior Suganuma Kyokusui. It has been eight years since he lived there—nothing remains of him now but his name, Elder of the Phantom Dwelling.

I too gave up city life some ten years ago, and now I'm approaching fifty. I'm like a bagworm that's lost its bag, a snail without its shell. I've tanned my face in the hot sun of Kisakata in Ōu, and bruised my heels on the rough beaches of the northern sea, where tall dunes make walking so hard.[5] And now this year here I am drifting by the waves of Lake Biwa. The grebe attaches its floating nest to a single strand of reed, counting on the reed to keep it from washing away

---

[3] The piece, written in 1690, describes a hut where Bashō lived for half a year on the southern shore of Lake Biwa east of Kyoto.

[4] In Bashō's time the Buddhist and Shinto religions had become so interfused that it was not uncommon for a Buddhist statue to be worshipped in a shrine dedicated to a Shinto deity such as Hachiman. The Yuiitsu school of Shinto strongly opposed such syncretism, but the more common Ryōbu faction looked upon the Shinto deities as avatars of the Buddhas—Hachiman was thought to be an avatar of Amida—and saw it as admirable that the Buddhas should set aside their dignity and deign to take on the form of local Japanese gods in order to save mankind.

[5] References to the trip to northern Japan that Bashō described in his famous travel diary *Oku no hosomichi.*

in the current. With a similar thought, I mended the thatch on the eaves of the hut, patched up the gaps in the fence, and at the beginning of the fourth month, the first month of summer, moved in for what I thought would be no more than a brief stay. Now, though, I'm beginning to wonder if I'll ever want to leave.

Spring is over, but I can tell it hasn't been gone for long. Azaleas continue in bloom, wild wisteria hangs from the pine trees, and a cuckoo now and then passes by. I even have greetings from the jays, and woodpeckers that peck at things, though I don't really mind—in fact, I rather enjoy them. I feel as though my spirit had raced off to China to view the scenery in Wu or Ch'u, or as though I were standing beside the lovely Hsiao and Hsiang rivers or Lake Tungt'ing. The mountain rises behind me to the southwest and the nearest houses are a good distance away. Fragrant southern breezes blow down from the mountain tops, and north winds, dampened by the lake, are cool. I have Mount Hie and the tall peak of Hira, and this side of them the pines of Karasaki veiled in mist, as well as a castle, a bridge, and boats fishing on the lake.[6] I hear the voice of the woodsman making his way to Mount Kasatori, and the songs of the seedling planters in the little rice paddies at the foot of the hill. Fireflies weave through the air in the dusk of evening, clapper rails tap out their notes—there's surely no lack of beautiful scenes. Among them is Mikamiyama, which is shaped rather like Mount Fuji and reminds me of my old house in Musashino, while Mount Tanakami sets me to counting all the poets of ancient times who are associated with it.[7] Other mountains include Bamboo Grass Crest, Thousand Yard Summit, and Skirt Waist. There's Black Ford village, where the foliage is so dense and dark, and the men who tend their fish weirs, looking exactly as they're described in the *Man'yōshū*. In order to get a better view all around, I've climbed up on the height behind my hut, rigged

---

[6] Zeze Castle and Seta Bridge, the latter where the Seta River flows out of the south end of Lake Biwa. See Bashō's hokku, "The pines," p. 281.

[7] The mountain is the site of graves or shrines associated with various poets such as Ki no Tsurayuki.

a platform among the pines, and furnished it with a round straw mat. I call it the Monkey's Perch. I'm not in a class with those Chinese eccentrics Hsü Ch'üan, who made himself a nest up in a cherry-apple tree where he could do his drinking, or Old Man Wang, who built his retreat on Secretary Peak. I'm just a mountain dweller, sleepy by nature, who has turned his footsteps to the steep slopes and sits here in the empty hills catching lice and smashing them.

Sometimes, when I'm in an energetic mood, I draw clear water from the valley and cook myself a meal. I have only the drip drip of the spring to relieve my loneliness, but with my one little stove, things are anything but cluttered. The man who lived here before was truly lofty in mind and did not bother with any elaborate construction. Outside of the one room where the Buddha image is kept, there is only a little place designed to store bedding.

An eminent monk of Mount Kōra in Tsukushi, the son of a certain Kai of the Kamo Shrine, recently journeyed to Kyoto, and I got someone to ask him if he would write a plaque for me. He readily agreed, dipped his brush, and wrote the three characters Gen-jū-an. He sent me the plaque, and I keep it as a memorial of my grass hut. Mountain home, traveler's rest—call it what you will, it's hardly the kind of place where you need any great store of belongings. A cypress bark hat from Kiso, a sedge rain cape from Koshi—that's all that hang on the post above my pillow. In the daytime, I'm once in a while diverted by people who stop to visit. The old man who takes care of the shrine or the men from the village come and tell me about the wild boar who's been eating the rice plants, the rabbits that are getting at the bean patches, tales of farm matters that are all quite new to me. And when the sun has begun to sink behind the rim of the hills, I sit quietly in the evening waiting for the moon so I may have my shadow for company, or light a lamp and discuss right and wrong with my silhouette.

But when all has been said, I'm not really the kind who is so completely enamored of solitude that he must hide every trace of himself away in the mountains and wilds. It's just that, troubled by frequent illness and weary of dealing with people, I've come to dislike society. Again and again I think of the mistakes I've made in my clumsiness over the course of the years. There was a time when I envied those who had government offices or impressive domains, and on another occasion I considered entering the precincts of the Buddha and the teaching rooms of the patriarchs. Instead, I've worn out my body in journeys that are as aimless as the winds and clouds, and expended my feelings on flowers and birds. But somehow I've been able to make a living this way, and so in the end, unskilled and talentless as I am, I give myself wholly to this one concern, poetry. Po Chü-yi worked so hard at it that he almost ruined his five vital organs, and Tu Fu grew lean and emaciated because of it. As far as intelligence or the quality of our writings go, I can never compare to such men. And yet we all in the end live, do we not, in a phantom dwelling? But enough of that—I'm off to bed.

Among these summer trees,
a pasania—
something to count on

In Praise of Unchiku[8]

The Kyoto Buddhist monk Unchiku drew a priest with his face turning the other way, probably a portrait of himself, and asked for words in praise of it. He is about sixty, and I'm already near fifty. We are both in dreams, appearing in dream forms. I add words spoken in sleep:

Turn this way; I'm lonely too, this autumn evening

Life of Tōjun[9]

Old Tōjun was of the Enomoto family, and his grandfather was a farmer-squire in Katada in Gōshū by the name of Takeshita. The Enomotos were the family on Shinshi's

---

[8] Kitamuki Unchiku (1631–1702), a calligrapher, who influenced Bashō.
[9] Enomoto Tōjun (1622–1693). Father of Takarai (Enomoto) Kikaku, here called by one of his other pen names, Shinshi.

mother's side. Seventy-two years old this year, he looked at the autumn moon from the bed where he lay ill, and enjoying flowers and birds, sorrowing over the dew, his soul remained undisturbed till the end. Then he left a hokku on Sarashina[10] as a keepsake and died peacefully through his faith in the Lotus Sutra. When young he learned medicine and made it his source of income; receiving a stipend from Lord Honda, he had little trouble making ends meet. Nevertheless, he came to dislike his worldly routine and discarded the accouterments of his reputable profession. That was when he was already in his early sixties. He turned his city residence into a mountain hut. He enjoyed himself, never letting his brush go, never leaving his desk, for about ten years, and the amount he wrote during that time was more than enough to fill a cart. Born near the lake, he died in the eastern plain.[11] He was no doubt "a great hermit living in a city":[12]

After the moon has set, a desk's four corners

[10] Known for Mount Obasute where, legend says, people too old to work were taken to die; also known as a good spot to view the moon. Tōjun's hokku: "Son or old woman, who would want to change the moon today?"

[11] That is, Lake Biwa and Musashi Plain (Edo).

[12] Allusion to a proverbial Chinese saying that a truly great hermit lives in the middle of a city, rather than far away from it.

RENGA

Under a Tree

[Composed in the third month of 1690 by Matsuo Bashō, Hamada Chinseki,[1] and Suganuma Kyokusui[2]]

Under a tree both soup and fish salad are covered with cherry blossoms	*Bashō*
the westerly sun peaceful, it's fine weather	*Chinseki*
a traveler passes scratching louse bites as spring ends	*Kyokusui*
he hasn't learned how to sport a sword with sheath-cover properly	*Bashō*
come the bright moon, promotions are made at the temporary palace	*Chinseki*
the woodcutter made a rice-huller swiftly[3]	*Kyokusui*
to the saddled three-year-old horse the autumn has come	*Bashō*
the rain changes its name in various ways[4]	*Chinseki*

[1] Hamada Chinseki (died ?1737), a doctor.
[2] Suganuma Kyokusui (died 1717), a samurai who committed suicide.
[3] Transition from the preceding part is not clear. One possibility is that "temporary" made Kyokusui associate some swift action; another is that the promotion ceremony was held suddenly and forced people to make quick preparations.
[4] In Japan rain is differently called according to time of day, location, and season.

men and women bathe in a Suwa[5] hot spring as eve-   *Kyokusui*
ning grows dark

among them a tall exorcist   *Bashō*

pushing an argument off to one side   *Chinseki*

from a tenuous point her love has grown intense   *Kyokusui*

when lost in thought, she's prodded to eat   *Bashō*

looking at the moon, her face—sleeves laden with   *Chinseki*
dew

on a boat in an autumn wind she's scared of the sound   *Kyokusui*
of waves

geese fly away toward Shiroko, Wakamatsu   *Bashō*

a thousand scrolls recited at Ishinden under blossoms in   *Chinseki*
their prime[6]

a pilgrim died on the road where heat haze rises   *Kyokusui*

above all a butterfly in reality stirs pity   *Bashō*

not enough strength even to write a letter[7]   *Chinseki*

---

[5] Suwa is a mountainous area where weather is particularly changeable.

[6] Shiroko, Wakamatsu, and Ishinden are in the same region. Recitation of a thousand scrolls of Buddhist scriptures is a service performed at a temple in Ishinden.

[7] Reflections on life's transience associated with a butterfly made the person here lose heart; or, the butterfly is associated with someone, preferably of noble stock, who is too pampered or languid to do anything.

with a silk gauze a noble figure avoids the sun   *Kyokusui*

he weeps, insisting, "I'd like to see Kumano"   *Bashō*

at Ki the barrier guard with a short bow is obstinate   *Chinseki*

his bald head must be due to excessive drinking   *Kyokusui*

so dark now the dots on the dice are peered at   *Bashō*

facing his temporary altar he says prayers[8]   *Chinseki*

"Say what you will, I sit on the earth floor and suffer   *Kyokusui*
no fleas!"[9]

"I am, in this village, a butt of derision"[10]   *Bashō*

he's hated for being a busybody over the dance festi-   *Chinseki*
val[11]

night after moonlit night, the moon until dawn   *Kyokusui*

the pampas grass, having beckoned for too long, is now   *Bashō*
withered

his is simply a square grass hut with dew   *Chinseki*

---

8 Association by contrast: a gambler and a religiously devout person.
9 The "temporary altar" made Kyokusui think of someone, possibly a
traveler, without enough money to pay for a regular room.
10 From the defiant tone of the preceding part Bashō thought of an eccentric.
11 The Bon festival in August when people dance at night, sometimes
from evening to dawn.

"I've sent back the money, saying, 'That's bother-   *Kyokusui*
some' "12

the decision is not to take the doctor's drugs   *Bashō*

when blossoms come into bloom he runs about places   *Kyokusui*
like Yoshino

getting bitten by gadflies in springtime mountains   *Chinseki*

A Kite's Feathers

[Composed toward the end of 1690 by Mukai Kyorai, Matsuo Bashō, Nozawa Bonchō, and Nakamura Fumikuni13]

A kite's feathers, too, have preened in the first shower   *Kyorai*

a sweep of wind, and the leaves calm down   *Bashō*

still in the morning his pants get wet as he crosses a   *Bonchō*
stream

a small bamboo bow for scaring badgers14   *Fumikuni*

an ivy crawls on a slatted door under the evening moon   *Bashō*

his famous pears are given to no one15   *Kyorai*

---

12 The money was possibly a gift. Suggests a hermitlike eccentric.
13 Nakamura Fumikuni (dates uncertain), a doctor.
14 The bow may be carried by the person described by Bonchō; it can
also be a device set up on the ground to frighten off animals.
15 May allude to an episode in Yoshida Kenkō's (1282–1350) *Tsurezure-
gusa* in which the author happens upon a secluded hut; he is moved by it
until he sees an orange tree, its branches bent with fruit, "sternly surrounded" with a fence.

as he dashes off ink drawings to enjoy himself, autumn ends	*Fumikuni*
"I'm so comfortable in these knit socks"	*Bonchō*
all is quiet while nothing is said	*Kyorai*
a village comes into view, and someone blows a conch for noon	*Bashō*
a frazzled sleeping mattress from last year, losing its shape[16]	*Bonchō*
lotus petals scatter, fluttering[17]	*Fumikuni*
"This soup with Suizenji weed is excellent"[18]	*Bashō*
"I have to go about three *li*"	*Kyorai*
this spring too, Lu T'ung's manservant stays on[19]	*Fumikuni*
his cutting rooted on a moon-hazy night	*Bonchō*
he put a stone basin, though mossy, alongside the blossoms	*Bashō*
"My anger this morning has cured itself"	*Kyorai*

[16] Possibly offered to the mountain exorcist suggested by Bashō.

[17] As related to the preceding part, suggests someone engaged in meditation.

[18] Suggests a tea ceremony in a temple garden.

[19] Lu T'ung (died 835), a T'ang poet who wrote the oldest treatise on tea drinking, had, according to a poem Han Yü (768–824) wrote to him, a loyal "manservant, long whiskers, head unturbaned."

"I've eaten two days worth of food in one sitting"   *Bonchō*

snowy and cold, the island's north wind   *Fumikuni*

come darkness, he climbs to a hilltop temple to light   *Kyorai*
the lamp

all the cuckoos have stopped calling   *Bashō*

lean-fleshed, she still isn't strong enough to raise herself   *Fumikuni*

borrowing a neighbor's space he pulled in his   *Bonchō*
carriage

"He's the one who saddens me—I'll let him through the   *Bashō*
syringa hedge"

now at parting she hands him his sword   *Kyorai*

hair hurriedly scratched with a comb[20]   *Bonchō*

"Look at this determined death struggle!"[21]   *Fumikuni*

daybreak moon in the blue sky, as the morning comes   *Kyorai*

autumn over the lake water, first frost on Hira   *Bashō*

a brushwood hut: the man makes a poem when his   *Fumikuni*
buckwheat gets stolen[22]

---

[20] Suggests a prostitute, as well as a warrior preparing for battle.
[21] Allusion to a passage in volume I of the *Taiheiki*, a fourteenth-century narrative of a series of civil wars in the same century.
[22] Allusion to Chōe, an eccentric monk described in *Kokon chomon jū*, a thirteenth-century collection of instructive tales.

"I'm becoming used to wadded clothes these windy evenings"   *Bonchō*

after sleeping in a crowded room he again rises from his rented pillow   *Bashō*

when the clouds from the foundry are still red in the sky   *Kyorai*

one house makes cruppers with blossoms by its window   *Bonchō*

among the old leaves of a loquat, buds begin to sprout   *Fumikuni*

At a Fragrance of Plums

[Composed in the spring of 1694 by Matsuo Bashō and Shita Yaba[23]]

At a fragrance of plums, a blob, the sun appears on a mountain path   *Bashō*

here and there a pheasant call rises   *Yaba*

he begins repairing his house while there's nothing to do in spring   *Yaba*

news from Kansai raises the price of rice   *Bashō*

in the evening there was some pattering—now the moon among clouds   *Bashō*

23 Shita Yaba (1663–1740), a shop clerk.

talking with a bush in between—the autumn, the loneliness   *Yaba*

"My boss offered to *be given* my chrysanthemums, dammit!"   *Yaba*

"I wouldn't let anybody see my daughter, absolutely not"   *Bashō*

he frequents Nara—the same face, a man of scanty funds   *Yaba*

"This June we have no rain at all"   *Bashō*

someone sent to the other bank of the river to fetch bean paste kept for them   *Yaba*

intensely he begins to talk about his mom   *Bashō*

all night he tried to assuage the nun's chronic pain   *Yaba*

only *konnyaku* is left after the superb moon[24]   *Bashō*

first geese—he tries the cushion on the packsaddle[25]   *Yaba*

with dew as the opponent a sword drawn in a flash[26]   *Bashō*

townspeople are soaked and sodden under cherry blossoms[27]   *Yaba*

---

[24] *Konnyaku* is a loaf made from starch of tubers of the devil's tongue. Though Bashō is known to have liked it, it's not the best part of any meal. The observation suggests a moon-viewing party that lasted all night.

[25] In the Edo period, a pack horse, in addition to a regular load, typically carried a human being, hence a cushion on the packsaddle. Suggests someone leaving on a trip after a farewell party.

[26] A young samurai testing his sword.

[27] Yaba takes the person in the preceding part to be a street vendor showing his special skill to attract potential buyers of his ware.

| jostled at the gate for Mibu prayer-shows[28] | Bashō |

| each waft of east wind spreads the stifling odor of manure | Bashō |

| just sitting around he's bothered by arthritis of the elbow[29] | Yaba |

| "The master across the street is back and telling what's going on in Edo" | Bashō |

| "We need our millstones but I let his wife use them" | Yaba |

| from all directions the noise of bells for *jūya* services[30] | Bashō |

| high above the paulownia tree the moon is clear | Yaba |

| "I closed the gate and went to bed, wordless, for the fun of it" | Bashō |

| he changed the straw mat covers with the money he found on the street[31] | Yaba |

| for Hatsuuma[32] he treats his wife's relatives[33] | Bashō |

| this spring too, the masterless samurai hasn't found a job | Yaba |

---

[28] "Mibu prayer-shows" (*Mibu nembutsu*) are the pantomimes performed at Mibu Temple from the fourteenth to the twenty-fourth of the third month.

[29] As a contrast to the busy farming season suggested by Bashō, Yaba depicts an idler.

[30] *Jūya* is the service from the sixth to the fifteenth of the tenth month observed by the Pure Land sect of Buddhism.

[31] The eccentric suggested by Bashō becomes here someone who did something unconscionable.

[32] Hatsuuma is the Inari festival in the second month.

[33] Not enough money to treat all his relatives.

people see off an exorcist from the hot spring, the   *Bashō*
blossoms at their prime[34]

down from the path by the paddies green wheat is   *Yaba*
doing well

every house has its eastside window open   *Yaba*

"I'm sick of eating fish stew on this shore"[35]   *Bashō*

plovers call, and night by night it gets cold   *Yaba*

they try endlessly to figure the amount of unpaid tax   *Bashō*

they've brought in a bride without even letting their   *Yaba*
neighbors know[36]

by a screen I see a tray of cookies   *Bashō*

Broad Bean

[Composed in 1694 by Koizumi Ko'oku,[37] Matsuo Bashō,
Taisui,[38] and Ikeda Rigyū[39]]

"Visiting Fukagawa"[40]

Broad bean flowers have bloomed alongside a wheat   *Ko'oku*
field

daytime, a clapper rail darts by in a rivulet   *Bashō*

[34] Association by contrast.
[35] Suggests somebody staying temporarily in a fishing village.
[36] Income too low to have a wedding ceremony.
[37] Koizumi Ko'oku (dates uncertain), a shop clerk.
[38] Taisui (dates uncertain). Little is known about him.
[39] Ikeda Rigyū (dates uncertain), a manager of a commercial house.
[40] Where Bashō lived.

rain but not enough to come through the jacket	*Taisui*
a furtive look inside, and they're carousing	*Rigyū*
no one's sleeping in the bedroom—the evening moon	*Bashō*
with a thud a fence falls in the autumn wind	*Ko'oku*
a cricket begins to chirp from under firewood	*Rigyū*
she makes plans for work during the night	*Taisui*
her young sister was asked to be a bride by a good family	*Ko'oku*
she first sends a letter to the priest	*Bashō*
the wind is gentle and a daybreak crow flies by, calling	*Taisui*
he goes to see the spot where a house was swept away by a flood	*Rigyū*
loach soup[41]—he's better at it than young men	*Bashō*
he puts on sale at a lower price the tea he bought	*Ko'oku*
this spring, I'd say, flower-viewing was quiet	*Rigyū*
I feel sorry for the withered willow at this late date	*Taisui*
the remains of snow peeled off, and the hazy moon	*Ko'oku*
after rolling up the bedding she's lost in thought	*Bashō*

41 "Loach soup" was considered an aphrodisiac.

"We've broken up with our insolent neighbor"   *Taisui*

    he lets in a beggar-monk   *Rigyū*

something that makes him weep secretly happened in   *Bashō*
    his reed hut

    he asks about the money he left   *Ko'oku*

sleeping with his clothes on, stiffened, he perspires   *Rigyū*

    seeing the guest off, he holds up the candlestick   *Taisui*

while there's time he measures the thickness of snow[42] *Ko'oku*

    he was praised for having paid his taxes   *Bashō*

"Grandpa's healthy, I should congratulate him on his   *Taisui*
    gray hair"

    "I can't stand this Tanabata sun"[43]   *Rigyū*

"I want my yams to mature in time for the bright   *Bashō*
    moon"

    panting, he carries sweetfish that have just spawned   *Ko'oku*

the traffic at this station has lately dwindled   *Rigyū*

    the bell at the foot of the hill is almost inaudible   *Taisui*

---

[42] In light of the following part, this suggests a farmer with the old belief that heavy snow is good for the coming crop.

[43] Rain on the Tanabata day (the seventh of the seventh month) was welcomed for the crop. An implication of this part as related to the preceding part is that "grandpa" is *too* healthy.

a gentle wind begins to blow on banners of clouds   *Ko'oku*

above bleaching cloths skylarks sing   *Rigyū*

only women are out to view the blossoms   *Bashō*

picking no plants but violets, dandelions   *Taisui*

UEJIMA ONITSURA

(1661–1738)

TWENTY-THREE HOKKU

The spring water's visible here and there

Leaving Itami in early February:
Daybreak: at the tips of wheat blades, spring frost

I poured water in the basin and received a camellia in it

Monk Kūdō asked me, "What's your haikai eye like?" I
replied on the spot:
In the garden, blooming white, camellias

A gargoyle spits out a sparrow to a peach tree

Spring day: a sparrow sand-bathing in my garden

Late spring:
Here again, blossoms falling, I dozing, dozing

At the opening of Chikubu's collection of haikai:
Because they bloom, because I look at them, because the blossoms
bloom

Remembering with feeling:
Once in the past I stepped on a snail and crushed it

On my way home:
Evening—I see the bellies of sweetfish in river shallows

I think the May rains are meant just to go on falling

In spring they croak but in summer the frogs bark

Cooling off in the evening:
Saying, "What heat today!" I blow dust off a stone

Under flying sweetfish clouds flow in a stream

Profusely in confusion—the pampas grass

The night grew late in Kuzuha Village in Hirakata, but as the river waves tapped out their notes under my pillow, no dreams formed, my mind lucid:
Cool, cool, the moon too is white in the autumn wind

In the mist something's visible—a waterwheel

Bright moon: after an illness
With feeling, standing, I look at today's moon

Early autumn:
Tree leaves flutter, and autumn begins

The thirteenth year of Genroku [1700], the year my boy Toshiaki died; on the night of the fifteenth of the eighth month:

This autumn, without my son in my lap I look at the moon

A fir stands sveltely under the moon

Why are some icicles long, some short?

A water bird, looking heavy, floats

TAKARAI KIKAKU

(1661–1707)

THIRTY-THREE HOKKU

At a grass hut I eat smartweed, I'm that kind of firefly

Shoes going over rocks have fins—running sweetfish

The year's first day, the charcoal vendor's ten fingers are black

Sleeping butterfly, what do you do night after night?

Evening dusk: flying in the middle of the town, a butterfly

A swallow has erased a rainbow above the face of the sea

Darkening mountains are distant, but the way the deer look

Yearly regret:
If I had a child how old would it be at this year's end?

Lightning: in the east yesterday, in the west today

Bashō's old hut:
For a while, gentle: the evening sun on leafless trees

Amused at my own figure while traveling:
A screech owl laughing alone?—this autumn evening

Even swallows seem to have no time to dry in the May rain

Slashed in a dream—was that real? a fleabite

The evening shower has washed and separated the colors of the soil

Lightning: again the sky's morning glow

On charcoal dust, a not-at-all lowly leaf

Haziness is the blackness of pines in the moonlight

Bright moon: on the straw mat, the shadow of a pine

A winter river: a raft sits in a field of grass

Think it's your snow, and it's light on your hat

Against the morning glories for a while a butterfly shines

The autumn sky has detached itself from the mountain-top cedars

Voice hoarse, the monkey's teeth are white—the moon at the peak

Began drinking sake at fifteen, and today's moon

Even on the bridge there's no wind this evening

A woman on a spring night—it's my daughter!

An evening shower—a woman alone, looking out

In the tree-searing wind a fox's tail looks frozen

In the sleet too, the heron in the pond poises himself ready

In an evening shower ducks walk around the house, quacking

Winter comes, and a crow perches on a scarecrow

A young woman plants seedlings toward her crying baby

He goes, his horse as his shield against the cold

MUKAI KYORAI

(1651–1704)

TWENTY HOKKU

A distant sailboat never quite
clearing Awaji Island—
shell-digging at low tide

He doesn't seem
to move at all—
man working a field

What's this?
wearing a long sword
for cherry-viewing?

That mountain I crossed
day before yesterday—
its cherries in full bloom now

The cuckoo sings
at right angles
to the lark[1]

Too dark to tell the gate—
I'll rap at a break
in the deutzia flowers

[1] The lark ascends, while the cuckoo's flight is horizontal.

Every boatman in
the village off at work—
poppy flowers

The waters of the lake
have risen—
early summer rains

So hot the melons
tumble out from under
leaf covers

Deep in the family shrine,
the fondly remembered face
of a dead parent

Poem of parting:

Your hand among them
waving—
plumes of pampas grass

Point of rock—
here too, a lone
admirer of the moon

Fall breezes—
time to try out the
white wood bow

Full sail, reefed sail
all you can handle
in an offshore squall

"Coming, coming!"
but rapping continues
at the snowy gate

How to tell
head from tail?
sea cucumber

On the death of his younger sister:

Firefly
fading away pitifully
on my palm

In this heat
even rocks and trees
glare in my eyes

Rocky shore—
flocks of plovers
nimbly running

Close of day—
a row of cloud peaks
side by side, bald

NAITŌ JŌSŌ

(1662–1704)

FIFTEEN HOKKU

Just seen the bottom of the water—that's the way the small duck looks

Thinking I'm after them, loaches squiggle away as I pick parsley

Blackening the offing, the shower moves along

White beach: a dog barks at today's moon

Waiting on Bashō as he lay ill:
Crouching—the cold under the medicine kettle

Wolves' voices harmonize this snowy evening

A hokku gathering at an inn:
From my sleeve a katydid flies to a lantern

A dragonfly catches a fly under my hat

I run into fireflies—a valley wind

The bottom of loneliness falls off in this sleet

Below the boulder where I sit, legs folded, wisteria flowers begin

On the boulder at the bottom of the water a leaf settles

Colder than the snow: white hair under the winter moon

Ill in bed:
Amid insect chirpings I wake, coughing

Both fields and mountains, robbed by the snow, having nothing left

.

NOZAWA BONCHŌ

(died 1714)

TWENTY-ONE HOKKU

In a shower, black chopped wood by a house, its window lit

I try to call him back, but the carp vendor's no longer visible in hailstones

An elongated line of a river through the snowy field

A razor blade rusted overnight in the May rain

Dark night: a child begins weeping in a firefly boat

Fording a stream I stop and peer at weed flowers

A blowing wind's companion—the moon in the sky, alone

"Not a bird singing, the mountain is all the more quiet":[1]
A noise: a scarecrow fell by itself

In the heat haze a fox lets her cubs play

---

[1] A line from the poem, "Mount Chung, As Observed," by the Chinese poet Wang An-shih (1021–1086).

At an eagle's nest on dead camphor branches, the sun goes down

The town smells of things under the summer moon[2]

The ash pail has stopped dripping—now a cricket[3]

The spring rain isn't even enough to wash away the dust

A crow wipes its beak on young grass

Meeting Etsujin:[4]
A handsome face drinking water—this autumn moon

A patch of cloud rides the moon tonight

Every bit of water in the paddies is frozen this morning

From the porch, in various ways, fallen leaves

At this dilapidated hut, slugs are the hinges for the door

A paulownia tree drops dead leaves, mindless of the wind

An abandoned boat, frozen inside and outside, in a cove

---

[2] Followed by Bashō's wakiku, " 'It's hot! It's hot!'—voices at each doorway."

[3] The water filtered through ashes was used for cleaning and other purposes. Followed by Bashō's wakiku, "the oil has run dry and I go to bed early—it's autumn."

[4] Ochi Etsujin (1656–1739), a haikai poet.

KAAI CHIGETSU

(?1634–?1708)

THIRTEEN HOKKU

I sleep alone; throughout the night a male mosquito's lonely voice[1]

I know and I don't know what I am—sad this autumn evening

In a wide garden peonies open amply

Loving my grandchild:
I'll make a straw house for this tree frog

Each morning a wren comes, bit by bit

Lying awake endlessly in old age:
Snow-tanned: each night I blow on my grandchild's hands

Despite myself I become so childish at flying fireflies!

A cricket chirps in a scarecrow's sleeve

In autumn a dove looks as if loneliness were only his

---

1 Written soon after her husband's death in 1686.

On the anniversary of Bashō's death, I visited his grave in Kiso:

I'd like to open the door and show the buddhas the blossoms in bloom

The fifteenth of the eighth month:

If only my heart were as it is normally—today's moon!

Today's moon—if there were another, a fight would surely ensue

Unaware I'm growing old, the blossoms are in their prime

HAIBUN

On Letting a Sparrow Loose

With lower branches of a willow visiting my window, plum fragrance beckoning under the eaves, and the sunlight clear, I was dusting the paper sliding doors rather than sweeping with a broom on the year's first day of the rat,[2] thinking, "Someone unexpected is coming to see me," when I heard a noise at the door in the corner of the room. I went to look and found a baby sparrow lying with his wing injured, probably chased by a falcon or a hawk. "Poor thing! But I couldn't have had a chance like this even if I'd wanted one," I thought, and petted him and did everything I could for him. It all seemed useless, until I got hold of an herb called bastard gentian, which perked him up. As each day passed, I felt as if the sparrow grew more attached to me than my grandchild. Soon, the moment he heard my footsteps, he would turn to me and open his beak, waiting for food. Ugly old woman that I am, I wouldn't do a thing like cutting off his tongue, I told him,[3] and I would even stop children from playing harmless tricks on him. I also thought of Murasaki's childhood games.[4] So the spring passed, then the prime of the summer, and it was already the middle of autumn when, finally deciding that I wouldn't have a chance if I waited another day, I opened the door of the sparrow's cage and let him loose. But the next day, and the day after, he returned to his empty cage and stayed near it, acting as if he missed it. Seeing that, I felt sorry for him and gave him some more food:

Come to me on the spring equinox, sparrow friend, you don't need
   your crutch

---

2 Reference to the old court custom of presenting the empress with a broom for sweeping the floors of the silkworm chambers on the year's first day of the rat.
3 Allusion to a children's story about a wicked old woman who cut out the tongue of a friendly sparrow.
4 Reference to Chapter 5 of *The Tale of Genji* in which Murasaki, a child at the time, complains that someone has let loose her baby sparrows and is told that it is a sin to keep birds in a cage.

SHIBA SONOME

(1664–1726)

FIFTEEN HOKKU

"Spring water and spring wind come at once":
Ice has vanished—don't be left behind by the wind, waterwheel

At the ferry on the Miya River the night was still deep:
With a hint of some coloring, a spring day breaks

A robin's call has stumbled on a rock

Not content, the violets have dyed the hills as well

Rouge vendors come during rice-planting breaks

Busy, the winter clouds don't even stop to rest

Violets have withered between my folded tissues

The child I carry on my back licks my hair—it's so hot!

The heat's so intense I dry my towel on my parasol

So cool: brow laid on the green straw mat

Spilled from a tree-searing wind, a bull's midday voice

After a wind a firefly drops and turns upward

The leaves of trees rend and scatter in this cold

Evening dusk: crowned with fans, white peonies

Each time they roll in, the beach waves break up the plovers

FROG MATCHES

FORTY-ONE HOKKU ON FROGS

[In the spring of 1686 Bashō and his fellow poets gathered at his house in Fukagawa and matched hokku on frogs. The meeting was apparently prompted by Bashō's famous piece on the frog, printed at the outset of the text, published in the intercalary third month of the same year.[1]]

I

An old pond: a frog jumps in—the sound of water[2]   *Bashō*

Innocently a frog squats on a floating leaf   *Senka*

2

Frogs in rain—as their croaks rise, pity grows   *Sodō*

Right next to a mud turtle a frog sets up house   *Bunrin*

---

[1] Because of the convention, the host of the meeting—Bashō, in this case—and the poet paired with him are left uncontested. The decisions on the other matches are (2) Sodō, winner; (3) Ranran, winner; (4) draw; (5) Kyorai, winner; (6) draw; (7) Kōrin, winner; (8) Sensetsu, winner; (9) Kimpū, winner; (10) Kifū, winner; (11) Ryūsui, winner; (12) draw; (13) draw; (14) draw; (15) Shōda, winner; (16) Kashiku, winner; (17) draw; (18) draw; (19) Totaku, winner (By this time, "both the judges and the scribe were wearied by the slow day and weren't quite themselves. Accordingly and therefore, the decision isn't clear. The first must have won."); (20) undecided.

[2] Followed by Kikaku's wakiku: "suspended over young rush blades, a spider's web."

3

Shifty-eyed, the frog keeps his cheekiness   *Ranran*

At human footfalls a frog makes a knowing face   *Ko'oku*

4

Under a tree a frog gets covered by a blanket[3]   *Suikō*

Carrying his wife on his back a frog hides in the grass   *Jokushi*

5

The straw-coat vendor saw the frog last year   *Rika*

One paddy ceases croaking for a while—the frogs   *Kyorai*

6

After their bells stopped, horses in the stable rest amid   *Yūgo*
frogs

The frog has legs, yes, but the bull stepped on him   *Kiju*

7

Where was the monk? Frogs at evening too are lone-   *Shugen*
some

A narrow path: frog, which clump of grass have you   *Kōrin*
leaped into?

8

Evening shadow: frogs call out clouds over Tsukuba   *Hōjū*

At daybreak frogs begin saying Buddhist prayers   *Sensetsu*

9

This moonlit evening, on the path through the paddy a   *Kimpū*
frog dries himself

Hopping frog—is a cat chasing you, deep in Ono?   *Suiyū*

10

The sound of rain dripping annoys me because of those   *Tonan*
frogs

Pitifully baby frogs struggle up a water pipe   *Kifū*

11

A hopping frog—as if saying, "I envy herons"   *Zempō*

Hidden in water plants, a frog peeks at the affairs of   *Ryūsui*
the world

12

What can I do?—frog dumped with dirt from the fishnet   *Ransetsu*

Deep in the bamboo grove, are there reeds nourishing   *Haritsu*
frogs?

13

Undulating, a frog undulates with the willow *Hokukon*

A frog climbs up a willow, holding on with his hands *Kosai*

14

Arms spread, a frog floats in the water, asleep *Chiri*

Beside a dewless, noonday mugwort a frog croaks *Santen*

15

Lodging in the puddle from the straw coat I took off— *Kitsujō*
    a frog

On a young rush blade a frog stretches himself along the *Shōda*
    flow

16

A frog crawls out and rubs his back against the grass *Kyohaku*

Among floating weeds, frogs play with their children *Kashiku*

17

A frog has lifted a fallen blossom on his back *Sōha*

Morning fodder: a frog attached to a horse *Ranchiku*

18

A mountain spring: near the black sleeve dipping water,   *Sampū*
a frog[4]

His tail fell off, but the frog doesn't know how to croak   *Bunsoku*
yet

19

Out from the moat, a frog waits for someone all day   *Totaku*

You hook it, but it's no fun—if it's a frog   *Kyōsui*

20

When you're depressed, a toad's distant voice too—this   *Sora*
rainy night

Here and there frogs croak in a river of numberless stars   *Kikaku*

Postscript:

> When I visited Kashima,
>   at the Joined Bridge of Mama:

Looking like a guide to the Joined Bridge: a hopping   *Fuboku*
frog

---

[4] "Black sleeve" of a monk.

CHIYOJO

(1703–1775)

SEVENTEEN HOKKU

WILLOWS[1]

A green willow's quiet, wherever you plant it

To tangle or untangle a willow, it's up to the wind

The willow flows away and again returns to its trunk

At the ferry in Kuwana:
Looking at the willows, one ends up forgetting them

BUTTERFLIES
Butterfly: what's it dreaming of, moving its wings that way?

From time to time, a butterfly fans itself out of the haze

Dandelion: from time to time, it awakens a butterfly from dreams

Butterfly: now in front, now back of a woman along a path

By its own wind, a small butterfly blows itself down

[1] Hereafter, headings in small capitals in hokku selections are kigo, "season words," that specify one of the four seasons.

FIREFLIES

Only over the river, darkness flows: fireflies

CLEAR WATER

I forget my lips are rouged, at the clear water

I go on, and the clear water meets me again

I raise my hands, and the clear water has no seams

"Truth is one":
Clear water has no front or back

SUMMER MOON

Touching the line from a fishing pole: the summer moon

WINTER BIRDS

The wind spills plovers, picks them up, and leaves

Mistaking birds for leaves—lonely, a winter moon

TAN TAIGI

(1709–1771)

TWENTY-NINE HOKKU

Eyes open, I listen to spring in the four directions

A village child with spring grass tied to her hair

Sound of casting a net downstream under the hazy moon

With a faint scent of river an east wind spreads itself

Warbler: leaves hiding it move in the water

A servant, taking leave, says farewell to the horses at the stable

A spring night: I frighten a woman with a story I made up

I peer into quietness: a willow on a rainy night

Angry, is he, a wasp drinking water from a washbasin

The way it walks, the snail seems not to have slept during the night

I feel someone dying of an illness—it's that hot

Many mosquitoes bloated with blood during Zen meditation

The sound of the rain can't overpower a mosquito's voice

The water of a shallow river is blown away by a field cleaver

A rat has dropped into the water jar—this night's cold!

Autumn night: I question and answer myself—I must be losing heart

I lie down, I get up, living the long night alone

A long night: I wake up at someone's, drunk on sake

In the waves rolling in, a single snipe not quite standing

A shower: on a raft the pole gets plied faster

The stream's clear: five inches of water above fallen leaves

The other end of this long bridge is hidden in the blizzard

Cold moon—the sound of the bridge I cross alone

I swept and ended up not sweeping the fallen leaves

Tree-searing wind: wrinkles of age begin to show on my hands

Near a fence, young, small grasses in the winter rain

At daybreak when plovers call, a woman returns

> Kyūkō and I stayed at Rittei's; the next morning we parted on the road:

We turn to look: both are now snowmen

Beautiful sunlight has come over the snow

YOSA BUSON

(1716–1783)

EIGHTY-SEVEN HOKKU

Spring

PERSISTING COLD

The barrier guard's brazier, small in the persisting cold

SPRING EVENING, NIGHT

Waking from a nap—the spring day has darkened

A huge gate and its heavy doors: spring at dusk

Spring at dusk—no one but those far from home

DEPARTING SPRING

Departing spring: on the carriage my lady murmurs

Departing spring: a boat with brushwood seems not to be moving

Departing spring: I've lost the eyeglasses that don't fit my eyes

SPRING MOON

In the pear orchard someone stands under the hazy moon

SPRING RAIN

Spring rain: small clams on a small beach get wet

Spring rain: telling stories, a straw coat and an umbrella walk past

Flowing in the spring rain—a wide river

HEAT HAZE

Suburb

Heat haze: a bug I don't know the name of flies white

SPRING WATER

Spring water flows through the mountainless land

Spring water flows, wetting violets and the ears of reeds

SPRING SEA

The spring sea sloshes, sloshes all day

FLYING KITE

A flying kite, in the spot in the sky where it was yesterday

WARBLERS

I mistook a warbler for a sparrow—that's part of spring

Wattled Fence

Distant from warblers all day—the person in a field

FROGS

Looking at a passing cloud, a frog shifts his stance

Swimming, a frog looks as if it had nothing to hold on to

BUTTERFLIES

A butterfly settles on the neckplate of a warrior in ambush

Coming out of the privy, I'm surprised at a butterfly

Settled on a temple bell and asleep—a butterfly

PLUM

(Buson's last hokku)

For white plum blossoms, time has come for the day to break

CAMELLIAS

Into the darkness of an old well a camellia drops

A camellia drops and spills yesterday's rain

RAPE FLOWERS

Rape flowers: the moon in the east, sun in the west[1]

---

[1] Followed by Chora's wakiku: "far along the base of a mountain a heron flies through the haze." Allusion to Hitomaro's tanka on p. 30, "In the east."

Summer

SHORT NIGHTS

Coming out of the dark of the short night—Ōi River

Short night: on a hairy caterpillar, a bead of dew

HEAT

Sitting at an edge, avoiding wife and children, because of the heat

Waving flies off a sick man's shoulders—it's so hot

COOLNESS

Coolness: separating from a bell, the bell's voice

MAY RAIN

Even the floating weeds sink, almost, in the May rain

May rain: paddy by paddy, it has turned into darkness

May rain: the muddy water thrusts into the blue sea

May rain: in front of a wide river, two houses

EVENING DOWNPOUR

Evening downpour: clutching grass blades, a throng of sparrows

SUMMER MOUNTAINS, RIVER

Summer mountains: across the span of Kyoto a heron flies

Walking a flatland and weary of traveling: peak with clouds

At Kaya in Tamba
Delight of crossing a summer river, sandals in hand

CLEAR WATER
The stonemason cools his chisels in the clear water

Sparks from a stonemason flow in the clear water

GREEN PADDIES
The mountains are low, I feel, beyond green paddies

RICE-PLANTING
Though divorced, she steps right in for rice-planting

I look around: humans like green stalks at this rice-planting time!

BLUE HERON
Evening wind: the water strikes the shins of a blue heron[2]

FIREFLIES
As the tides flow, in the rain, over a rivulet, fireflies

MOSQUITO
A mosquito whirs each time a woodbine flower falls

---

[2] Followed by Saiba's wakiku: "a few acres of cattails grow luxuriantly."

YOUNG LEAVES

The young leaves have left Fuji alone, unburied

PEONIES

Peony in a wide garden, on one side of heaven

FLOWERS OF A BRIAR

The path ending, a fragrance and close by, a briar in bloom

MELONS, EGGPLANTS

I met Monk Seihan for the first time, but we talked like old friends:

In a water pail, nodding at each other: a melon and an eggplant

Autumn

EARLY AUTUMN

That the autumn has come—a sneeze makes me understand[3]

COLD OF NIGHT

Chipped away, the moon disappears into the cold of night[4]

AUTUMN EVENING

An Old Man's Thoughts

Lonelier still than last year, you know, this autumn evening

[3] Allusion to Fujiwara no Toshiyuki's tanka (Kokinshū, no. 169): "That autumn has come isn't clearly visible to the eye, but the sound of the wind startles me."

[4] Followed by Kitō's wakiku: "in the silence of autumn, a round of Nō recitation."

Leaving my gate, I too am someone on the road this autumn evening

Lonely—still, I've forgotten my stick this autumn evening

In the autumn dusk a woman wipes a mirror with her sleeve

MOON

Moon at heaven's center: I pass through a destitute town

The bandit chief composes a tanka for the moon tonight

DEW

A warrior walks, swishing the dew aside with the ends of his bow

White dew: one drop on each prickle of a briar

LIGHTNING

Lightning spills a noise: a dewdrop from bamboo

TANABATA

Love in many forms: threads for wishes begin in white

BON DANCING

Asked for a word on Hanabusa Itchō's painting:
The moon about to set on four or five dancers

CRIMSON LEAVES

Mountains, darkening, have robbed the crimson leaves of scarlet

Friends went hiking in Takao and gave me a branch of red maple leaves. It was about the tenth of the tenth month, and the old leaves could not withstand frost. The way they soon fell off, scattering, was especially moving:

Burnt in the fireplace, crimson leaves clutch the smoke

CHRYSANTHEMUMS

In the candlelight in my hand yellow chrysanthemums lose their color

MORNING GLORIES

"The valley stream collects in pools the color of indigo":[5]

Morning glories: a single flower the color of a deep pool

PAMPAS GRASS

The mountains darkened, the fields in twilight with pampas grass

ACORNS

As I visited Kyōtai at Genjūan[6] where he was staying while on a trip:

From the acorns on a round tray I'd like to hear the sound of the past

GLEANERS

The gleaners walk toward where the sunlight is

---

[5] A sentence in Soku 82 in the *Hekiganroku*.
[6] See Bashō's "Phantom Dwelling," on pp. 292–95.

Winter

WINTER MOON, COLD MOON

Suburb:

A woodland of silent oak trees: winter moon

Cold moon: amidst dead trees, three bamboo poles

SHOWER

A shower silently wets the roots of a camphor tree

Dead of winter: crows are black, herons white

SLEET

In an old pond a sandal lies sunken, in the sleet

WINTER WIND

Winter wind: pebbles in a plowed field are visible

Winter wind: the voice of water tearing through the rocks

Winter wind: blowing pebbles against a bell

WINTER FIELD

Not yet dark, but stars glitter above the withered field

PLOVERS

Each time a wave rolls in, plovers walk sidewise

FALLEN LEAVES

The footfall of someone I wait for, distant on fallen leaves

The roof repairman steps on dead leaves above my bedroom

After the venerable Bashō's hokku:[7]
In an old pond a frog ages while leaves fall

WINTER WOOD

Chopping with an ax, surprised at the fragrance, in a winter wood

SCALLIONS

I buy scallions and go home through leafless trees

[7] See Bashō's hokku on p. 282, "An old pond."

LETTER

Dear Yakō,[1]

This incessant rain surely is a nuisance. I'm pleased to know you are getting along better than ever. I was gratified that you visited me the other day. Seeing you after such a long while, I mistook you for someone else and greeted you in a very careless manner. I hope you will forgive my rudeness.

For our regular hokku meeting on the tenth of next month, the topics are:

    lotus   caterpillar

I'll be glad if you think about them to amuse yourself. When you have something to do in this part of town, please be kind enough to drop by. I'd like to talk about all the rest when I see you.

                  Twenty-fourth of the fifth month[2]

May rain: in front of a wide river, two houses

Moon after rain—who's that! a night fisherman's white shins

Coolness: separating from a bell, the bell's voice

None of these is much good, but I just happen to have made them, so I've written them down for your amusement. They are somewhat different from the kind of hokku fashionable at the moment. I don't like the tanka or renga that are fashionable now, either.

[1] Little is known about Yakō, except that he was a haikai poet.
[2] 1777.

Running out of the nets, running out of the nets—the water, the
  moon

> I can't fix on a definite season for this hokku, but the scene
> must be a summer one, so I include it among the hokku on
> summer.

Buson

Mourning for My Teacher Hokuju[1]

You left at morning, my heart at evening in pieces—
how far away!
Thinking of you I go to the hillside and wander.
The hillside—why is it so saddening?
Yellow of dandelion with shepherd's purse blooming white,
there's no one to look at it.
Is that a pheasant? I hear it call over and over;
I had a friend, he lived with a river between us.
Smoke that transforms you abruptly scatters, the wind from the west
  blowing
so hard on the fields of low bamboo and sedge
there's no place to escape.
I had a friend, he lived with a river between us. Today
there's no cooing call.
You left at morning, my heart at evening in pieces—
how far away!
Light before my hut's Amida image not lit,
flowers not offered, disheartened I stand here—tonight
you are more than ever venerable.

---

[1] Hayami Shinga (1671–1745), a haikai poet.

RENGA

Peony Fallen

[Composed in 1780 by Yosa Buson and Takai Kitō]

Peony fallen, and a heap of two or three petals	*Buson*
the twentieth of Deutzia Month,[1] in the daybreak light	*Kitō*
coughing, the old man is opening the gate, it seems	*Kitō*
the spirit has come to select a bridegroom	*Buson*
an aged hackberry tree axed on the street	*Buson*
over the hundred miles of land I have nowhere to settle	*Kitō*
a book on poetics—the malaria left me yesterday, today	*Kitō*
in the paddies on the hills, time to harvest early rice	*Buson*
after the evening moon has faded, chickadees fly	*Kitō*
autumn and wistful, he stands by the door, alone	*Buson*
eyes ailing, he sips a bitter medicine	*Kitō*
sending back to Taima a *furoshiki*[2] and a letter	*Buson*

---

[1] "Deutzia Month" is a literal translation of *uzuki*, an old name for the fourth month.

[2] A *furoshiki* is a square cloth for wrapping and carrying things.

next door, he's still talking, that oil vendor   *Kitō*

   the snow has piled up three feet in the dusk   *Buson*

famished wolves must be lurking near the house   *Kitō*

   his harelipped wife weeps and weeps   *Buson*

a temple in blossoms—for the bell to be cast she cuts her   *Kitō*
   hair

   spring passes, and the sun inclines to the west   *Buson*

Lord Noto's bowstring faintly heard in the distance[3]   *Buson*

   the astrologer in retirement divines the times   *Kitō*

a horse with a load of millet dropped dead, says the bird   *Buson*

   chinaberry trees bloom, scatter flowers along the road   *Kitō*
   through the paddies

a buffeted rainbow and smoke from Asama[4]   *Buson*

   happy to offer lodging to the imperial envoy   *Kitō*

in a basket the fish caught in the bay have red bellies[5]   *Buson*

[3] Lord Noto, or Taira no Noritsune (1160–1185), is a general who was good at archery. At the famous Dannoura sea battle he failed to capture the enemy general Minamoto no Yoshitsune (1159–1189) and committed suicide by drowning himself. In the following part, Kitō takes Buson to be referring to the old custom of humming a bowstring for divination.

[4] Asama is an active volcano.

[5] At the court in ancient times, fish with red bellies were presented to the emperor on the first day of the year.

though the sun is shining, again it hails   *Kitō*

acolyte I love, march out for the hall service   *Buson*

"I don't like people to touch me on the head!"   *Kitō*

even for the dark moment on the sixteenth, pressed to do   *Buson*
      things[6]

they're beating cloths with mallets in Bamba, Matsumoto   *Kitō*

no one to carry the palanquin with in the autumn rain   *Kitō*

both the kite and the crow keep their faces turned away   *Buson*

the small, curse-bringing shrine in the paddies looks   *Kitō*
      awesome

already the minister seems to have lost his lawsuit   *Buson*

to him, who's alien to blossoms, only rice and soup at the   *Buson*
      inn

still before dark, in spring, a lamp is lit   *Kitō*

---

[6] By the lunar calendar, the moon is full on the fifteenth and rises slightly later on the sixteenth than it does on the fifteenth. The suggestion here is that there are people too busy to have a respite even during that brief moment of darkness.

KATŌ KYŌTAI

(1732–1792)

SIXTEEN HOKKU

Melting snow—
among deep mountains clouded over,
crows caw

The sun has set—
coming down from Mii Temple,
someone in spring

Nights when the muddy river
smudges the sky—
the moon in spring

Quivering
in the heat waves,
single-petaled poppies

A column of mosquitoes
there where the
jujube flowers drop

The waves are hot,
echoing angrily
against the rocks

On her way, the little nun
picking, tossing away
bushclover blossoms

Cold night,
pasania nuts rolling down
the shingled roof

Falling leaves
fall and pile up,
rain beats on rain

The wind is mournful,
the moon's shape
withering night by night

Daybreak—
whales trumpet
in the frosty ocean

Winter shut-in—
a single fly
keeps circling me

Day ending
and again it starts
to snow

Observing as I go along—
eggplants rotting
beside an old road

Leaves falling
on top of the smoke
of the leaves I burn

Start of winter—
showing my two-year-old
how to hold chopsticks

MIURA CHORA

(1729–1780)

SEVENTEEN HOKKU

I first see the spring light on the feathers of birds

Seeing the stars through a willow makes me feel lonesome

A mountain temple: no one comes to worship the image of Buddha
entering Nirvana

Delightful at night, quiet during the day—the spring rain

I think of flowers and birds through the night's spring rain

I turn to look: everything behind me is covered with cherries

Even the day with cherries scattering has turned to evening

As the evening shower clears, the moonlit night

An insect spills its notes on the grass, fluttering

Out of the grass in a storm, today's moon

Brushing aside the clouds, drifting in the clouds, the moon in the wind

A white chrysanthemum makes its surroundings as elegant as itself

The heartache of love, the distress of poverty, the pain of illness—all reveal one and the same truth; falling ill and not dying is equal in emotion to falling in love and not meeting, and the poor woman who had to sell her house on the Kamo River bank is no different from a samurai who is laid up by illness. Recently afflicted with an illness, I've been enjoying its torment:
I broil shrimp and play with my illness in this cold

Brightness: not even a wind blowing, the moon in the cold

The moon in the cold: the wind from the river chisels the rocks

Glancing near the hands cutting a sea bream—hailstones[1]

It's dark around the earth mortar in the evening shower

[1] Allusion to Minamoto Sanetomo's tanka, "As the warrior reaches up," p. 220.

TAKAI KITŌ

(1741–1789)

TWENTY-FOUR HOKKU

A warbler escapes next door and gives his first warble

"I came to see the plum blossoms":[1]
Warbler, what are you afraid of? ready to get away!

I see the shadow of a warbler—and his first warble

An ugly sight—a burn mark on the straw mat by the shadow of a
    plum

Parting:
Love for love, the willow grows distant from our boat[2]

Escaping a dog, a rooster flaps up into a willow tree

A tumble, fall, crash, then silence—cats in love

---

[1] An anonymous tanka (*Kokinshū*, no. 1011): "I came to see the plum
blossoms, but the warbler, resenting me, keeps saying, 'Someone's come,
someone's come!'"
[2] Followed by Buson's wakiku, "growing luxuriantly, the grass awaits
another butterfly."

Anyone who hears "River wind so cold the plovers cried"[3] is supposed to feel chilly even in intense heat. Again, "A frog jumps in," in so observing the sound of water,[4] leaves much unsaid, suggestive. Though mine is far from attaining the exquisite status of the two poems:

When evening comes, plovers fly over the spring water

A skylark rises through the dawn by a mountain

Stepping on violets, they climb a stone wall to make love

A woman who has crossed the river has flowering weeds on her calves

I drink water and my stomach bulges—it's so hot!

On my stupid face I see white in the beard this autumn morning

Pitying a woman who has many affairs:

Would she at least want time for combing her hair tonight, when the stars meet?[5]

The winning wrestler leaves, gently parting the people

Sitting quietly at night:

An insect voice has separated from the folds of grass

---

[3] Ki no Tsurayuki's tanka, "My longings unbearable," p. 134. The observation on feeling chilly was made by Kamo no Chōmei (1153–1216) in his *Mumyōshō*.

[4] Bashō's hokku, "An old pond," p. 282.

[5] Refers to Tanabata; see note on p. 46.

The bright moon: a crab walks with his eyes in the sky

Yawning and praising the moon—my neighbor

Water lowers and stones show:
By a winter river a crow's pecking at something unsightly

Out of sadness I eat fish this autumn evening

Daybreak: in its madder-red, a stand of winter trees

A stand of winter trees: the moon enters my marrow tonight

As I went by the foot of Mount Asama, there were no trees and grasses growing though the springs and autumns of three years had passed since the volcanic fires, and even boulders were buried under the ashes. After going over Usui Pass, my palanquin bearers told me that the red soil showing about ten feet below us was just about where the old road used to be. In the fields and paddies burned sand was raked into piles, and things looked quite desolate:

Even the soil is withered and saddening in this winter field

Love:
Frozen hands and feet come and gladly meet at night

NINE KYŌKA

HEZUTSU TŌSAKU

(1726–1789)

Dawn Cherries

On the crest of the hill,
"Cherry blossoms!"
"No, no—clouds!"
till the dawn sun rose up
to squelch the argument

Affluence—define it as:
pickled greens,
rice for supper,
wine, one container,
modest but never empty

AKERA KANKŌ

(1740–1800)

Autumn Wind

In the blasts of wind
chestnut burrs
skitter over the ground,
burr-headed village boys
hot in pursuit

Year End

Under a ragged loincloth
some things can't be hid—
my debts too
protrude through the
frayed ends of the year

YOMONO AKARA

(1749–1823)

The young fiddlehead ferns
lift up their tight fists,
in the spring wind
shaking them
right in the face of the mountain

The season greeter,
tipsy with toasts,
weaves unsteadily
down the avenue—
lo, the New Year has come!

YADOYANO MESHIMORI

(1753–1830)

When it comes to poets,
the clumsier the better—
what a mess
if heaven and earth
really started to move![1]

KINO SADAMARU

(1760–1841)

Though this body, I know,
is a thing of no substance,
must it fade, alas,
so swiftly,
like a soundless fart?

JIPPENSHA IKKU

(1765–1831)

Deathbed Verse

By your leave,
O world—
for leave I must—
and may a whiff of incense
waft me on my way

[1] Reference to Ki no Tsurayuki's preface to the *Kokinshū*, which says that great poetry "can move heaven and earth," see p. 107.

FORTY-SEVEN SENRYŪ

Setting out on the road,
the second goodbye
spoken with the hat

Mount Yoshino—
looking at pines awhile
to rest your eyes

Ox driver in a sudden shower,
sentenced to his
plodding pace

Poking with his ruler,
measuring the snow—
he keeps a journal

A warning of dog shit
passed from person to person
down the line

One bite
and I'm doing a dance—
red peppers

That's his specialty—
bawling out
his beautiful wife

Home from work,
the bachelor sniffs
at the leftover rice

Hair washed,
she wrings it out
like a wad of pickled greens

Workmen eating lunch,
with a side order
of gripes

Off to work,
the burglar to his wife:
"Lock up tight when you go to bed!"

First childbirth—
her husband feels like
he did half the work

The wife won—
and she never
said a word

Rasping in his throat:
"Chin whiskers
need more soap!"

The icehouse keeper—
how often he dreams
of sunlight streaming in

"Don't worry!" he says,
and then tells you something
that really gets you worried

Half asleep,
chanting a Nō play,
his rear end for a drum

Night rendezvous—
mosquitoes squashed to death
ever so softly

Beaten
to the privy,
he praises the moon

Lotus Sutra—
the lips are busy with it
and that's about all

Housebreaker types—
that's the kind
she goes for

In the cold forbidding capital
he learns
to write poetry

Lord of a castle—
her beauty reduced him
to a dried-up moat

Aired in the sun,
even the nun's pillow
has an earthy smell

Yelled at
for praying in his underwear
at the family shrine

The town fire-watcher in his tower—
rainy nights sometimes
he pees over the side

Days I've got
my umbrella with me,
I'm absolutely fearless!

Laying a fart—
no humor in it
when you live alone

A covered boat
where they're not gambling—
what are they up to, you wonder

Stopped to piss—
and missed
the ferry

The unfaded patch
of floor mat
where the divorced wife's dresser stood

Back from the fields,
leaving himself just enough daylight
to wash his feet by

What was he thinking of,
hauling out his Buddhist rosary
in the Confucian temple!

The amateur play fell through—
all they did was bitch
about the parts they got

Snatched from his wife's hand,
it turned out to be
a letter from her Mama

Ferry service suspended,
he polishes the wording
in his travel diary

"Best scene
in the whole play!"
(much blowing of noses)

Mementos of the dead—
not necessarily doled out
to those who bawl the loudest

The way the chicken walks—
like it wanted
to say something

Slip a little something
into his sleeve
and watch the sour expression fade

When you're trying to get it
unwound in bed,
nothing's longer than a kimono sash!

So many people
found out about it,
our affair fizzled out

My loneliness—
I snuggle it up
against the back of another

He goes up the staircase,
stomping on
his anger

Things hard to say
are easily said
inside a mosquito net

The gaudy leaves of autumn
won't let the temple
be temple-like

Swirls of dust,
and in the midst, unblinking,
a blind man

RYŌKAN

(1758–1831)

TANKA, CHŌKA, and SEDŌKA

Though I lie here
legs snuggled
close to the embers
tonight's cold
goes right through my stomach

In the mountain's shadow
my grass hut's
so cold
I'll be up burning firewood
all night long

All through the night
in my grass hut
burning brushwood,
how we talked on and on—
when will I forget it?

"Mingling with the Wind"

Mingling with the wind
the snow comes falling;
mingling with the snow
the wind comes blowing;
by banked coals
I stretch my legs,
idle, idle,

in this grass hut
a shut-in,
and counting, find
that the second month too
like a dream
has come and gone

Water to draw
brushwood to cut
greens to pick—
all in moments when
morning showers let up

Wait for moonlight
before you try
to go home—
the mountain trail's
so thick with chestnut burs!

Dew on it,
the mountain trail will be cold—
before you head home
how about a last drink of sake?

Taking Leave of Mount Kugami

[Probably written in 1826, when Ryōkan left his hut in the Otogo Shrine at the foot of Mount Kugami and moved to the village of Shimazaki]

Slopes
of Mount Kugami—
in the mountain's shade
a hut beneath the trees—
how many years
it's been my home?

The time comes
to take leave of it—
my thoughts wilt
like summer grasses,
I wander back and forth
like the evening star—
till that hut of mine
is hidden from sight,
till that grove of trees
can no longer be seen,
at each bend
of the long road,
at every turning,
I turn to look back
in the direction of that mountain

The Rabbit in the Moon

[The poem is a retelling of one of the Jakata tales that deal
with the Buddha in his earlier incarnations. It relates the tale
to the old Chinese legend of a rabbit in the moon.]

It took place in a world
long long ago
they say:
a monkey, a rabbit,
and a fox
struck up a friendship,
mornings
frolicking field and hill,
evenings
coming home to the forest,
living thus
while the years went by,
when Indra,
sovereign of the skies,
hearing of this,
curious to know
if it was true,
turned himself into an old man,

tottering along,
made his way to where they were.
"You three,"
he said,
"are of separate species,
yet I'm told play together
with a single heart.
If what I've heard
is true,
pray save an old man
who's hungry!"
then he set his staff aside,
sat down to rest.
Simple enough, they said,
and presently
the monkey appeared
from the grove behind
bearing nuts
he'd gathered there,
and the fox returned
from the rivulet in front,
clamped in his jaws
a fish he'd caught.
But the rabbit,
though he hopped and hopped
everywhere
couldn't find anything at all,
while the others
cursed him because
his heart was not like theirs.
Miserable me!
he thought
and then he said,
"Monkey, go cut me
firewood!
Fox, build me
a fire with it!"
and when they'd done
what he asked,
he flung himself
into the midst of the flames,
made himself an offering
for an unknown old man.

When the old man
saw this
his heart withered.
He looked up to the sky,
cried aloud,
then sank to the ground,
and in a while,
beating his breast,
said
to the others,
"Each of
you three friends
has done his best,
but what the rabbit did
touches me most!"
Then he made the rabbit
whole again
and gathering the dead body
up in his arms,
took it and
laid it to rest
in the palace of the moon.
From that time till now
the story's been told,
this tale
of how the rabbit
came to be
in the moon,
and even I
when I hear it
find the tears
soaking the sleeve of my robe.

For the parents of a dead child:

You fondled him
piggybacked him
reared him, fed him the breast—
and today bear him away
to the withered fields

For the children who died in a smallpox epidemic:
When spring comes,
from every tree tip
the flowers will unfold,
but those fallen leaves
of autumn, the children,
will never come again

KANSHI

"Green Spring"

Green spring, start of the second month,
colors of things turning fresh and new.
At this time I take my begging bowl,
in high spirits tramp the streets of town.
Little boys suddenly spot me,
delightedly come crowding around,
descend on me at the temple gate,
dragging on my arms, making steps slow.
I set my bowl on top of a white stone,
hang my alms bag on a green tree limb;
here we fight a hundred grasses,
here we hit the temari ball[1]—
I'll hit, you do the singing!
Now I'll sing, your turn to hit!
We hit it going, hit it coming,
never knowing how the hours fly.
Passers-by turn, look at me and laugh,
"What makes you act like this?"
I duck my head, don't answer them—
I could speak, but what's the use?
You want to know what's in my heart?
From the beginning, just this! just this!

[1] Grass fights and *temari* refer to children's games.

"Finished Begging"

Finished begging at the village crossroads,
now I stroll through the Hachiman Shrine
when children spot me, call to each other,
"That crazy monk from last year's back again!"

"Breath of Spring"

Breath of spring bit by bit milder;
rattling the rings on my staff, I head for the east town.
Green green, willows in the gardens;
bobbing bobbing, duckweed on the pond.
Alms bowl smelling sweet with rice from a thousand houses;
heart indifferent to ten-thousand-chariot glory.[2]
Following in tracks of old-time buddhas,
begging for food, I go my way.

"Done Begging"

Done begging in a rundown village,
I make my way home past green boulders.
Late sun hides behind western peaks;
pale moonlight shines on the stream before me.
I wash my feet, climb up on a rock,
light incense, sit in meditation.
After all, I wear a monk's robe—
how could I spend the years doing nothing?

"Rags and Tatters"

Rags and tatters, rags and tatters,
rags and tatters—that's my life.
Food—somehow I pick it up along the road;
my house—I let the weeds grow all around.

[2] The glory and wealth of a ruler with an army of ten thousand char-
iots; an old Chinese expression.

Watching the moon, I spend the whole night mumbling poems;
lost in blossoms, I never come home.
Since I left the temple that trained me,
this is the kind of lazy old horse I've become.

"On Peaks Before"

On peaks before, peaks behind, snow glinting white;
my grass gate shut tight, west of the rocky stream.
Through the long night in the firepit I burn sticks of wood,
pulling on my beard, remembering times when I was young.

Long Winter Night

I remember when I was young
reading alone in the empty hall,
again and again refilling the lamp with oil,
never minding then how long the winter night was.

Dialogue in a Dream

Begging food, I went to the city,
on the road met a wise old man.
He asked me, "Master, what are you doing
living there among those white-clouded peaks?"
I asked him, "Sir, what are you doing
growing old in the middle of this red city dust?"
We were about to answer, but neither had spoken
when fifth-watch bells shattered my dream.

Drinking Wine with Yoshiyuki and Being Very Happy

Older and younger brother meet—
both with white eyebrows drooping down.
And what delight in this time of peace,
day after day getting drunk as fools!

To Inscribe on a Picture of a Skull I Painted

All things born of causes end when causes run out;
but causes, what are they born of?
That very first cause—where did it come from?
At this point words fail me, workings of my mind go dead.
I took these words to the old woman in the house to the east;
the old woman in the house to the east was not pleased.
I questioned the old man in the house to the west;
the old man in the house to the west puckered his brow and walked
    away.
I tried writing the question on a biscuit, fed it to the dogs,
but even the dogs refused to bite.
Concluding that these must be unlucky words, a mere jumble of a
    query,
I rolled life and death into a pill, kneading them together,
and gave it to the skull in the meadowside.
Suddenly the skull came leaping up,
began to sing and dance for me,
a long song, ballad of the Three Ages,
a wonderful dance, postures of the Three Worlds.[3]
Three worlds, three ages, three times danced over—
"the moon sets on Ch'ang-an and its midnight bells."[4]

[3] The three ages of past, present, and future; the three worlds of desire, form, and formlessness.
[4] The last line is taken verbatim from a poem entitled "For the Monk San-tsang on His Return to the Western Regions," by the ninth-century Chinese poet Li Tung.

KAYA SHIRAO

(?1738–1791)

TWENTY-ONE HOKKU

HAZE
The tides carry the haze along the country

SKYLARK
A skylark rises, and a beach sparrow dances a bit in company

CHERRIES
About the time I miss someone and light a lantern, cherries fall

Rafts are moored to cherries in far and near places

WISTERIA
I put aside a story and look at the flowering wisteria

CUCKOO
A bowman listens to a cuckoo, holding his bow

BABY DEER
For eight or nine yards I watch a baby deer through the wood

PEONIES
In the dark garden at night, quiet peonies

POPPIES

Sparrows, mating, have dropped into flowering poppies

MAY RAIN

Asking a guest to stay longer at my hut:
Wait a while—this is an evening shower in the May rains

COOLING OFF

There's even someone combing her hair, cooling off at her doorway

HEAT

The floating cloud before my eyes makes me hot, though I'm in the
shade

LIGHTNING

Lightning gets to be terrifying when you are alone

KATYDID

A katydid stops chirping, then the sound of its flying

SCARING BIRDS

In the setting sun even its shadow is light—the scarecrow

SNIPE

Just one evening snipe stands in the shallows

AUTUMN FISH

Pity the sweetfish after spawning—one, two, three traps

HAILSTONES

In a field with scentless winter trees, evening showers

Night hailstones fall so hard I can't help getting up to look

COLD

On a dark night, as long as it's dark, it's cold

WINTER MOON

Cold moon: a white sheet of paper flies after hunting is over

RICE-PLANTING SONGS[1]

From *Morning Songs*

Opening a little the wheeled door at the back, I look out:
    morning sun's rays better than gold.
Today the morning sun shines so. A fine morning sun!
The morning sun's rays blaze on the hill to the east.

Morning, about six, as I look at the rim of the hill,
is that mist or haze?—as I look at the rim of the hill,
a thick mist rises and dances round Misen's hips.
Cloudy morning—is it cloudy to let the sun shine later?
To let out the rain—morning mists round Misen's hips.
Leave your straw coats and hats, rise to your feet. Look, the clouds
    are going, it's clearing!

Out for a morning meal a little crow, drenched with dew,
    passes by with melancholy caws, drenched with dew.
This morning my lord looks merry indeed!

On first-paddy maidens deep in the hills, blossoms have opened!
    opened, opened, blossoms have opened eightfold!
On the lovely treetops blossoms are in bud.
Blossoms have opened so the domain may increase.
The landowner was called a big pile, a millionaire!

[1] A selection from a total of 134 "songs" recorded in the early nineteenth century.

"Buy me a Kyoto comb, yes, a Kyoto comb!
    Yes, a Kyoto comb to make my hair sleek!"
"I've bought you a comb. Comb your hair, girl.
Your hair, longer than you're tall,
your long hair, look! as you walk, it gets tangled in your sandals."

This morning, in the faint light of dawn a pheasant called, lords,
    a pheasant and a hawk called, passing by.
A pheasant calls and stretches its wings.
A pheasant calls and becomes a hawk's food.
Wings stretched, it will fall on that hill.

The bird's call this morning was a fine bird call.
    Twenty bushels an acre isn't at all a bad crop.
The good bird sang of eighteen bushels of rice.
The bird sang, deep at night—I had to tell my lord to go home.
Let's listen to that bird's auspicious call!

You work fast in the morning, ladies, as you plant the seedlings.
    Reap them this fall, pile them in the storehouse.
Plant early rice, and the stalks will put on ears first.
The stalks have leaned toward the storehouse—rustling, they've
    leaned.
From the stalks piled this year in the storehouse, we'll get seed.

From *Noon Songs*

How far shall I go with our lunch maid? To the Barrier Mount, to
    Barrier Mountain, Barrier Temple, Chambers, Chamber Barrier.
Now at the trip's end, look, Thrust Island of Gourd!
Hurry, slow girl, the tea shop on the hilltop's near!

Let's give sake to the planters today.
  Come on, let's give it in a cup of longevity!
Give them a drink, all of this sake that makes them young!
Help them to Kaga's Chrysanthemum Sake,
for a snack, Kyoto's salted early beans.

  When they drink, poor fellows, those planters!
  When they drink, they get only nasty words.
  Sing a song, paddy god, you've had three drinks!

This white sedge hat came from Kyoto yesterday.
  Why shouldn't I lend my man this white sedge hat?
Lean on me, I'll let you wear this Kyoto-curved hat.
If you lean on me, I'll let you wear this lovely little sedge hat.
You're too young—I won't let you row in the swampy paddies with-
  out a hat!

What did the cuckoo bring?
  He brought a measure, a leveler, and straw rice bags.
He brought straw rice bags and put them in the northwest corner.
Keep taking them, those straw rice bags in the northwest corner—
  they never decrease.
The stalks are good, so make many rice bags.

The birds called warblers are fancy mountain birds,
  fancy birds that hide in mountains and recite poetry.
When your voice gets croaky, borrow the warbler's voice.
Raise your voice and sing, warblers in the fields.
We never tire of hearing your voice, your reedy voice!

Swallows, when your wings are full grown, fly off into the distance.
    Raising you, your parents suffered.
Wing to wing, they've flown off to the Timeless Land.
May your parents' hearts rest in peace!
Wing to wing, they've flown off, all at one time.

"Come, come, let's go home, look at today's sun.
    The sun's gone down, look at today's sun."
"I left my knit hat at the tea shop, I dropped your fan in the town.
I'll buy you one when I go to Miyoshi Town again."
"Perhaps the town doesn't have them, he doesn't bring the fan!"
"The summer passes. Let's put the fan away!"

From *Evening Songs*

Let's make sake, strong and clear, from early rice.
Let's extract sake, using the clear water under the willow.

How far shall I go with our lunch maid? To Kaji Island,
    to Kaji Island—Gourd singing for love!
Now at the trip's end, look, Thrust Island of Gourd.
What's fancy—Gourd and Temple to the West.
What's good to touch—a shamaness' skin, her rice-cake skin!
Touch it one night, you'll get stuck seven days, her skin's that good!

Bandō warriors are skilled with their bows.
    One shot down a bird rising to the sky.
How skilled he is—he shot down a crane dancing in the sky!
The young man shot the bird darting through the sky—
yes, he shot it, how marvelous his bow!

"Look at the path, look at her waving her sleeve!
  Don't spill your charm on the path.
Come out and look, how she spills her charm!
Let's play to the tune of her charm."
"She's a girl, she's young, don't let her wave her sleeve!"

What fun to work the mountain paddies!
  A monkey rubs the *sasara*,[2] a badger beats a drum!
Good sound on the badger's drum, what fun this is!
From the old days the monkey's been good at the *sasara!*
How long will the scarecrow be in the mountain paddies?

If only I could pretend to be a bow woven with rattan
  and hang on to the shoulders of a Bandō lord!
Pretending I'm a bow I've fallen in love with a Bandō lord!
Why doesn't my body go to him, as I wish?
Sheer beauty—that's what my Bandō lord is!

When he kicked the ball under a plum tree,
  a blossom fell, fluttering, and the ball stayed in the sky.
Kicking the ball high is what a good player does.
How I love my lord in pale blue *hakama*,[3] as he kicks the ball!
My lord is good at playing ball.

A true young woman, yes, for midnight,
  her voice fine, yes, for midnight!
If only the sun sets, her voice is good!
The May girl's voice is fine as it grows dark.
For her fine voice I'll gladly give my sword.
It's fine, sing, first-paddy maiden!

[2] A simple musical instrument made of bamboo.
[3] Formal skirtlike trousers for men; kickball was a game for aristocrats.

I gave my musk scent to her white *kosode*,[4]
  I slept with a Kuruhara lady and rubbed off on her.
Musk and incense, move, become the fragrance of her sleeve!
Say what you will, I can't forget the Kuruhara lady.
I'll never forget the way she lay, hair disorderly.

"My lord must be secretly coming in. The wheeled door at the back
  squeaks, squicks—that wheeled door at the back!
My secret lover—is he a dog?—couldn't open the door and groaned!"
"Dagger by the pillow, sword at the screen joint,
I'm coming secretly. Where are you sleeping?"

"Get a lovely spray of cherry blossoms when you come to me.
  Get one to decorate my bedroom when you come to me."
"What will you do with blossoms? My sword is your bedroom
  decoration!"
"For my bedroom decoration, blossoms from that hill!"

Against the sunset, two snipes go to the west.
  There's a pond to the west, I am told.
The snipes fly down to the small mountain pond.
Are they making love? Their calls are high.
Together, the two of them, how loving they are!

Today's landowner planted stacks of paddies,
  built eight rows of storehouses, and attracted virtues.
Let's grow rice that rustles, let's build storehouses everywhere.
Kyoto blacksmiths will make the storehouse keys.
Today's landowner's called a millionaire loaded with blessings!

---

4 A kimono with simple sleeves.

TWO FOLKSONGS

Hay-Making Song: Miyazaki Prefecture

Here on this hill hay-making is over.
Tomorrow in the paddies let's reap the rice.

Sun's already sinking. Valleys grow dark.
Horse, we're going—carry the hay on your back.

Autumn's over. On the path between the paddies,
that must be another bride—five lanterns.

Rice-Planting Song: Aomori Prefecture

When spring comes, from the paddy dam, small dam,
water rushes. Loaches, bullheads, leap for joy,
thinking they're in the sea.

When summer comes, the paddy dam, the small dam,
warms up. Loaches, bullheads, leap for joy,
thinking they're in a hot bath.

When autumn comes, the fields, mountains, and hills
turn red. Loaches, bullheads, stick out their heads,
thinking it's a forest fire.

When winter comes, in the paddy dam, small dam,
ice forms. Loaches, bullheads, are freezing, freezing,
thinking now they have a ceiling.

KOBAYASHI ISSA

(1763–1827)

FORTY-FOUR HOKKU[1]

Awakened by a horse's fart, I see a firefly in the air

    Poor house:
Cold night: I keep a vigil on my own body

Lying on the ground, I pick young herbs in the sunlight

Awakened by someone gnashing his teeth—night's cold

Pissing and trembling—laugh at me, crickets

Just one mosquito raises a fuss all day near my pillow

Departing wild geese rudely stare at my face

In the autumn wind a beggar compares himself with me

By a clump of grass, how that frog gripes and complains!

Wild geese gone, the cove looks cleared of all trouble

---

[1] Arranged in rough chronological order.

Mountain mist: a horse-dung cleaner has a beautiful voice

A frog looks at me and screws up his face

Firefly: a frog opens his mouth a bit

A blossom drops, and that as their cue, small sweetfish hurry

The great sky splendidly darkens while it's hot

I've survived, I've survived, in this cold

I know, I know it, but still I'm cold, I'm poor

Beautiful—the sky after a lark has called

A butterfly comes and takes a butterfly away from my garden

A door-latch rusted scarlet in this cold

I let the sparrows play on my straw mat

Frogs play hide-and-seek in the blades of grass

Must be a good day—the fleas are dancing, leaping!

Among the fleeing silverfish, there are parents, children

Through a long night the demon in my heart tortures me

Falling leaves, making no sound, intensify the cold

Snow gone, the village fills up with children

A willow tickles awake a big dog

Another round of farting contests begins as we hole up for winter

Dragonflies' resting place, a scarecrow

A big cat teases a butterfly with his tail

Lending a branch of his antlers to a dragonfly, a deer sleeps

A huge firefly, undulating, passes by

A kitten twirls around at scattering leaves

On the heavily loaded bull's head, the snow accumulates

A mosquito larva plays alone in a lacquered tub

A laconic crow flies by in the autumn rain

A shrike call takes a persimmon thief by surprise

From a brat's sleeve an icicle comes out

A sparrow goes in and out of jail

Sparrows' friendship breaks up as a shower strikes

On a potato leaf, by a dewdrop, a snail

A frog keeps still, while sniffed at by a horse

Snowy day: the temple hall's packed with pigeons, sparrows

HAIBUN

Fire in Yokkaichi (eighth month, 1806)

28th. Clear. Around two at night a fire broke out in Yokkaichi. In the first month, when a fire broke out in Aomono-chō, I managed to escape it and congratulated myself on my luck. On the fourth of the third month, another fire started in the direction of Shiba. It covered a distance of three *li* with smoke, as far as those parts of Asakusa where the green grass grows, the calamity extending, as they say, to the fish in the pond. All this area was turned into a field where pheasants call.

Still, mindful that life can't go on without some way to make a living, we turned to the hills and the sea, until finally we more or less had set up shop again and were beginning to feel some sort of relief, when, about ten days later, another fire struck, this time from a neighborhood behind us. Thus, in a brief time, we met sudden disasters that severed our roots and made our leaves wither.

Among the most pitiful was Matsudaira Heisuke, a book dealer I know. Not at all uninformed in the ways of business and probably blessed by the Princess of Fairs, he had one stroke of luck after another. Like the rising sun or a flourishing pine, he prospered day by day, over the years and months accumulating considerable numbers of Chinese and Japanese books. But all of them were reduced to ashes in a moment. To be subjected to such hardship three times this year alone—even to a casual observer like myself, it seemed a bitter lot, and as I thought how he must feel, my heart was chilled:

Blow on the burnt pilings and cool them soon, autumn wind

Murder of a Masseur (ninth month, 1806)

24th. Clear. Frost.

Around seven in the evening, on Fifth Street in Aioi-chō where I live, someone stabbed a blind masseur with a spear and ran away. Some of us immediately gathered around the victim and asked, "Where do you live?" But he barely finished saying, "I live in Yokoami" before he died. Since this past spring, I'd heard rumors that this kind of outlandish thing happened from time to time, but when I saw it right in front of my eyes, I felt terror, pity, and bitterness, and a chill ran down my spine.

If he had been a normal person, someone said, he could have grappled with his attacker. But simply because he was blind, he lost his life with the unexpectedness of a bird flying into a net in the dark or a fish getting poisoned in a stream. We shed tears, though we were all strangers. The attacker was not a thief who was after the man's valuables, nor was he trying to avenge some grievance. And yet, the fact that this kind of calamity takes place makes me think the Demon King or someone like that is trying to throw the world into confusion, and I feel barely alive, auspicious though the present reign may be. We are just onlookers this time, we said to each other, but we've no assurance that we won't meet with the same kind of fate tomorrow! We felt particularly chilled at heart that night:

Wait and see, the murderer too will turn into dew on the grass

DIARY

From *The Spring of My Life*[1]

Last summer, around the day for bamboo planting,[2] a daughter was born to us in this world so full of sad events. Though she may have been born stupid, we hoped she would grow up to be a clever girl, and decided to call her Sato.[3] This year, from around the day we celebrated her birthday, she began to laugh if we clapped our hands, and to nod her head if we patted it lightly.

Once, when she saw a child her age with what is called a pinwheel, she wanted it for herself badly and fussed so much that we hurriedly got one for her. But soon she was chewing on it noisily and then she threw it away. Without showing a drop of regret, she turned her attention to something else, and began breaking the bowls that happened to be at hand. Soon bored with that too, she started tearing the thin paper off the sliding door. We said, "Well done! well done!" as though praising her. She thought we meant it and, cackling, went on tearing away intently. Not a speck of dust in her heart, she seemed as bright and pure as the full moon of autumn. As if witnessing a superb actor, I felt the wrinkles being smoothed out of my heart.

Again, when someone came along and said to her, "Where's the bow-wow?" she'd point at a dog, and when asked, "Where's the caw-caw?" she'd point at a crow. From her mouth to the tips of her fingers she brimmed with charm and lovableness, and I thought she was gentler than the butterflies that play around the first spring herbs.

The child must have been protected by the buddhas.[4] On

---

[1] Diary written during 1819.

[2] The thirteenth of the fifth month. It was believed that bamboo planted that day would root easily. Sato's birthday was the fourth of the same month.

[3] The name is related to the word *satoshi*, "clever," "quick," "bright."

[4] The sentence, along with the one that follows, reflects the belief that everyone becomes a buddha after death. Among Issa's immediate family members who had died by 1819 were his grandmother, his parents, and his first son.

the evening before the anniversary of someone's death, as
soon as I lit a candle and tinkled the bell at our family altar,
wherever she might be, she would busily crawl up beside
me, press together the hands that were as small as sprouting
ferns, and recite "Nammu, Nammu"[5]—her voice touching,
elegant, stirring, admirable. Speaking of such things, though
I'm old enough to have my head crowned with frost and
waves of wrinkles gathering on my brow, I still have not
learned to trust Amida Buddha, but mindlessly waste the
months and days. In the presence of this daughter of mine
barely one year old, I feel ashamed, but as soon as I leave the
family altar I start sowing the seeds that will send me to hell
—hating the flies that swarm on my lap, cursing the mosquitoes that circle my table, and worse still, drinking sake, a
practice Buddha forbade.

I was lost in such thoughts, when I noticed the moon
shining on our gate, and that the air was very cool. Outside,
there were voices of children dancing. Sato immediately
threw away her little bowl, crawled out on her knees, and
raising her voice, imitated the children, looking quite happy.
As I watched her, I thought that if I could make her old
enough to part her hair and dance, she would be far more
wonderful than the pipes and the strings of the twenty-five
bodhisattvas. Thus I managed to forget the years piling up
on my body, and drove away my melancholy thoughts.

As the days passed, Sato never stopped wiggling her hands
and feet, even for a period as short as the summer deer's
antlers, and worn out from play, she would sleep well into
the morning until the sun was high. That brief interval was a
New Year's holiday for her mother, who would, during that
time, cook, sweep, clean as much as she could, and try to
cool off, fluttering her fan. The sound of crying from the
bedroom was the signal that Sato was awake. Her mother
would then quickly pick her up, let her pee in the field at the
back of the house, and give her the breast. Sato, sucking
noisily, would thump her mother's chest and look up with a
smiling face. Seeing that, her mother would forget all about
the pains of the long months when the child was in her

[5] A child's imitation of the Buddhist recitation, "Namu Amida Butsu."

womb, or the dirty diapers every day, and as if her daughter were a jewel she had found sewn in her clothes,[6] she would pet and caress her, all happiness:

Counting the fleabites while suckling her baby   *Issa*

I have here put together the pieces, like companions in play, that I've written on children from time to time:

A child jumps out of a willow, saying, "Boo!"

A child says, "Nammu, Nammu," to an Immortal Island[7]

Asked, "How old?" a child shows its palm—time to wear new clothes

In celebration of a child's future:
We can count on you—your first clothes so shrunken!

"Get me that bright moon!" the child cries

Our child, our treasure, cackles at the fire in the firepit

"This is mine, this is mine"—the child lays the rice cakes in a row

How our child carries them piggyback—rice cakes for neighbors!

---

[6] Allusion to a parable in Chapter 8 of the Lotus Sutra.
[7] The island home of the immortals in Chinese legend. Here, a New Year decoration in the shape of the island.

Under the tree with rice-cake flowers[8] a child claps her hands, laughing!

He ties him to a breezy tree—that's his son

The brat, tied up, calls to fireflies

Hokku on the same subject by other poets:

Ah, he stood up, stood up by himself this year!   *Teitoku*

"I'm tired of children"—to anyone who says that, no   *Bashō*
flowers

For their son who wears his first *hakama*, they carry   *Shidō*
sandals[9]

Say "flower," say it again, our little child   *Rakō*

Spring rain: a child's hands stuck out of the lattice   *Tōrai*

A young woman plants seedlings toward her crying   *Kikaku*
baby

Breaking a branch off my cherry tree—but that's my son   *Kikaku*

---

[8] Freshly-made rice cakes were attached to willow branches for decoration.

[9] Reference to the celebration for boys upon becoming five years old. *Hakama* are skirtlike trousers for men worn on formal occasions. The parents are so proud of their son they don't mind waiting on him.

The day she began using chopsticks:
A shrike calls when I kiss my infant's cheek   *Kikaku*

A woman who, disliked by her husband, was living with
her parents, wanted to see her son on his first boys' festival
day But she could not do so during the day, because too
many people would have seen her:

Sent away, I look at the banner above the gate during   *Anonymous*
the night[10]   *Woman*

Here, I'm touched by the woman's real feeling for her
son. This must be the kind of sincerity that "soothes the
heart of the fierce warrior."[11] However much of a demon
her husband may have been, if he happened to hear about
this hokku of hers, how could he help but call her back?

It's said that even the beasts have their ties of kinship from
generation to generation.[12] How can there be any difference
between thinking fondly of parents and loving children?

A human parent chases a crow away from sparrow nest-   *Onitsura*
lings

On a summer hill a doe appears and cries for her fawn   *Gomei*

A frog emerges with its child on its back, letting it croak *Tōyō*

[10] "Banner" hoisted on the boys' day.
[11] See the introduction to the *Kokinshū*, p. 107.
[12] Allusion to or quotation from a Buddhist text. The meaning is uncertain.

A parent deer hurries back at the wind over the bamboo   *Issa*
   grass

Midnight shower—that crying must be a childless deer   *Issa*

Trying to hide her nestlings, a skylark cries—away from   *Issa*
   the bush

When joy has reached its height, sorrow arises—such is the way of the world. A little pine tree that was far from having had half the fun of a thousand years, our child with her second leaf just out and full of laughter was marked by the harsh god of smallpox with the abruptness of water swamping a person asleep, and in no time she was covered with blisters. Like the year's first flower hit by muddy rain as soon as it opened, and wilting—even someone merely standing by could see her pain. Two or three days later the blisters began to dry and the scabs came off, crumbly as the mud on a slope after a thaw. We rejoiced, applauding our luck, and then made what's called a rice-bag top, went through the motions of bathing her in sake, and sent the god away.[13] But she grew weaker and weaker, looking less encouraging today than yesterday, until finally, on the twenty-first day of the sixth month, she faded from this world with the bloom of the morning-glory. Her mother clasped the dead face and burst out sobbing—who could blame her? But the child's time had come, the flowing water would never return, the scattered blossom would never go back to its branch. We tried to resign ourselves without speaking words of regret, but we could not stop thinking of her, because of the bonds of love:

The world of dew is, yes, a world of dew, but even so   *Issa*

---

[13] A ritual celebrating the recovery of a smallpox victim. Upon recovery, the patient was normally given a hot bath with sake added to the water, but Sato was too small and weak and so the bath had to be simulated.

NATSUME SEIBI

(1749–1816)

TWENTY-SEVEN HOKKU

Standing by a plum, a penniless poet, clean and lean

A topic for a painting:
Houses, and again willows, as far as one can see

On the anniversary of my father's death:
Scolded in a dream—a willow whip

The hazy moon has detached itself from willow branches

Reading the *Analects:*[1]
Spring night: a neighbor comes to get some vinegar

Somehow I can't help looking at a bird's empty nest

A spring bird—thinking of what? chest puffed up

Sleeping in the grass, laying myself amid butterflies

---

[1] Allusion to *Analects* IV, 25: "Virtue never dwells alone; it will always have neighbors."

Reading an "Ode to a Widow":[2]
Waking from spring dreams, I hear the neighbors talk

Once when my five-year-old daughter was out playing with her mother, digging violets and picking ears of reeds, some ladies accompanying a certain aristocrat viewing the blossoms strolled by, and one of them asked her: "Little girl, what is your name? How old are you?" Looking down, my daughter said, "My name is Ito. My age is this," and spread her fingers. Everyone thought that was lovely, and laughed. This telling of her name to exalted persons was to become the greatest honor in her life, for she died in the sixth month of the same year [1793]. This year, longing to see the place with the blossoms, I went and walked alone with a stick by the Sumida River, but my heart was not consoled at all. Only the willow by her old gravestone stirred in the wind, as if obeying it, as if resentful of it:

"I want to die"—at times I think, looking at the cherries

On the violets of the field quietly a crow walks

Useless acquaintances increase as spring passes

White peonies about to collapse—I've watched them for two days

The summer night has turned to dawn, earthenware wet

The traveler I saw yesterday returns in the May rain

Is that the person I once loved?—walking in a summer field

[2] Nothing is known about the ode.

A wild cat steps over kudzu vines to get to the clear water

Lightning: a man walking is so slow

A butterfly dying right in front of its eyes, a quail cries

Deer in the morning look edgy and lost

Even gulls appear to feel cold at the falling leaves

Under how many layers of fallen leaves am I to be?

An old man's thought:
Just falling asleep is accidental under the frosty moon

Visiting my wife's grave:
Frost on your tombstone: I'm about to turn to moss as well

Having eaten fish, my mouth smells raw in the midday snow

"Not home! Not home!"—I make my house parrot say

When mother died:
Motherless I have become, I've become

RAI SAN'YŌ

(1781–1832)

*Setting out from Hiroshima, Saying Goodby to My
Father*

[Ninth month, eleventh day, 1814, starting off for Kyoto
after a visit with his father Shunsui and other family
members in Hiroshima; Shunsui died two years later.]

Hurrying, hurrying, we've downed our cups of wine;
slowly, reluctantly, I go out the neighborhood gate,
turning my head, asking my cousins
to be good enough to look after my parents for me.
The boat moves forward, islands shift, city receding in the distance;
far off I see my well-wishers turn back from the shore.
One tree like a carriage top looms in the gathering dusk:
I can still make out the camphor that grows by my father's gate.

Coming Home

[Third month, eleventh day, 1819; returning to his home at
Nijō Takakura in Kyoto after over a year of travel in western Japan.]

To the end of the alley sloshing through new mud,
dawn rain coming down now in thin threads;
the nearer home, the more nervous I feel,
wondering if I'll recognize the old house.
My wife recalls the sound of my step,
so filled with joy she seems to be grieving.
Two years, my first time home,
face black with dust of the road.
She heats water to wash my feet,
but the wood is damp and slow to burn.
Slow to burn—what does that matter!
Happiness enough in this meeting alone.

Shortly after I Married, I Had to Go into Mourning for My Father. Now I Have a Son. I Wrote These to Express My Joy.

[The first three of six poems written on the birth of his son Tatsuzō on the seventh day of the tenth month, 1820]

1

No fields, no house, one poor scholar,
but I have a child, and to my delight it's a boy!
A few paintings, a pair of old inkstones:
your father offers them to you—but will you accept them?

2

So stupid of me to hope you'll take to books;
a scholar all my life, I want to raise you the same way.
Baby squalls that to other ears are nothing but noise—
sooner or later they'll give way to the student's drone.

3

Fist like the mountain fern half unfurled,
skin like the pomegranate when the blossom has just dropped;
all you do is howl, searching for your mother's breast;
beautiful baby eyes that have not learned to tell their father.

The Cat in Cold Weather

[One of four "Songs of the Cold" written in 1821 and inspired in part by a similar series by the Ch'ing poet Chiang
Shih-ch'üan, 1725–1785]

Witless and dull, I curl up in the hut I love,
laughing that my laziness is so much like yours.
A cramped room all smoky—what rat would live here?
My poor kitchen grown cold—you'll find no fish there!
Through the long night on the quilt corner you share my sleep,
in midday warmth sit with me by the brazier's side.
And now you're off yowling for your lady love—
silhouetting the plum by the eaves next door, a moon just coming up.

New House

[Late in 1822, San'yō moved to a new house on the west
bank of the Kamo River. The poem was written on New
Year's day, which, according to traditional reckoning, marks
the beginning of spring.]

In a new house greeting the first of the year,
opening doors on bright clear weather:
below the stairs, shallow water flows,
rippling already with the sound of spring.
Bending by the current, I wash my inkstone,
purple of the stone reflecting green of hills.
In such an out-of-the-way spot, few visitors—
I'm pleased to be spared all that greeting and goodbyeing.
A place to live this peaceful—
it fits exactly with what I've always wanted;
only I regret that business of my mother,
not arranging to have her come live with me.
How can I share this wine with her,
see her gentle face smiling as she lifts the cup?
I grind some ink, write a letter home
in a drunken hand that keeps straying out of line.

*I Accompanied My Uncle Shumpū on an Outing to Lake
Biwa and Wrote This to Commemorate the Occasion*

[Third month, 1825; Hirai Kisō lived at Ōsaka Barrier on
the road between Kyoto and Lake Biwa.]

My father and my uncle
once accompanied my grandfather—
so often I've heard of that youthful expedition,
how they bought wine, drank in a tower by the lake;
their old friend Hirai Kisō
served as host along the eastern road.
Now my father, my grandfather, and my father's friend
all are logged in the ledgers of the dead;
only my uncle is still with me
as we set out to retrace that former outing.
I live now by the Kyoto bridge,
take his hand carefully, help him along.
At the stone landing we rent a little boat,
riding together, listening to the gentle oars.
He points out spots of that earlier trip,
some forty-five years ago:
"Weather was clear, the lake calm,
not like the rain we've run into today.
From the lake we could see the mountains
ranged peak by peak, all plainly in view!"
The dead will never see them again,
and the living—how often will we be together?
Uncle and nephew have a chance to tip the cup;
where shall we buy our presents for those at home?
I'm learning to wash away my cares with wine,
dancing a crazy dance to delight the elders.
Still I can't help worrying about my boy,
troubled in mind by the sickness that racks him.[1]
But why speak of wife and family—
my uncle is the guest of honor today.
I've written this poem to mark the occasion,
a footnote to add to the family records.

---

[1] The poet's five-year-old son Tatsuzō, who had been stricken with
smallpox and died shortly after this was written.

Reading Books

[The third and sixth of eight poems with this title written in 1828]

1

This morning, splendid breeze and sunlight,
north window where the new rain passed;
visitors sent off, I open my book;
then my wife comes with her story:
"No money coming in—all these relatives—
eight mouths—how can we get along alone?
No one important ever comes to call—
poverty and cold—that's all we'll ever know!
If only you'd be a little less sharp—
try being pleasant to others for a change—"
My illness, who can cure it?
The bones I have are the ones Heaven gave me.
If I'd stayed in my father's fief
I'd never have forgone official service.
But if I went back to that petty routine,
wouldn't I be false to my father's hopes?
Go away—don't bother me!
I'm trying to converse with the men of old.[2]

2

Eastern hills—dense and lush,
turning purple in the evening sun.
Kamo River ripples have all subsided,
only here and there the glint of a white gem.
Our family ducks know the day is ended;
they quack to each other, time to go home!
I too put away my books,
call to my wife to get out the cask of wine.
Fresh fish from the river, just right for grilling;
bamboo shoots—we dig them ourselves.
I'm going to sit by the eastern eaves,
share a drink with the hills over there.

[2] Despite the gruff tone, San'yō was apparently very devoted to his wife, and in fact was known in current parlance as a *rakuda* or "camel," a man who, contrary to custom, takes his wife along with him on outings and social visits.

Escorting My Mother Home: A Short Song for the Road

[In the spring of 1829 the poet's mother came to visit him in
Kyoto. In the fall of the same year he escorted her part of
the way back home to Hiroshima.]

East winds to greet my mother when she came;
north winds see her on her way back home.
She arrived when roads were fragrant with blossoms,
now suddenly this cold of frost and snow!
At cock crow already I'm tying my footgear,
waiting by her palanquin, legs a bit unsteady.
Never mind if the son's legs are tired,
just worry whether her palanquin's fit for riding.
I pour her a cup of wine, a drink for myself too,
first sunlight flooding the inn, frost already dried.
Fifty-year-old son, seventy-year-old mother—
not often you find a pair lucky as we!
Off to the south, in from the north, streams of people—
who among them happy as this mother and son?

Farewell Talk with Saikō by a Rainy Window

[The intercalary third month of 1830. Saikō is Ema Saikō
(1787–1861), daughter of the physician and scholar of Dutch
learning Ema Ransai of Mino. She studied *kanshi* writing
under San'yō. San'yō fell in love with her in his early thirties
and asked his friend Yanagawa Seigan to arrange a marriage.
Saikō's father refused to consent, and though he later re-
lented, by that time San'yō had given up hope and in 1815
took Hikita Rie as his second wife. The poem suggests that
San'yō was still in love with her fifteen years later.]

A parting meal, low lamp—stay and enjoy it a bit longer;
new mud on the road home—better wait till it dries.
On peaks across the river, clouds only now dispersing;
strings and songs in the house next door just beginning to fade in the
    night.

Intercalary month this spring—my guest lingers on,
though last night's rain heartlessly scattered the cherry flowers.
From here you go to Mino—not a long way away,
though, growing old, I know how hard it is to meet now and then.

Delighted That Jippo Has Come to See Me in My Illness, I Wrote This

[Ninth month, ninth day, 1832. Kōda Jippo was a physician who evidently journeyed from the eastern side of Lake Biwa to visit the poet.]

I'm ashamed, with this set of discordant bones,
to be lingering still between heaven and earth.
Who told you of my sudden turn for the worse,
troubled you to come journeying across lake and hill?
You rowed the waves from Yabase landing,
in wind palanquined over Ōsaka barrier.
An old man with nothing but tears
greets you, but can't seem to manage a smile.

A Parting Talk with Seigan

[On the seventeenth day of the ninth month of 1832 Yanagawa Seigan, about to leave for Edo, called on Rai San'yō to inquire of his health. San'yō knew it was the last time he would see his friend; he died six days later.]

Lamp by the yellow chrysanthemums,
     close onto midnight;
tomorrow morning you set off
     to tread the Shinshū clouds.
Our one pot of wine gone,
     but stay a little longer—
in this sickness near to death,
     must I say goodbye to you?

TACHIBANA AKEMI

(1812–1868)

THIRTY TANKA

Scenes in a silver mine:

Deep in mountain caves
where no sun rays reach
they enter,
torches flaming,
digging out the metal

Stark naked,
the men crowd forward,
flailing hammers
to smash
lumps of ore

Deafening noise!
treadling pestles,
pounding the lumps of earth
that glint and shine,
turning them to powder

Soaked in sluices
fed from valley streams,
it yields up silver dew
that trickles through the fingers

Sending up billows
of black smoke,
they smelt the ore,
never resting till
the silver avalanche tumbles down

Ingots of silver,
stacks of them
packed in boxes,
stoutly corded,
raced off by horseback

The servant:

The gourd of wine
he buys and
brings home from the market—
it never warms
his chilly night

Stepping through the sleet
that falls and collects in puddles,
shivering, shivering,
he follows
after others

"Happiness is when":

Happiness is when
you fall over asleep
beside the fire
and don't even know
when they try to shake you awake

Happiness is when
you borrow a rare book
from someone
and open to
that very first page

Happiness is when
you spread out the paper,
take a writing brush,
and write in a much better hand
than you expected

Happiness is when
you struggle with a poem
for a hundred days
and then suddenly
it turns out just right

Happiness is when
you and your wife
and children all happily
put your heads together
and dig into a meal

Happiness is when
you've been asked to write something
and then the person
pays a handsome price
as though money meant nothing to him

Happiness is when
you get up in the morning
and see a flower
that wasn't there
yesterday

Happiness is when
you find some rice
in the rice bin you thought was empty
and know you're all right
for another month

Happiness is when
you buy a fish
from the peddler who comes around
and smell the aroma of it
cooking in the pot

Happiness is when
you're reading along
aimlessly in a book
and come on someone
exactly like yourself

Happiness is when
you're sick of reading a book
and just then
someone with a familiar voice
knocks at your gate

Happiness is when
you've got some passage
that's supposed to be so difficult
and all by yourself
you figure out the meaning

Happiness is when
you wake up
and find that
while you were napping,
a shower wet down the garden

Happiness is when
with what little you have
you call people in
and tell them
"Drink! eat!"

Happiness is when
there are five people
in your family
and not one
has so much as a cold

Happiness is when
nobody comes to call,
nothing's going wrong,
and you can really
get your mind on your reading

Happiness is when
you make some tea
and stuff
a big round cake
in your mouth

Happiness is when
somebody you don't like
comes around,
but then stays hardly any time,
and goes right home

Happiness is when
you're talking in bed
with the covers pulled up
and while you're talking
you drop off to sleep

Happiness is when
you get a good writing brush
and first you soak it in water
and then you lick it
and try it out

Happiness is when
in this age
of foreign fads
you see someone
who hasn't forgotten about Japan

Happiness is when
sunset finds you in some country temple
or mountain village
and they say "Stay the night!"
and you do

The Modern Age

MASAOKA SHIKI

(1867–1902)

THIRTY-NINE HAIKU

From the firefly
in my hands,
cold light

A cricket singing
somewhere back of
the shoe closet

Lonely sound—
simmering in the firepit,
wood chips with snow on them

Above the treetops,
far away
fireworks explode

Long night,
when the waterfall
makes all kinds of noises

Always someone resting there—
a single rock
in the summer field

Getting lazy—
taking my socks off
after I get in bed

A dead squid
with the ink it spit out—
low tide

Fluttering, fluttering,
butterflies yellow
over the water

Where the castle stood,
daikon radish
blooming on the hilltop

In the hospital at the Suma seashore:

At daybreak
a white sail goes by
outside my mosquito net

In a strong wind at the Suma seashore:

My summer jacket
wants to get rid of me
and fly away

People going home—
after the fireworks
it's so dark!

Summer storm—
all the sheets of blank paper
blown off my desk

Sky blazing—
as I go down the gravel path,
husks of dead butterflies

Country road—
boys whacking at a snake,
wheat in autumn

Morning fog—
one man's got a fire going—
construction workers' shed

Peeling pears—
sweet juice drips
from the knife blade

Written when sick in bed:

I keep on asking
how deep
the snow's gotten

Airing books—
today I'll do
the haiku collections

Twilight cicadas—
the shadow of the pasania tree
presses on my desk

Written when sick in bed:

I'm trying to sleep—
go easy
when you swat the flies

After I'm dead:

Tell them
I was a persimmon eater
who liked haiku

I pulled on a creeper
and all this fruit
came falling down

This year
I took sick with the peonies,
got up with the chrysanthemums

I checked
three thousand haiku
on two persimmons

Forsythia blossoms gone,
leaves of the plantain
still unfurled

Summer grass—
way in the distance
people playing baseball

I think I'll die
eating apples,
in the presence of peonies

Fall rains—
scum collecting on
the garden pool

A stray cat
shits in my
winter garden

Crickets—
in the corner of the garden
where we buried the dog

For eating persimmons, too,
I think this year
may be my last

Clog with a broken thong
discarded in the
winter paddy

Home alone,
my mother off cherry-viewing—
I watch the clock

They've cut down the willow—
the kingfishers
don't come anymore

Daily routine,
sketching a plant or flower—
we're into autumn

Sketching from life—
eggplants are harder to do
than pumpkins

A purple so deep
it's almost black—
the grapes

FIFTEEN TANKA

I, who
hear the drums
from Yoshiwara[1]
and alone late at night
sort out haiku

I, who
listen to a man
tell how he climbed
Mount Fuji
and rub my skinny legs

I, who
think so often of
the fun I had as a boy,
and watch the fireworks
more intently than a child

[1] A famous brothel district near Shiki's house.

I, who
plant the pit
in the little garden,
waiting for the time when a tree
will flower and bear fruit

The sprays of wisteria
arranged in the vase
are so short
they don't reach
to the tatami

Sprays of wisteria
arranged in a vase—
one cluster
dangles down
on the piled up books

When I look
at the wisteria blossoms
I think of long ago,
the Nara emperors,
the emperors of Kyoto

When I look
at wisteria blossoms
I want to get out
my purple paints
and paint them

If I were to paint
the purple
of the wisteria blossoms,
I ought to paint it
a deep purple

Sprays of wisteria
arranged in a vase—
the blossoms hang down,
and by my sickbed
spring is ending

Last year in spring
I saw the wisterias
in Kameido—
seeing this wisteria now,
I recall it

Before the
red blossoms
of the peonies,
the wisteria's purple
comes into bloom

These wisterias
have blossomed early—
the Kameido wisterias
won't be out for
ten days or more

If you stick the stems
in strong sake,
the wilted flowers
of the wisteria
will bloom again like new

I don't know when
I'll get well again,
but I'm having seeds
for fall flowers
planted in the garden

SHIMAZAKI TŌSON

(1872–1943)

Song for the Burial of My Mother

> *Wide sky with*
> *scarcely a drifting cloud—*
> *in the moonlight*
> *this fine rain falling*

On your grave
 are yellow chrysanthemums,
on your grave
 are *sakaki* branches

On their leaves
 the dew lies thick—
are they heavy, perhaps,
 these tokens?

Some day will you wake
 from your sleep?
Some day will you come back,
 my mother?

The sprightly children
 the strong men—
all end as
 dust and mire

Ah, do not
 wake again!
Ah, do not
 return!

Though in spring
  the cherry flowers
bloom and scatter
  on your grave

Though in summer
  the tangled lights
of fireflies
  stream above your grave

Though in autumn
  the sad rains
of autumn
  soak your grave

Though in winter
  the pure white snow
may freeze
  upon your grave

Pillowed and dreaming
  in your long sleep,
have no fear,
  my mother

Birdless Country

Bats in a birdless country,
Sōsuke put his hoe on his shoulder,
Kōsuke took his net in hand,
Sōsuke to the mountain, Kōsuke to the sea

Cucumber flowers that bloom in the twilight,
cicadas singing in the leaves of a distant mulberry,
mountain paths cool with dew—
Kōsuke by the sea dreamed of them with envy

Tasty beach grasses on dunes near and far,
boats drying by the distant summer tide,
the voice of the sea resounding in the eelgrass—
Sōsuke on the mountain dreamed of them with envy

And the world changed, as change it will—
Kōsuke put the hoe on his shoulder,
Sōsuke took the net in hand,
now Kōsuke to the mountain, Sōsuke to the sea

Beginning in mist, ending in frost,
springs and autumns passed swiftly by,
and hope was like the bloom on the grass,
a thing buried in sand and lost from sight

What becomes of the blue clouds of ambition
that for a moment swell up in the breast?
Not a trace left to be seen
of Sōsuke's dreams, Kōsuke's dreams

Once again the lilies flower,
once again the plums are green,
and in the deep blue shade of the trees,
Sōsuke and Kōsuke come home perplexed

The Coconut

From some faraway island whose name I do not know
a single coconut has washed up here.

Since you left your homeland shore,
how many months have you spent on the waves?

Is the tree that bore you alive and green?
Can its fronds still offer shade?

I too have the beach for my pillow,
a lone traveler who sleeps on the waves.

I pick up the coconut, hold it to my chest
and taste anew the wanderer's sorrow.

As I watch the sun sink into the sea,
a stranger's tears come coursing down.

My thoughts drift over the eightfold tides—
when will I go back to my home again?

Song: Thoughts of a Traveler on the Chikuma River

Yesterday it was this way too—
today again it will be like this.
Why fret your life away
forever worrying about tomorrow?

How many times have I gone down into the valley
where dreams of glory and decay still linger,
seen the uncertain drift of the river waves,
sand-laden water that circles and returns?

Ah, what is the old castle saying?
What do the waves along the shore reply?
Be still and consider the ages gone by—
a hundred years are like yesterday

Chikuma River willows are hazy,
spring is shallow, the water flows on.
Alone I wander over the rocks,
binding my sorrows to this shore

YOSANO AKIKO

(1878–1942)

THIRTY-NINE TANKA

Hair, five feet long, loosened and soft in the water—I'll keep my
virgin heart secret, won't let it go

Camellia, yes, and plum, yes, that too is white; I see in peach the
color that doesn't ask of my sin

The girl, twenty—her black hair flows through her comb, how
arrogant, how beautiful her spring!

Who shall I tell of the color rouge? my blood wavers, thoughts of
spring, life in its prime

"I must go now, goodbye," said the god of night:[1] I touched the skirt
of his kimono, my hair became wet

With your other hand support me at my slender neck, god of night,
you are going away

To Kiyomizu, through Gion, with the moon above cherries—people
I meet tonight are all beautiful

[1] The "god of night" may be Yosano Hiroshi (1873–1935), a poet,
whom Akiko met in 1900. Earlier in the same year Hiroshi had founded his
New Poetry Society and, when he started a magazine called *Myōjō*, Akiko
became a member of the society.

Not even trying to touch the hot blood-tide under my soft skin, aren't you lonely, you who teach the Way?[2]

I won't let you go, this spring evening turns dark, my hair on a small harp, tangled, entangled

When I reflect on it now, my feeling is that of a blind person unafraid of the dark

"I don't want to take a beautiful bud," said the god, but now I've done what I wanted to

Having changed my tangled hair into Shimada style in the morning, I shake my lover awake, whom I'd told to rest a while

After throwing a parasol to the grass on the other bank, I cross the rivulet warm with spring water

Hugging my breasts I lightly kick the door of mystery—the scarlet of the blossom here is intense

In the spring dusk I find our next-door painter handsome; this morning, near the kerria rose, his voice was young

For some reason I thought you'd be waiting for me, and came out to this field of flowers under the evening moon

I bathe and step out of the spring; what touches my soft skin then is this world's cruel fabric

[2] If by "you who teach the Way" Akiko meant Hiroshi, that was because he headed the poetry society to which she belonged.

Sliding down two feet of my gossamer sleeve, a firefly streams away
into the blue night wind

This evening rainfall is merciful. Traveler, my love, don't ask for a
shortcut, but take a room with me

As I wait for you in the grass with lilies blooming, the end of the
field becomes fragrant, and a rainbow appears

Wondering, I touched it with my young lips—it was cold—the dew
on a white lotus

Another look like his mixed me up again—you really play tricks on
me, don't you, gods of love

Shall I receive the spring rain dripping on swallow wings, and with it
smooth my morning hair?

"You picked a white chrysanthemum and smiled—your look I caught
this morning!"—someone wrote to me

You think of him, and so do I; our hearts now, separate, can't be
separated: you are White Bush Clover; I, White Lily[3]

"The three of us are relatives not doing well in this world," I said it
first, at an inn in West Kyoto

[3] Akiko and her poet friend, Yamakawa Tomiko (1879–1909), met
Hiroshi and fell in love with him about the same time. Toward the end of
1900 the three of them traveled to Kyoto together. Akiko's nickname was
Bush Clover, and Tomiko's, Lily. This and the following five tanka are
about that trip.

"At least, at least in his dreams"—so thinking, I murmured to our god
Lily's poem on dew

"Our friend's feet were cold," the morning we set out traveling I said
to our young teacher heartlessly

Just one room away, from time to time you sighed—that night, did
you dream you held White Plum?[4]

Saying nothing, asking nothing, just nodding to each other we parted,
two and one—the day was the sixth

Black hair, a thousand strands of hair, tangled hair—my thoughts so
tangled, my thoughts get tangled!

"Can't say that now, you have little spring in your heart!" I closed
my eyes and clung to your hand

"At least let it burn just as it burns!"—that way I feel, as spring begins
to end

"Spring is short! Who says our life's immortal?" I said, and made his
hands caress my strong breasts

Yesterday feels like a thousand years ago; at the same time I feel your
hands still on my shoulders

To smear poisoned honey on my lips that lust for someone's love—
this wish I have!

[4] "White Plum" may refer to Hayashi Takino, to whom Hiroshi was
married at that time.

The way morning looks in the plum valley, haze scarlet—the hills are beautiful, and so am I

Not speaking of the Way, not thinking of the future, not asking the names, here we find ourselves, you who love me, I who love you

You are ill; let me put my slender arm around your neck and kiss your lips dry from fever

KITAHARA HAKUSHŪ

(1885–1942)

Memory[1]

Is a memory, like the uncertain touch past noon
of a firefly with a red nape,
an airy bluish glow
that does not seem to glow?

Or a faint flower on a cereal grass,
a gleaner's song,
the white flare of feathers plucked from a dove
on the warm southside of a wine cellar?

If it's a tone, something of a flute,
an evening when a toad croaks
and a physician's drug is fondly remembered,
the harmonica someone plays in the half light.

If it's a smell, that of velvet,
the eyes of a card queen,
the somewhat lonesome feeling
on the clownish Pierrot's face.

Not as hard to bear as a dissolute day,
not with the luminous pain of fever,
nonetheless, soft as late spring,
a memory, or else, my autumn's legend?

---

[1] The original title is *Joshi* (Proem), the poem being introductory to
a collection called *Omoide* (Memories).

First Love

In the dim light, red and red,
the girl dances all alone.
In the dim light, shedding tears,
the girl fades, too, all alone.
In the dim light, for memory,
the dancing person, the one alone.

Time Passes

Time passes, just as a steamer's red belly moves by,
like a flare of sunset by a granary,
the beautiful ringing in a black cat's ear,
time passes, unnoticed, softly casting a shadow, it passes.
Time passes, just as a steamer's red belly moves by.

Water Hyacinth

Moon white? No, it was not.
Dim sun? No, it was not.
And yet, that faint smell,
why is it still part of me?

Yes, it was a dream of a pale scent.
By the faint twilight beach,
I, again lying behind you,
what did we sing, what did we speak?

I don't know; though it was a day
when everything was young, now forgotten,
I know, the two of us drowned,
I glimpsed a flower of water hyacinth.

Terror

She was a wet nurse,[2] but I was afraid.
Night and day, "My child," she sobbed,
"I'm all bones," and saying, "If I die,"
with love fiercer than mother's,
held me tight. —As if to say, "I'll be sad."

She was a wet nurse, but how afraid I was.
Devotion, a moment before death;
her tearless, aged eyes
with love fiercer than mother's
stared at me—bluish white.

She was a wet nurse, but I can't forget her.
Aggrieved, confused with doubts,
she huddled up like water when I cried,
"My child, it's me" (must have been two at night)
"I'm your mother"—her face turned pale.

Memory of Pinks

Why did those people laugh?
I don't know,
I couldn't know,
because it was long ago, when I was only two.

It was a hot day.
It was a noiseless summer day, a bright midday.
Stifling, curious, suggestive of some meaning.

Whose house it was, I don't know.
I only know about a lantern Grandpa made, that was yellow,
know about the odor of tiny clams that exuded blue juice
that an old woman with poor eyes was splitting on the earth floor.

[2] Kitahara's second wet nurse, who died after a terminal illness when he was ten years old.

When I woke from a sensuous dream during a nap,
a woman's ample hands
with the hasty, hot strength of a spring
collected me, took me to the shining porch.
There were flowers, tiny red flowers, flowers of pinks.

Innocent urination. . . .
The child was restlessly staring.
The red, red, flowers of pinks reflected in his eyes almost painfully,
something ticklish behind him. Was it the antique touch of a picture
    book?

What was so funny?
A great many young fishermen and unclad women gathered,
their souls uselessly moved to see
what was curious, fearful.

His head pressed down with soft breasts,
the child felt something suspicious.
Forever and ever, persistently, like a fond memory, helplessly,
the woman rubbed her body against him, breathing.
The odor of her sweat was strong, stifling, maddening,
whatever was fearful was behind him.

Why are those people laughing?
I don't know,
I couldn't know,
because it was one day long ago, when I was only two.

It was a hot day.
It was a noiseless bright midday by the briny river.
Out of a steamy childhood fear
I was peeing . . . while staring
at the red flowers, tiny flowers, flowers of pinks that hurt my eyes.

Caterpillar

Caterpillar, caterpillar, blue caterpillar,
where are you crawling?
This summer evening, on frosted glass
lightly clouded and cold,
how beautiful your belly, faintly, faintly, transparent!
Does the light outside make you lonesome,
do you miss the little flute inside?
Caterpillar, caterpillar, blue caterpillar,
where are you going alone?

Cat

Under the summer sun, a blue cat—
I hold her lightly, my hands turn itchy;
her hair shifts, and my heart
catches a cold, body a fever.

Is she a magician? Her golden eyes
breathe deeply, terrifying;
throw her, she falls airily,
perspiring green shines.

Though in such sunlight,
she hides an air of invisibility.
All her skin turned into an ear,
in the smell of barley, what is she watching for?

Under the summer sun this blue cat—
I rub my cheek against her, how beautiful,
deep, elegant, terrifying—
I'd rather hold her till I die.

One-sided Love

Acacias' gold and red are falling.
Falling at dusk, in the autumn light.
One-sided love, light flannel, my melancholy,
as I walk by the water in "Towboat."[3]
Your soft sighs are falling.
Acacias' gold and red are falling.

Okaru and Kampei[4]

Okaru is crying:
like a velvet hollyhock trembling in prolonged twilight,
like the soft touch of flannel,
like the daylight about to fade from a field of buttercups,
like dandelion fuzz drifting away airily.

She cries and cries, but doesn't run out of tears.
Kampei is dead, Kampei is dead,
my young beautiful Kampei disemboweled himself. . . .

Okaru cries, longing for the young man's smell;
she thinks it was a strong stimulus like stifling onion in a malting
    room.
The soft touch of his skin was like the outdoor sun of May;
his breathing feverish as black tea,
when he held me tight, the salt farm gleamed blue in the sun,
my white parsley flower nerves turned sharp, and wilted, pale.
His inner thighs, which were trembling, and my lips I let him kiss,
on the day we parted, his white hands had gunpowder moistness
    soaked in them,
until just before getting on the palanquin—I was, lost in thoughts,
    cutting fresh vegetables. . . .

But Kampei is dead.

[3] Hikifune, here translated Towboat, is a place name in Tokyo. Quotation marks are part of the original.

[4] Two characters in *Kanadehon chūshingura*, a puppet play based on a historical incident in which forty-seven samurai avenged their master. In the play, Kampei disembowels himself, believing erroneously that he killed the father of Okaru, his wife. The play was written in 1748 by Takeda Izumo, Miyoshi Shōraku, and Namiki Senryū. See Donald Keene's *Chūshingura* (New York: Columbia, 1971).

Like an orphan in a greenhouse,
Okaru, incited by various memories of sensuality,
is indulging in her own happy pleasures.

(Beyond the glass window of the puppet theater, red oranges blaze in
the autumn sunset, and from the bottom of the city streets comes the
whistle of a riverboat.)

Okaru is crying.
With her beautiful gestures, as if despairing of herself, of this world,
accompanied by the pressing samisen,
riding the narrative push,
she cries and cries, as if drowning to death,
Okaru is crying.

(Colors, smells, music.
Kampei can go to hell, for all I care.)

Larch Trees[5]

1

Passing through a wood of larch trees,
I looked at larch trees, for the first time.
Larch trees made me lonesome.
Traveling made me lonesome.

2

Coming out of a wood of larch trees,
I entered a wood of larch trees.
Entering a wood of larch trees,
the path again continued, narrow.

[5] The stanza arrangement is that of the poem as originally published.
Later, stanza 7 was moved to a position after stanza 3 and an extra stanza
was added at the end.

3

Deep in a wood of larch trees,
there was a path for me to take.
It was a path that misty rains shrouded.
It was a path that mountain winds haunted.

4

Passing through a wood of larch trees,
for no reason my walk hushed itself.
Larch trees made me lonesome,
larch trees and I murmured to each other.

5

Coming out of a wood of larch trees,
I saw smoke rise from the Asama peak.
I saw smoke rise from the Asama peak.
Above and beyond the larch trees.

6

The rain in a wood of larch trees
made me lonesome, but quietened.
There was only a cuckoo calling.
Only larch trees becoming wet.

7

The path in a wood of larch trees
was haunted by me, and by someone else.
It was a path one haunted, all narrow.
It was a path one hurried by, alone.

WAKAYAMA BOKUSUI

(1885–1928)

FORTY-FOUR TANKA

Written while traveling:

In the spring night's fragrant darkness, here and there lie the hills
with budding trees

My train passes Ono Station—in the spring night an old station worker
stands motionless (ON MOUNT TAKAO)

The sun's light and the water's light muddy one color, at dusk I cross
the Great Tone

How many mountains and rivers to cross—to a country where loneliness ends? Today again I travel

Through the blue, blue, moonless night the tides of the great ocean
come in, then go out again (LOOKING AT THE SEA OF JAPAN)

Mountaintop: as far as I can see, there and elsewhere, rivers glisten in
the sunset country (AT KAI IN ŌSUMI, HYŪGA)

My ship stopped, I've come upon this country where in the sky full
of stars a mountain rises fragrantly (AT ABURATSU IN HYŪGA)

The mountain soars and the sea lies on its side—between them, narrow and white, a strip of summer sand

Huge swells move blue against the winds, crowned with waves of white beads

Leaning on the chest of your seasick young mother, are you delighted with the sea, little baby?

Sucked into the hillside darkness my ship has entered port—a prolonged whistle

The clouds burn, the sun sets, the red ochre faces of ship travelers, and their silence

I drank yesterday, I drink today—not dying of sake, laughing idiotically, I go on traveling

Lodging the firelight from a fire, night clouds, lighted red, flow in the sky (IN WAKAYAMA)

Stars in the great sky fall in confusion—under them, through the dark of one mountain to another, my train goes (GOING OVER IGA)

On drinking:

Turn on the light, and the water looks more like green; it's called sake, you pour it for me constantly

How lovely! getting drunk faster than I do, you've fallen asleep, your arm for a pillow

Wholly drunk, I see only the large vermilion ring of a blossom that blooms on a small maid's sash

Parched, throat ashen, while sobering up—a girl with bangs peels an
apple for me

For Sonoda Saeko:[1]

On the day the two in love set out on a sad trip, surrounding their
ship sea birds cry

Ah, our kiss—may the sea remain as it is, the sun stay, and birds, dancing, die and cease now!

Look at the mountain—on it the sun shines; look at the sea—on it the
sun shines. Now give me your lips

I weep aloud—may my voice reach the bottom of sea's dark green,
reach its indifferent ear!

A white bird cries in a hushed manner, as if resentful of the dead
calm sea

When you smile, the sea becomes fragrant, those hundreds of waves
this spring day hush themselves

I'm lost in the sea under the shining sun, in midair, and near your
breasts where melancholy sleeps

Eyes closed, you lean on a tree and listen to the sea. What is hidden
in that distant sound?

At times you fall silent—don't watch the sea, it might take you away!

[1] A woman Wakayama met in the middle of 1906. He spent about ten
days with her near Nemoto, Chiba, from the end of 1907 to early 1908.

At midday when the sea's visible in the window, through the pine
trees, I kiss the hair of someone sleeping peacefully

In the dark night it's light where the waves lap; crouching there, I
look at the pale-blue sea

Does its pounding pierce the sun in the sky? Blue and blue, the sea
thunders, ah, the blue sea thunders!

A white bird—is it not sad? not dyeing itself the sky-blue or the sea-
blue as it drifts

Sadly stars fall; two in love have lain side by side for the first time
tonight

Not speaking many words, going there, coming here, the two sadly
collect shells

A bird flies away quietly on its white wings, toward that part of the
sea where the evening is bright

In front of me the sea lies on its side, gleaming in the sun. This sorrow—what am I fearful of?

Thousands of white wings wheel in the morning wind, toward the
green sea, toward the sun, toward the great sky

By chance I find a strand of your hair in my sleeve—with my lips on
it, I look at the morning sea

How long our kiss was! Returning to heaven and earth I look at your
dark hair again

"Don't leave me, ever!" she said, and then was asleep, my arm for a
pillow

Arm for a pillow, fragrance of hair—since lying with you, then parting, how many spring nights have I slept?

By a window where evening silence falls and keeps falling, our lips
meet—do not ask how long

Used to lying together, the two of us have nothing to say, and grieve;
by this house cherries bloom

Such loneliness! if I could carve in stone a giant, bound, wordless,
standing

ISHIKAWA TAKUBOKU

(1886–1912)

FORTY-SEVEN TANKA IN THREE LINES[1]

From *Handful of Sand*[2]

By the eastern sea, on the white sand of an island beach,
drowned in tears
I play with a crab

On the sand of a sandhill I lie on my belly
and think this day
of the pain of first love as something remote

Sadness of the lifeless sand:
rustling,
it falls through my fingers as I clutch it

For fun I carried mother on my back,
she was so light I cried
and couldn't take three steps

Heart felt
as if being sucked into a very dark hole,
tired I was, asleep

---

[1] By Ishikawa's time, the convention of printing tanka in one line had been firmly established. Toki Aika's *NAKIWARAI* (Crying and Laughing), published in 1910, was the first to break the convention in book-length form. Later in the same year Ishikawa followed the practice with *Handful of Sand*.

[2] Ishikawa's first collection of tanka published in December 1910.

"Die for a thing like that?"
"Live for a thing like that?"
Stop, stop arguing

The little man I always see on the streetcar—
his cutting look
bothers me these days

Coming in front of a mirror store
I'm startled:
how shabby I look, walking

All I'd wanted was to get on a train.
Off the train
I have nowhere to go

It rains,
and the people of my house look depressed.
Rain, clear up

Act like a wizard
and the desolation afterward—
what can I compare it to?

No better than the ordinary in talent
this friend—
pitiful, his deep bitterness

Uneventfully
and pleasantly I go on putting on weight.
Something's missing these days

I get anxious to die, at times.
I hide away in a privy
and make frightening faces

Let down, I stood in the hall:
violently I pushed the door,
and it just opened

The water spurting out of a pump
looks so good.
For a while, feeling youthful, I watch

Name known, but no relations or kin in this place—
the inn's cheap,
like my house

Calling out the station name as if singing,
that young station hand
with mild eyes that I cannot forget

Even while pillowing her lap
my thoughts
are all about myself

That creepy feeling you have
putting on dirty socks—
some memories are like that

When was it?
I heard it in a dream and was happy.
That voice is something I haven't heard for a long time

I said those words casually,
and you heard them casually, I guess.
There's nothing more to it

Parted, I came away and years have passed;
each year my love increases
because of you

Taking off my gloves, my hands stop—
what is it?
a memory flits through my mind

A useless letter, long, yet to be finished,
I suddenly miss people
and go to town

Like a weak-minded scout,
fearful,
in the late-night town, alone I take a walk

That kiss from the past—
startled:
a sycamore leaf falling had touched me

From *Sad Toys*[3]

Though I close my eyes,
nothing comes to my mind.
        Desolate, and again, I open my eyes.

[3] Second collection of tanka published posthumously in June 1912.

On the way, a whim, I changed my mind,
I didn't go to work today either
but wandered around the riverside.

I got out and for about five blocks
I walked like someone
with something to do, but—

Wishing someone would
bawl me out to his heart's content.
What's the matter with me?

I believe in the coming of a new tomorrow, I say—
these, my words,
aren't false, and still—

Come to think of it,
there seems to be something I really want, but there isn't.
I polish my pipe.

I look at my dirty hands—
it's just like
coming face to face with my mind these days.

Everyone's
heading in the same direction.
And me, watching from the side.

For thinking somehow tomorrow will bring something good,
I scold myself
and go to sleep.

Cover myself with the quilt,
pull up my legs,
and stick out my tongue, at no one in particular.

Chin buried in the collar of my overcoat,
late at night I stop and listen.
So much like that voice.

Somehow,
I feel there are more people than I expect,
who think the way I do.

By accident I broke a rice bowl,
and thought, "It feels good to break things,"
again, this morning.

Those days I didn't even notice
the misspellings, so many of them,
in these old love letters!

Old letters!
I was on such familiar terms
with that guy, five years ago.

I push the door and step out—
to the eye of a patient, endless,
the long hall.

The nurse's hand taking my pulse,
warm some days,
cold and hard other days.

A vague sadness
comes with night
stealthily and sits on my bed.

As if my thoughts were secretly listened to,
I jerked my chest away—
from the stethoscope.

I scolded my child,
weeping, she went to sleep.
    I touched her face asleep with her mouth open a little.

SAITŌ MOKICHI

(1882–1953)

Mother Dies[1]

PART I

Broad leaves turn themselves on the trees, gleaming, hiding, never restful

As the drooping flowers of white wisteria fall, it touches me—the way their pods now begin to show

Mother far down the road—to have a look, to have a look at her life, I simply hurry

In the sun-shining capital, at night, looking at the redness of lights, my heart does not settle down

As I hurry to have a look at mother's eyes, sweat comes out on my brow

The way I go out of the capital where lamps are red—will people think I'm going on a casual trip?

Faintly have I slept, in the running train, have I slept?

---

[1] A sequence of tanka Saitō wrote in May 1913 when his mother, Iku, died.

As snow blazes on Mount Azuma, the train has entered the country
of my mother far down the road

Morning cold, frost formed on mulberry leaves, getting closer to
mother, the train runs

From the blue light shimmering over the marshes do you say my
melancholy comes? LAKE HAKURYŪ

At the Upper Mountain station I got off and saw my brother, young,
now a widower

PART 2

From far off I have brought medicines, she watches me because I am
her son

I go near her, she watches me and says, she says something because I
am her son

On the vermilion-lacquered spear on the wall-beam I see dust; close
to mother, in the morning, I see it

I have offered prayers to the sunlight coming out of the mountains.
The flowers of columbines continue to bloom

Lying by mother, who's close to death, night hushed, frogs in distant
paddies are heard in heaven

Mulberry fragrance drifts blue at daybreak, it is unbearable, I call to
my mother

Going near the eyes of mother who's close to death, I said, Columbines are blooming

It's spring, light flows, and I'm sad. Perhaps by now, gnats are born in the grassfields

As I rub the forehead of mother who's close to death, my tears keep flowing—as I come to myself

Away from mother's eyes, for some time, I watch—how sad the silkworms asleep

My mother, my mother who is going to die, mother with sagging breasts who gave birth to me

With two red-throated swallows perched on the crossbeam, mother with sagging breasts comes to death

People who are alive gathered and saw my mother's life go to death, go to death

I come alone, stand in the silkworm room, and my loneliness becomes extreme

PART 3

Young oak leaves shine and turn—unreal, these mountain silkworms are blue, mountain silkworms just born

The sunlight filters in, mottled, and is saddening. The mountain silkworms are still small

On the funeral road, sorrel blossoms, bemused, on the funeral road, were they not falling?

Along the road through the field where windflowers with red mouths bloomed, light flowed as we went

I hold the fire with which I must cremate my mother. In the skies there is nothing to look at

Under the night sky where the stars are, red and red, mulberry mother went on burning

Deep into the night, I looked at the funeral fire of my mother; simply red, it went on burning

As we guard the funeral fire, this night becomes old. The heavens tonight are awesome

We guard the fire, the night is old; my younger brother sadly sings a song of life

Single-minded, I will keep watch over the faintly red rising smoke, the smoke

We have picked mother in the ashes. In the morning sunrise we have picked mother

The bone fragments we carefully collected on rhubarb leaves—we have put them all away in the urn

Languidly into heaven a lark climbs singing; on snow-mottled mountains no clouds stay

Both stinkweed and thistle flowers are found burnt, as heaven dawns
at the crematorium

PART 4

Because spring of heat haze has come, tree buds have all sprouted
near the mountain where I go on walking

On the mountain where faint akebia flowers fall, a wild dove coos,
its voice lonely

Near the mountain a pheasant called. Near the mountain hot water
comes out—how sad it is

In sour hot water, body sadly immersed, I saw light blaze in the sky

Coming back to my birthplace, the village where my house is, I pickle
the flowers of white wisteria and eat them

The snow left unmelted on the mountainside is saddening; I push apart
bamboo grass, hurrying

Pushing through the bamboo grass field, I go and keep going, though
I am not looking for mother

The acid hot water that comes out at the foot of a fire mountain—I
was immersed in it one night, sad

Near the mountain where faint flowers fall, mists, flowing, have gone
away

A fire burning far off on a mountain beyond the valley—its scarlet,
and my mother, saddening

On the mountainside, in the distance, fire burning red and red, its
smoke moves though I'm sad

Picking buds of devil's walking sticks, I walked. The pass by the
mountain narrowed as I walked, lonely

Bearing up with loneliness I push into the mountain; there, darkly,
akebia flowers are falling

Far into the view, avalanching down the mountainside, blooming mag-
nolias appear faint

Thinking the mottled snow on Mount Zaō may blaze, as evening came,
I went to a cliff

It touched me—the way the rain was falling. The earth near the mountain was red—how pitiful it was

The cloud flowing in distant heaven has no soul-ending life, they say,
and that makes me sad

Between the mountains the sun has set, all of it; now the fragrance of
hot water pervades, drifts

After sleeping two nights at a hot spring, I ate water shield and felt
sorrow again

Because I'm on the mountain I eat bamboo shoots. Mulberry mother,
mulberry mother! (WRITTEN IN MAY)

TAKAMURA KŌTARŌ

(1883–1956)

To Someone[1]

No, no, I don't like it
your going away—

Like fruit coming before blossom
like bud sprouting before seed
like spring immediately following summer,
that's not logical, please don't do
so unnatural a thing.
A husband as if cast in a mold
and you with your smooth round handwriting,
the mere thought makes me cry.
You, who are timid as a bird,
willful as a gale,
you are to be a bride

No, no, I don't like it
your going away—

How can you so easily,
how shall I say, as it were
put yourself on sale?
Because you *are* putting yourself on sale.
From the world of one person
to the world of millions,
and yielding to a man,
yielding to nonsense,
what an ugly thing to do.
It's like a Titian
set out for shoppers in Tsurumaki-chō.
I am lonely, sad.

---

[1] Written to Naganuma Chieko (1886–1938), whom Takamura married in December 1914. Chieko became insane and died in a hospital.

Though I really don't know what to do,
it's just like watching
the large gloxinia you gave me rot,
like watching it leave me and rot,
like seeing a bird fly off into the sky
not knowing where to,
it's the sad abandon of a wave as it shatters,
brittle, lonely, searing
—But it isn't love
Mother of God
No, it isn't it isn't.
I don't know what it is
but I don't like it
your going away—
you're going away to be a bride,
offering yourself to the will of a man you don't even know

In Adoration of Love

Body's desire that knows no end
the terrible power of a rising tide—
in the fire that flares up still more, perspiring,
salamanders twist and turn, dancing.

The ceaseless snow throws a feast of *vol nuptial* late at night
and shouts out joy in the hushed air.
Shattered by beauty and power
we then immerse ourselves in an esoteric flow
breathe in an aroused rosy haze
and reflected on the jewels in Indra's net[2]
mold our lives inexhaustibly.

The cradling demon's power that lurks in winter
and the raw heat of sprouts that bud in winter—
what burns inside everything pulsates with time
and lets electric currents of ecstasy echo through our bodies.

[2] Indra is the principal deity in Vedic mythology; the god of thunder
and hail, later the god of warfare. In Buddhist tradition, each jewel in
Indra's net contains the reflection of every other jewel in the net and is
likewise reflected in its entirety in each of them.

Our skins wake ferociously
our bowels thrash about in the glee of existence
hair becomes phosphorescent
fingers acquire their own lives and crawl clinging all over the bodies
the world of chaos, of sincerity, that stores the word
swiftly reveals itself above us.

Full of light
full of happiness
all discriminations circle a single sound
poison and manna share a box
unbearable pain convolves our bodies
supreme rapture illuminates the mystery, the labyrinth.

Buried warm under the snow
we melt in natural elements
feed on endless earthly love
and praise our life, in the distance.

Cathedral in the Thrashing Rain

O another deluge of wind and rain.
Collar turned up, getting drenched in this splashing rain,
and looking up at you—it's me,
me who never fails to come here once a day.
It's that Japanese.
This morning
about daybreak the storm suddenly went violent, terrible,
and now is blowing through Paris from one end to the other.
I have yet to know the directions of this land.
I don't even know which way this storm is facing, raging over the Ile-
de-France.
Only because even today I wanted to stand here
and look up at you, Cathedral of Notre-Dame de Paris,
I came, getting drenched,
only because I wanted to touch you,
only because I wanted to kiss your skin, the stone, unknown to anyone.

O another deluge of wind and rain.
Though it's already time for morning coffee,
a little while ago I looked from the Pont-Neuf,

the boats on the Seine were still tied up to the banks, like puppies.
The leaves of the gentle plane trees shining in their autumn colors on
    the banks
are like flocks of buntings chased by hawks,
glittering, scattering, flying about.
The chestnut trees behind you,
each time their heads, spreading branches, get mussed up,
starling-colored leaves dance up into the sky.
By the splashes of rain blowing down, they are then
dashed like arrows on the cobblestones and burst.
All the square is like a pattern,
filled with flowing silver water, and isles of golden-brown burnt-
    brown leaves.
Then there's the noise of the downpour resounding in my pores.
It's the noise of something roaring, grinding.
As soon as human beings hushed up
all the other things in Paris began at once to shout in chorus.
With golden plane tree leaves falling all over my coat,
I'm standing in it.
Storms are like this in my country, Japan, too.
Only, we don't see you soaring.

O Notre-Dame, Notre-Dame,
rock-like, mountain-like, eagle-like, crouching-lion-like cathedral,
reef sunk in vast air,
square pillar of Paris,
sealed by the blinding splatters of rain,
taking the slapping wind head-on,
O soaring in front, Notre-Dame de Paris,
it's me, looking up at you.
It's that Japanese.
My heart trembles now that I see you.
Looking at your form like a tragedy,
a young man from a far distant country is moved.
Not at all knowing for what reason, my heart pounds
in unison with the screams in the air, resounds as if terrified.

O another deluge of wind and rain.
How furious these four elements of nature
that would, if they could, snuff out your existence, return you to the
    original void.
Smoking phosphorescent shafts of rain.
Scales of the clouds flying, mottled, not quite touching your top.

Blasts of the persistent clinging gales, trying to snap off at least one
column of the bell tower.
Innumerable, small, shining elves that bump against the rose window
dentils, burst, flow, and flap about.
Only the gargoyles, the monsters on the high architectural rims, visible between splashes,
taking on the flitting flocks of elves,
raise their paws, crane their necks,
bare their teeth, blow out burning fountains of breath.
The many lines of mysterious stone saints make eerie gestures, nod to
one another,
the enormous arc-boutants on the side reveal their familiar upper arms.
To their many arms that form arcs aslant,
O what a concentration of wind and rain.
I hear the reverberation of the organ during Mass.
How is the rooster at the tip of the tall slender steeple doing?
Flapping curtains of water have dammed up all directions.
You stand in them.

O another deluge of wind and rain.
A cathedral standing in it
solid with the weight of eight centuries,
a mass of many millions of stones piled and carved by believers of old.
A great scaffold for truth, sincerity, and eternity.
You stand wordless,
you stand, taking on, motionless, the force of the blasting storm.
You know the strength of nature's force,
have the composure of mind to leave yourself to the rampant wind
and rain, till the earth shakes.
O rusty gray iron-colored skin of stone glistening in the rain.
My hands touching it
feel as if they were touching Esmeralda's white palm.
And along with Esmeralda, the monster
Quasimodo who delights in storms is hiding near some molding.
A just soul crammed into an ugly body,
a firm strength,
silently absorbing on his back
the words of those who wounded, those who whipped, those who
would do wrong, those who despised, and not to say the least,
those who were petty,
he ground himself to serve God,

O only you could give birth to that monster.
How many non-hunchbacked, non-deformed, more joyful, more daily
     Quasimodos
have been born since then
and nurtured on your breast full of solemn, yet protective motherly
     love, and gentle.

O Cathedral in the thrashing rain.
Baton swung down abruptly at the sudden
turn of the wind and rain that took a breath and has driven itself
     harder,
all the instruments of the heavens gone berserk,
the dance swirls around them.
O Cathedral, you who at such a moment keep ever more silent and
     soar,
Cathedral, you who watch motionless the houses of Paris suffering the
     storm,
please do not think me rude,
who, hands on your cornerstone,
has his hot cheek pressed on your skin,
it's me, the drunken one.
It's that Japanese.

Comic Verse[3]

As long as you've got inherited provisions stored in your cellar,
go ahead and look hungry,
play at being poor to be chic.
When you tire of the Parthenon and Notre-Dame,
fine, go on to lanterns, Mount Fuji,
Hiroshige, Harunobu, Bashō, Buson,
throw in Taiga, back to Sesshū,[4]
praise the blank paper.
Pick, as you please,
tanka or haikai.

[3] Its first published title was "Comic Verse Given to a Certain Kind of
European Poets Who Amuse Themselves with the Orient."
[4] Andō Hiroshige (1797–1858), Suzuki Harunobu (1725–1770), Ike
Taiga (1723–1776), and Sesshū (1420–1506) are all painters.

But I, who know the thing about your cellar,
won't join your playing at being chic.
You may tap me on the shoulder,
but I won't feel good.
With your wooly hands
you may tug at me
and try to seat me on the Great Road to cheap instant Enlightenment,
but I'll have to excuse myself.
You see, like those fellows in the *Kojiki*,
I just like to shuffle about in the sun;
to tell you the truth,
—*Japon, Japon, Japon, Japon, Japon*[5]—
ah, you're too noisy.

Knife Whetter

Wordless, he is whetting a knife.
Sun already going, he's still whetting it.
Pressing the back blade and the front,
and changing the water, he's again whetting it.
What on earth he wants to make,
as if he did not know even that,
with split-second concentration on his brow,
he whets the knife under green leaves.
His sleeves gradually tear,
his mustache turns white.
Fury, necessity, or innocence,
or is he chasing an infinite sequence
simply, prodigiously?

Spouting Whale

As May came to the Kuroshio off Mount Kinka,
the sea suddenly enlarged,
brightened like a tent of blue cellophane.
The waves flowing, glittering, batted their eyes at the midday sun,
their course getting somewhat closer to the land.

---

[5] "Japon" happens to sound like an onomatopoeic Japanese word that means something like "splosh."

The sperm whale, after spouting once, dived again deeply,
put the giant weight of his head on the water;
pleased with this warm current, salt-thick and smooth,
he let his mind loose and indulged in endless thoughts.
That I am not a dolphin, not a grampus,
but a sperm whale,
makes me the happiest thing in the world, the whale thinks.
Ah, you can't beat the present.
The whale looks at nothing but the present.
He always tastes the peak of existence,
he doesn't touch hypotheses, he doesn't get into metaphysics.
Drunk with thoughts resembling drowsy sleep,
the whale senses the unknown land drawing near
and is half afraid, half glad.
Once again he rose up, and into the May sky
raised a full-breath spout, a rainbow.
On the Ojika Peninsula, at Ayukawa Port, the siren is on,
but this massive optimist is utterly unaware of it.

Lemon Elegy[6]

So intensely you had been waiting for lemon.
In the sad, white, light deathbed
you took that one lemon from my hand
and bit it sharply with your bright teeth.
A fragrance rose the color of topaz.
Those heavenly drops of juice
flashed you back to sanity.
Your eyes, blue and transparent, slightly smiled.
You grasped my hand, how vigorous you were.
There was a storm in your throat
but just at the end
Chieko found Chieko again,
all life's love into one moment fallen.
And then once
as once you did on a mountaintop, you let out a great sigh
and with it your engine stopped.
By the cherry blossoms in front of your photograph
today, too, I will put a cool fresh lemon.

[6] Chieko died on October 5, 1938.

Beautiful Dead Leaf

In front of a police box I picked up a dead leaf.
A large dead leaf of a plane tree.
By its stem I hold it against the sun:
half gold, half verdigris
dye this slightly crinkled feather fan.
I like dead leaves of any kind.
Always abundant and warm,
rustling, never cloying,
they fly off if wind blows,
and before you know it, again pile up all around
and are bathing in autumn sun.
The smell of dead leaves is the smell of your native land,
above all, how friendly the blue smoke of burning leaves.
Ah how graceful those people of old
who kindled crimson leaves in the woods and heated their wine.[7]
Although there's no wine to heat now,
friend, burn the dead leaves piled mountainously in your garden
and obtain potash for the farm behind your house.[8]
I'm thinking how I should carve in wood
this leaf of a plane tree that I have picked.

Shōan Temple

At Shōanji, an old temple of the Jōdo sect,
in the rustic town called Hanamaki, Ōshū,
on the anniversary of your death, in recurring autumn showers,
I had a truly modest service for you.
The town of Hanamaki was also bombed
and the Shōanji, completely burnt,
was a shed, a two-mat place
with an altar in it.
The rain blew in through the papered doors behind me,
wetting the skirt of the priest's robe.

---

[7] Allusion to a poem of Po Chü-yi (772–846), "Seeing Wang Eighteen (Wang Chin-fu) off on His Return to the Mountains and Writing of the Old Days at the Hsien-yu Temple," which has the lines: "Among the trees we heated wine, burning red autumn leaves;/on the stone we inscribed poems, brushing away the green moss."

[8] The poem was written toward the end of World War II, when food shortages were becoming acute and city residents were encouraged to plant vegetables in their gardens and backyards.

The priest read the One Page on Salvation[9]
as prescribed, in a quiet voice, feelingly.
The terrifying truth of the confession of someone in the ancient past
who cast himself out, believing in the Buddha,
struck me, living now, as very much alive.
In front of the Buddha in the shed-altar of Shōanji
I again remembered intensely
the procession of your life, which, your trust boundless,
burned up for me.

From "A Brief History of Imbecility"[10]

Sculpting in the Imperial Presence[11]

Father, unusually tense,
cleaned his workshop and carved wood for seals.
In an instant he finished and showed the result to everyone,
including me, a child.
On the splendid stem of cherry wood
was a deer carved with a single knife.
His society was going to have an Imperial visit the next day,
and he was ordered to sculpt in the Imperial presence, father said.
The carving was a rehearsal.
Father took a bath, purified his body,
and the next day had flints sparked on himself and left home.
He's going to show it to the Emperor, in person.
So fortunate for him.
"May he be free from any mistakes,"
mother said, and prayed at the Buddhist altar.
A child, I was much agitated
that he didn't come home though the sun had set.
At the rickshawman's cry, "He's home,"
I flew to the front door.

---

[9] A "one-page" commentary on the Jōdo sect by its founder, Hōnen (1133–1212).

[10] A sequence of twenty autobiographical poems written partly in response to accusations of "war responsibilities" raised against Takamura for his activities in support of the military before and during World War II. The three poems that follow are from the sequence, written in 1947.

[11] Takamura's father, Kōun (1852–1934), was a sculptor. The emperor in the poem is the Meiji emperor, Mutsuhito (1852–1912).

Cooperative Council[12]

A cooperative council was going to be set up
to convey people's wishes upward, I was told.
A man whom I had long respected came one night,
talked at length about the faults of the nation as it was,
and told me to become a member.
It wasn't an age when one could be surprised at abruptness.
If people's wishes could be conveyed upward,
I had a mountain of things I wanted conveyed upward.
In the end I became a member.
Once it begins to turn,
all the cogs move, like it or not.
Would people's wishes brought in by individuals
be conveyed upward?
A weird sort of pressure, on the contrary,
pressed down from above.
The cooperative council became an organization
that followed a certain will.
From the fifth floor where the council was,
I could see the mausoleumlike Diet.
The poem in which I mentioned the mausoleumlike Diet
was returned from a newspaper with a red mark.
The council had a suffocating air,
the wild animal inside me
was poisoned by the smell of bureaucracy
and roared, every night, toward a deserted land.

[12] The council is the Central Cooperative Council, which was set up to
aid military causes.

The Day of Pearl Harbor[18]

What I heard before the declaration of war
was that there was a battle near Hawaii.
At last we're going to fight in the Pacific.
Listening to the Imperial Proclamation, I trembled.
At this grave moment
my brains were distilled by an alembic,
yesterday became a remote past,
the remote past became now.
The Emperor in danger:
that phrase alone
determined everything for me.
The childhood grandfather was there,
father and mother were there.
The family clouds and mists of my boyhood days
rose and filled my room.
My ears were crammed with ancestors' voices:
His Majesty! His Majesty!
my consciousness panted, reeled.
Now I can only give myself up.
I'll protect His Majesty.
I'll give up the poetic and write poems.
I'll write a record.
I'll prevent the wastage of compatriots, if possible.
That night, in Komagome Heights where Jupiter shone large,
simply, seriously, so did I decide.

[18] Japan attacked Pearl Harbor on December 8 (Japan time), 1941.

HAGIWARA SAKUTARŌ

(1886–1942)[1]

Night Train

In the dawn twilight,
cold on the glass door a fingerprint,
the vague whitening rim of hills
is as funereal as mercury
but the travelers still not awake from sleep,
tired sighs of lamps alone are clamorous.
When the cloying smell of varnish
or the smoke of cigarettes, there, not there,
feels desolate to the tongue ravaged on the night train,
how badly the married woman must take it upon herself and grieve.
Have we still not passed Yamashina?
Loosening the metal valve of her air pillow
and letting it sigh—the way she feels;
the two of us, sad, nestle to each other
and look out the window of the train near the eastern clouds:
in a mountain village, place unknown,
flowers of columbines blooming quite white.

Cherry

Under cherries many people have gathered,
what are they doing to amuse themselves?
I too stood under a cherry tree, just to see,
but my heart was cold,
as petals scattered and fell, only tears came down.
How touching,
now at the noon of a spring day
when I did not force myself to watch sad things.

---

[1] Roughly in the order in which they first appeared in magazines.

On a Trip

Though I think I'd like to go to France,
France is too far away;
I would at least put on a new jacket
and go on a carefree trip.
When the train takes a mountain path
I would lean on an aquamarine window
and think, alone, of happy things
on a May morning when eastern clouds gather
leaving myself to my heart with fresh young grass flaring.

An Impression of Early Summer

Because insect blood flows and seeps in
and everything exhausts its semen
this earth is bright,
from a woman's white fingers
a gold coin slips down on my hand.
The time is the beginning of May.
Infant trees swim out onto the streets,
chirping, buds grow out to flare.
Look, the landscape has come, valiantly flowing;
floating up distinctly in the blue sky
it really clearly reflects people's shadows.

Bamboo

Something straight growing on the ground,
something sharp, blue, growing on the ground,
piercing the frozen winter,
in morning's empty path where its green leaves glisten,
shedding tears,
shedding the tears,
now repentance over, from above its shoulders,
blurred bamboo roots spreading,
something sharp, blue, growing on the ground.

Sickly Face at the Bottom of the Ground

At the bottom of the ground a face emerging,
a lonely invalid's face emerging.

In the dark at the bottom of the ground,
soft vernal grass stalks beginning to flare,
rats' nest beginning to flare,
and entangled with the nest,
innumerable hairs beginning to tremble,
time the winter solstice,
from the lonely sickly ground,
roots of thin blue bamboo beginning to grow,
beginning to grow,
and that, looking truly pathetic,
looking blurred,
looking truly, truly, pathetic.

In the dark at the bottom of the ground,
a lonely invalid's face emerging.

Spring Night

Things like littlenecks,
things like quahogs,
things like water-fleas,
these organisms, bodies buried in sand,
out of nowhere,
hands like silk threads innumerably grow,
hands' slender hairs move as the waves do.
A pity, on this lukewarm spring night,
purling the brine flows,
over the organisms water flows,
even the tongues of clams, flickering, looking sad,
as I look around at the distant beach,
along the wet beach path,
a row of invalids, bodies below their waists missing, is walking,
walking unsteadily.
Ah, over the hair of those human beings as well,
passes the spring night haze, all over, deeply,
rolling, rolling in,
this white row of waves is ripples.

Sunny Spring

Ah, spring comes from afar, smoky,
under puffy swollen willow buds,
eager to press its gentle lips close,
and suck in a virgin's kiss,
spring comes from afar riding a *rubber*-wheeled rickshaw.
In the absent-minded landscape,
the white rickshawman's legs hurry,
but going, going, the wheels turn backward,
gradually the shafts begin to lift away from the ground,
then too, the good passenger is *oddly* unsteady about his waist,
all of which looks much too precarious—so saying,
at the least expected moment the spring gives a snow-white yawn.

Lover of Love

I painted *rouge* on my lips,
and kissed the trunk of a new birch,
even if I were a handsome man,
on my chest are no breasts like *rubber balls*,
from my skin rises no fragrance of fine-*textured* powder,
I am a wizened man of ill-fate,
ah, what a pitiable man,
in today's balmy early summer field,
in a stand of glistening trees,
I slipped on my hands sky-blue gloves,
put around my waist something like a *corset*,
smeared on my nape something like nape-powder,
thus hushed, assuming a coquettish *pose*,
as young girls do,
I cocked my head a little,
and kissed the trunk of a new birch,
I painted rosy rouge on my lips,
and clung to a tall tree of snowy white.

White Public Benches

Along a path in the woods,
is a row of snow-white public benches,
around there, on the lonely mountain,
shades of green are very deep,
looking through the woods,
there too a lonely stand of trees is visible,
and a row of benches with elegant, snow-white legs.

The Hand Is a Cake

Look at the way it's truly lovely, and ample
look at the way it's round and full, swelling like a cake
take the fingers—they are svelte, *graceful*
and just like tiny blue fish
the way they are gently wafting, I can't stand it
ah, I want to kiss the hand
want to put my mouth on it and eat the whole thing
what clear-cut roundness of the fingertips
look at the air of this mysterious flower blooming in the valley be-
    tween the fingers
its fragrance is like musk, and it looks like a slightly perspiring peach
    blossom.
A woman's fingers ever so elegantly polished
fingers perfectly fitting, snow-white and slender
fingers that hit the *piano* keys
fingers for labor that hold a needle and sew silk
the way fingers work—they snuggle up to a shoulder yearning for love
let their nailtips touch lightly
the particularly sensitive skin
scratch it with nails lightly
and pretend to press it lightly, firmly
the joy of love that trembles visibly, the fingers that tickle violently,
    shrewdly
the standoffish and mean forefinger
tricks of the cowardly, spry small finger
the thumb's obese beauty and truculent brutality
ah, I would like to gratefully receive one smoothly polished finger
have it slip into my mouth and suck on it, suck on it forever and ever
the back of the hand is the soft rise of a *waffle*

and the fingers the cold appetite of crystal sugar
ah, this appetite
a childlike, greedy, shameless appetite.

Twilight Room

The tired heart sleeps well through the night
I sleep well
the owner of a lonely heart in flannel
what is it, there quietly moving in dream a suckling
freezing from cold a fly's whimper
bumm bumm bumm bumm bumm bumm.

I feel sorrow over the dust-white light of this room
I feel lonely about the powerless tremor of this life.

My love
you're sitting there, by the pillow on my bed
my love, you're sitting there.
Your slender neck
your hair you've grown long
listen, my gentle love
please stroke my miserable fate
I feel sorrow
I watch
there a painful emotion
the melancholy of a landscape that sickens and expands
ah, from a corner of the lachrymose room, tired, wandering over the
      floor, the ghost of a fly
bumm bumm bumm bumm bumm bumm.

My love
maiden sitting by the pillow in my room
what do you see there
what do you see about me
are you looking at my emaciated body, the shadow that thought left
      in the past
my love
as if smelling a sour chrysanthemum
I smell your mysterious passion, your pale faith
come let us unite ourselves body to body
your white hand laid on this, hand laid on this warm thing.

My love
the light in this quiet room is faintly red
there again a powerless fly's whimper
bumm bumm bumm bumm bumm bumm.
My love
my piteous heart is like a child clinging to your hands and your breast
my love
my love.

The Army

impression of a passing army

This weighty machine
presses the ground down solidly;
The ground, powerfully trodden
reacts
and raises swirls of dust.
Look at this giant-weight sturdy machine
passing through the daylight;
it's a dark-blue, greasy
fantastic, stubborn giant-body
a gigantic group's power machine
that presses the ground down solidly.
thud, thud, crash, crash
crunch, crunch, crunch, crunch.

Wherever this vicious machine goes
the landscape discolors
turns yellow,
the sun depresses in the sky
the will becomes heavily overwhelmed.
thud, thud, crash, crash
one two, one two.

O this weight-pressing
gigantic pitch-black crowd
just as a wave pushes back and comes back
through the muddied flow of heavy oil
ranks of heated gun-barrels pass
innumerable tired faces pass.
 crunch, crunch, crunch, crunch
 one two, one two.

Under the dark oppressive sky
a heavy machine of steel passes
innumerable dilated pupils pass;
the pupils, open in the heat,
rove vainly, powerlessly
in the shadow of the yellow landscape, the terror.
Becomes fatigued
exhausted
dazzled.
 one two, one two
 mark time!

O these multitudinous pupils
above the road where dust hangs low
they see the sunlight of melancholy
see the white illusion, the city streets
feelings darkly incarcerated.
 thud, thud, craunch, craunch
 crunch, crunch, crunch, crunch.

Look at the dark-blue, fantastically greasy
giant-weight sturdy machine
now moving through the daylight;
wherever this vicious machine tramples
the landscape discolors
the air turns yellow
the will becomes heavily overwhelmed.
 thud, thud, craunch, craunch
 thud, thump, crash, crash.
 one two, one two.

In the Horse Carriage

In the horse carriage
I've fallen asleep peacefully.
Beautiful lady,
do not shake me awake;
we've run through streets with bright lamps,
passed the countryside of cool green shades
and before we know it the smell of the sea flutters near where we're
    going.
Ah, with the sound of hoofs clopping,
I pursue reality in reality;
beautiful lady,
until we come to the inns' flowering eaves,
do not shake me awake.

A Barren Area

With strollers loitering
here, you see, is a street in a lonesome alley of the eighteenth century
    or so,
blue, green, red flags moving flabbily,
in a bay window of the past a tin hat is on display.
Why is there a town like this, so deep with feeling?
the sundial's time has stopped,
there's no store or market to shop in, anywhere.
Things like fragments of an old shell were dug out
and they were, you see, rusted black in the sand of the fort grounds
I don't know what to do
I'll be walking only the barren areas where human beings live their
    lives like this.
The figures of elderly ladies
are much like ducks and chickens
and in that part of the retina that reflects, a scarlet cloth flutters.
What a sad twilight;
things like elephants swarm
and roam here and there in front of the post office.
"Ah where shall I send my epistolary letter?"

Out of the Inner Shell of a Certain Landscape

Where shall this lust open its mouth?
A big sea turtle is asleep like a mountain
and near the Paleozoic sea
the shell of a giant clam weighing about four tons in thickness is sur-
    veying it all.
What slow dark sunrays!
From behind the island at each cape misty with sprays
a mysterious hospital ship form emerges
and it is, you see, dragging the hawser of its sunken anchor.
Listen! my love
how long are we going to sit here, side by side on these sad rocks here
the sun is boundlessly distant
and where the rays of light beam in, low booms a conch sounds.
My love!
As we sit lonely like this, side by side like penguins
both love and my liver seem to turn into *icicles*.
My gentle love!
I no longer have hope or the consolation of a peaceful life, you know;
everything drives me to maddening melancholy
oddly the seasons turn and turn
and both spring and damson plums have already been entangled in a
    messy net of delusions.
What shall I do, my love!
We are trembling like large clam flesh on the seashore of a terrifying
    solitude.
Besides, there's no way of speaking of lust
and you don't understand such a helpless heart, do you? My love!

Pinks and a Blue Cat

Under the flowers of green pinks, one illusory corpse sleeps
her black hair flows on the floor
arms and legs feebly thrown out, she lies supine on the bed;
under the curtain of this secret chamber
surreptitious, noiseless, comes up one pale mysterious lust.
It's tormented by stifling musk
it suffers, is bashful, and knows all the sensual thoughts.

Ah, now, close to the lamp of spring night
happily it sniffs and fondles the body of dead wax.
It smears oil on the gentle lips and fondles the silky white limbs.
It's one lonesome blue cat
love, do not be frightened by a dream demon into blaming me for this
    playfulness.

The Corpse of a Cat

to a woman I call Ula

In a spongelike landscape,
and moist, swollen with dampness.
Nowhere are humans and beasts visible,
and an oddly sad-looking waterwheel seems to be weeping.
Then too, from under a blurring willow,
a gentle person you are waiting for is visible, I say.
Her body wrapped in a light shawl,
dragging a beauteous, gaseous costume,
and roaming quietly like a spirit.
Ah Ula, lonely woman!
"You, you're always late, aren't you?"
We have no past, have no future,
then too, we've disappeared from actual things. . . .
Ula!
In this landscape that looks peculiar,
why don't you bury the corpse of the muddy cat?

The Octopus That Does Not Die

In a water tank of a certain aquarium, for a long while, a starving octopus was kept. In the underground dim rock shadows, pale crystal ceiling beams always drifted sadly.

Everyone, all of the people, had forgotten about this dim water tank. It was thought that the octopus had died long ago. And only rotten sea water stagnated in the dusty sunlight, always in the glass window of the tank.

However, the animal did not die. The octopus had been hiding in the rock shadows. And when he woke up, in the unhappy forgotten tank, for days on end he had to endure terrible starvation. When he had nothing to eat anywhere and had completely run out of food, he tore off his legs and ate them. First, one leg. Then, another. Then, finally, when all of them were utterly gone, this time he turned his body inside out and started to eat a part of his intestines. Little by little from one part to another. In neat order.

Thus the octopus finished eating all of his body. Epidermis, brains, stomach. Every part, leaving nothing at all. Completely.

One morning, when the keeper happened to come by, he found that the water tank was empty. Behind the clouded dusty glass, transparent indigo salt water and willowy seaweed were moving. And in no corner of any rock was the creature visible any more. The octopus had actually, utterly, vanished.

However, the octopus did not die. Even after disappearing, he still was eternally alive *there*. In the antiquated, empty, forgotten water tank of the aquarium. Eternally—most likely through many centuries—an animal with a horrible deficiency and dissatisfaction was alive, invisible to the human eye.

Yoshiwara

Surrounded with tall board fences
it's a shadowy gloomy district.
Still, in a vacant lot a ditch flows
a tree grows
and everywhere the smell of white carbolic acid.
Yoshiwara!
Like a frog lying dead on an embankment
it's a pleasure zone, its belly exposed white.

In the sad enclosure of board fences
I heard the woman I fancy weeping
all night long.
Then she ate indigestible noodles
and was lying under a sooty electric lamp.
"Come again, please!"

Even on a day of cloudy weather of despair
a photograph is posted on the brothel billboard.

OZAKI HŌSAI

(1885–1926)

ONE HUNDRED HAIKU IN FREE FORM

The sea becomes light, a window is open

The sound of the florist's scissors, I'm sleeping late into morning

I walk over a moistened bridge, how bright the rain

The Lord Buddha's yellow flowers, without fragrance

The snow has cleared, the sun shines on children's voices

Children are shouting, in the evening sun, jostling houses

Holding a child's hand intently, my big hand

In the great wind, in the sky, ringing, a bell

After scolding my wife, I go out into the hot sun

I release a turtle, into noon-deep water

Here's a dying invalid, listening to maneuver gunshots

Mountain water, trickly, washes rice bowls snow-white

One or two, immersed in darkness and returning, people

He moves his quiet shadow and pours tea for his guest

Moonlit night I return and begin a long letter

I look back at the shore, not one of my footprints

In the darkness of the well I find my face

In a pond of silence a turtle floats to the top

Just the ants at the bottom of the burning sky, what the world has
    come to

In the mountain sunset the graveyard tilts toward the sky and sea

A pomegranate opened its mouth, mad love

Carrying fresh water with both hands, I pass a dark road

A snake, killed, lies under the burning sky: I walk over it

Farewell said, cover lowered, those white fingertips

Morning-glories' white continues to bloom, insufferable

The cigarette is dead, I cast away the loneliness

It's been raining for days, the sparrows and I are watching

Already dawn, before the Buddha's altar some rice, spilled

Rejecting a slanderous mind, I shell beans

I'm thinking of sweeping off the dead leaves on the roof

Having washed the gravestone and fanning himself

On the straw roof grass grows, so flowers bloom

Snap, the thong broke, in the midst of the dark

Wallet gone completely empty, and a cold nose

Leaving only the noise of dead leaves burning, I go off

The heart that seeks something, I release it to the sea

Right under the big sky, I don't wear a hat

Carved into Buddha's form, a stone sits

A single set of footsteps coming, a child's footsteps

With a face saying I caught something, the child came out of the bush

A crow wordlessly flew away

Getting time off from the Buddha and doing the laundry

Thinking about something I crossed the whole bridge

Walking down to eat my meal, my footsteps

A woman in dark glasses resting on the stone, that's all

Ants stopped coming out of the ant hole

Unable to put thread through a needle, I look at the blue sky

Wears dirty clogs, yet remembers to powder herself

The big pine's darkening, time to wash my bare feet

I rescue a needle from the ashes, no one to talk to

I slip a boiled egg out of its shell and let a child have it

A praying mantis drops with a thud and doesn't forget to pray

In the sun, counting the money she got from selling persimmons

I hold a dog, my skin has no hair

Biting hard pears, arguing

Their many children each reading a different book

We drained the pond, it has become a puddle, a cold moon

To one of the ears, she comes to tell a secret

The snow fades into the river, without even the sound of waves it
darkens

These are the mornings and evenings at a temple with only big trees

Daybreak, big waves, the clear sky, are before me

Frost-packed morning, I scold a dog

A handkerchief still lying there, on my way back

The snowy sky turns into a single crow and darkens

Supper eaten, still blessed with the sun

In a sharp wind trying to part

The small rural newspaper, in a minute I've read it

Splashing hot water over my navel, alone, midnight, a hot spring

For laughing, front teeth have started growing, wow

For a hollow mind, two eyes are open

An early morning road, a dog

Wonderful breasts, here's a mosquito

There it was, my face, I bought the tiny mirror and came home

Late night wheat flour spilled on the straw mat

It's wet around the well, evening wind

The woman in the newspaper on the wall is always crying

Houses are crowding the town, a peddler calls

I'm looking for a single flea, midnight

Ran and caught up, in the wind

A late moon, shut out of the town

A festival, letting a baby sleep

Althea nodding all day, it has darkened

From the pipe pointing the way for me, smoke is coming out

It came as a stray dog and still is

I leave the paper doors open, the sea has gone dark

Driving huge bulls up the hill, the morning haze

I know the footsteps of the sparrow walking on the straw mat

Blowing the evening sun against the bamboo grove

The sparrows all at once are gone

Clipped the nails, the fingers, there are ten of them

Where the autumn sun shines, on a stone, he puts down the child from
his back

I have no vessel, I receive with both hands

I cough and am still alone

Chrysanthemums have all withered, a bit of the sea is visible

A pine cone, as it is, has turned into fire

A gun, glinting, deep snow

I go around to the back of the grave

I look at the evening sky and then pick up chopsticks for supper

On a warm roof, working

Emptying the boat, they all climbed up

MIYAZAWA KENJI

(1896–1933)

Spring & Asura[1]

Out of the gray steel of imagination
akebi vines entwine the clouds,
wildrose bush, humus marsh
everywhere, everywhere, such designs of arrogance
   (when, more busily than noon woodwind music
   amber fragments pour down)
how bitter, how blue is the anger!
Below April's bright atmospheric strata
spitting, gnashing, rushing
I am Asura incarnate
   (the landscape sways in my tears)
Shattered clouds to the limit of visibility
   in heaven's sea of splendor
      sacred crystalline winds sweep
        April's row of *Zypressen*[2]
          absorbs ether, black,
            at its dark feet
              the snow ridge of T'ien-shan[3] glitters
                (waves of heat haze & white polarization)
              yet the True Words[4] are lost
            the clouds, torn, fly through the sky.
        Ah below April of brilliance
      gnashing, burning, rushing
   I am Asura incarnate

[1] Asura: According to Buddhist belief, all living things are bound, depending upon the good or evil they have done in the past, to be reborn in one of the six realms of existence: those of the devas, humans, demons, beasts, hungry ghosts, and hell-dwellers. Ranking between humans and beasts, the demon or *asura* world represents the realm of anger, arrogance, contention, and suspicion.

[2] German word for cypress.

[3] Mountain range west of China where important trade routes ran to central Asia. Buddhists venerate T'ien-shan ("Heaven's Mountain") because their religion came through the region.

[4] Refers to the Shingon ("True Word") sect of Buddhism.

(chalcedonous clouds flow,
spring bird, where do you sing?)
The sun shimmers blue,
   Asura and forest, one music,
     and from heaven's bowl that caves in and dazzles,
       throngs of clouds like calamites extend,
        branches sadly proliferating
      all landscapes twofold
     treetops faint, and from them
    a crow flashes up
      (the atmospheric strata become clearer
      & cypresses reach heaven, hushed)
Something comes through the gold of grassland,
casually assumes a human form,
a farmer in rags, he looks at me,
does he really see me?
Below the sea of blinding atmospheric strata
   (the sorrow bluer and deeper)
Zypressen sway gently,
the bird severs the blue sky again
   (the True Words are not here,
   Asura's tears fall on the earth)

As I breathe the sky again
lungs contract faintly white
(body, scatter in a million pieces, in the sky)
The top of a ginkgo tree glitters again
Zypressen darken
sparks of the clouds pour down.

                 1922/4/8

The Landscape Inspector

That forest
has too much verdigris poured on it.
I might overlook it if the trees were in fact like that
and it may be partly due to the Purkinje effect,[5]
but may I suggest
we request the clouds to send a few more olive-yellow rays?

[5] A psychophysical discovery made by J. E. Purkinje (1787–1869).

Ah what a commendable spirit!
The frock coat shouldn't be worn
only in the stock exchange or the parliament.
Rather, on a citrine evening like this,
in guiding a herd of Holsteins
among pale lances of rice,
it is most appropriate and effective.
What a commendable spirit!
Yes, his is beancake-colored, tattered,
and maybe a little too hot,
but the serious manner in which he stands erect,
such a pious man in the landscape,
that's something I have never seen before.

1922/6/25

Traveler

You who go through rice paddies in the rain,
you who hurry toward leviathan woods,
you who walk into the gloom of clouds and mountains,
fasten up your raincoat, damn it.

1922/9/7

Bamboo & Oak

You say you suffer.
If you do suffer,
you'd better stay in the woods of bamboo & oak
when it rains
        (*You* get your hair cut)
you'd better stay in the blue woods of bamboo & oak
        (*You* get your hair cut.
        Because you have hair like that,
        you think things like that.)

1922/9/7

The Last Farewell[6]

Before the day ends
you'll be far away, my sister.
Outside, there's sleet and it's oddly bright.
From the clouds, reddish, gloomy,
the sleet comes down thick and clumsy
  (Get me some snow, Kenji)
To get snow for you
in these two chipped ceramic bowls
with blue water-shield designs
I flew out into this dark sleet
like a crooked bullet
  (Get me some snow, Kenji)
From dark clouds the color of bismuth
the sleet sinks thick and clumsy.
Ah, Toshiko,
now so close to death
you asked me
for a bowl of clean snow
to brighten me for the rest of my life.
Thank you, my brave sister,
I too will go by the straight way
  (Get me some snow, Kenji)
In your harsh, harsh fever, panting,
you asked me
for a last bowl of snow that fell from the sky,
the world called the galaxy, the sun, the atmospheric strata. . . .
. . . Between two pieces of granite
sleet makes a solitary puddle.
I will stand on them, precariously,
and get for my gentle sister
her last food
from this gleaming pine branch
laden with transparent, cold drops
that keep the white two-phase system of snow and water.
Today you will part with
the indigo designs of these bowls we've seen
since the time we grew up together.
Yes, today you will part with them.
Ah, in that closed ward,
behind the dark screen and mosquito net,

[6] Written for his sister, Toshiko (1898–1922).

my brave sister,
you burn gently, pale.
No matter where I choose it
this snow is too white, everywhere.
From that terrifying disturbed sky
this beautiful snow has come.
On these two bowls of snow you will eat
I pray from the bottom of my heart:
may this turn into the food of Tushita Heaven[7]
and soon bring to you and all others
sacred nourishment.
That is my wish, and for that I will give all my happiness.

1922/11/27

Okhotsk Elegy

The sea is rusted by the morning's carbon dioxide.
Some parts show verdigris, some azurite.
There where the waves curl, the liquid is fearfully emerald.
The ears of the timothy, grown so short,
are one by one blown by the wind.
       (They are blue piano keys
       pressed one by one by the wind)
The timothy may be a short variety.
Among dewdrops, morning-glories bloom,
the glory of the morning-glories.
       Here comes the steppe cart I saw a moment ago.
       The head of the aged white draft horse droops.
       I know the man is all right
       because on that empty street corner
       when I asked him, Where's the busiest section of the shore?
       he said, It must be over there
       because I've never been there.
       Now he looks at me kindly from the corners of his eyes
       (His small lenses
       surely reflect the white clouds of Karafuto[8])

[7] The region presided over by the Boddhisattva Maitreya. According to Chapter 28 of the Lotus Sutra, those who reverently copy the text of the sutra will be reborn in this realm.

[8,9,12] Saghalien is an island in the Sea of Okhotsk north of Hokkaido, Japan. Divided between Russia and Japan in 1905, the southern half became known as Karafuto. Eihama, now called Starodubskoe, was a port town in Karafuto.

They look more like peonies than morning-glories,
those large blossoms of beach roses,
those scarlet morning blossoms of beach eggplant.
  Ah these sharp flower scents
  can, I insist, only be the elves' work
  bringing forth numerous indigo butterflies—
  here again, tiny golden lancelike ears,
  jade vases and blue screens.
Besides, since the clouds dazzle so,
this joyous violent dizziness.
  Hoofmarks, two by two,
  are left on the wet quiet sand.
  Of course not only the horse has passed.
  The wide tracks of the cartwheels
  form a soft series.
Near a white thin line waves have left
three tiny mosquitoes stray
and are being lightly blown off.
Piteous white fragments of seashells,
blue stalks of day lilies half buried in the sand.
The waves come, rolling the sand in.
I think I'll fall upon the pebbles of white schist,
hold in my mouth a slice of seashell
polished clean by the waves
and sleep for a while.
Because, for now, from the sound of these waves,
the most fragrant wind
and the light of the clouds
I must recover the transparent energy that I gave
to the morning elves of Saghalien[9]
while I lay on the fine carpet
of blue huckleberries bearing ripe black fruit
among the large red blossoms of beach roses
and mysterious bluebells.
Besides, first of all, my imagination
has paled because of tiredness,
becoming a dazzling golden green.
From the sun's rays and the sky's layers of darkness
there even comes the strange wavering sound of a tin drum.[10]

[10] Because of two words Miyazawa may have coined or misused, the meaning of the line is unclear.

Desolate grass ears, the haze of light.
The verdigris extends serenely to the horizon
and from the seam of clouds, a variegated structure,
a slice of heaven's blue.
My chest retains the strong stab.
Those two kinds of blue
are both characteristics Toshiko had.
While I walk alone, tire myself out, and sleep
on a deserted coast of Karafuto,
Toshiko is at the end of that blue place,
I don't know what she's doing.
Beyond where the rough trunks and branches of white and silver firs
are in confusion, drifting, stranded,
the waves roll many times over.
Because they roll, the sand churns
and the salt water is muddy, desolate.
        (Eleven fifteen. Its palely gleaming dial)
On this side of the clouds, birds move up and down.
Here a boat slipped out this morning.
The rut engraved in the sand by the keel
with the horizontal dent left by a large roller—
that's one crooked cross.
To write HELL with some small pieces of wood,
correct it to LOVE,
and erect a cross,
since that's a technique anyone uses,
when Toshiko arranged one,
I gave her a cold smile.
        (A slice of seashell buried in the sand
        shows only its white rim)
The fine sand that has finally dried
flows in this engraved cross,
now steadily, steadily flowing.
When the sea is this blue
I still think of Toshiko,
and the expressions of distant people say,
Why do you mourn for just one sister so much?
And again something inside me says:
        (Casual observer! Superficial traveler!)[11]
The sky shines so, it looks empty, dark,
three sharp-winged birds fly toward me.

[11] Original in English.

They've begun to cry sorrowfully.
Have they brought any news?
There's pain in half my head.
The roofs of Eihama,[12] now distant, flare.
Just one bird blows a glass whistle,
drifting away in chalcedonous clouds.
The glitter of the town and the harbor.
The ibis-scarlet over the slope on its back
is a spread of fireweed flowers.
The fresh apple-green grassland
and a row of dark green white firs.
        (*Namo Saddharmapundarika Sutra*)[13]
Five tiny sandpipers
when the sea rolls in
run away, tottering
        (*Namo Saddharmapundarika Sutra*)
when the wave recedes flatways,
over the mirror of sand
they run forward, tottering.

                                1923/8/4

"Spring" Variation

Various flowers' bowls and cups
as they open their forbidding lids
and spurt blue and yellow pollen
some of it
falls, as it comes, into the marsh,
turns into whorls or stripes
and is quietly gliding, avoiding now here, now there,
the water stone-leek roots that poke out glaring green leaves.
Yet those girls standing on the platform,
one of them just never stops laughing,
all the others stroke her on the shoulders, on the back,
and do many things, but no matter, she doesn't stop laughing

                                1924/8/22

[13] In Sanskrit: Buddhist recitation, which may be roughly translated:
"I revere the Sutra of the Lotus of the Wonderful Law."

The Prefectural Engineer's Statement Regarding Clouds

Although mythological or personified description
is something I would be ashamed to attempt,
let me for a moment assume the position of the ancient poet
and state the following to the black, obscene nimbus:
I, a humble official, hoping to wash both mind and body
in the vast air glimmering above this summit,
and in the cold wind passing here with a fragrance of roses,
and in the terrifying blue etching of mountains and valleys,
have managed from today's business schedule
a few moments
and stand here, knowing their full value.
But, first of all, black nimbus,
against my wish
you bring to mind an abnormal anxiety
and make me feel as if I were, in the words of the *Kojiki,*
"treading on air."
Let me explain, since you ask the reason:
For two-thirds of this past May,
obscene nimbus family,
you covered the river and the valley to the west and did not move.
As a result, sunlight fell below the normal level
and all the rice seedlings grew excessively
or acquired red splotches.
Under the circumstances, as outlined,
I could not regard without grave concern
the season's rice growth in this prefecture,
I looked up at the skies and uttered anguished cries
more than several times a day.
Last night, however,
the veteran weather bureau chief
forecast it would be absolutely sunny,
and this morning, the sky blue, the air fresh,
I enjoyed letting my cigar smoke flow out the train window,
the fifty miles among valleys and twenty-five miles through plains,
happy to be on schedule. But now, past noon,
what deceit, what breach of trust!
As I scan the vast expanse from this summit,
I am gnawed by anger:
First, that you, from here to the east,
disguised in the color of the nightingale,
cover the long stretches of land mass

going to the limit of visibility
to rape the ocean;
second, that you rush northward,
going against those cirrocumuli
and the blue void;
third, that above the mountains covered with larches
you, dark atmospheric sea cucumbers,
are all too brazen,
now disappearing, now transmogrifying yourselves
into all sorts of lascivious lights and forms.
To summarize all this,
soft, dubious nimbus,
although you allow me to enjoy several chinks of sensuous sunlight,
although you send me rude fragrance in the wind,
your intention cast out in the entire sky
with your gray black wings and tentacles,
your fluid mass of great baritone,
is too evident to hide.
Therefore, I, a humble official,
considering all the positions I occupy, public and private,
give you, these last moments,
a glare brimming with outrage,
ready to leave this summit
as swiftly as I can.

1927/6/1

The Breeze Comes Filling the Valley

Ah
from the south, and from the southwest,
the breeze comes filling the valley,
dries my shirt soaked with sweat,
cools my hot forehead and eyelids.
Stirring the field of rice stalks that have risen,
shaking the dark raindrops from each blade,
the breeze comes filling the valley.
As a result of all kinds of hardship,
the July rice, bifurcating,
foretold a fruitful autumn,
but by mid-August
twelve red daybreaks

and six days of ninety percent humidity
made the stalks weak and long,
and though they put on ears and flowers
the fierce rain yesterday
felled them one after another.
Here, in the driving sheets of rain,
a fog, cold as if mourning,
covered the fallen rice.
Having suffered all of the bad conditions,
few of which we thought we'd have,
they showed the worst result we'd expected,
but then,
when we thought all the odds were against their rising,
because of the slight differences in seedling preparation
and in the use of superphosphate,
all the stalks are up today.
And I had expected this,
and to tell you of this recovery soon
I looked for you,
but you avoided me.
The rain grew harder
until it flooded this ground.
There was no sign of clearing.
Finally, like a crazy man
I ran out in the rain,
telephoned the weather bureau,
went from village to village, asking for you,
until, hoarse,
in the terrible lightning,
I went home late at night.
But in the end I did not sleep.
And, look,
this morning the east, the golden rose, opens,
the clouds, the beacons, rise one after another,
the high voltage wires roar,
the stagnant fog runs in the distance.
The rice stalks have risen at last.
They are living things,
precision machines.
All stand erect.
At their tips, which waited patiently in the rain,
tiny white flowers glisten
and above the quiet amber puddles reflecting the sun

red dragonflies glide.
Ah, we must dance like children,
dance we must, and that is not enough.
If they fall again,
they will rise again.
If, as they have,
they can stand humidity like this,
every village is certain to get
five bushels a quarter acre.
From the horizon buried beneath a forest,
from the row of dead volcanos shining blue,
the wind comes across the rice paddies,
makes the chestnut leaves glitter.
Now, the fresh evaporation,
the transparent movement of sap.
Ah, in the middle of this plain,
in the middle of these rice paddies rustling as powerfully as if they
    were reeds,
we must dance, clapping our hands, like the innocent gods of the past,
dance we must, and that is not enough.

1927/7/14

Night

When with hot palms, unable to fall asleep,
people got to sleep, from long ago,
gripping a crumpled towel,
or holding a black clay-slate stone.

undated

Rest

On the ground cedar and zelkova roots
entangling, robbing each other
stand out like terrifying veins
from the grass and moss of this lean soil,
in the sky, clouds silently flowing east,
the cedar top withered,
the zelkova tip looking as if
it lives on snatches it takes from the wind

. . . sometimes the cedar withers the zelkova
    sometimes the zelkova withers the cedar. . . .
          (Harvest the rice, eat the rice, what for?
          Eat the rice, harvest the rice, what for?)
The technician shouts over there,
the trees, blurring, look half-melted in the sky,
and again, suffocating, the blue rice stalks.

                    undated

November 3rd[14]

neither yielding to rain
nor yielding to wind
yielding neither to
snow nor to summer heat
  with a stout body
      like that
without greed
never getting angry
always smiling quiet-
      ly
eating one and a half pints of brown rice
  and bean paste and a bit of
          vegetables a day
in everything
not taking oneself
      into account
      looking listening understanding well
and not forgetting
living in the shadow of pine trees in a field
  in a small
    hut thatched with miscanthus
if in the east there's a
    sick child
going and nursing
    him

[14] Written in a pocket notebook Miyazawa is thought to have used beginning late 1931. The typographical arrangement is as faithful to the original as possible.

if in the west there's a tired mother
going and for her
          carrying
               bundles of rice
if in the south
     there's someone
                         dying
going
   and saying
          you don't have to be
               afraid
if in the north
               there's a quarrel
                         or a lawsuit
saying it's not worth it
                    stop it
in a drought
     shedding tears
in a cold summer
     pacing back and forth   lost
called
     a good-for-nothing
               by everyone
neither praised
nor thought a pain
     someone
               like that
is what I want
          to be

NISHIWAKI JUNZABURŌ

(born 1894)[1]

Shepherd in Capri

Even on a spring morning
my Sicilian pipe makes a sound of autumn
retracing thoughts past thousands of years

Rain

The south wind has brought gentle goddesses,
has wet the bronze, wet fountains,
wet swallows' wings and golden feathers,
wet the brine, the sand, the fish,
wet quietly temples, baths, theaters;
this procession of quiet gentle goddesses
has wet my tongue.

Cup's Primitivism

Along the river where daphnes bloom
and shine,
passing by an angel with an apple and a saber,
a blond boy runs,
holding firmly between his fingers
a fish called red-belly
with its milk-light eyes.
The golden dream inclines.

---

[1] Selected from a group corrected and approved by the poet. Roughly
in chronological order.

Ceylon

The natives were all in their houses
I walked alone in the burning sun
A lizard lay on the sewage pipe
Eggplants gleamed
Violets flared
The hot sand that had collected on the leaves of violets
Spilled on my hand
Ceylon in the old days

The Modern Fable

The fable at the end of April is linear.
On the peninsula the bronze wheat and aloe-green rape
were rusted like the Gentle Woman's robe.
One thinks; therefore, existence ceases to be.
Man's existence is after death.
When one ceases to be human one merges
with greatest existence. For the moment
I don't want to talk a lot.
With the people in the poppy house
with the people studying metaphysical mythology
I take a hot bath in Ochiai where mustard grows.
I think secretly of Andromeda.
In the house over there the Gentle Woman, lying on her side
plays go with a woman, her friend.
She ponders, her hand stuck out of the front of her robe.
We philosophers gathered before the broken waterwheel
and holding azalea and sweet flag in our hands
had a photo taken, had another hot bath
served ourselves an arrow-head liquor
and indulged all night in geometrical thoughts.
I think of a friend of the days
when we talked about Beddoes' suicide theory
as we climbed Dōgenzaka, and also thinking
about the white-haired Einstein walking
in an American village, I cannot sleep.
I run along the Nekko River alone.
Early in the morning I walk the white road to the inn at Seko.
A damson tree with white blossoms stands
crooked on the roadside. I turn toward a bush warbler's

song and see the blossoms of mountain cherries already fallen.
The pale violets clinging to the rocks; cattails
drooped in great masses in the mist;
my hair has turned badger gray.
All of a sudden an Ophelian thought—
wild strawberry, vetch, buttercups, wild roses,
violets I picked.
I hold this full bouquet together with a pencil in my hand
for the Gentle Woman, for the never-ending love,
for the curses of Pascal's and Rilke's women
and for this water spirit.

Katherine

The parabola thrown
from the woman
to the hedge
is the lifeline of
a man who yearns for beautiful human solitude
The Greek goddesses too try to avoid
the line
At the end of December and into January
it gets extremely lonely here
The concrete road
as wide as the Champs-Elysées
runs beyond the racetrack thrown away toward Meguro
to Kakinokizaka
its backdrop a wonderful evening sun
the mountains of Sagami undulating black
If you saw this sunset sky
you would as I do
feel so lonely you'd be moved to tears for
the infinitude of love the solitude of man the origin of human seeds
The apricot sunset
The woman like dew
becomes a shadow like a wildcat
From spring to summer from summer to autumn
on this concrete road
human beings were awfully talkative
The dreams to be dreamed are exhausted and life is uselessly solitary
blackthorn bloomed

fructified again and my dear man came
made gin and left
If I go a little further   turn off the road
and go down to the valley I know that among frost columns
thistles are budding and yet
I keep walking straight to the west
Next to the store selling stamps with the head of the queen of Antigua
a flower shop
had mistletoe branches piled on the roadside
A Polynesian woman in boots wearing kasuri[2] pants
was fumbling around
"At Christmastime I sold them   you know
to Americans   A branch for 100 yen
Now I can give you one for 10 yen"
The branches like dark blue rubber
had transparent yellow berries
like salmon eggs
"So you know that   heh-heh-heh-heh-heh"
She was pleased how vegetable
the Western mythologies are
About the time the afternoon assumed the look of
a withered rose leaf I discovered an antique shop
Between an oil stove and a brass bed
there happened to be in a frame a picture
of a Walton by an eighteenth-century painter
The portrait of a boy on his way back from fishing
yes that country boy wearing
a silk hat with a feather as blue
as a gentian flower those daces
that silk line that float as
light as your earring
Dangling the small fish skewered on a willow branch
he is looking at the buyer
is dreaming up the fish that got away
Oh well I don't think I'll send you this letter

---

[2] An old technique of dyeing.

Autumn

I

On the morning that a typhoon was blowing
I went to a neighboring stationer
and bought that foreign-made yellow pencil
as light as a cigarette,
the soft wood—
you burn the shavings
and they smell of Brahmanism.
I close my gate and think:
tomorrow morning, and it will be autumn.

II

I'd like to talk about copses and all that:
But I sat on a log and was thinking
"People are beginning to polish
gourds for the divine liquor.
The festival is so near at hand."

Far down the Kōshū Road

Far down the Kōshū Road the clear-tone cicadas sing
and the dockmakie has scarlet fruits. "The Rape of the
Sabine Women" perhaps? Look, a Corinthian stone
house. Here lives an old maker of fish-shaped wooden
drums. With his lodger, a teacher of French, one
day, I acutely drank palm liquor with eggplant pick-
les and raw dace—it numbed the roots of my tongue.

Sorrow

Over the granite
spring has come
in the mountain depths of Jōshū
plum blossoms white
about the 20th of March.
On my way from funeral rites
I hurry toward the capital
the dead person laughs,
born of a rose,
behind trumpet lilies.
Now I can only read Aesop's *Fables*
except those sermons,
there's that wonderful pastoral tragedy;
to the greatness of that nameless
illustrator I consecrate carnations, mimosa,
freesia, violets.
A man in a triangular hood,
in briefs, wearing
a dagger, fishing,
Which race is this costume of?
neither a Greek nor a Malay;
I should never have
thought about it before;
it's a costume for a children's book
by an English illustrator during the Ansei era[3]
harvesting wheat with a sickle like a crescent
and surprising skylarks
a man and a perch talking
a fox and a stork stand talking
beggars and travelers loitering
pricked by a thorn in a hedge
bleeding,
a wasp, a locust, an ant, a water jar
wind, sun grapes, an adder
an old oak, a drowning child
a tower, distorted in the distance.

[3] 1854–1860.

January

The monk's season has come.
A monk of God knows what country was it
who discovered the fragrance of narcissus?
What's beautiful is not so much a nude goddess
as the way a nude tree twists.
A season of crystals and roots that form in black earth.
A man sticks his hand out of a yellow bamboo grove
and takes gems, the seeds of vines.
An oak like a broken harp
hangs a tress of green hair.
There's neither bee nor woman to play lonely spring.
The human being still squats
among brambles, thinking.

Loquat

Volcano   portulaca   rain
Gauguin's gamboge golden
Flesh   exquisite   on a silver plate!
In the shriveled Tahitian gourd
In the forgotten gods' dark blood
I glimpse dangerous seeds
The hands of a woman traveler
With a bird's eyes
Peeling a fruit of the towering loquat
Are unlimitedly white

Winter Conversation

The black copper sun paled the hunter's cheeks.
The wing-flapping
pheasant,
a woman's footsteps
disappear into brambles,
tapping the life of a sleeping tree,
a woodpecker—at the isolation
of its vertical sound effect
reality pales.

The vagrancy of the heart that drinks secret honey
from the blindness of the universe
is a crooked ash stick.
In this empty roadside summer
the withered hips
decorate a shepherd's purse.
Whose drinking cup is this
crooked liquor bottle?
The acorns that burn at fire's dreams
warm the beggar's hat.
It's the twilight of
a bullfinch's wings.
What remains in the dark of the eye
is the cleft in the hedge
is the border of infinity.

The Way to the Lighthouse

The summer wasn't over yet.
On the way to the lighthouse
I thought of the darkened branches of
the pasania tree on the rock,
of various human beings,
of the bird country,
thought as I walked
of the story of the "old man of the sea"
drinking a nut liquor on someone's shoulders,
of the story of the "hemp-beater"
whom Renan, the scholar who wrote the life of Christ
saw in his boyhood,
and of other things various human beings said.
I looked in a bush, thinking, "It certainly must be there,"
and there it still was
the garish, poisonous-looking blue of spiderwort.
The water-pepper had turned feeble.
Before going into the tunnel penetrating the rock mountain
I saw a tree called *tobera*[4] hanging branches from the cliff,
pulled off a twig bearing nuts,
and cracked a green nut as hard as a plum stone.

[4] *Euonymus tobira.*

Many seeds as red as a Persian rug
were hiding in its core.
I felt terribly sorry
that I surprised the lovely lives
living happily in the dark.
One shouldn't expose such a lonely secret of nature.
They must have wanted to remain
hidden in that dark.
I began again to think of human beings, rocks, plants
and walk along the way to the lighthouse.

Decorations

The hedge
the leaning tower
the gourd
the lamp
are all decorations
that people have left.
Are the greatest monuments humans have made.
There's nothing more to say.
When autumn comes I visit the village of Windsor.
From peasants, father and son, like those
in Victorian illustrations of Aesop's *Fables,*
I bought a yellow pear,
peeled it with a shiny crescent-shaped
Sheffield knife, and ate it.
That itinerant bear-tormenting man had stopped coming.
With a child wearing a silk hat
I exchanged hips for acorns.
Women's dreams can only pass into the wind and tremble.
There's nothing more to fear.
At a riverside bookstore I bought a botanical dictionary
        (technicolor) showing edible
and poisonous mushrooms in Britain
and came back by horse cart.

Travelogue

1

Near the village where quails call
there lives a man:
walks, thinking always
of a woman.

2

There was a man
whose head in the photographs
looked like a monk's.
"On the fence in my garden
the rosebuds
have swollen: summer has come"
so he sang,
put on a new rush hat, and went out.

3

Walks, almost touching millet ears;
something happens and craning its neck
a quail flies up
heavily: its eyes
sharply
gleam in the dark
of Andromeda.

Slope

When in a dent of the cliff
white blossoms
jut out on a devil's walking stick
with its swarms of thorns
I walk down the narrow slope before a ruined pub.
The cut rocks are moist.
The rotten smell of the bushes
of the gods spurned and turned
into plants by Jupiter
powerfully stimulate the brain.
The eternity that hides
in the nervous system
suffers a transparent thrill.

Broadax

Summer noon
I passed under a large *kihada*[5] tree,
turned to the left,
reached a stone fence with wax-pinks,
passed a temple gate,
walked down a small path, to the right.
When I passed through a village of suffering people,
a young man
who looked like Dylan Thomas
came out of a house.
He walked before me
in sportswear and wooden clogs;
he crossed to the right.
He dropped in
at the house of his neighbor acquaintance.
"You there, people,
would you lend me a broadax?"
Eternity.

5 *Phellodendron.*

For Memories

For memories
I raise a moon cup
and toast.
But the white melancholy
still wore
the candlelike skin.
Beyond a cucumber garden
the noon sun was knocking
on a Chiangching tree.
I break off a branch,
and a sap raw-smelling as a skink
comes out.
Country people abhor it
as Medusa.
On memories' plate
Salome's black lips like fancy beads
quiver.
A tendril, severed by a memory,
trembles for fear in a bush
with a man.

Memories are twisted
as the Western man's pipe
that parasitizes the roots
of the lawn grass,
are lonely
as the breath of a goddess
blown in man's pores.

Pheasant

Another turn around the sun,
and dreams in endless fields have started.
The woodcutter stares at pheasant plumage
and ponders in the haze—
the tail warps crescent
and yearns for a distant place.
Here, an illusion of God knows what design,
a woman's winter letter:

writing done with a hatchet's head
or a self-consolation of a pitiful man,
these words have come again,
drifting over infinity's gentle waves!

In an Abandoned Garden

Autumn is about to leave.
The memory of the lost earth
goes down among the ferns dead decayed
by the meteorite rust in the garden.
Pan plays a skinny naked note,
his pointed lips
turned to the existence of lead.

The consciousness of crystal water
moves like the evil spell of bronze
of village clouds
of the clouded blood
of a rusty man.

The pale traveler
accursed with the sufferings of mercury
narrows an eye
and peeps through a hole
on a torn holly hedge.

Sad

The sad history of mankind
that wetted the traveler's sleeves
is blurred in his pale notebook.
Perhaps the modern man's melancholy
comes from the amplitude of logic;
the joy of hanging from a cliff
the ancient man's atavism
only is the fear of cruel dreams every night.
The sap of the violet torn at the tip of a rock
darkens the woman traveler's diary.
The fields have grown invisible.

The glitter of lightning from the wheatfield
falls in the cup, and the liquor turns into a spider.
Tomorrow too it will rain
until the marrow of the hollow stone in the temple begins to drip.
In the broken mud fence there may be talk of
sowing but I can't hear it POPOI.
There may be plum blossoms but I can't see them POPOI.
Tomorrow too someone in glasses
and with a camera will cross before you.

Afterword

In the distance,
blue as a Persian cat's eye,
mountains undulate
& through the basin runs a single
dusty highway: long ago—
various travelers hurry their ways;
passing by the village station,
I feel dizzy
& sit at a tea hut, to rest;
eating pale *tokoroten*,[6]
ankoromochi[7] wrapped in mulberry leaves,
& salted *myōga*,[8]
I gaze at the feet of the travelers who pass before me;
an iris-like woman resting by my side
talks to me
"I thought so, *uuuun*"
I can only reply
in a broken Yellow River dialect;
soon
a bearded man,
wailing loudly, pushes aside
the villagers
& goes away.

[6] Summer food made of seaweed; eaten cold.
[7] Ricecake with sweet bean filling.
[8] *Zingiber mioga*, used for seasoning.

KANEKO MITSUHARU

(1895–1975)

Sharks[1]

I

On the sea's face, sharks
lie about like logs.

The sharks don't move.

And, positions yielding on their own, they come to lie side by side,
    athwartwise,
or, far beyond it all, dimly,
float up like balloons;

endlessly gangly, beyond your height,
blue as bamboo, yet muddily dark, salty, dizzying salt water—into it
stone-packed, jagged cans
fall weightlessly, spinning in the water.

The sharks won't bite at you.
Because their stomachs are full.

In the stomachs of these fellows, humans are so packed they almost
    bulge out.
One arm with its severed part ripened and burst,
parts below the crotch they've bitten off in slow chunks,
pillowlike torsos—

"Don't want nothing," the sharks, eyes half-closed,
are now drowsy, drowsed.

Irrelevant crosseyes, insidious, fiendish fellows.
The sharks gather outside the white breakwaters of Malacca and
    Tandjung Priok.

[1] Written in 1934, when the poet traveled in Southeast Asia.

Where the red turnips, the roofs of pilots' offices,
are splashed by the waves from the oil pot.
Corpses.
From where have you brought them in your mouths?
From the *kampung*[2] on the water, from the mouths of bays,
from the rotten mouths of rivers—
corpses from bubonic plague that float and block the stream. Corpses
    from fever. Corpses of children.
Corpses with bellies like blue gourds.
Again they wait patiently for a burial at sea,
their harpoon-point snouts glued to ships' hulls.
The sea between Minicoy Island and Africa scorches, suppurates,
    spouts up mists, purrs deeply, pulls about a biscuit thrown to it,
    a coffin, plays with it, and smacks its lips.
Corpses.
. . . Wax-colored corpses that wear out like soap.
Corpses.
. . . Corpses with not a drop of blood left.
Corpses. Loitering. Drifting corpses.
Corpses kicking about like hydras. Intestines like strings.
Large heads like seashells in which water has collected.
The sharks, like cutting machines, hack them off.

The sharks, lying about,
wait for any length of time for servings of humans.

Their skins are slimy, blue-smelling,
an unpleasant odor, pungent, pierces your head.

Hauled up on deck—the sharks.
Like large ceramic bathtubs,
no heads,
no tails.
But in their familiar seas, they are as colossal as heavy guns, and
    malignant, muzzles darkly, oppressively, smoldering.
They, like the Mosaic miracle, slit apart the waters of the world with
    their backs, take a chunk out of the beach as with Death's scythe,
    emerge majestically, and disappear swiftly.

The shark.
He's a steel blade.
He's the danger of a steel blade. Just sharpened.

[2] Village.

A blade's glittering, fine, irritations.
The shark.
He has no heart, he's the brutal one who rides this world.

. . . .

2

Searching for Christians and spices we have reached this place.
These words of Vasco da Gama as he landed in India
are as good as:
—Searching for slaves and plunder we have reached this place.
Jan Pieterszoon Coen built gun bases in Batavia,
Sir Stanford Raffles grasped the gate of Singapore and set up a strong-
hold to twist the arms of Siam, Japan, and China.
The fleets of these fellows, grown thick and fat like agaves, with
white powder all over them,
remain quietly open.

Are warships only *kebon*[3] simply to make grand spectacles?
Do you say they are defenses for peace?
Are they merely trying to maintain their dignity in solemn fashion?

No, no, no, it's just that for the moment their stomachs are full.
Their stomachs are stuffed with indigestible corpses of human beings,
but impudently enough, they turn their stomachs and signal me, wink-
ing a narrow eye.

The sea water is pretty, and bitter. Stings the eye.
Washed, bleached, it smarts.
In this water, shadowlike water spiders.
Coral fragments.
Old guns rusted cinnabar-red.
And the sharks leisurely stretch their large bodies, white as rich West-
erners', in this pool.
Cheeks fragrant as grass, as after shaving.

In the water that stretches and shrinks like a magic mirror,
these sharks.
Embarrassing but naked.
Yes. Floating on this prickly salt water,
even the fleets, in the water's reflections and swayings,
all feel ticklish in their bellybuttons.

[3] Floriculture.

Through such waves, dizzy,
I'm reeling, holding a black umbrella overhead.
Five years, seven years, soon ten years,
pitiful, fingers bitten off one by one, this part and that part of my
    body lost, now reduced almost to half,
I am sometimes hurried forward, sometimes left behind, by mysteri-
    ous currents.
Under the equator, in Sumatra Strait.

People jeer at my lameness, and even for that I depend on them.
What a miserable game. Silly endless circling.
Still, my intestines, rinsed too much in sea water, are too clean, and
    hurt.
As if wrung, blood oozes.
When those fellows slid by me,
my guts floated up, a puffball, and I lifted my hat a little and greeted
    in Charlie's style.
But a passing shark's nose nudged me
and turned my direction a little—that was all.

Why don't they eat me?
Does my heart have poison in it?
Does my flesh taste bad? Is it rotten?
They start eating me all right, these days, but as soon as they do,
    they spit me out.
They do it, just for the fun of it.
Their stomachs are overloaded. They do it to lessen their loads.
They can't possibly have the sensitivity, anything fine like that, of
    choosing their food.

3

Singapore sits on top
of coke that's just begun to kindle.
Cracked burnt stones, cockspur coconut palms. Hindu *kering*. Malay-
    sians. Baba Nangking.[4] Ghastly odors of their scorching bodies,
    these human beings.
Sutra[5] flower blue sky.
Tongkang.

Spitting betel blood—red bedazzlement.

[4] Chinese in the South.
[5] Silk tree.

The sharks' nozzles are beginning to suppurate in the Lysol.
Their eyes are scarlet, puffy, swollen.

On white mosquito nets,
on plastered walls,
pale rose geckos dart.
Sweaty, twitching bodies with fast-beating hearts—they wear bracelets
    of pure gold on them.
A Cantonese girl pushing a makeup ball on her hairless skin.
Siamese women decorated like phoenix-palanquins.
Singapore durians:
their bodies are hot, lethargic, and empty, as they lie about twining
    around "bamboo-ladies."
Looking in through the brothels' square bars,
men hurl the worst insults at them.

Turned into maggots of coal, coolies squirm.
Iron roasts. Water sizzles.
Thirsty. Furious. Totally blackened, they carry cement. Boil tar.
In the *kaki rumah* of the bleak town, they raise feeble whimpers after
    the Hari Raya Puasa.
They're naked, constructing a battery they'll turn against themselves.

The sharks have chomped arms
off them.
And leisurely turn around them,
mimicking the seven trips around the holy place in Mecca,
making fun of them.

The sharks, like autos, are disgustingly shiny,
and gradually grow in the stinging water.

The nickel-colored water of the Strait of Malacca.
To the breakwaters where the water slides on the boulders just as you
    might unfurl curled plantain leaves,
the sharks roll their bodies close.
Shadowless fish
and glass shrimp.

Yes. A man's blood or a woman's, blood, in the sea water, is only a
    drop of port wine.
Sucking on my lips that have lost blood,

this is a woman. Just the same, hers is a bloodless tongue.
—Damn. No one has anything like blood.

The water with a hangover, painful, is washing the wounds
of Singapore, smarting.

4

Where has he drifted from? this capricious, facetious fellow.
Emden—
no, more like a bum. Or,
a floating mine.
In the narrows flickering like numberless fireflies and covered with
    small wrinkles, he's reeling, from Tandjung Bunga to the Strait
    of Malacca.
By a difference of one or two millimeters, the sharks' snouts don't
    touch this explosive as they pass by.
They know;
proud they've cheated him,
they're sneering with eyes like needles.

But this shark had part of his face sliced off slantwise.
He had the face of Governor-General Clifford,
and looked like Hitler, too.

His haughty, insolent, spacious, coarse, totally unreceptive, cruel, blue
    whetstone-like profile—the profile says, untroubled:
—You are no loyal citizen. You're no believer, either. You're a drifter.
    A beggar. A phony. You're someone at the end of the line.

A woman and a child with me,
I can't make any retort.
The woman's legs get torn off, the child's small ass gets nibbled off.
Threads of white flesh sway in the water.

I shut my eyes tight and threw myself at them.
They're a wall. A barricade called "society" that doesn't accede to
    anything.
And, over the sea, it's rain.
On the waves, small patterns; a lonesome promenade.

Waiting for a second floating mine,
I was swaying in the waves, as I drifted to some place.

5

I'm now lost outside Telukbetung Port of Sunda, under the equator,
in Macassar Bay, in the narrows of Bintan and Batam of the Riau
Archipelago, in the water with blue moss-rust floating on it, in
the dark water, through the dark seaweed forest.
A river thrust like a kris into the throat of a jungle. Black Death.
Pahang, Batang Hari, Perak Rivers soak *nipah* palms, push muddy
water into the sea,
and sago palms, fallen low, smolder darkly.
In amber pools the color of a plantain leaf,
mosquitoes are clamorously singing.
Customs. That's Pera Anson.[6] Kuala Kubu. Palembang Port.

Rubber rots, crumbles, and turns into a stream of tar.
People can't eat it, can't stuff it in their *kayu*[7] and suck it in place of
candu.[8]
The haaj caps, eyes looking enfeebled,
squat quietly the whole length of the jetty.
As I pass by, watching one port after another,
the sun scorches my head floating on the water after deaths, filth,
floods.
Latrines on the water, pickets—
leeches and snakes with fins flap on them.
A blue heron atop a *pohon sengon*.
On the reddish-brown full water a bleak landscape shows as much as
a sash, sitting on top of the water, looking as if about to be over-
whelmed by it.
Water surface garish as a reflector.
Those sharks.
Here, too, they follow me.
Their bellies white as a chip of a cup
pass before me in the yellow muddy water.
Their seven cutting edges in a row.

Sharks—they're as persistent as a dog.
Sharks. Weep or laugh—it's no use.
No good to threaten them either.
They run me down till I'm against the wall.

6 Unidentified; spelling uncertain.
7 An unidentified word, here used in the sense of "pipe."
8 Opium.

I'm now staggering about in the coral-reef zone off Karimun Lombok
  at latitude 8° south and longitude 115° east.
Scarlet tortoise-shell dyed in menstruation,
and coral stars like mantles.

Among the waves fine as peacocks
I was drunk.
Acting as if I'd downed too much good peppermint. But that was ter-
  rible methyl.
The salt water is bitter. A single butterfly. A Borneo ship is being
  kneaded.

From Bostiro Timor Island to New Guinea
the sea is utterly, like a virgin forest, deep.
I am lonely as if I entered a wealthy man's salon.

The sea deceives me, deranges me, confuses me.
But I know. Will you stop kidding me. That which floats up to the
  surface, in the sea, palely white. An abyss. What it is, is the
  shark.
The shark softly checks up on my body
with his narrow, lozenge-shaped nostrils.

They say all at once:
Friendship. Peace. Love of society.
They then form a column. It's law. Public opinion. Human values.
Shit, again, with that, we fall apart.

6

Ah. Me. Corpse of a corpse. Only, child's soul turning in rebel's will.
  Body.
A dream that detests normality. Betrayal to coupling, wandering that
  turns against intimacy. I wouldn't be cured of my anger even if
  I destroyed this great earth of hurt feelings seven times with a
  sledgehammer.
Feigning an air of composure, detached from the world that hates
  me, blames me, laughs at me, and considers me its enemy,
I play on the tottering surface of the sea
and splash over myself the sour water of the *rambutan.*

Over a view wasted and gone rusty, water without hope, red-hot
    hardship.
Among spit, piss, and watermelon rinds, from east to south, from
    south to southwest, me, having grown thoroughly sick and tired
    of roaming,
ah. Why do I, I, go on roaming?

The woman twines around my arm.
The child clings to my neck.
No matter what, I can't do anything but face up to them.
I'm infirm. But no room for hesitation. No technique of cheating
    them, no means of playing the coquette for them.
Robbed of everything I had, body torn into shreds, just cocking my
    head,
I slapped the flesh on my chest, just to see.

Sharks.
Sharks, however, wouldn't move.
With eyes narrow as a *topeng*'s, they're glaring at us, wall-eyed fash-
    ion.
You'll be our food sooner or later—that seems to be what they're
    saying, but now they're so stuffed they'd have to make an effort
    just to move their bodies.
In their stomachs, arms and legs of human beings lie about, undigested.
The sharks turn their asses to me, by turns.

On their bodies blue rust forms in places.
Like torn tin-plate funnels,
with dents and warps,
some even have blunt dots here and there,
bullet holes.
And smell offensively of new paint.
Sharks.
Sharks.
Sharks.
Let's curse them. Let's destroy them.
Otherwise, they'll devour us all.

POET'S NOTES

Malacca: The old capital of Malacca on the Malay Peninsula. Before Singapore Port was developed, it was the number one port of the colony on the Strait [of Malacca]. It used to be in Portugal's hands; today it's in Britain's.

Tandjung Priok: The new port of Batavia, the capital of Java.

Minicoy Island: An uninhabited island on the way from the Persian Gulf to the Red Sea.

Vasco da Gama: A navigator who went around the Cape of Good Hope for the first time and landed in India.

Jan Pieterszoon Coen: Second Dutch governor-general in Java. Brave and dauntless.

Sir Stanford Raffles: A far-sighted man who bought Singapore Island from the Johor Court and developed Singapore as it is today.

Charlie: Charlie Chaplin.

Hindu *kering:* An Indian tribe of tall, skinny people mainly engaged in hard labor.

tongkang: Large, tub-shaped barge.

betel blood: Tropical people have a habit of chewing betel nuts to dispel heat. "Blood," because they spit out blood-red juice anywhere.

gecko: Many flesh-colored geckos live on the wall of all the houses.

makeup ball: Chinese use solid balls of powder by partially melting them with water.

durian: Called the king of fruits. During its season, the native people are said to forfeit their properties, even their wives and concubines, for a durian. It has a terrible odor. As large as a football, it has prickles all over it.

bamboo lady: A long pillow one holds to cool oneself while sleeping in hot weather.

brothels' square bars: In Chinese brothels, square wooden bars are put up horizontally to lock the doors.

kaki rumah: In a tropical town, the eaves of buildings facing the streets are made wide, so that one can shelter under them when showers hit.

Hari Raya Puasa: A one-week fast in conformity to an Islamic commandment, in which people do not eat while the sun is out; when the fasting ends, they have a great festival.

seven trips in Mecca: Muslims make it their life dream to go to Mecca, and work and save money for it. Colonial governments, taking advantage of it, organize pilgrimage ships to Mecca and rob the people of what little they have. In Mecca, people walk around the "black stone" seven times.

Tandjung Bunga (Cape of Blossoms): A beautiful spot in Pinang Island on the Malay Peninsula.

Clifford: A governor-general of Singapore famous for confronting the native people with a ruthless policy.

nipah palms: Palms that grow in watery areas.

sago palms: Palms from which starch is extracted.

Palembang: The most important port in Sumatra.

haaj cap: A white Turkish cap that indicates the rank of haaj; a Muslim who has made it to Mecca gets it. The cap is regarded as a supreme honor, and those who have it are treated with respect.

pohon sengon: An enormous tree.

rambutan [spelling uncertain]: Fruit resembling but slightly larger than the longan fruit.

topeng: Masks used in Javanese drama.

TAKIGUCHI SHŪZO

(1903–1979)

ÉTAMINES NARRATIVES

1

As a copper and a white rose form a consonance sleep with wings begins to scream. In it is a bullet trace as tough as a rainbow kicked off to an area where unusually blue grass flourishes. The countryside is beautiful like the ground dragon but because its palms trembling for fear of cold are accurate they offer a sufficient gravity to cover the face. Like any material that emits sound did that sleep too belong to the will? From there a brain, a brain as detailed as the moon, is visible. Adhering to the sub-zero mirror surface are innumerable gods. The foundation of this moment is as pretty as a flower. The two eyes of an architect with a cigar-colored throat scheming a new architectural trick by means of overflowing useless things by means of a flower's will are artificial eyes. And conscious of his name gradually changing into inorganic matter. A ray of golden light pierces a bird's vocal organs. Rational 7 A.M.

2

The breast part of the full moon that makes an unstable flight to a tower that opens its rose eyes remembers a wind wounded blue. Is kind to a girl who after taking a medicine of Paradise is looking at a simple landscape. A perfect swindler rushes. He collides. With a garland-like ocean. With a star-colored dog. With two finds that can't be compared. And with an unknown ray of light. Finally cannot drown and die in an infinitely amputatable petal.

3

Inhales a boy who puts his head on a changing book of poetry. Inhales a cup. The skeleton of a bird tries to become gold. A ray of light doesn't drop. A rose and she return to the first moment during the night that has come to a standstill. A fruit doesn't smile. The fruit, like a compass, is knowledgeable about poetry. The fruit becomes oblivious of the noises in a flower and bursts out laughing concerning an enfeebled green window.

4

The sturdy bird clearly sees through their city from high in the sky above the ocean and turns its chest to the soul as dizzying as a solitary gem conversing on a cold protuberance. The city that puts makeup on the aquamarine mole of the petal merchant who turns his back to the virginity of dynamic force doesn't have anything that appeals to language. In the form of a bird, doesn't give a kiss to the imperfect lips of a crocus. A restricted angel after brightening the bird's sympathy suddenly resets its new eyeballs.

5

Transfers into the eyeballs of a fish with a good posture a glossy mountain-water drawing which is in the brains of innumerable gods. The words that are born at the fingertips that smash themselves do not know yesterday and today. When delicious tears flow down green-grass-like cheeks, look at the swift walk of the infant Aphrodite who rushes over the precise clock face, the lake water. Look at the development of a spring season in a circling race. That is the very elegant unanachronistic basket.

6

The vertical drunkenness of a mirror surface assaults a cold flower in early morning. Love of milk passes through laconic glass windows of towns and disperses. A farmer who takes his hat off voluntarily before a blinding imbalance does not take his supreme order except from the ground dragon from whom chlorophyll spills. Greets in two golden moon rays. Shouts gently like two stars. Becomes bashful at the evidence of resplendent life and dies like a wedding dress that does not know the season. Two windpipes are there that do not defend themselves against poetry.

1927

Fragments

—danse des impuissants de la creation. Tristan Tzara

The ruby of the body gleamed on my body that did not die. The ruby felt the cold of three seconds. The perfect neck of Venus in her youth consoles me. The ruby of the body is on her finger. The ruby of gray is on my finger.

Night and all other things keep a balance on a resplendent scale. I look at Mars. The night wraps my soul. I look at a hyacinth. The night wraps the hyacinth. A cruel ennui moves me. A girl's nude soul, about to be amputated like a reed, is trembling. I walk away from everything.

A demon of fantasy has possessed her. She becomes like an idiot and shows me her white fingers. My soul that does not know words begins to swell like a white lily. Why has she metamorphosed? The libertine's breasts become feminine like the inside of a new shell. My eyes can see them for the first time. The puzzling posture she takes.

A crowded smile that doesn't resemble any flower. A flower hairpin that wants to change infinitely. Ah fearful analogy!

She sobs for loneliness.

Becoming some extreme female, and wrapped in a kimono. I become a simple hydrangea. She, carrying an unknown portrait with her, tried to bring a change to my art. She puts out before me her bruised bewitching arms. At last the demon of fantasy caught me. I tried to turn her attention to a photograph of the iron bridge of Brooklyn. Suddenly she becomes a hydrangea.

If the body dies I do not love her.

A breeze of exactly the same style continues three days. She is out on the beach and is curiously rubbing her knees that extremely resemble avian eggs. She seems to have lost most of her body. She confessed that she would feel sorrowful if grapes abided eternally. She eats her meal before me like a marble statue. The girl is unaware of various words pouring on a live white lily. When innumerable gods are surprised it is already daybreak.

May 1928

DOCUMENT D'OISEAUX: DOCUMENT OF BIRDS

The angel who entered the constellation Carp peered in the plum pith mirror and for the first time knew me. Adorned my hair with wheat flowers and ran away. A fish with a beautiful heart, when spring comes, steals the angel's costumes. This experiment is performed at my fingertip where a bud is about to spill over. In the glass waves groan, close. It was the first dinner born of the conversational instinct between the first snow on my fingernail and the cataract under my armpit. As my eyelashes are already dyed the color of evening sun, my angel walks away from a large fruit shop, almost formless. I deny this angel's profession. And just as I crack a doll, I cut this peachlike angel. He was an angel filled with bliss. There, a single pitiful green seashell explodes. I am a dangerous virgin. A rose that tempts me skillfully, however, is also no more than a flounder that swims eternally. Look at the pebblelike sun of pure yellow rising along my nape.

This is purely a virgin's imagination. Now I give feathers to all the birds that come through my gold earrings. I give all breezes the clothes on which stars fly. My miracle was to impregnate a cluster of heaven's diamonds. By the light of the class Pisces, the angel's shadow falls on me. His smile was truly a god's feat. His voice had the effect of a boundless fortress of an incomparably transparent cobweb. Already, however, his lips fossilize as they are, vermilion. Beautiful angel like the one family Felidae that has become nameless. I wish I could once again pass through thy soul of a crystalline wheat ear. I thank the granite that sends blood. A shower is the angel's assassin as much as a hydrangea express train. A virgin stung by a rainbow filled with sap is me. The eagle's core at last yearns for the angel's rosy hair. It is an ideal universal gravitation. The flowering of violets at the wavetips this year as well is its result to be feared. Every sea coast is almighty, and the pine trunk also conceives an Apollo. Look at the photograph of a guiltless demon in its marrow. It glitters more beautifully than a diamond. Angel. Dost thou know thy future by the neon ad under this pine bark? Corpse of the blue sky of the angel who has stretched his hands this way. The bird is amiable. His mother too is amiable. I who have conceived carry into the sea a bright candle along with delight. Is that poisonous to the class Aves? Nay, now is the season when all poisons become extinct. An esthetic iceberg too is in its child-bearing season. Even a single goldfish shines atop the wall of a fortress. A cigar burns on the supreme sea coast. It's a secret that that is a recent phenomenon in the aquarium. The air is a boneless beautiful princess. Inside a straw she is the Virgin

Mary. In the PIAZZA of its throat, dropped a gem like a white rose. That white world was neither an island nor a bird. This sole memory will make me a devil. When morning comes all the angels rise from their beds. They again expose their eternal, immortal breasts. The morning wind was again refreshing to them.

Because I secretly saw God sculpturing a peach, I die. I am dead, holding a magnificent breast in my mouth, hugging a bouquet of sky-blue roses. That's a fair, youthful adventure. By that a fly and a gem are not surprised. For the sea is no more than a new musical instrument. The lion of beautiful sound who harbingers spring was a perfect heavenly body, which was unable to distinguish a morning glory from a man, and which held overhead a cobalt parasol. This was a dramatic spectacle. Theater on the horizon. Outside are the four seasons, birds of love are warbling. Keep silent about the turning of a seal into a seven-string lyre. The shadowless sun is a yacht I get a ride on. I see a pure white divine horse bucking on the deck. See, in the document of birds, that a Muse is now putting her makeup on.

July 1929

MIROIR DE MIROIR: MIRROR OF A MIRROR

A looking glass of a cherry's ash has a cherry's footprints. Long ago, a bird with pebble-ears fell in a looking glass in a wood, owl of eternal future solitude, thy nude body can be mistaken for golden glass, a great fire breaks out in Berlin, owl, listen. My sympathy was all poetry. Owl children, what is the lightbulb that is above the ninth infant girl's eyebrows and shines the most? Listen to these pebbles laughing. Do you see the snow of innumerable loves falling in tomorrow's winter? Wheat's illusion changes year by year and grows year by year more elegant like a beautiful girl's costume. By a machine that sniffs at goldfish, I knew it was snowing in the waterway as precise as a heart. In a mirror where wheat dries, a whalebone structure moves like the morning sun. Moves like a beautiful girl's magnet. Wheat is disturbed. Wheat's stone breasts are a mackerel actress's mirror. The voluptuous sparrow that painted waves there and left was asleep in my palm. The most beautiful purple bird that flies off from my fingers returns to its nest. The fish that brocade a threadbare coast with golden threads drink hot spring water among clouds. A peacock of zero will sip water from a yellow mirror, and a millionaire's cataract will wrap the white clipper on an owl's head. That is the rebirth of an infinitely white pelican of infinite time, strangely

breasts, this is the milk of a great forest that has brought up copper and owls. Milk of a milk star of a black cloud,
the lady dove who bore my seven mirrors sucks my milk before noon. The pasturage of my mirrors has now grown taller than the dove's chest and is crowned with a butterfly's brain, the hearts of the doves in the dark between its two legs are reciprocal. Blossoms of kisses open on plum blossoms. It's the hour for the nude body of the lady dove, the hour for an iceberg to talk, the hour for a starfish to laugh. Listen to the beautiful voice of a blue butterfly surrounded with rock cliffs on four sides, owl children in my pupils. Decorations on the calendar of your skin. Heaven's love pours into the chandelier on the marsh bottom and into a carp's lovely gloves. The gold of a gold treasure is a painting one heavenly body one sign a polar bear OUI
Seven perfect natures on the lake the infinite sun's enticing chests mounting the animals of ribs of ripples sport blossoms according to their custom. A Muse of the secret heart of thunderclaps wrapped with clouds is related by marriage to a cactus flower. The waves of the river of my joined hands, my hen's voice that is a knee, (1) which is ruby, and (2) which is marble, a blossom of a ship on the lake visible from a window, a boy who is a natural stone kowtows to an infant carp under the waves under the clouds like underground water. In an express train I am a field of gems. This is the midsky of rape flowers. Cloud candy of a ritual, descend from heaven, hanging from a breeze's cheeks *bonbonbon* . . . the sculpture of a bird on the round-shaped lake of the cheeks is eternal. The ship of heaven's lake water that reflects in the water on the land, I, dressed as a rose in one of its dressing rooms, am an infinitely tall sailor. A white abrupt wave destroys a statue of hydrangea the newest love. An angel's egg-shaped bedroom where the civilization of snow's dreams emerges on his elf's ring flourishes blue on the horizon. Elf, love thy elf.

July 1929

Kiss toward the Absolute

A woman of pure intuition who storms into the guest room wet with sprays of a waterfall inside my golden fingernail. I do not ask whether or not a hunter had trampled into the diamond that gleamed on her finger. Her at once horizontal and vertical breasts are wrapped in a garment like a saturated scale. Of the natural disasters in a wax country, her thin moustache tells. She is moving on the back and the front, to the right and the left, of the lens of the lipstick that is burning time. Secrets of a personal pronoun. Senses of time. O a trace of time makes the hexahedral interior of my room transform violently like snow. A bed of light that generates in the sable fur that was slipped down. Her fainting has an eternal egg-shape. The beautiful game that confuses water and land will in a while draw near its denouement. A dry star will be raising a din on a breakfast plate. Marine elements and so forth will soon have crept into a bookshelf. Soon the sea consisting of three straight lines will rush in my palm. Her totality, like a dot on a die, turns sometimes white, sometimes purple. The copulation of the sky. The voice of a crab in a pupil, a rainbow in a cupboard. The mid section of her arm, that does not exist. She becomes eroded like Venus, for only one moment. She is heat in a hot wind, iron in the iron. But her song, which is the class Aves in the ash. Starfish flow in her capital. Her curves are leviathans. Her torso is a virgin plain of differences, a letter of flame where a tombstone of mercury becomes pregnant, it is a level of one bright noon a bright noon between the pubic hair as between clouds. Her hurricane. Her legend. Her nutriment. Her socks. Her corroboration. Her ovaries. Her sight. Her meaning. Her canine teeth. The advent of innumerable factual examples plays a coincidental game in an innocent display window that falls from the sky. Rainbow-hued sparks of corned beef. The public property right of a mirror of cheese. The death of a lady's hat. A swarm of Greek pantheons in bread. When a soul's fuss and noise dies, will all matter travel carrying a saturated briefcase—who can answer that? The scarlet star in her semen is insoluble. Just as a wind caught her green garment (which like an old miracle evokes my memory), space was a green flower. Her judgment leaves a time-like trace on my lips. Why was that love? When a Chinese with a green collar knocked on the door, a simply nameless ignorance pulled my fingers. Everything was flooding. Everything was singing. A supreme bliss was shining like noctilucae on used tea leaves of the untrodden land. . . . (*sans date*)

ONO TŌZABURŌ

(born 1903)

Stealing

In the garden by the street
I decided to steal an amaranth.
The amaranth was broken easily,
with a truly pleasant snap.
—And the air was filled with quiet, chaste autumn sun.
There was no one to shout, Thief!
I had wanted to hear that voice.
If at that moment someone had shouted,
how comically, delightedly
I could have started running down the late fall Ichijō Avenue
brandishing the amaranth overhead!
But I stole it too easily, banally, untroubled,
in a manner so natural as to be insipid.
Now casually
from this bridge, I'll throw it away.

Landscape: 6

The wind is rough
and the ground is frozen.
The roadbed for the sidetrack is rusted red;
here and there
nut grass still spreads its roots.
Today, too, toward the sea
there are the clouds with only their hems effulgent, and that makes
    you feel cold.
On the track, sooty, tank-shaped freight cars, strung together, stand
    still.
Every one of them has thick sulfuric acid or carbon sulfide liquid.

Landscape: 7

At a high place
a large glass pane shakes noisily.
Uttering a groan from time to time,
a wind is raging outside.
There, over the reed plain
and near the estuary, it must be terrible,
but the smoke, pent up on the horizon, doesn't move.
The world below looks mysteriously quiet.
Only, amid the crowded roofs
there's a patch of grassland showing a bit of its ruddy skin
with a dog in it.
He's too far, and sad,
but probably he's supposed to chase a rubber ball or something thrown
    to him.
I've just seen him
make a leap as cute
as love itself,
run out from the shadow of the house,
and run back.

One Plant for Man-made Oil[1]

Between the rusted railways
evening primroses put out fewer seeds each year.
On the burnt sand is a row
of gigantic, silver-gray globes
coated with aluminum paint.
The utilization of solar energy and the tides that popular science books
    preach
doesn't excite me a bit.
My fantasies are extremely modest.
That raw-smelling, black mud that's supposed to be all dug out of this
    earth in another twenty or thirty years is the future, they say.
Look at the sea.
Evidently
when one design

---

[1] Ono says he had a coal-liquefying plant in mind. Japan's coal technology was among the most advanced in the world during the 1930s.

begins there,
the landscape on the earth looks almost hatefully wasted.
I'll get there
a trifle earlier
than matter.
A trifle earlier
than the accumulation of inventions, capital,
steel frames,
and tracks.

Dislike of Nature

I don't know many
names of trees,
names of grasses.
I don't know names of birds, names of insects.
I've forgotten them all.
Calling on my terribly inaccurate knowledge and memory
I look at the grass and trees outdoors, point to the crops,
call the birds by name.
Nature doesn't respond.
For a long time I've done without it.
This morning, on that filled-in land
I suddenly saw something like a lark dance up to heaven.
    (Probably that was a lark.)
In the world neither trees, grass, birds, nor insects exist.
In a complete loss of memory
I have remembered many names such as
Woods, Fields,
and Fish.

Extinction of Plankton

What's the matter here?
What happened?
This color of the tide.
This red, lukewarm, dirty, poisonous juice.
All around,
corpses of fish gone soft.

Rolling them in,
not knowing what to do with them,
thudding, thudding heavily,
dog day waves wash the windless, burning sand beach all day.
—Come, do something with them, do something!
the sea cries out.
The scarlet sea choked with muddy heavy oil and factory discharge.
The clouds that melt
like the fume from fuming sulfuric acid.

Today's Ferns

Near the sea
the ground's partitioned off.
The winter sun shines, and it's quiet.
The air contains a faint bit of blue vitriol,
and iron, electricity, and carbide are there.
From sometime in the past they've been there.
Look at the reeds rusted red.
Like ferns turning to carbon,
grasses gradually complete spiritual assimilation
with this desolate field.
Then too, certain kinds of birds, dragonflies, and hairstreaks that are
    already transparent.
Their tiny souls.
Human beings follow far, far behind.

Sparrow Flock

In the distance
a sparrow flock flies.
In the flight of their group
something bursts incessantly,
something keeps exploding incessantly.
Bloody afterglow of the harvest day!
The earth shines upside down
in the heavens.

Sparrow Bathing

Catching the water that drips
from a hose dangling from a water tower,
a baby sparrow is bathing.
It trots up to it, flaps its wings,
and trots back again.
It's repeating the same movement many times over.
Yes: No matter what happens to the world,
sparrow, stay there, repeating your movement eternally, without resting.
There's rumbling in the C61 boiler.

In the Eyes of a Screech Owl

On the diesel train's
shaking floor
there was a screech owl.
Night's bird of prey caught alive on a foggy, northernmost mountain,
with its large, brass-colored eyes glinting,
was firmly holding on to the wire netting of the perchless cage,
bending its sharp, pointed nails.
As I looked in,
it arched its upper body, half-opened its beak,
made as though to leap fiercely
at my face.
What at that moment suddenly came close
and filled the owl's
wide-open eyes
must have been something like the pockmarked surface of the half-
moon a reflecting telescope caught.
I drew my face closer
and went into the eyes of the screech owl.
It was pitch-dark there.
Within that palpable volume
something was packed and was moving.
I smelled blood,
raw, but clean.
I smelled intestines.

MARUYAMA KAORU

(1899–1974)

Estuary

The ship lowers its anchor.
The hearts of the seamen also lower their anchors.

From the freshwater, seagulls greet the creaking halyards.
Fish come near the bilge hole.

The captain changes his suit dyed by the salt winds and goes ashore.
It gets so that even after nightfall he seldom returns.
How many more oyster shells have grown on the hull already?

Each time the dusk thickens,
his son, a sailor, alone lights the blue lamp at the bowsprit.

Anchor

The captain is drinking rum.
Drinking and singing something.
His song, hoarse, is as sad as the block slowly turning with the hal-
    yard;
a seagull, wingbeat hushed, went through the half light astern, whis-
    pering.
Soon the moon must rise at the estuary.

The captain's chest too is at full tide with red rum.
At the bottom of its flow
tonight too the tattooed anchor wavers blue.

Song of the Sail

The wings of the gull flapping in the dark sea sky, if I turn my
   shoulder, may touch my shoulder.
The voice of the gull calling in the dark sea sky, if I stretch my hand,
   may be grasped in my palm.
It seems within my grasp, but I can't see it, probably because the lamp
   hung from my neck is flickering.
I will blow the lamp out.
And wait for the gull to come and perch on the cinder of the blown-
   out lamp.

Song of the Lamp

Beyond my sight, deep into the darkness, the anchor chain disappears
   on the face of the sea.
Beyond my sight, high into the darkness, the halyard escapes toward
   the mast.
My light is meager. It can only shine on my blind face.
Staring at me in the distance, in the darkness I cannot see, a gull
   called.

Song of the Gull

Even I myself cannot see my figure.
How can the lamp or the sail that reflects the lamp see it?
But I can clearly see the lamp and the sail.
Frozen and distant, I only circle in the darkness.

Sad Parting

A gull is whispering to the anchor's ear.
Suddenly—without a word, the anchor slides and falls.
Surprised, the gull gets away.
For a moment, the anchor pales in the water and goes down.
The thoughts that remained in the gull's chest turn into sad calls and
   scatter in the sky.

Gun Base

The fragments were trying to huddle into one.
The cracks were trying to smile again.
The gun barrel was trying to rise, to sit again on the gun carriage.
All were dreaming of their fragile original shape.
With each wind, they were buried further in the sand.
Invisible ocean—bird of passage flashes.

Fragments

In the gun muzzle a crow had nested.
In the collapsed gun carriage a bat was hiding.
The earth and sand were piled high;
in the thoughts entwined with rust,
each lived, crisscrossing the day and night.

Crane

What else does a crane spreading its torn wings have
other than torn wings?
Tilting your torn wings fully like sails,
crane, what are you trying to shield from the wind?

Funeral Song

Let's scatter petals on the coffin.
Let's hide the petals with a lid of sand.
Let's nail the lid with tears.

Dark Sea

The flock of gulls, voices swallowed in the dark sea, must be
already rising to their feet on the face of the sea far in the darkness.
The lamp was at least illuminating the rain at the bow.

Dusk

The river is black—a single white flower lit on its breast.

TACHIHARA MICHIZŌ

(1914–1939)

For a Certain Night

We will pause. In the mist.
The mist will flow far from the mountain, brush the moon
like a cast arrow, and will wrap us
like a cloth of ash.

We will part. Without knowing—
without being known, like the cloud
we came across, we will forget.
Like a waterway

the road will be silver. We will go off
alone, separately . . . (How is it
one has learned to wait for another in the evening?)

We will not meet again. The moon,
reminding us of the past, reflects the night,
we will simply keep saying.

For a Memory

The dream always went back to a lonely village by the mountain—
by the path through a hushed, afternoon wood
where the wind rose among smartweeds
and crickets did not stop singing.

The sun was peaceful in the blue sky, the volcano slept.
—And I went on talking
of the things I had seen: islands, waves, capes, sunlight and moonlight,
knowing no one was listening.

The dream goes no further, now.
When it tries to forget everything
and forgets it has forgotten it all

the dream will freeze in midwinter memories.
And it will open the door and pass, in quietude,
by the road lit by stardust.

Rainbow and You

A gentle wind after the rain stirred,
the grass thickets still wet with dewdrops, the cobweb shining like a
    rosary;
in the sky to the east hung a slow rainbow,
and we stood, silent. Silent!

Ah everything remains the same. You were then
looking up at me. Because I had nothing to do.
(Though I loved you)
(Though you loved me)

Again a wind blows, again a cloud moves.
In the bright, blue, hot sky, as if nothing had happened,
birds' songs echo, the colors of flowers are fragrant.

Upon your eyelashes too, a small rainbow must be resting.
(But you no longer love me,
I no longer love you)

In Mourning for the Summer

My times that passed away
have turned my heart to gold. So as not to be wounded, so wounds
    may be cured soon,
between yesterday and tomorrow
a deep indigo gulf has been made.

What I tossed away
was a small piece of paper stained with tears.
Amid foamy white waves, one evening,
all, everything, vanished! Following the story line

then I became a traveler and passed many
villages on the moonlit capes, many
hot, dry fields.

If I could remember! I'd like to return once again.
Where? To that place (I have a memory of,
that I waited for and quietly gave up—)

Soon Autumn . . .

Soon autumn will come.
Evenings talk to us, friendly,
trees cast shadows bare like gestures of old people
darkly toward the night,

and everything wavers with uncertainty,
oddly, like quiet, shallow sighs. . . .
(Because it's not yesterday, it will be tomorrow)
our thoughts will whisper to each other.

—So the autumn has returned.
And the autumn pauses again, and
like someone asking for forgiveness. . . .

soon, for having not forgotten, as a keepsake,
but leaving no keepsake, it will pass by.
The autumn . . . and . . . again, one evening—

For a Lost Night

The burnt eyes burned.
The eyes were neither blue
nor brown. Twinkling,
they stabbed my heart.

They seemed to make me cry,
but did not.
Twinkling, they caressed me,
licked my spoiled heart.

The burnt eyes did not move.
As if they were both blue
and brown, forever

the burnt eyes were quiet!
Having forgotten the sun and fragrant grass,
they burned sadly, twinkling, twinkling.

TAMURA RYŪICHI

(born 1923)

Nine Prose Poems: A Sequence

Etching

A landscape he saw in a German etching lies before him. It looks like a bird's-eye view of an ancient city, dusk turning to night, or, he thought, like a realistic picture depicting a modern precipice, midnight being led to daybreak.

The man—that is, he about whom I began to speak—killed his father when he was young. That same autumn, his mother, beautifully, went mad.

Sunken Temple

People all over the world want proof of death. But no one has ever witnessed death. In the end, people may be a mere illusion, and reality the greatest common divisor of such things. Instead of people, objects begin to ask questions. About life. About its existence. Even if a chair questions, I must be afraid. Reality may be the least common multiple of such things. Incidentally, how can a man unable to feel melancholy about the fate of people stake his life on this world of disturbances? On occasion geniuses have appeared, only to make nothingness more precise. The self-evident, too, has merely deepened the turmoil in broad daylight.

Maybe he tried to tell them something. But I'll write only about facts. First, his knees gave in, hit the ground, and he fell. Among the people who ran up to him, a young man just about my age murmured, "A beautiful face. And worse, he believes in the world like a flower!"

Golden Fantasy

He was afraid of naked thought. Beautiful things never fail to kill. That's what he used to say.

It's no longer a matter of seeing with the eyes. Nor trying to draw with the hands, either. In broad daylight, in this city, in the autumn of 1947, I witnessed: the logical proof of death which someone incises in golden calligraphy on a breast of white wax.

Nothing is sad, but somehow he stops, eyes filled with tears. And without saying a word, he is absently looking in my direction.

Autumn

The bandaged rain turned and left. After making a round of the sleepless city.

That autumn, I went to a recital. A concert hall shut in by dry doors. A cold, cruel pianist seated on a hard chair. There the dark dream rejected by sleep silently handed over all weapons to you. You may arm yourself. Love, love your life.

Outside, the rain smelling of fresh gauze turned another corner to the harbor, from the harbor at twilight to the dark sea, to the world of illusion without stars.

Lips became wet. Soon my hands dried. Goodbye. The woman walked past me and went out. Out the door. A tall man waits for me, getting wet in the rain. To live or to die, with a door between us, we load our guns.

Bless us. Even to us the solitary ones, the enemy has appeared. In the mirror my features totally change. A raw fiction that gives you gooseflesh! Out the door. The sleepless metropolis and its satellite cities. The seven oceans and the enormous desert. From the summer of Petersburg to the winter of Paris. The woman sang ferociously. I still love you, still love you. And Tokyo. Autumn! The world constructed by my hands is dreaming underneath antennas. At this point, ask yourselves about the moment of awakening through the sonata form. . . . I pray for the freedom to die. Applause has begun. I stand up from my seat. Mother!

Voice

The fingers begin to droop. On the gray musical scale unearthed here.

Hold your breath. Talk in voiceless sounds . . . love is a twilight symbol caused by a dissonance of genitals and the dead. On rainy days she is beautiful. That same autumn, at daybreak, she invites a golden smile. Suddenly I turn my back. The blue that plummets the eye! Death is familiar to me. I witnessed his obscene silence and sacred disintegration. To witness is to experience. I knew the process, first accompanied by screams, then gradually turning to vocatives beginning with *tu.* Sometimes he talked a lot. It was when autumn turned to winter, when fog filled the aquamarine capital. Decline thought. It possesses time. Get out of time. Toward the painful space where you can totally feel. Feel. To feel thoughts with your body. The fingers begin to droop. On the gray musical scale unearthed here. The sounds were selected by my fingers. The sounds were pure matter. A unity was born. Twenty-five years do you have any last words. In the corridor and in the yard, mother is incessantly calling me. It seems it's becoming *tu.* Never pray for the fulfillment of our youth. Weep. If you do, weep like father. If you do, do not weep for father.

Premonition

The afternoon arrives suddenly. He, as a person, is pushed into the bottom of the chair. His arms hanging slack, the world begins to darken. The world's sufferings drive him into his single being. The world's sorrows gouge out his eyes. Like an empty socket, the door, opened, leads directly into the past, it seems to him.

From the window the town where he was born is vaguely visible. Rain is falling on the town. For the past twenty years, between the wars, the rain has soaked the ground. The town has changed its shape many times. And the town of his childhood memory is expunged from this town. Once mother was beautiful, and grandmother must live in the real world as well. The past goes through the door, wordless. And it becomes connected to a part of the future. The rain collides with time. Before his eyes, the rain is wounded. A bandage! An ordinary middle-aged man walks past holding an ordinary black umbrella.

What can he do? Innumerable hands come through the opened door onto his shoulders, and with a slight pressure cold lips lie on his lips. A kiss without passion. And it's painful, that he tastes deep bliss.

You came to kill me.

The Image

Beads of death,
in this brown city,
in the rain, throngs of twisted entrails,
black umbrellas, dead experiences, their flow.

The man is not my father, nor is he my solitary friend. I am merely the same existence, the same experience as he, and a man with common images. And like him, I was born during the first world war and surely died in the second.

To fall the way a chair falls! That was my old image, and a hope for death which the eye in the mud dreamed of.

From the gouged eye, the cracked forehead, the dull gleam of the hair, and the black clothes wet with sea, the storm, and the huge illusion, the silent screams, the fierce arias of a shipwrecked man, resounding from them, when he appears out of the weekend night fog that flows when autumn turns to winter, I have to call out, "Where did you come from?"

My tongue hangs out like a dog's.

The Emperor

There is an eye in the stone. There is an eye closed with melancholy and tedium.

He passes by my door in a black robe. Winter emperor, my lonely emperor! With your white forehead reflecting the shadows of civilizations, you walk to the graveyard of Europe. The sun shining on your back, your self-punishment is painful.

Flowers! You extend your hands for them. At the end of the age of reason and progress, the winter of the world is about to begin.

The beautiful European woman is an illusion, and who will kiss your hand? Is there a budding stage in your palm which has run dry with brown fate?

Flowers, scars like flowers!

Winter Music

One can't say it is impossible. At some end of the earth, unknown to me, surely in a basement in a foggy city, a thin twenty-five-year-old just like me, his hair blond, eyes gray, talks in a Scandinavian language about the principle of revolutionary action. Is it madness or sentimentalism? Even if it were vomit in the winter of 1947, who would now believe it was someone else's business? Possibly, like Modigliani's men, he's cocking his head on a thin neck, staring. It's not definite what his eyes are looking at. It's no longer clear. No longer definite. No longer clear, the universe. He is like a man awake in it.

Do not laugh. Even if you met a worm's fate, do not laugh, not now. Whether you refuse it or drag it with you, caress that incomparable, invincible fate.

You, alone, are perhaps the first and last man! I abandon a drama, in a far larger drama.

The singing voice recedes. Arms hanging slack, the noise of innumerable footsteps disappears. From the basement room. From the desert. And the lights of the city turn off and on. Melancholy time forms, solemn rentier's life, farewell!

Even if it is related to a boyhood memory on a summer day or the lonely smell evoked on a snowy night, can you imagine a raw vision unsupported by ideas? But after the pianist, I try to support and to constantly amend a raw vision with my eyes and fingers. The wind begins to blow. Good. The universe gradually turns cold. Eye in the stone! The fingers wish desperately to keep their balance. Should I call an eye larger than my eyes eternity? These moments? The eye has appeared. Hiding a smile, he questions. Regarding the self-evident conquest. An order to massacre! Into the space between the eye and the fingers, into the graveyard of culture, I settle. The winter music.

A Study in Terror

10

An evening
when you hear a needle
hit the floor.
A whisky glass on a table breaks
and from the drawer
of countless pasts
emerge unfamiliar cards
incomprehensible codes
the notes
of a mind that is missing.
This is
a world of light and shadow
a world of negatives:
the files of records of the K University Hospital surgical ward.
Blood vessels like the veins of an orchid
make ash-white rivers,
the skin and subcutaneous fat enfolds
a world of darkness.
The dull tactile sense
suitable for touching by rubber gloves,
the overripe flesh
suitable for groping
with tweezers and knives of alloyed metals.
If the flesh enfolds a dead heart
ask a poet you like
what bread he can imagine,
ask a painter you like
what wine he can see
in the flow of milky blood.
Ah
a slight intrusion of meaning
and any modern city becomes shattered,
a slight intrusion of light
and the world of negatives collapses.
The needle leaps up from the floor.
The milky rivers turn into the color of blood
and under the smooth skin
appears the heart that has feigned death.
The window opens.
The door opens with a violent noise

and someone goes out.
Or
someone comes in.

9
If the heart has died,
any attempt at reviving it
will be useless.
For his resurrection
what rituals
what mobs
what powers
what traitors
what doctrines
what skies
what horizons are there?
Perhaps Breughel
might have silently painted large trees
with tones heavier than gravity.
To make blanks.
Because he can only answer it with blanks
because he wants a blank perspective no matter what
because he wants to hear a blank rhythm.
Incidentally
if it's a missing heart
you can't bury it casually.
There's no trouble forging
a death certificate
or a cremation permit
but you can't forge a heart.
Perhaps Mozart
would need a flute.
With a flute
the boy with curled hair would set out on a journey,
with a flute
he would roam countries of all living things.
From all thirsts
the boy would find a uniform dream.
Perhaps Miro
would give the uniform dream
a uniform color.

From the uniform color wild lines would be born
and soon the lines would cross,
dots echo each other,
and toward a center
paint a fertile territory.
The black earth
where all beings were born
and all beings died,
the black earth will spread its wings as wide as it can
and divide the sky and the horizon.
Sometimes
showers will come
or they will accompany thunderclaps as well.
Lightning will pierce the space,
numerous dolphins copulate
and gigantic whales spout rainbows.
Often
the trade wind will be sent to the Ivory Coast
and Henri Rousseau's
dark green trees will flourish.
In the East the stars yet to be named will twinkle
and by the time their light reaches the earth
St John's
John Donne's
Baudelaire's
and Mallarmé's metaphors will be created.
By these metaphors
billions of days and nights part,
millions of days and nights keep harmony
and oh
in my mind
four thousand days and nights engage in battle.

8

Where day and night part
where there are harmony and order of day and night
where there are battles between day and night
this is
the tip of a needle
the tip that shines by the light of unnamed stars
the spear of history's fire
the tip of the trembling spear

7

to the tower
to the fort
to the mansion
they rush
they roar
they loot
they rape
they arson
they express
they express the domain of every art
the white-heated rhythm
the image that multiplies
the original metaphor
the dangerous simile
the exposé-type manifesto
the most hypocritical art movement that suppresses hypocrisy

6

If you really want to see things, gouge your eyes.
If you really want to hear rhythms, slash your ears.
What connects image to image is the king's power.
What creates image from image is the angel's glory.
Submission is the slave's joy.
Enjoyment is the secret pleasure of the ruled.
Therefore
the king must be greater than the mass.
Therefore
the angel above must be more powerful than any king.
All critics on earth, get lost.
Look at the eyes of generations of kings:
their eyes were gouged thousands of years ago,
their eyes are in the stone.
Look at the ears of the angel. If
you can see your own angel
his ears are in his wings.

5

the trembling wings
the trembling tongue
in the backyard of the K University Hospital

I saw the pink legs of a wild pigeon
the trembling tongue
the ripping tongue
on the premises of Kaizen Temple on the Kamikawa route, Shinshū
I saw a genuine blue snake
the trembling tongue
the beautiful tongue
in Rokurigahara in the autumn wind
I met Sakuraiwa Kwannon

4
where
a needle lies
light comes from anywhere
the darkness is in the voice of the wild pigeon
in the resplendent design of the snake
and in
the hands of Sakuraiwa Kwannon

3
from the deer's horn
to the french horn
from the blokfleute
to the flute
the histories of musical instruments belong to light and dark
to the blank
of the heart that is missing
from Mozart to Debussy
from the deer's horn
to the french horn
from the blokfleute
to the flute

2
the light drives the heart
into rhythm
the darkness drives it into instrumental form
as the hunter chases his quarry
as hunger chases a wild beast

I

where there's a needle
there's a silence

where the angel above intercepts
there's a trembling tongue

I see a tower
our life is too long to commit sins

I see a castle
our life is too short to atone for sins

the soul is a form
from the deer's horn
to the french horn
from the blokfleute
to the flute

O

TANIKAWA SHUNTARŌ

(born 1931)

Nero

—To a small loved dog

Nero
in no time again the summer comes
your tongue
your eyes
the way you napped
now clearly come alive before me

you knew only about two summers
I have already known eighteen summers
and now I'm remembering various summers, some mine, some not
Maisons-Laffitte summer
Yodo summer
Williamsburg Bridge summer
Oran summer
and I wonder
how many summers have human beings known already?

Nero
in no time again the summer comes
but it isn't the summer you were in
it's another different summer
quite a different summer

a new summer comes
and I'll go on learning various new things
beautiful things, ugly things, things that encourage me, things that
        make me sad
and I'll question
what on earth is it
why on earth is it
what on earth should I do

Nero
you died
going alone far away so no one could know
your voice
your touch
even your feelings
now clearly come alive before me

but Nero
in no time again the summer comes
a new infinitely broad summer comes
and
I will still go on walking
to welcome a new summer, welcome fall, welcome winter
welcome spring, expect yet another new summer
to know all new things
and
to answer myself all my questions

Night

No matter how fast I run
I can't help standing like a tree;
arms spread as if looking for something when there's nothing to look
       for
I try to rest my heels temporarily on something reliable

Not into the night
but into something the night exposes by darkening it
I enter;
while hesitating where to put the lamp for not losing sight
what I can illuminate disappears;
and so the depth grows ever more exposed,
which I try to pull toward myself;
but before even kissing it I spread my arms
and go on falling, and while falling,
thinking I ought to wake up, uselessly—

—Even when a flock of distances supported me somewhere
because I did not know the origins of those distances
I couldn't say they were not a dream;
there was no pain to wake me

I go on spreading without stopping
but like a clumsy tree I'm certain only of my spread,
I'm not at all certain of my position;
even if the sun begins to shine now
because I can see the ground, see the sky
and I can't see anything else
and even if the night comes again
I can see the things the daytime hid
even then I still can't see anything

Sounds

—To John Cage

The sounds
flow not wanting to become a river
but before you know it the sounds are gone
and there a river flows

The sounds at first tried to become a new river
but too fast or too slow
it wasn't a river
except even though clouds reflected in the river of sounds
even though people looked back at it
and ran along with it
when trees budded on the river banks
the river of sounds understood it had neither spring or fall
but when the sounds forget what they become
and flow, modesty and foolishness together, as if tired
exposing themselves completely
they somehow become a river
and the sounds no longer notice that they are a river
they don't care what they are
throwing themselves out
as if not caring that they are not sounds, not a river
before long spring comes and the summer
and they don't even notice that they have become a tree

The sounds, not looking at themselves
are in what keeps them alive

the sounds no longer make people dance
no longer make people weep
the sounds mingle with the world
like the circling of the moon, without end they are singing
like the circling of the moon, without making them aware they are
   among people

. . . In that manner the sounds go home.

kiss[1]

I close my eyes, the world recedes,
and only the weight of gentleness ascertains me without end. . . .

The silence becomes a quiet night
and turns round us like a promise;
it is now not something that separates
but rather a gentle distance that encloses us;
because of that we suddenly become something like one person. . . .

We explore each other
in a manner more certain than talking, seeing,
and we find us
when we have lost sight of ourselves—

What did I want to ascertain?
Gentleness that has returned from the distance,
in the silence that has lost words, that has been cleansed
you are now only breathing. . . .

You now are life itself. . . .
but even these words will be punished
when soon gentleness fills the world
and I fall in it to live.

[1] Original title in English.

On Love

What did you want to welcome,
blooming?
Had you understood
the darkness?

Had it ended in joy?
I merely passed through you.
Did you know
that I tried to return endlessly?

Love was too large for me.
Did you make certain
of flesh,
which I believed in and passed by?

Did you not explore?
Were you not uncertain?
Was joy that total?
Could you believe in me that much?

I was in your joy.
In you love was total.
But the darkness had not ended.
I was staring.

I could not make certain.
Where were you?
I went far.
. . . Would you forgive me?

Kiss

She came home, smelling of another man.
And so I could not kiss her.
Then the two of us got under the quilts
that still held the sun's heat.
That day the weather was nice all day.
And yet I could not kiss her.

She pressed her breast close to my breast.
And yet I could not do it.
I felt she was a different woman.
It was like before the two of us met.
It was like the days when I still didn't know that part of her
and went fishing alone on Sundays.
It was like the days when I watched the thin winter sun by that small
    marsh
and was waiting to meet someone.
I was afraid.
And yet I could not do it.
And in time I fell asleep.
It's a night like a vast prairie
no matter how long I run, how long I run

Two Portraits

C

I see a woman
it's a woman who was my lover

Above a swaying balance
a heart alive

A paper boy's shrill call
turns a street corner

What I couldn't catch
I see an n number of faces of the world

Film changing color
a choo-choo train chasing a horse

A variety of angels held down with insect pins
a martini glass that is lifted

A turning record
I see a faint scratch on the record

D

I see a woman
I see my wife

I see tears welling up slowly
I see translucent milk being squeezed out

I see an expansive back
absorbent cotton being torn

A hard ripe fruit
and an infant sketch of the fruit

I see all of the things I have seen enough
I see myself who doesn't try to see them again

A polished, long corridor
runs away like a snake

Under a hot shower
I see lips suddenly coming close

On Obscenity

No pornographic film
can be as obscene as a husband and wife making love.
If love is of humanity
obscenity is also of humanity.
Did Lawrence, Miller, Rodin,
Picasso, Utamaro,[2] *Man'yōshū* poets
ever fear obscenity?
It isn't that films are obscene,
but that we are, as we are, obscene.
Warm, gentle, strong,
and this ugly, shameful,
we are obscene.
Every night, every day, we are obscene.
Whatever it is, we are obscene.

[2] Kitagawa Utamaro (1753–1806), an ukiyo-e painter.

Beginning of Love

Though I'm thinking of you ceaselessly,
I can't somehow remember your face.
I come to myself, and realize I'm humming over and over again
a tune of some music that caught my ear.
Though I think I'd like to see you
it's not so much a passion as a curiosity:
I'd like to make certain of what's what with myself,
in front of you, once again.
What comes after doesn't come to my mind.
I can't imagine holding you either.
Only, the world other than you is quite wearying,
and like an actor in a movie filmed at high speed
I light my cigarette slowly.
Then, living without you
begins to look like a pleasure.
You may be by chance one of the time-honored beautiful sculptures
I saw in another country.
By it, a fountain was sparkling high in the sun.

Reason for Your Suffering

The reason for your suffering
couldn't have an answer, even if I asked.
As you pushed your eyelids hard with the fingers of both hands,
your face for a moment warped like that of someone from a different
      star.
I have not yet even held your hand,
but I am already one of the men who have left you.
If my holding your body
without mouthing any word of consolation
could soothe you as much as a cup of hot tea,
that should do—
even such a thought, to me, looks as featherbrained
as a line in a "personal advice" reply.
Just as I cannot touch your suffering
so I cannot touch your body—
this thought of mine comes not from gentleness
but from a fear of gentleness.
After that there'll be nothing but silence,
though that too may be merely a deception.

That Act

I don't think I'm being manipulated.
But to do something one can't do anything about
as if by one's own will
is comical, sad, and yet peaceful.
While lying by you like this,
waiting for our breathing to calm down,
there's no way of thinking about things like love.
What were they—
those smooth, hot, and endless things?
Just because those odd things touched each other,
even my heart relaxed and breathed deeply,
my eyes looked at the starless darkness,
my ears heard moans that could not form words,
and I was about to melt and cease to be,
when you became unfathomably gentle and rich,
and in the void where any relation between persons doesn't catch up,
the very first thing of this world,
trying to be born, spurted out of me.
Out of this total silence now
what can I begin to say?
I simply rise to my feet in the darkness, for a glass of water.

ISHIGAKI RIN

(born 1920)

The Pan, the Pot, the Burning Fire I Have in Front of Me

For a long time
these things have always been placed
in front of us women:

a pan of a reasonable size
suited to one's strength,
a pot in which it's convenient for rice
to begin to swell and shine, grain by grain,
the heat of the fire inherited since the very beginning—
in front of them there have always been mothers, grandmothers, and
    their mothers.

What measures of love and sincerity
they must have poured
into these utensils—
sometimes red carrots,
sometimes black seaweed,
sometimes crushed fish

in the kitchen, always accurately
for morning, noon, and evening, preparations have been made
and in front of the preparations, in a row, there have always been
some pairs of warm knees and hands.

Ah without those persons waiting
how could women have gone on
cooking so happily?
their unflagging care,
so daily a service they became unconscious of it.

Cooking was assigned oddly
as the woman's role,

but I don't think that was unfortunate;
because of that, her knowledge and position in society
may have lagged behind the times
but it isn't too late:
the things we have in front of us,
the pan and the pot, and the burning fire,

in front of these familiar utensils,
let us also study government, economy, literature
as sincerely
as we cook potatoes and meat,

not for vanity and promotion
but so everyone
may be served for mankind
so everyone may work for love.

Roof

The Japanese house has a low roof,
the poorer the house, the lower the roof;

the lowness of the roof
weighs on my back.

What makes the weight of the roof?
I walk away ten steps to look:
what's on top of the house
is not the blue of the sky,
but the thickness of blood.

What holds me and blocks my way,
what confines my strength in the narrowness of one house
and consumes it

my sick father lives on the roof,
my stepmother lives on the roof,
my brothers live on the roof.

A wind blows
and the zinc roof twangs,
it can be easily blown away,
the four hundred square feet of it at the most—
look,
white radishes also lie on it,
rice lies on it,
and the warmth of the bed.

Bear it, they say;
under the weight of this roof
a woman, my spring darkens,
in the distance, the sun goes down.

Landscape

If you wait, he won't come,
if he won't come, who will wait—
I tell myself
and because he doesn't come, I wait.

You've receded too far to call to,
you no longer show even your back—
you come from the horizon,
rushing in like the tide,

you rush in
but never make me wet,
stopping short at the tide-line far below,
irritatingly undulating.

On the hillside
I turn dry like sand.
Behind my eyelids
the seascape again dims into night.

Clams

At midnight I woke up.
The clams I'd bought in the evening
were alive in a corner of the kitchen,
their mouths open.

"In the morning
I'll eat you,
every last one of you."

I laughed
a witch's laugh.
After that
I could only sleep through the night,
my mouth slightly open.

Island

I stand in a looking glass.
A dot,
a small island.
Separate from everyone.

I know
the island's history.
The island's size.
Its waist, bust, hip.
Differently dressed in each season.
Singing birds.
A hidden fountain.
Fragrance of flowers.

I live
on my island.
Cultivate it and build it up.
And yet
I can't know

all of this island.
Can't settle on it forever.

In the looking glass I gaze
at myself—a far-off island.

Tsuetsuki Pass

Near Lake Suwa in Shinshū,
I visited a distant relative.

The old woman I hadn't seen for years was ill,
had lost words,
and was lying quietly.

The ridge showed the rises and falls of the many years
of bringing up eight children—
where its small span ended,
the dent in her round buttocks, from there
she dropped a lively steaming form.

I climbed to the height, Tsuetsuki Pass,
the Hachigatake range opened into view;
the snow-cloaked mountains
lay in the distance.

The coldness of the white underwear that the winter had her change
     into,
the warmth of her flesh showing under its collar—
my hands believed in them, somehow:
naked trees growing fluffily like down,
clouds rising in the valley.

I found myself standing
at an overlook commanding two natures.
Under the clear sky
I pinched my nose and put up with the large beautiful thing.

Festival of the Blind

A person has
two faces.

On the head, eyes, a nose, and a mouth,
on the body,
another set of eyes, a nose, and a mouth
(This set, since some time in the past, has remained concealed)

The two breasts are
unseeing eyes;
the blind one knows
that though unseen, something is there.

What is there
she tries to make sure, touching them.
One day
at the joy and sorrow of what she made sure
the woman's eyes became moist,
she shed white tears endlessly.

A child who grows with white tears.

The tiny dent in the middle of the belly
is the primeval nose,
which in remote days, from its mother's womb,
sucked up mysterious things.
From there blew in
smells of flowers,
fragrances of tides,
the winds and the light.
The nose has those first memories
deeply tucked
in its soft folds.

Below the nose, a grass bush,
a woman, or a man,
has ferns growing around an old marsh,
beneath the ferns insects chirp,
many tongues flare.

The tongues know
of the good food about to be arranged
on the sea-like table:

fruits
rare in any country,
resplendent dinner
no cook knows how to make,
liquors of fire.

People the world over
throw away all their clothes
and go to the table.

The festival of the blind,
drums of the festival,
bonfires without heat, without color.

ANZAI HITOSHI

(born 1919)

Hitomaro[1]

Like green fruit, many dawns
have tumbled into an abyss.
Under alder blossoms the eyes of a lone deer moisten,
in the villages and valleys live only those with love and those without;
trying to wake, yet unable,
the ghosts of the pristine dead
gleam like pure gold among the boulders.
In souls' province without a bridge
a singing voice alone runs ahead,
trying to embrace what is beyond.
(Melancholy sunrise . . .)
for some time a man in hunting clothes stood in heat haze,
looking back at the moon, a pallid world declining at the end of the
field.[2]

Random Thoughts on the Shinkokinshu:[3]
Fujiwara no Teika[4]

"What does it have to do with me, the crimson banner?"[5]
The aristocratic youth bit the orange, laid out a pallid poem-scroll.
His stuffed soul in the shape of a court cap whispered in his ear.

[1] Kakinomoto no Hitomaro, pp. 28–37.
[2] Allusion to Hitomaro's tanka, "In the east," p. 30.
[3] The eighth imperial anthology, completed in 1205.
[4] Fujiwara no Teika, pp. 192–218.
[5] Reference to the famous September 1180 entry in Teika's *Meigetsuki*
(Diary of the Bright Moon), which says in part: "The world these days is
nothing but rebellion and attack, but although the reports of it fill my ears,
I pay no attention. Red banners and punitive expeditions are no concern of
mine." In the previous month, Minamoto no Yoritomo (1147–1199), leader
of the Genji clan, had revolted against the ruling Heike clan. The Heike
warriors carried red banners, and the Genji, white banners.

The lantern oil had boiled to the last drop.
The shoulder of his court dress, like a small cliff, let the frost slip off.
During the imperial regime, in a corner of the night sky, the scale
    had gradually tipped.

"*Non!* I see no blossoms, no crimson leaves."[6]
He was holding down with his palm the gray esthetic the night wind
    was trying to peel away.
The flowing water moving clouds flowers birds winds moons made
    negative creaks.
Barren darkness froze on the desk.
In the cold daybreak the smell of heated ashes flowed.
The revolution was about to take place both in February and June.

Warbler

Quitting kickball, the gods
went out to prepare for war.
Picking up the globelike ball that was left and holding it by his side,
a bridegroom, a god, walked quietly
to the house made of white wood, fresh with fragrance, and hid in it.
Suddenly, from there
a sound as limpid as a birth cry came out, running,
and in the clear cold dawn, in a bush, spilled a plum blossom.

Meigetsuki

In *Meigetsuki*, the diary of Fujiwara no Teika, poet toward the end
of the imperial regime, I find a record of an unfamiliar star written
for an entry in early November of his sixty-ninth year, and before I
know it, my eyes wander off to dwell on a corner of the boundless
universe.

Here's a paraphrase: At the time of Emperor Goreizei, in the second
year of Tenki, near Taurus' right horn, a new star lodged and blazed;
its brightness was about that of Jupiter. Taurus is the constellation
raging against Orion the Hunter, with its neck adorned with the
Pleiades once extolled by Sei Shōnagon in her *Pillow Book*.[7] How-

6 Teika's tanka, "As I look out," p. 193.
7 Sei Shōnagon (born c. 965) mentions the star cluster in section 224 of
her *Makura no sōshi* (Pillow Book).

ever, since the light that glittered near Taurus' horn was a disturb-
ance more than a hundred years before the court poet was born, perhaps he learned about it from a Chinese book. In China, a volume on
astronomy in *The History of Sung*[8] has a similar record; thus, a star
that suddenly emerged in A.D. 1054 has since then become invisible to
the naked eye. On the European continent they must have missed this
new star. Since they relied on Chinese literature for it, they called it
the Chinese NOVA.

Admiring in a sort of trance a collection of Mount Palomar Observa-
tory photographs of heavenly bodies, I am slaking my vague thirst
with the green tea my wife offers. I am looking for a gaseous world
shaped like a lettuce, named the Crab Nebula. It is a truly mind-
boggling entity that continues to expand, three thousand light-years
away, at a speed of one thousand and several hundred miles a second.
How was the Crab Nebula born? About nine centuries ago, somewhere near there an unknown star's life exploded. At that moment it
must have blazed several hundred million times brighter than the sun,
astronomers estimate. In other words, that was the identity of the star
that casts a lone light in Fujiwara no Teika's diary.

The year A.D. 1054 is the year that the Greek Orthodox Church and
the Roman Catholic Church split. Almost an illegitimate student, I
memorized that particular page of Western history and crossed in a
state of dream the bridge of the Middle Ages, I feel. Later I learned
about the history of the Greek Orthodox Church, the Soul of the
Slavs, and so forth, all unworthy knowledge acquired in bits and
pieces, which always left me irritated and disappointed. Because my
earth was too antiquated and petty, I could only let drip on my lap
the pathos of exploring an existence far fainter than a nebula three
thousand light-years away. One thing, though: before closing, I'd like
to talk about an image of a blue skull—that is, St. Nicholas Church in
Tokyo. Come to think of it, how many years has it been since parting with a youth in that church that had long lost its Slavic smell? I
saw him walk away, my hand on the shoulder of my wife then still
young—that was a late autumn night when the Pleiades push themselves up even in the dusty Tokyo sky. My wife was in love with the
youth. I believe in the beauty of the foreign word, Ascension, only in
his case. He was killed in the war.

----

[8] In 496 volumes, completed in 1345.

Slaughter

It was when the war was at its peak. The council of a small city where I was stationed as a reporter for a bureau of a newspaper voted to slaughter the large animals kept in the zoo. One broiling day, the mayor, councilmen, reporters assigned to city administration, and slaughterers filed in and, as if performing a somewhat shady ritual, shot the caged beasts one after another.

Poisoning was avoided so they could be used for food later. Indeed, the councilmen relished several pounds of tiger meat, and the reporters were rationed several pounds of hippopotamus; how the meat of other animals was diverted is not precisely known to me.

We watched, with cigarettes stuck idly in our mouths, a pair of lions being slaughtered at the end. First, the male lion, absorbing two bullets in his brow, turned without much ado into a pliant corpse. The female lion put her forelegs on his corpse and, glaring at the slaughterers outside the cage, roared again and again.

Soon she too sucked three bullets into her head, piled down on the male lion, and expired. The slaughterers looked at each other's tired and perspiring faces and put on a forced smile whose meaning was undefinable.

More than ten years since then, I still cannot talk about that tiny incident without tasting a bitter grain of sand on my tongue. Because, aside from the raw aftertaste of the hippopotamus meat I tried in secrecy, people read into this episode various parables and morals— that's it! nothing but interpretations that please them, and smile. In the face of such a smile, I can only shut up and quietly wipe away something like blood, that drips from my brow.

If there were any existence I could believe in this world, it would be nothing other than a definite death—a death with a clear outline in which the body heat remains with putrefaction yet to begin. I could not believe any other death than such death. Let alone any other life than such death.

No. This too will amount to no more than my suggestive affectation. I must strictly behave myself. I must stop scheming like people who deal with words, that is, poets. Only, I hear: the monotonous cicadas that often sing in my ears. They're the agitating echoes of silence that flowed in between the shots of that midsummer slaughter. I love the pure time, the precise corpse, that keeps putrefying as one talks about it.

Village Hairdresser

I have a friend, once "Hey, war buddy!"
now a fishing partner and a rival in go.
His old lady, a graduate of a women's normal school and barren,
is always working in the fields, like a grub.
He has only one bad habit:
he learns by heart more of my wretched poems than I do.
The only way to deal with a reader and critic like this is to drink him
        under the table,
so about once every two months I go by train
with cheap whisky that smells like medicine.
He entertains me with local sake that smells like dust.
His old lady's stew is good,
such pungency! the soy, saturating, makes me weep.
Disproportionate to the narrow village, a zelkova tree soars,
and that's his sole real estate.
Each of us dropped our names
in a distant battlefield, or in a brothel.
Since I have no manual work, he calls me "poet."
Because he uses razors, I call him "barber."
Crowned with the village name, he is "The Barber of Sebira."
When he gets drunk, he likes war songs.
"An enemy yesterday, a friend today,"
that antique is his favorite.
What's this!
Isn't that a song from the war our grandpas went to?
Today the two friends with hangovers put fishing rods on their shoul-
        ders
and pissed together on a narrow path, under the blasting sun.
In the field, leaves of sweet potatoes
swaying like a chest-roentgenogram,
swaying in a row like blue wraiths—
hey! our good old war buddies.

Winter Evening

How could I have possibly said
I'd be waiting by a small bridge like this?
For some time the trains passing on the girder bridge by me
have had their lights on.
When there are so many warm stores I frequent
on the other, bustling side of the girder bridge,
how could I have possibly promised
to meet in a chilly spot like this?
I like busy streets.
I like Russian restaurants, Korean restaurants.
I like planetariums, underground movie houses.
I like beer halls where waitresses are like nurses.
I like to watch the new titles like young girls
cramming the bookstore shelves.
I like the alley with a cook who makes good jokes,
piling up fresh fish right before your nose.
I like casual gaiety,
crowds that don't have much meaning.
And what I'm waiting for is
an ordinary errand,
an ordinary promise,
an ordinary tryst.
The narrow river unlikely to attract anyone
flows, purling at evening,
and I wait, thinking that's lovely.
In the faint dark flow
something like a lump of garbage is caught
and pointing up from it, aslant,
I see a bamboo stick,
but why doesn't it move?

May Song

Day for life, so helpless, so shy. Balancing, we stand on the low gun-
wale. Look: scintillating on the water, small rainbows. The sea's sloe
eyes. Caught in their serene look, a sinuous May island hurries. Near
the breast of a reclining peninsula, sand glistens. Insignificant as a
dimple, a red buoy. A distant cape where the midday hours stop.
Above the cape, as if it touched something, a somersault of a bug, an
airplane. The launch utters a shrill whistle shriek, snuggles its shoul-

der, and tosses a rope. My shoes are a little wet. Coming out of the
sea in a soft wind, you are beautiful. A shop selling abalones and
boiled eggs. An omnibus enjoying a respite, facing the sea obliquely.
A man irritated for something is by turns rapping on a window of
the car and drinking soda from a bottle. A violet on a stone wall. On
the shrine premises, slightly obscene camellia blossoms. The latticed
hall packed with deer antlers. Near the edge of a wheat field I lie on
the ground, looking at the sky. Suddenly you whiff away from me.
For some time you cease to be. All I hear is a thin clear voice, and
soon, like a skylark, on flaring wings, you descend straight to my
face. That's the island's elementary school. A teacher is making my
friends laugh at me, a clumsy boy, on the Swedish bars. That's the island's quarry. On a distant cliff in my mind a small pick twinkles.
Lying on the rocks, naked men are talking. They're too far to hear.
You take out a mirror from your sash. A light makeup. Behind your
face another layer of face falls slowly asleep. Bored, you catch the
sun in your mirror and let it flicker in the foliage of whitish trees.
Leaves are blinking. A trembling bird. My dry tongue. Sand. A word
that doesn't form a voice. Suddenly, bitten by the white teeth of de-
risive waves, the sand letters on my chest collapse. O. Palms that hide
the bashful cheeks. Like the fingers of those palms opened in trep-
idation, a sparse stand of pine trees—through it I look at the sea. The
sluggish stagnant sea behind the sun sick of wasted efforts. That's already too far from the shore, too desolate to be called a landscape.
Bitter eternity. From my dry eyes a modicum of aroma of old pine
needles has spilled.

YOSHIOKA MINORU

(born 1919)

Pastorale

Wheels fall innumerably
From the palms of God
Further, waves rise
Play the flute
Rain-wet blue blades of reeds
The sheep expand and contract
The path to an abandoned garden becomes invisible
I wipe the inside of a lamp
And turn the piling butterfly wings
The dagger which did not come in time pierced the moon
And petals incessantly overflowed

Still Life

Within the hard surface of night's bowl
Intensifying their bright colors
The autumn fruits
Apples, pears, grapes, and so forth
Each as they pile
Upon another
Goes closer to sleep
To one theme
To great music
Each core, reaching its own heart
Deliberately reposes
Around it circles
The time of rich putrefaction
Now before the teeth of the dead
Those fruits and their kind
Which unlike stones do not strike

Add to their weight
And in the deep bowl
Behind this semblance of night
On occasion
Hugely tilt

The Past

The man first hangs an apron from his thin neck
The man, just as he has no will, has no past
Holding a sharp blade in his hand, he starts to walk
To a corner of the man's wide-opened eyes rushes a line of ants
At each illumination by both sides of his blade the dust on the floor
    begins to stir
Whatever is going to be cooked
Even if it's a toilet, probably
That object will shriek
Will instantly spurt blood from the window to the sun
What now quietly waits for the man
What gives him the past
That he lacks
A motionless stingray is placed on a board
Its back, mottled, large, slippery
Its tail seems to hang deep into the basement
Beyond it, only the roofs in winter rain
The man quickly rolls the sleeves of his apron
And thrusts the blade in the stingray's raw belly
There's no resistance
In slaughter not to get any response
Not to get one's hands soiled is a terrible thing
But the man bears down little by little and goes on ripping the mem-
    branous space
The dark depth with nothing to be spewed out
The stars that sometimes appear and fade
Work done, the man unhooks his hat from the wall
And goes out the door
The part which had lain hidden under the hat
The spot where the hook is, which had been protected from the terror
From there the blood with time's adequate weight and roundness de-
    liberately begins to flow

Confession

I don't tell the others what I don't know. Nor do I walk around the plaster that the others' voices create. But I'm exasperated, trying to touch with a short ax in which the force of the whole concentrates. If it's standing, I push it on a stone until it falls. If it's lying I leap on it. If it's turning, I entwine it in my arms. Until it cuts into my dark flesh. And I yield the path to lines of moths and blood vessels who go out, lonely. If it's a woman, I thrust her back into her eyes. I must wait patiently until she brims with consummate suppleness and a cold lake. If it's food, I vomit it. In the dark under the table where bottles and vessels have gone down, I decapitate fish and birds one after another and sort out things useful and things useless. But there can be an error. When there is one, I wipe the froth off the feathers and scales and try to see what's happening outside the window glass: the children jumping rope, the mass of the smokestack that gives birth to one night. Eventually at the shriek of a tree that sleeps in the strata of its own grain, I start to run. As a naked figure, as a dark image that embodies training and endurance, I go in the rain, getting wet. Of this fact, here, I can tell the others.

Coolie[1]

The Chinese sleeps under his running horse.
His melon-shaped small head
laid alongside the horse's penis,
sometimes hanging from it,
he goes defecating over the winter topography,
the spear blockades of kaoliang after the harvest.
The Chinese, drooling drivel that glitters with poison,
binds the horse's fat body with the ropes his limbs,
leaves behind the rolling hills
with profuse blooms of twisted irises under the full moon.
In search of a larger proposition,
when morning comes he jumps across the river.
Between the horse's ears
the Chinese feeds skillfully,
carries hot millet gruel into his mouth slowly with a spoon,
a feat incredible to ordinary men:

[1] Yoshioka says the poem reflects his observations of Manchuria and Manchus during the four years he was stationed in Manchukuo.

this is no operation for profit or show
but, say, a secret rite that natural souls mainly perform.
With the tail bundle made incessantly
to stream out of the cage of the running horse's hind limbs
the Chinese wipes the sweat off one being, himself and horse,
and through the membranes of the horse's fiercely opened eyes
glances at a red-eyed infant·a ruined clay house·a coffin wrapped
      with the green of a weeping willow
a yellow sand tornado
and the Chinese hates the history of diseases.
The horse keeps running for its master inhabiting it inseparable,
and dying attempts a leap.
When ready to make a flight
the echo of its last fart
tears apart the floating horse buttocks.
The Chinese instantly forces his exhaustion
to meet the impulse of lust,
takes a wife from the direction of his back,
and achieves the prosperity of his race.
At daybreak when myriad-branched clouds
give birth to petty matters and great premonitions,
the Chinese continues to despise himself,
heads for the Forbidden City · the Enemy
to inflict on it sinister punishments.

Ode to an Old Man

The old man accompanies
A lonely naked infant and pelican
Against the time that he will die king of invalids
Confirms the virtue of flesh and the isolation of heart
Saws the entirety of forest trees
And as slowly as possible
Constructs a ghost ship
It showed from under his nightgown
Only chipped teeth were loaded
The old man goes out of his native land
Of hemorrhoids and lung diseases
Rides a deep swell that's continuous from under his skin
And prostrates his hirsute wife
With a toxin of her black breasts

Even human mind is clamorously disturbed
Even the jellyfish body is clouded
The old man laughs without reserve
Banzai
Banzai
Because death for once is a new experience
On the night to cross the unhinged border
The fish belly yet to be torn incessantly gleams
Incessantly contracts
And besides adding pressure terribly
Is erotic
And doesn't let the courteous old man sleep
With the sensuality of a gauzy moon
The old man reminisces
To put it correctly, creates
For the stomach and bladder
A desert night without shifts
Calls of hyenas and vultures
A city where stars and sands rank equal
And sitting at the center of flames in a hut
Tries to boil the sumptuous blood
In the king's heart the bowl
An existence like a basket
Left upside down in vain
No splendid nude dancer shows up
In the uneasy world of hair
The master of a barbershop flashes his razor
And shaves the old man's large head
Coldness of plaster
As a beautiful dead man
As the guardian deity of the infant and the pelican
He is moved to a place where he won't get in the other's way

Diarrhea

I have diarrhea. It's not my wish, nor do I have a means of resisting
it, but under cover of the night doubly reflective of historical change
and personal work, I have diarrhea. Scarlet flowers and the water in a
basement where phlegm that dyes the twilight sky is spat out. Is it a
phenomenon of mine alone? Today too I have it, yesterday too I had
it. Come to think of it, peering into the inner rooms of a wax gourd

with a blue skin in the memory of old days, diarrhea is our daily habit. The world's toilets just washed are collected. My diarrhea gulps down my spirit, is communicated to the many minds of other persons, and goes on rotting the aliments of the hungry populace. From then on sprawl crowds of old and young, men and women. Their negligible voices. The movements of their pathetic hands and feet. Love of excretion which is proof that they are alive. Everyone in the position of driftwood. From some place a little higher I become directly covered with ash. To take masochistic meals I have comical metaphysical diarrhea that a horse or a dog would not even experience; confirm that I am powerless, that I'd rather live; see a soaring tower in a place that pain leads to, the space where combats of thunder end. When the flow of the blood of martyrdom in which my body that is to die resounds, heightens, I have diarrhea. On the sloping land that is being plowed, under the rocks and stones where the spring to be dipped from never stops, I sever for good the entrails that are the trigger of a civil war of heart. I am forgotten. I forget people and things. Because they are friends encountered in a supposition. I come out of a cold diarrheal modern ugly squatting hypnotic state, and the darkness of astonishment that recovers changes its dimension. Repeats the contact of natural light at its center. In the garden of the twentieth century I become a healthy man as a synthetic body. Begin by eating a pear first. Here begins a new relation·a dialogue.

Negative

Drawn out into the light
The eggs and such till now sunken
Begin to move in unison
With flies buzzing around them
Cross the marshes of sweet lovers' faces foreshadowed by death
And responding to the music of tree leaves performed accidentally
Sparkle the color of rose
Emitting magnetism on one side
The eggs and such
Roll thoroughly
Go from the place for escapers from the life of sorcery
Through the city of weapons where the hero was assassinated
To the front of a mirror

Each and every egg goes on confining
Transitory women's thighs
No doubt the domination of sleep
Letting dark water flow endlessly
The bathroom attractive and deprived of spiritual coitus
Enumeration of the eyes and tongues of the dead which repeat their
    linkage every night
For this view could there be coexistence of love and death
Some eggs go over the other eggs
Uncorresponsive, terrible transformations
The innumerable mouths of the dead are not clearly visible
Until the teeth of healthy men and women are opened
The eggs and such drag their shadows
Can't they toss and turn to the world of ideas
On the rug of soft weed of the sea
They show a fierce passage
The eggs and such devoid of an axis
Seek the other shore devoid of any scheme
A plane devoid of light and heat
If it's no good, for a while
Detained behind cold-blooded flesh
The plucked-off eggs and such
Are swiftly crowned with a relentless orb

Quiet House

Parsley leaf green's
Swelling form
We're happy to have wives
A man's shouting
That does not mean he is in a suit
Still looking for acidity
And flying past the joints of tall blue bamboo trunks
A black swallowtail, in whose darkness gold powder
A vegetable human
Looks drowned
What's a wife?
She is eating on a shelf
The center of marmalade
Each husband's <<Here begins the desert>>
A meal begins

A bottle into a bottle being stuffed
In addition evening
On the breath
Visible from the flame tongue
On the descending slope the bell the tongue is medievally
Plump
And goes down along a cross
Well then from what earth
Is cinnamon brought?
Toward the beloved lips
Headed by two children
Who wet even Victoria's frog with rain
It comes
A spring storm!
Is this real lyrical?
The pillar inside mother
The sextuple that can't describe its hair
Assimilated with forests
Gathering birds
Whose upturned, black, fragmented
Sufferings in heels
After all, a wife is a floral decoration of baroque art
Can spurt out?
Toward the front of the building
Can you see the vine leaves reviving again?
If eternal preservation is possible
Of religious stained glass
Push it open dazzlingly
In the scattering volume
Seeds of barley
The husband who must accept in advance
Prints
A silk-ripping vermilion-coated small painting
There beyond the cedar tree
Is a river in which flow flowing horses and soldiers
Whose world is silent
A housemaid comes home alone

Lilac Garden

The purple color, night's tribute
So all music may sink with ease
Foaming little by little
Erases stars from the garden
It is when the surrounding lilacs bloom
A stone statue is whispered to
Dangling a chipped earlobe
Which in jealousy or in love
Outlines abstract ennui
From its shadow
The beautiful wife is lured
Through the heart a wet bird runs past
And her immoral sash, in the orange man's arms
A leap of pure love
An angle to be made only once
The woman is supported by the weight of an olive branch
A ripping of underwear of delightful sin
When sensual silk legs tangle
The bearded man the lord of this mansion jumps out and yells
A dog runs out, cats guard the lamp
The bearded man goes on expanding large rings of lust
At the center of flower's floundering
Lays down his own mistress the woman in green
Other flowers than the lilacs that have failed to bloom
Listening to their awakening voices
Manservants dance the toy monkey's dance
Maidservants dance the toy snake's dance
Under flower clusters of lilacs
Don't strike the match
Don't make nightingales sing
The seashore winds that bewitch the mansion's candlelight
Are all waved into
The beautiful wife's many-creased robe where
Engraving on stone the depths of the breasts of the woman who belies
    love
The echoes of the autumn sea grow fainter
In the sky above the garden where the figures are no more
The nightingales pass singing
The flowers of other seeds begin to emit their fragrance
The yellow moon rising deranged
Is the approaching dawn's tribute

Holy Girl

The girl is our hypothetical enemy, you know!
Lies outstretched on summer grass
And shows modestly her crotch with blue hair
Ambiguous form of love
What are its insides made of?
Plastic
The girl with her ruddy face walks over a large watermelon
And looks for the eternal unicorn
That's in every flesh!
Takes the subway
And with a baby bottle
Ducks under a far-off arch of white bones of our hypothetical old
man
Toward a lodging holing up in winter
Hans Bellmer's[2] doll
To its globular girl abdomen
And joints, relates
And twists twists
Flourishing pampas grass · karukaya[3]
As the weather gets better
Scorpion appears
After words
A killer of others, a younger brother, will be born!

[2] Polish artist (1902–1975) who did erotic paintings and made dolls.
[3] A kind of pampas grass.

ISHIHARA YOSHIRŌ

(1915–1977)

Horse and Riot

When two horses run
inside us
another horse runs
between the two.
When we go out to riot
we run with
that one horse.
It's that horse
that goes out with us to riot,
not the two horses
on its sides.
Therefore what runs out
from us
when we halt
is that one horse,
not the two horses
on its sides.
When two bandits run
inside us
another bandit runs
between the two.
When two hollows run
inside us
still another hollow runs
between the two.
What goes out with us to riot
is that last bandit
and that last hollow.

Funeral Train[1]

What station we started from
no one remembers.
Only, through a strange land where it's always midday on the right
and midnight on the left
the train goes on running.
Each time it gets to a station, invariably
a red lamp looks in the window
and along with dirty wooden legs and worn-out boots
coal-black lumps
are thrown in.
They are all alive,
and even while the train runs,
they all remain alive,
but in the train nevertheless
odors of corpses pervade every corner.
To be sure, I am there among them.
They are each already half-wraiths,
they lean on one another,
they snuggle to one another,
they still eat and drink,
a little at a time,
but some are already transparent around their asses,
about to fade.
Ah to be sure, I am there among them.
Leaning ruefully against the window,
sometimes one of us
begins to chew on a rotten apple,
myself, my wraith—
so all the time
we overlap with our own wraiths,
separate ourselves from them,
waiting for the train to get to
the unbearable, remote future.
Who is in the locomotive?
Each time we cross a huge black iron bridge,
the girders rumble ponderously,
many wraiths, for a moment,
stop their eating hands
and try to remember
what station they started from.

[1] After World War II Ishihara was captured by the Russian army in
Siberia and was sent from one concentration camp to another.

Commerce in the Caucasus

from a certain retribution

At that moment you were leaning
on the blade of an ax.
Or it can also
be said, an ax
was leaning on your back.
Who else but an ax loved so much
your shieldlike back
that was appropriate
to the blade of an ax?
It could have been any morning.
For a wind to rise in the stone
the blade of an ax had only
to wake in the ax.
In the beginning of the value
of things that happen
only in the morning
the ax was pulled off the trunk
and struck into your back
gently, directly.
Like a rolling pin
the ax had a straight-faced handle
that had a golden-haired hand.
In the mountain area of the Caucasus, even now,
there are three republics
but the commercial custom
of buying back with a steel ax
what was sold
for twenty pieces of silver
remains as it was.
Exchanges of eyes as vivid as
the rainbow that spans from ax to back
make up the commerce in the Caucasus.
To the end of the earth where you lie
Caucasian prices
follow you
but the splendid value settled on you
is something
you must approve of firmly.

The Last Enemy

Like a rose, a scar
fragrant behind his earlobe—
Is it forbidden
to see such a man?
A man one can face without unfolding one's arms
under splendid invitation lamps—
Is it forbidden
to see such a man?
Like a steeple in the evening glow
anger shines on his forehead.
In his eyes, turned toward
a crossroads in the distance,
a typhoon seems to be gently
hesitating.
When he passes in his boots
silence spreads through the town,
in a far-off basement
gamblers hush their hands.
There should be one or two boulevards
unable to forget
the seriousness of his back that turned away
just before pursuit.
Shoulders like a balance
that incline gently toward pain
and a steep chest
that repulses any future
are the signs of his sincerity
one recognizes wherever one comes across them.
Among the enemies he made enemies
and striding over a whip
he would not turn on us, to the end.
Above all, on the day of conclusion,
over the road
where sunflowers higher than towers
bloom like anger,
he will come
and effortlessly open
our folded arms
more stubborn than bolts
and press
on our chests
that odd hot fire.

Sancho Panza's Homecoming

Stacking countless lights of relief
the night welcomes the hometown.
Look! Appearing at all the doorways
all the widows hold their voice.
Donkey, put authority on the ground.
Squire,
write the time on his fur.
My authority drowns in the distance of madness
and your authority
drifts to the hometown of relief.
Donkey, turn back to the distance,
to the predawn hours of laziness.

Voiceless, I will soon
be welcomed into the garden of barren women,
turn, again voiceless,
into a plant,
and place a definite shadow
on the ruins of the territory.

Donkey, you who will after this
modestly restore the sovereignty of laziness,
in your master's night of relief,
you must not leave anything,
you must not leave anything.

Song of the Ringing in the Ear

The man I left behind
likes for example the ringing in the ear.
Likes for example the small cape
in the ringing in the ear.
Likes the smoldering smell of a matchlock.
And the sky is always
on this side of the man.
With a chest where stars stir like a wind
the man is ashamed of me like a medal.
When ringing begins in my ears
then abruptly
the man begins.
In the distance wheat sings to his hair,
and he firmly
looks around.
The man I left behind
likes for example a stuffed donkey.
Likes for example a red mane.
Likes for example a copper horseshoe.
Likes a sunset that resembles a gong.
As if making a whip meet the flesh,
he makes me meet the future.
When ringing begins in my ears
he is perhaps the man that begins
but when he begins abruptly
there's another man
that begins
and all the other men that revive at a stroke.
At the end of their blood-smelling line
there's a tower standing gently
like a lipstick.
Doubt my ear if you will.
Beyond the illusory ringing,
nevertheless, gently
the tower remains standing,
and the one who still firmly
believes in it
is the man
I left behind.

Fog and Town

I wouldn't say night with fog
is particularly free.
No matter where we come across you
there's no line between you and us,
in this town leveled marvelously
by crossfires of accusation,
wherever someone walks
is a boulevard,
but when if rarely an honest wound
peers over your shoulder,
the night with fog, or without,
makes a difference
to your bad conscience.
In the festival-noisy, witch-hunt town,
only its centroid pushed to the top,
even that bastard
passes as a Jacobin,
but if a stone hammer, wherever you swing it down,
sparks the same color,
if a gold coin, whoever flips it,
turns the same face or back,
fog, don't hesitate
to come down in this town
where whip and spur collude!
I wouldn't say night with fog
is particularly free, but if
only the petty thieves who haggle,
get their wayward shadows, and walk off the fair
and the pennies wet with lamp oil
scatter onto distant pavements,
even if the man who placed the night on a whetstone
whirls off in a gust,
until the day breaks
unexpectedly
between your legs blocking the way,
the fog comes to draw the line
to this faceless town
where daybreak repeats daybreaks,
where sunset repeats sunsets.

You Heard Him Say Lonely, Now

You heard him say lonely, now,
didn't you. Right behind
your back pressed close,
unshaven,
to the mud fence,
you heard him say lonely, now,
didn't you.
There
at the only spot
warm as an animal's belly,
with shadows, unrestrained,
piling, lost,
there between the odd
hatreds, back to back,
there certainly was one
who said lonely,
there certainly was one
who heard it.
Between the mouth that said it
and the ear that heard it,
an unexpected
lid lifts,
and like a joke, hot water
boils over.
Caught off guard, the mud fence, or I,
may jump back,
but there certainly was one
who said lonely
and there certainly was one
who heard it. As long as that's the case,
that pasania tree,
the horse chestnut,
the sunset, and the lake,
all of them are mine.

Night Robbers

When they realize it's no longer evening,
one rises to his feet
and strangles a chicken,
one rises to his feet
and strangles a pillar,
one rises to his feet
and twists up his own arms.
In response to the depth of night he schemes,
each of the night robbers
will be a night robber.
For example, the one who steps on the back
of a prostrate night robber and runs, is also
called by custom a night robber.
No matter how short
the distance night robbers run through
from beheading to whipping,
the daybreak that seems to be cut off and discarded
equally concerns
all the night robbers.
Fire bells clanging, whiskers burnt,
something like reason
pressed on his back,
he runs home through naked noon,
then the one who catches up with him
must also be a night robber.
On occasion, supported by logic,
a night robber runs past
a night robber.
Something like an apple
that the night robber bites and tosses away,
something like a rope
that the night robber tears off and tosses away,
these things that concern
the morning of the momentary escape.
The boulevard like a cutting board,
washed by a shower,
is the distance to broad daylight.

Night's *Invitation*

Outside the window, a pistol shot,
the curtain instantly
set on fire,
and so comes the hour I waited for:
it's night, like a regiment,
framed with cellophane—
France,
be reconciled with Spain,
lions, each of you,
lick your tail.
I suddenly become tolerant,
hold hands
with someone who's ceased to be anyone,
and take between our enclosing hands
the generous adult's hour.
Sure, in the zoo,
there's got to be an elephant,
next to it
there's got to be another elephant.
The hour that can't but come
comes,
how splendid.
Allow the severed flowers on the table
the act of pollination.
Now, little time
remains
unresurrected.
The night is rolled back,
the chair shaken,
the card flag pulled down,
crayon melts in the palm,
and the morning comes to make a promise.

Myth

In truth that morning had no succession. It can be said that it was limited to a single generation. For there was finally neither afternoon following the morning nor evening dusk following the afternoon. The morning was there with no clue, by itself, a morning. We all awoke at once, and had nothing to do. Between a quieter sea and a far quieter coast, in the vivid silence after those with courage to escape had all escaped, carelessly we simply exchanged greetings. Were the greetings then any different, for example, from the way the two halves of a clam close? With no hopes to put in the greetings, after raising our voices as in a chorus, we fell into a further silence. We bundled hay, pulled down the lever-iron, and in that posture could only wait for the time to have ourselves cut down. Unless cut down, the morning would have to remain simply a morning. Yes we hoped for it. That the morning in its mediocrity be a morning. If in the end there was nothing to come after that, we would already be able to be vegetables. In any case, before the morning was a morning, we ourselves had to be a morning. We did not wait singlemindedly for our last years, we were not promised a next generation. We held our breath and waited for the next ennui. For the time when the serene repetition of water and shore would finally, unrelatedly, mature into a myth.

Meal

It may be that I was then having what could be either lunch or supper in a corner of a restaurant. Light seemed to flow in from outside, or flow out from inside.

"Here I am," I asserted, in a low voice, lucidly. After the assertion, for the first time, I had an oppressive hesitation. With that hesitation, for the first time, it could be an assertion. Then it could be a chair, could be a picture frame like a window, or it could be a white, lucid plate.

"Here I am," I repeated. In the assertion lingering leisurely, I finished the meal resembling light.

TOMIOKA TAEKO

(born 1935)

Between—

There are two sorrows to be proud of

After slamming the door of the room behind me
After slamming the door
Of the entrance of the house behind me
And out on the street visibility zero because of the rain of the rainy
    season
When the day begins
What will I do
What am I going to do
To neither
Am I friend or enemy
Who can I ask
This concrete question
I hate war
And am no pacifist
The effort just to keep my eyes open
The sorrow that I can make only that effort

There are two sorrows to be proud of

I am with you
I don't understand you
Therefore I understand that you are
Therefore I understand that I am
The sorrow that I do not understand you
The sorrow that you are what you are

Let Me Tell You about Myself

Because both Dad and Mom
Even the old midwife
In fact every single prophet
Bet that I'd be a boy
I tore out of the placenta determinedly a girl

Then
Because everybody praised it
I became a boy
Then
Because everybody praised it
I became a girl
Then
Because everybody bullied me
I became a boy

When I came of age
Because my sweetheart was a boy
I had to be a girl
Then
Because everybody except my sweetheart
Talked about how I had become a girl
I became a boy to everybody
Except my sweetheart
Because I regretted being special to my sweetheart
I became a boy
Then because he said he wouldn't sleep with me
I became a girl

Meanwhile several centuries passed
This time
The poor started a bloody revolution
And were being bossed around by a slice of bread
Therefore I became a medieval church
Saying love is the thing
I visited back alleys   distributing old clothes and balls of rice

Meanwhile several centuries passed
This time
God's kingdom had come
And the rich and poor were great friends

So I hopped in a private helicopter
And scattered agitation leaflets

Meanwhile several centuries passed
This time
The bloody revolutionaries
Were kneeling before a rusted cross
I saw a fire of order in the disorder
So in the pub and in the den
Byron   Musset
Villon   Baudelaire
Hemingway   girls in black pants
And I played cards   drank
Talked nostalgically
About things like the libertines peculiar to
The country in the East called Japan
And mainly
Made fun of things like
Simultaneity of love

Because both Dad and Mom
Even the old midwife
In fact everybody said I was a child prodigy
I was a cretin
Because everybody said I was a fool
I became an intellectual and set up a residence somewhere in the rear
I didn't know what to do with my energy
When the rumor became widespread
That I was an intellectual somewhere in the rear
I began to walk out in the front
The walk I walked
Was the same as my Dad and Mom's
I the pervert was confused
Was tormented for the pervert's reputation was at stake
And so
I became a good solid girl
I became a boy to my sweetheart
And wouldn't allow him to complain

Just the Two of Us

You'll make tea,
I'll make toast.
While we're doing that,
at times, early in the evening,
someone may notice the moonrise dyed scarlet
and at times visit us
but that'll be the last time the person comes here.
We'll shut the doors, lock them,
make tea, make toast,
talk as usual about how
sooner or later
there will be a time
you bury me,
and I bury you, in the garden,
and go out as usual to look for food.
There will be a time
either you or I
bury either me or you in the garden
and the one left, sipping tea,
then for the first time, will refuse fiction.
Even your freedom
was like a fool's story.

Please Say Something

To a man eating a pear
you pose a question
like
why the hell
is he turning the light
on and off
only when
you're sitting like an insect
on a chair
in the dark of
an autumn house
and revenge and such crap
doesn't count.
Which reminds us, doesn't it,
how yesterday

a nine-year-old girl
got out of her kimono
better than her mom does.
Then
an insect like a golden green
glass bead creeping up
an outstretched arm, oh I know,
all of these stories are too good.
For a midnight snack,
have a pancake or something,
and think it over,
will you?

see you soon

you guys
like spring
sat face to face
then with hands and feet
touched similarly
only the details
tomorrow and the day after
I'm already yours
three days from now in the evening
you'll be
in a relationship
with those long arms
eating
don't cry
before the night ends
gargle please

There's Nothing to Do in New York

so
I have time to wonder
how come she still
isn't liked by people
and
wonder too

what she was
eating
and by the way
wonder
why
grammar is passionate
and why
a person does good
to persons
and why
Americans
grill their meat
without sprinkling pepper or salt.

Ever since summer
we've had a slight fever in our muscles
we took off our underwear at a doctor's
and always came home with only outerwear on;
that was because of laziness
and had no relation with spirit or history.
And we were suddenly
buying photographs of nudes in Times Square;
this too
like death, was unrelated to us.
And we were suddenly
talking with a Jew
in a shack on the East Side,
in a toy shop.
And we were suddenly
riding the daytime subway with no one else on it
and, never killed,
were suddenly alive;
this too
is unrelated to anyone's joy.
We are
unrelated to what,
we have
no relation with what,
if that's the question
I was having relations
with you buddy,
that is

the cigarettes and change in your
pockets
are every day
scattered in the street called the Bowery
to have incessant relations with fear,
that's what you believed.

Today too
persons were visiting persons;
there were no incidents
except
both in winter and in spring
wind was blowing.

Outside the landscape
their long overcoats were lined up
they were eating still lifes
and shitting purple shit
they were torn scalps
they were relative pronouns
they were inclining surfaces
they were still alive.
English
doesn't shout
like a human being;
we can only
timidly enter a coffee shop
from outside
and throw away the absurdly large lemon rinds
afloat in the cups.
Nothing happens.
What is performed
is the progress
which is continued
like the long long earrings
that hang eternally
from old women's circumcised lobes.
That is,
those auburn women,
drinking auburn coffee
and turning auburn,
those pink women,

drinking pink coffee
and turning pink,
have long been staying
in this world, or so they say.
Since yesterday
I've been out of stock
of things I can talk about;
I haven't had with me
things to illustrate things with;
if you alone die
that won't make an illustrative story.
All I know
is that no one shouts.
For the last several hundred years
no one has heard a human voice.

Today too
various persons
were visiting various persons.
People
clogged their throats
sometimes with food
sometimes with drinks.
The born child was asleep.
Toward a river
we were walking.
Someone lives there,
that we were sure of.
Our secrets
were what they were tasting.
Their secrets
were the same as ours.
But
the long bridge spanning the river
had already fallen down
just as at a convenient moment
a woman you love dies.

Today too
the sky was bright;
when it rains here
it rains all over this country,

that's a trick,
it seems to me.
We have yet to come across
a funeral procession on this island.
In short
neither of us
was the type to see to the last
the end of man's world.
Except I am
concerned
about your noisy
festival-like kindness
hanging from your ribs.
You
don't you have anything to say?
In the lover's
mouth
a wisdom tooth grew;
then
you
always opened the refrigerator;
then
you
like a picture in a picture
became accurate
and in an extremely tiny
dim place
sat cross-legged
and tore sheets off the calendar;
you and your short temper.

Today too
persons visit persons
you are
ice
cream
and molding is
an exclamation point;
from between your
thighs
numerals
have fallen.
Please make some tea
for me.

Age

In front of the stove the dog, brown, is sleeping.
By the dog I, human, am also lying.
The dog, brown, is two years old and male.
I, human, am forty years old and female.
I am watching the brown dog's sleeping face.
At times the dog
busily moves its four legs as if it thought it were racing in a field.
I decide the dog is having a dream that it's running in a field.
Sometimes the dog sleeps
with its belly turned up, four legs floating in the air.
Because the pose reveals the dog's great security I feel secure too and
    sleep.
Sometimes the dog opens its eyes and looks at me with its grape-
    colored pupils.
I get shy and turn my eyes down.
The dog gets to its feet and tries to scratch its belly with its hind leg.
And yet the leg doesn't reach the itchy spot.
I scratch the itchy spot for it with my hand.
Then the dog comes and licks my nose-tip.
That's the dog's word of gratitude.
Again the dog's lying, asleep.
I, human, sleep also by the dog.
Until now I have never
taken a nap feeling so secure.
Sometimes I find the dog pushing me on the shoulder or hand with
    its front legs.
That means the dog is inviting me to get up and play.
But I'm sleepy and can't get up.
Sometimes, at the dog's sudden bark I jump up, surprised.
In a matter of a moment
the dog opens the glass window, jumps outside
and in a corner of the garden is barking loudly toward the back street.
The dog is barking at the animal signs
which I, human, can't sense.
Then the dog
sits in the middle of the garden and is intently looking the other way.
I don't understand what the dog's seeing, what the dog's listening to.
It's said that one year for a dog is seven or eight years for a human.
The brown dog, in the two years since it was born,
has lived fifteen to sixteen of my years.
From the time I was twenty until today,
I've lived only about two years of the brown dog.

TAKAHASHI MUTSUO

(born 1937)

Sleeping Wrestler

You are a murderer
No you are not, but really a wrestler
Either way it's just the same
For from the ring your entangling body
Clean as leather, lustful as a lily
Will nail me down
On your stout neck like a column, like a pillar of tendons
The thoughtful forehead
(In fact, it's thinking nothing)
When the forehead slowly moves and closes the heavy eyelids
Inside, a dark forest awakens
A forest of red parrots
Seven almonds and grape leaves
At the end of the forest a vine
Covers the house where two boys
Lie in each other's arms: I'm one of them, you the other
In the house, melancholy and terrible anxiety
Outside the keyhole, a sunset
Dyed with the blood of the beautiful bullfighter Escamillo
Scorched by the sunset, headlong, headfirst
Falling, falling, a gymnast
If you're going to open your eyes, now's the time, wrestler

Dream of Barcelona: My Ancient World

My Barcelona—the stone pavement shaded deep with weariness
The dry eyeballs are threshed down
The surface of the stone begins to turn
From there, flowing out in turmoil, darkly
Gradually giving forth luster, Diana's ocean
The ancient Mediterranean world
Wrapped in foam, from the bottom of heavy tides
Rising, growing clearer, bronze Hermes
A streak of light shouts on the dark half-face of this god of Hades
His profile devoid of the eye
A wide fig leaf covers
That part of his, once the shining center of fertility
Waves turn, coming closer, the voice of hard labor, of bitter rock salt
The salt, pungent, painful to the lips, the whips of burning heat, cruel
    to the young flesh
The galley with two decks of oars has sunk
The sunk plates, sunk slaves, sunk necks and armpit hair
The cry that disappeared, Silenus' vain song
Shadows, sailors, pass, the sea wind, Agrigentum
The turquoise sky between shattered columns
The island of palms and olives, the beach for wraiths
The wine that disappeared in the tideways
Rome, people swarming in the Forum
The thick eyebrows of young men selling melons
Jews selling dreams, Athenian male prostitutes
Crucified magnificent slaves, muscles twisting around the nails
Sunset, the wrestlers die
The sandals departed, the Colosseum in shadow
A breeze, the blood and mud greased on the coarse hair
High among their thighs, the fragrant areas wrapped with incense
    grass
Twin-horned ancient bulls lick the blood spilled on the ground
One of them cries sadly at the sky, the astrolabe
The bulls disappear, and the wrestlers
In my imagination, the ocean, Hermes' face of sorrow, spread over
    the map of Rome
Near his ear, filing out of night's gate
Expeditionary soldiers in an interminable line
The road leads to the four ends of the earth, the aqueduct spans
    heaven

Spears glint, in the dust, armor clangs
To Macedonia, to Numidia, and to Hispania, where the sun dies
Here, Hispania, the western limit of the woodblock map of the
     Roman Empire—
When I think of Barcelona, my dark flesh trembles
—Barcelona, the hidden gold
At the heart of this odd decadent labyrinth
The Ancient World is found unexpectedly innocent
Lamps come to reflect in the sweaty pavement—
Two young men holding each other in the inn's stable straw
Under their soiled underwear, become armored Roman soldiers
Become one shining flesh

Winter: 1955

Cold morning, in a public men's room
The warmth settling like haze

I was loitering
Dirty, lonely, hungry

The sycamores were bare
The street almost empty

A dog followed
A trash cart

My right hand slipped in
Through the hidden hole of my pants pocket

I was imagining with a hungry heart
One to love like a flame, in a public men's room

Light sliced in like a painful knife
And made the mud ahead blaze

"Forecome and Come"

from *Ode in 1,000 Lines*[1]

Eightfold camellia blossom that opens on my tongue full of love
Droplet of honeydew that collects at the tip of the petal
Drop of costly perfumed oil that trembles on the alembic
Thrust forward by thoughts of tender love, I press my lips
To the camellia, to the alembic, to the widemouthed jar—
Joyous glitter
That spouts and goes down into hell, my throat
Frothy honey liquor that brims over the widemouthed pot
And spills along the shapely furrow, leaving a gleaming trail—
It was stored through seasons of lasting fog and hail
By the ferocious barbarians of an unknown country
Way beyond the seas of waves tossing in winter storms
The men who fathered it are gutsy and rough
But the liquor that was born is smooth and gentle to the tongue—
Sacred water that wells up on Okeonos' purifying island
And is carried in the beak of a sapient dove
To Olympus, to the lips of the gods
Dr. Faustus' mercury, the spirit of the mercury-colored earth
Water that courses through the dark underground paths
A deep well one crackles by dropping a bucket on a dark night
A sudden spout in a winter park
The smoke a rocket ejects
Viscous fumes from a volcano
Lava that dribbles down toward the mountain foot
Time that trickles, a clepsydra
An avalanche, a glacier going down
Frozen waterfalls, icicles, frost columns
A firefly's saliva to feed its larvae
The dragon's slobber, a snake's tears, a slug's path
Saint James' way, the milky river made when heaven's big jar was
   overturned
In heaven, Ganymedes the beautiful boy amiably pours nectar
From a widemouthed *krater*
A shooting star, a shower of the starry host
Billions of well-washed pearls
Billions of incessant arrows
Sidelong glances, a row of arrows
Darts of light, arrows of words

[1] *Homeuta* (Ode), published in 1971.

Love God's arrows that escape the mouth of a boy in love
a krim namah[2] . . .
A swarm of honey bees, the sharp spring messenger the *Kokila* bird
Light, Holy Spirit, the tongue of a flame going down noisily
A jolly spring, joyful flow
Touched by light, Persephone's water cries out with delight
At midnight, a water-surprise
On a festival night, fireworks
A sudden visit
Brightly between the thighs, angels
The Word, what is eternally sonlike, overflows
Cheerfulness, innocence, directness comes forth

Myself Departing

A young man, crouching, ties his shoelaces.
Back turned this way, his nape, how gentle.
The slowly moving two lumps of flesh on the shoulders
And two knees at both sides of his waist are fresh and round
(The male nipples pressed against his knees are peach-colored).
The reticent young animal's untainted straight gaze
Stays on the movements of his fingers tying shoelaces
But the moving fingers themselves are tranced, dreaming
Of the time they'll play with the gentle Eros, rolled in thin skin,
Dozing in a soft grassbush pregnant with light,
A little above the movements of the fingers tying shoelaces,
Below the pliant belly like that of a starved young wolf.
The young man rises and, in his lace boots, nude,
Begins to walk, keeps walking, soon grows old.
The man grown old tightens his face and never turns to look
But behind the man grown old, many times does the young man
    crouch,
Tie his shoelaces, rise, and begin to walk
Many times.

---

2 Takahashi says it is a Hindu phrase, the meaning of which is unclear.

Myself of the Onan Legend

My face will be dark.
The glittering liquid that spurts out of my holy procreative center
Will not be received into that contractile interior, which is eternally
    female,
But spill, and keep spilling, on the cold lifeless ground,
So my sons, who are my shadows, will as transparent Leech-Children[3]
    make a round of the earth,
Make a round of the water maze at the bottom of the earth, make a
    round of the network paths inside the tree,
And, ejected from the skyward mouth of every leaf at the tip of the
    tree,
Will drift aimlessly in the empty blue sky and be lost,
So my face should have been the sons of my light, things which
Endlessly continuing glittering links of light wove,
So the overflowing light is behind me, and is not before me.
My face, the whole face as one large mouth of darkness,
Is shouting voicelessly in the overflowing spilling light.

Myself in the Disguise of an Ancient Goddess

Young man, you who stand in the stone-paved plaza of this castle city,
your origin, that you've come from the foul countryside,
is revealed in your bare feet wearing not even sandals.
Look, far up the worn stone staircase rising from your feet,
look at my frightful face as I stand filling the pantheon.
You who stand precisely at right angle to the ground as an innocent
    sundial
drag not only your own shadow in the summer afternoon,
you are dragging along with you the smell of country soil,
the smells of plants, smell of water, smell of cow dung.
I like the ignorant glitter of astonishment in your staring eyes.
I like the youthful darkness, almost fragrant, of your mouth, agape.
My lust must chew up your astonishment, ignorance, the whole of
    your youth.
My mouth slit to the ears is for kissing you,

---

[3] Allusion to the *hirugo* or leech-child, the first child of Izanagi and
Izanami in the *Kojiki*.

for sucking you to the marrow, beginning with the flesh of your lips
    it kisses.
The scarlet of my cheeks must be freshly re-dyed with your blood.
Come, young man, you've stared at me, you no longer can escape
    from me.
Behind the bloody wedding of you and me
the world will burn like the city of sin in the legend.
Our being is always burning like it.

Myself in an Anatomical Chart of Sexual Intercourse

The tip of my existence, the soldering iron of wet hot flesh,
Inserted in a death smith's gentle forge, quickly increases its volume.
The iron turns red hot, the iron turns white hot, and at the pinnacle
    of white heat, finally, melts from its cusp.
O, spurting, white-muddied, thick liquid at the moment of existence
    metastasizing into nothingness!
The liquid spreads like a cloud and enters the womb, depths of the
    burning force.
But look, the one who has accepted my existence, is not facing me.
The tongue tip sharpened like a hook swims in the air, trembling.
So, what I am invading is no womb, but a flexible male rectum.
From rectum to oral cavity, what puzzling swells and coils of entrails!
Like Arabian labyrinths, like the ant holes the legendary bull inhabits,
Like a thunderhead's interlacing corridors, they are entangled, com-
    plicated.
My liquid, which is myself, invading every labyrinth,
Every ant hole, and every corridor, all at once spreads throughout
    him.
But look again, this invader is not me,
Rather, the one invaded is no one but me!
I have, by a true existence, my rectum bloodied and disgraced,
And from my tip twitching in painful bliss, into space,
Not the thick liquid, but feeble air is radiated,
And continues to be radiated.

Myself with a Glory Hole

Lord, when will it be?
Will it be long before Your visit?
I crouch on the opprobrious floor, waiting, while before me
Are pictures of angels with wings, and of saints;
At the center of the wall adorned with holy words of gold and silver,
A holy hole—Your shining visitation through it,
Is it not yet time for it?
O then, I would kneel before You,
Madly open my lips parched and cracked from thirst,
And as that terrifying prophet said,
Fill my mouth with You.
Inside my mouth You would quickly grow large,
Your holy basket would violently overflow and splatter,
And to my popping eyes, my short nose,
To my crewcut head with a lot of young gray hair,
And to my narrow forehead, splatter all over, drip lazily,
And like trails of slugs, glutinously gleam—
In Your incomparable compassion, like one raped
I would close my eyes as if suffering, and pant. . . .
When will that be? Will it be long before the visit?

These words said, the face, like a pigskin sack from which liquor has
    leaked,
Deflated into wrinkles, was folded on its neck,
And together with the body mounting the john, slumped.
The perplexing incident just over, before the john
Stood the wall filled with base graffiti,
And from the other side of the hole in the middle of the wall, a glar-
    ing
Parched eye was looking in.

We Do Not Know the Name of the King

The king is someone who came from the dark water at the end of the
    east
Still, we do not know his true name
The king is a fist raised toward the shadow land at the end of the
    west
Still, we do not know his true name

The king is ten toes and two heels that crush and grind the people
Still, we do not know his true name
The king is a dazzling head which, lost in clouds, is invisible
Still, we do not know his true name
The king is commands to do this and that, falling from a dizzying
    height
Still, we do not know his true name
The king is a heart that pulses eternally with the timeless earth
Still, we do not know his true name
The king is lusts that spurt up ceaselessly toward the sun
Still, we do not know his true name

We send, for the king, ships of trade toward a thousand ports
Still, we do not know his true name
We offer, for the king, blood of ten thousand people in a field at the
    border
Still, we do not know his true name
We continue, for the king, to plow, legs weak in the mud
Still, we do not know his true name
We dig, for the king, coarse metals in the depths of the ground, blind
Still, we do not know his true name
We willingly leave, for the king, the women of our households to
    humiliation
Still, we do not know his true name
We are, for the king, robbed of the last bit of grain in our coffer
Still, we do not know his true name
We build, for the king, an everlasting abode, shortening our lives
Still, we do not know his true name

The king, some say, was once a base slave at the end of the east
The king's fist raised toward the end of the west, some say, is leprous
The king, some say, is fearful of his closest aides and defecates on the
    stool brought in under his bed
The king, some say, is a shabby-looking old man less than five feet
    tall
The king's voice giving commands, some say, is as irritable and high-
    pitched as that of a hysterical woman
The king's heart, some say, is constantly watched by ten doctors for
    its irregular pulse
The king's phallus, some say, always droops like the clothbelt of his
    robe
Of the king's one thousand ships, some say, nine hundred never re-
    turn

The ten thousand for the king's blood offering, some say, are collected
    from his own land
The king's mud, some say, is packed full of worms that destroy this
    land
The king's metal diggers, some say, have revolted at the end of the
    south
The women taken away for the king, some say, merely tire him
The king's key to his granary is in the minister's pouch, some say, and
    the king is starved
The king's everlasting abode, some say, is totally plundered, though
    far from completed

Still, we do not know the king's true name

GLOSSARY OF TERMS USED IN THE ANTHOLOGY

(Cross-referenced terms indicated in small capitals)

AZUMA ASOBI UTA (songs for the dances of the East) Ancient folksongs and TANKA adapted to be sung at Shinto festivals to accompany sacred dances. Some of them include dialect words and are older than the AZUMA UTA.

AZUMA UTA (Eastern songs) TANKA in the *Man'yōshū* and *Kokinshū* that use dialect words and show a mixture of courtly and folk styles.

CHŌKA (long songs) A poetic form of varying length, composed of alternating 5- and 7-syllable units, usually finishing with an extra 7-syllable unit, and longer than TANKA. In the *Man'yōshū*, the shortest chōka consists of 7 units, the longest of 149.

FŪZOKU UTA (genre songs) Folksongs of the Heian period that were used in court circles as well. Many of them are written in variations of the TANKA form.

HAIBUN (HAIKAI prose) Prose written by HAIKAI poets in such a way as to complement various stylistic and esthetic features of HAIKAI poetry.

HAIKAI (light, humorous, chic) A term used, with differing nuances of meaning, in TANKA, RENGA, and HAIBUN. Originally a Chinese term, the word HAIKAI was first used in Japanese poetry to designate a category of humorous poems in the *Kokinshū*. It later came into use to designate a humorous kind of RENGA whose effect was brought about by the use of daily or vulgar diction, double-entendres, riddles, and oblique references to high poetry. Early in the Tokugawa period, linked verse of that kind took on a lyrical character under Bashō. See also HAIKU, HOKKU.

HAIKU (light verse) A modern term for HOKKU. Some modern poets, such as Ozaki Hōsai, have ignored the 5-7-5 syllable pattern and the use of KIGO. Now almost completely dissociated from RENGA.

HOKKU (opening verse) The opening 5-7-5 syllable part of a RENGA. The hokku, as the most important portion of a linked-verse sequence, was required to stand on its own and began to be written independently during the fifteenth century. The hokku also had to incorporate a KIGO. See also WAKIKU and Introduction, pp. xxxii–xxxiii.

KAGURA (god music) Folksongs and TANKA adapted to accompany Shinto dances.

KANSHI (Chinese poem) A poem written by a Japanese poet in classical Chinese. The form was particularly important in the Nara and Heian periods but continued to attract attention down to this century.

KIGO (season word) A term used in RENGA and HAIKU. The use of words or phrases to indicate the seasons became important first in TANKA, then in RENGA, especially in HOKKU. Over the centuries the number of kigo has greatly increased, but some modern poets have advocated discarding them altogether.

KOUTA (little song) Popular songs of the Muromachi period and later, of which the *Kanginshū* is the first important collection. Some are in 7–5–7–5 syllables, some in 7–7–7–5, but many are in much looser forms.

KYŌKA (lunatic TANKA) Comic, satirical TANKA written mainly in the second half of the eighteenth century.

MAKURA KOTOBA (pillow word) Set phrases, usually in five syllables, used to introduce sounds, words, or phrases. Many of them had lost their original meanings by the time of the *Man'yōshū*. Similar phrases in twelve or more syllables are called joshi, or introductory phrase.

NŌ (accomplishment) The poetic drama brought to a peak in the Muromachi period by Zeami Motokiyo (1363–?1443), Komparu Zenchiku (1405–1468), and others.

RENGA (linked verse) A poetic form consisting of two to a hundred alternating 5–7–5 and 7–7 syllable parts, written usually by two or more persons. The form evolved from the tendency of TANKA to break up into two parts, the first half (5–7–5 syllables) and the second (7–7 syllables), and the Japanese poets' propensity to make poetry writing a group activity. At first a renga was simply a TANKA with the two parts composed separately by one or two poets. Later, alternate parts began to be added, and in the Kamakura and Muromachi periods the one-hundred-part sequence was popular, while in the Edo period the thirty-six-part sequence was most favored. The rules for renga composition are complex, but the basic one is that any two consecutive parts must form a coherent whole, but three may not. Because of this arrangement, the renga has been described as a series of shifting tableaux in writing. In content, renga are divided into two kinds: those with the stress on elegance in the court poetry tradition, and those with the stress on humor, earthiness, realism. The latter kind is known as HAIKAI NO RENGA or simply HAIKAI. See also HOKKU, KIGO, WAKIKU and Introduction, pp. xxxii–xxxiii.

SAIBARA (horse-preparing music) Ancient folksongs later set to music by the court in the ninth century.

SAKIMORI NO UTA (songs by frontier guards) TANKA in the *Man'yōshū* traditionally ascribed to men on military duty on the southern island of Kyushu.

SEDŌKA (head-preparing song) A poetic form consisting of two 5–7–7 syllable patterns.

SENRYŪ (named for the poet Karai Senryū, 1718–1790) Comic verse in 5–7–5 syllable patterns.

TANKA (short song) A poetic form in thirty-one syllables, arranged in a pattern of 5–7–5–7–7 syllables. Also called WAKA.

TSUKEAI (linking together) The process of linking 5–7–5 and 7–7 syllable parts or 7–7 and 5–7–5 syllable parts, either in RENGA or independently; also, the result of such linking. Wit and elements of surprise were essential to the technique.

WAKA (Japanese song) Broadly, Japanese poetry, as opposed to Chinese poetry; narrowly, TANKA.

WAKIKU (accompanying verse) The 7–7 syllable part that follows the HOKKU in a RENGA. See also the Introduction, p. xxxiii.

MAJOR POETRY COLLECTIONS
MENTIONED IN THE ANTHOLOGY

EIGA TAIGAI (An Outline for Composing Tanka) An important commentary on tanka composition and a compendium of 103 tanka chosen as examples, completed by Fujiwara no Teika about 1222.

INUTSUKUBASHŪ (Collection of Canine Linked Verse) An early collection of tsukeai and hokku in the haikai mode. The compilation of the collection is generally attributed to Yamazaki Sōkan, sometime between 1523 and 1532.

KANGINSHŪ (Collection of Leisure Songs) A compilation in 1518 of kouta, mostly short love lyrics, many of which are melancholy in tone.

KOJIKI (Record of Ancient Matters) The most ancient account of Japanese mythology and early history, compiled in A.D. 712 and covering events from the period of myths and legends until A.D. 592. The text contains a number of stories and poems.

KOKINSHŪ, or more fully, KOKINWAKASHŪ (Collection of Waka of Ancient and Modern Times) The first imperial anthology, compiled early in the tenth century by Ki no Tsurayuki and others. The collection contains twenty books and 1,111 poems, mostly tanka, along with some chōka and sedōka. The *Kokinshū* set the organizational and thematic patterns for the later imperial anthologies.

MAN'YŌSHŪ (Collection of Myriad Leaves) The earliest great compilation of Japanese poetry collected in the latter part of the eighth century by Ōtomo Yakamochi and others. The *Man'yōshū* contains twenty books and 4,516 poems.

RYŌJIN HISHŌ (Secret Selection of Songs) A collection of popular verse. Many of the selections are in the form of imayō, "poems in the present mode," (7–5, 7–5, 7–5). The anthology was compiled by Emperor Goshirakawa (1127–1192); only portions of the text remain. The manuscript was discovered in 1911.

SHINKOKINSHŪ, or more fully, SHINKOKINWAKASHŪ (New collection of Waka of Ancient and Modern Times) The eighth imperial anthology, compiled early in the thirteenth century by Fujiwara no Teika and others, which contains 1,981 poems in twenty books. The *Shinkokinshū* is generally considered the finest anthology of court poetry after the *Kokinshū*.

MAJOR POETS IN THE ANTHOLOGY

(Cross-referenced names appear in small capitals in the entries; poets are listed in the order in which they appear in the anthology.)

EMPEROR JOMEI (593–641) The thirty-fourth emperor of Japan, active in promoting diplomatic relations between China and Japan. His *Man'yōshū* poems are considered prototypes of landscape poetry.

PRINCESS NUKADA (seventh century) Her poem comparing the merits of spring and autumn began the tradition of literary debate in Japan.

EMPRESS JITŌ (645–702) The forty-first ruler of Japan, who took power at the death of her husband, Emperor Temmu. Officials who accompanied her on her travels wrote a number of poems on her outings; KAKINOMOTO NO HITOMARO was one of them.

KAKINOMOTO NO HITOMARO (active c. 700) Recognized as the greatest poet of the *Man'yōshū*, but little is known of his life, other than incidental details that can be gleaned from the poems and the notes to them. His chōka have always been particularly admired. By the time of the compilation of the *Kokinshū* in the tenth century, KI NO TSURAYUKI could already refer to him as a "saint of poetry."

TAKECHI NO KUROHITO (dates uncertain) He served the imperial court under EMPRESS JITŌ. His poems record his various travels and represent some of the earliest examples in the genre.

YAMANOUE NO OKURA (?660–?733) After a journey to China at the beginning of the eighth century, he occupied a number of government posts. His knowledge of Chinese literature and his social concern make him a distinct poet in the *Man'yōshū*.

ŌTOMO NO TABITO (665–731) An important official, he was governor-general of the Dazaifu in Kyushu later in his life. That experience, as well as his association with YAMANOUE NO OKURA, inspired many of his poems. More than eighty of his poems are included in the *Man'yōshū*.

TAKAHASHI MUSHIMARO (dates uncertain) Little is known of his life, although he was in government service from 717 to 723. Much of his poetry deals with early Japanese legends.

KASA NO KANAMURA (dates uncertain) Little is known about him, but the great number of his poems included in the *Man'yōshū* suggests he may have enjoyed greater esteem than his contemporary, YAMABE NO AKAHITO.

YAMABE NO AKAHITO (early eighth century) A minor court official under Emperor Shōmu (701–756), he has been particularly admired for his descriptions of nature.

LADY ŌTOMO NO SAKANOUE (early eighth century) Younger sister of ŌTOMO NO TABITO and aunt of ŌTOMO NO YAKAMOCHI. Her poetry is notable for its variety of subjects, intellectual poise, and sophistication.

LADY KASA (mid-eighth century) Her tanka written to ŌTOMO NO YAKAMOCHI make her one of the more famous poets in Japanese literature, but little else is known about her.

ŌTOMO NO YAKAMOCHI (716–?785) The eldest son of ŌTOMO NO TABITO and an important government official. Nearly five hundred of his poems are included in the *Man'yōshū*, and he is thought to have helped compile the anthology.

ARIWARA NO NARIHIRA (825–880) One of the greatest of the early tanka poets and a dashing and romantic figure, whose legendary amorous exploits are described in the *Ise monogatari* (Tales of Ise). His various love affairs have been the subject of countless later works of art.

ONO NO KOMACHI (mid-ninth century) Reputedly one of the greatest beauties of her age. Details of her life are few, but her beauty and her strong personality have made her the subject of a celebrated group of Nō plays.

SUGAWARA NO MICHIZANE (845–903) A brilliant scholar of Chinese, who rose to the position of Minister of the Right, only to be accused of treason and banished to Kyushu, where he died in exile. Later he was revered as the god of calligraphy. He is generally considered the finest of the early poets who wrote in the Chinese language.

LADY ISE (died 939) Lady-in-waiting during the reigns of Emperors Uda and Daigo (889–930). One hundred eighty of her tanka are preserved in imperial anthologies and a collection devoted to her work.

KI NO TSURAYUKI (c. 868–c. 946) A courtier-scholar who served as one of the editors of the *Kokinshū*, the first anthology of Japanese poetry compiled on imperial order. His preface to the anthology is one of the earliest statements on classical Japanese poetics. His *Tosa nikki* (Tosa Diary) has been a model of excellence in the genre.

ŌE NO ASATSUNA (886–957) A high court official, scholar of Chinese literature, historian, and calligrapher.

MINAMOTO NO SHITAGŌ (911–983) A government official, who was skilled in writing poems both in Chinese and Japanese. He was one of the compilers of the second imperial anthology of Japanese poetry, the *Gosenshū*.

LADY IZUMI (born c. 976) Lady-in-waiting at the court where Lady Murasaki, who wrote *Genji monogatari* (The Tale of Genji), also worked. Her poetic diary, *Izumi Shikibu nikki* (Lady Izumi's Diary), is a monument in the genre, full of intensity, passion, and self-awareness.

FUJIWARA NO SHUNZEI (1114–1204) A central figure in the development of court poetry, who did much to refine and promote the esthetic of *yūgen* (depth, elegance). His role as a highly respected arbiter in poetic matters can be seen in the touching portrait of him contained in the *Heike monogatari* (Tale of the Heike). He was the sole editor of the seventh imperial anthology of Japanese poetry, the *Senzaishū*.

SAIGYŌ (1118–1190) A member of the Fujiwara family who gave up his duties and became a monk at the age of twenty-two, Saigyō was one of the first of the important traveling recluse-poets who contributed so much to the tradition of the meditative travel diary, which climaxed in the work of MATSUO BASHŌ. Legends and stories about Saigyō's life and his poetry are found in all the Japanese arts, from painting and poetry to the theater.

PRINCESS SHIKISHI (died 1201) A daughter of Emperor Goshirakawa (1127–1192), who compiled the *Ryōjin hishō*, a collection of songs. Her tanka are among the most beautiful in the eighth imperial anthology of Japanese poetry, the *Shinkokinshū*, edited by FUJIWARA NO TEIKA and others. In later life she became a nun. As the Nō play *Teika* suggests, her name was evidently closely linked with that of FUJIWARA NO TEIKA during her lifetime, although there is not enough evidence to support rumors of a liaison between them.

MYŌE (1173–1232) An eminent Buddhist cleric of the Kamakura period, highly respected by laymen and religious leaders alike for his piety and diplomatic skill. His poetry serves as literary evidence for his mystical insights.

FUJIWARA NO TEIKA (1162–1241) The son of FUJIWARA NO SHUNZEI, Teika earned an enduring reputation as one of the greatest tanka poets in the court tradition. His work as a compiler of the *Shinkokinshū* and as an editor of various older texts, including the *Genji monogatari* (The Tale of Genji), made him the supreme arbiter of taste for his own and later periods. He was a renowned teacher of tanka composition and a superb essayist on the art and craft of composing poetry.

MINAMOTO NO SANETOMO (1192–1219) The third shogun during the Kamakura period, murdered by his nephew in a celebrated political incident. He studied poetry with FUJIWARA NO TEIKA, and his poems were collected and often anthologized. His reputation as a poet, however, remains controversial.

KYŌGOKU TAMEKANE (1254–1332) A great-grandson of FUJIWARA NO TEIKA, he continued to search for an innovative style in the increasingly staid court tanka tradition. A man of strong personality, he was exiled twice.

IKKYŪ SŌJUN (1394–1481) Zen monk legendary for his eccentric behavior. He is said to have been considerate to high and low, rich and poor, but harsh in exposing the hypocrisies of the religious.

GUSAI (1282–1376) A monk who helped set rules for renga in its beginning phases. He served as an important teacher to members of the nobility and the military class.

KOMPARU ZENCHIKU (1405–1468) A Nō dramatist. The famous actor and playwright Zeami Motokiyo (1363–?1443) held Zenchiku, his son-in-law, in high regard and passed on to him his subtlest and most mature teachings. Next to Zeami, Zenchiku is doubtless the finest playwright and theoretician in Nō.

BOTANGE SHŌHAKU, commonly known as SHŌHAKU (1443–1527) A renga poet from a noble family. He took nominal Buddhist vows in order to be free to pursue his scholarship in classical literature and the composition of poetry. A learned and elegant poet, he maintained close ties with SŌGI.

SAIOKUKEN SŌCHŌ, commonly known as SŌCHŌ (1448–1532) A renga poet, he accompanied SŌGI on many journeys. From a humble background, Sōchō had learning and eccentricities that made him attractive to many. His priestly ties were nominal. In writing renga with SŌGI he was careful to adjust his poetic personality to that of the man he regarded as his master. But his own poetry is often somewhat different in character.

IIO SŌGI, commonly known as SŌGI (1421–1502) The greatest renga poet of the Muromachi period. Learned in classical Japanese literature, he traveled widely, often to give lectures on famous tales and important poetic anthologies and to write renga. His life as a recluse-poet frequently on the road and the diaries he wrote about his travels became an inspiration to BASHŌ.

ARAKIDA MORITAKE (1473–1549) The first important writer of haikai no renga. He was the head priest of the Ise Shrine.

NISHIYAMA SŌIN (1605–1682) A haikai poet, whose pupils included the famous novelist Ihara Saikaku (1642–1693). The free and clever style he brought to the form also attracted BASHŌ, who considered Sōin his first master.

KONISHI RAIZAN (1654–1716) SŌIN's disciple. Precocious and a teacher of haikai at seventeen, he brought philosophical speculation to what had basically been a comic and satirical verse form.

MATSUO BASHŌ, commonly known as BASHŌ (1644–1694) The greatest of the haikai poets, who in his writings sums up many of the crucial linguistic and artistic concerns of Japanese poetry, recasting them in terms of his own unique sensibilities. Of samurai stock, he lived simply as a kind of hermit, earning a small amount of income from his disciples through teaching and judging poetry contests. His travels, in the manner of SAIGYŌ and SŌGI, took him through large areas of central and northern Japan and gave him the material for his remarkable travel diaries. Learned in Chinese as well as Japanese classical literature, Bashō created a literature as profound as it was cosmopolitan.

UEJIMA ONITSURA (1661–1738) Like BASHŌ, he looked beyond the witty ideal of the usual haikai poetry to search out *makoto*, or sincerity. Such a commitment was crucial in the development of the form.

TAKARAI KIKAKU (1661–1707) BASHŌ's pupil from the age of fifteen, he became his foremost disciple. His haikai was characterized as more sophisticated and urbane than that of his teacher, and much of it became difficult to understand by the time of BUSON, who admired him.

MUKAI KYORAI (1651–1704) One of BASHŌ's important disciples, he was devoted to his teacher and tried to attain in his haikai the spirit of lofty-minded melancholy he found in his master's work. The posthumously published *Kyorai shō* (Kyorai's Writings) records comments on haikai poetics by BASHŌ and his disciples.

NAITO JŌSŌ (1662–1704) A haikai poet and disciple of BASHŌ. The son of a samurai, Jōsō retired from service to his lord on grounds of ill health and became a monk before his association with BASHŌ. His work is often characterized as stern.

NOZAWA BONCHŌ (died 1714) A physician and haikai poet who became an important disciple of BASHŌ. After solid contributions to poetry, he was imprisoned for some crime and became estranged from haikai circles.

KAAI CHIGETSU (?1634–?1708) BASHŌ's disciple. Her husband was a freight agent. Her son and daughter-in-law also studied with BASHŌ.

SHIBA SONOME (1664–1726) A disciple BASHŌ admired. After the death of her husband, also a poet, she supported herself as a haikai judge and as an eye doctor.

CHIYOJO (1703–1775) A haikai poet. She began composing at fifteen and remained largely self-taught. She was visited by a number of famous poets during her lifetime and, by the time she took holy orders in 1755, had achieved a lasting reputation.

TAN TAIGI (1709–1771) A haikai poet who, along with BUSON, urged a "return to BASHŌ" or a more serious style. He covered a great variety of subjects in his haikai, but particularly excelled in describing human affairs.

YOSA BUSON, commonly known as BUSON (1716–1783) After BASHŌ, undoubtedly the greatest haikai poet. He spent much of his time in Kyoto, where he enjoyed a reputation as a painter as well. Both his poetry and paintings pay homage to the Chinese-inspired ideal of the gentleman-scholar highly appreciated during that period.

KATŌ KYŌTAI (1732–1792) He joined BUSON in an effort to improve the poetic level of haikai by a return to the spirit of BASHŌ. He especially admired NAITŌ JŌSŌ and helped publish *Kyorai shō* in 1775.

MIURA CHORA (1729–1780) An associate of BUSON, Chora lived in Kyoto and worked with those who attempted to restore dignity and artistic seriousness to the haikai form.

TAKAI KITŌ (1741–1789) A major pupil of BUSON, who succeeded him as the head of his haikai circle.

RYŌKAN (1758–1831) Poet, calligrapher, and Zen priest, Ryōkan lived as a traveler-recluse and wrote poetry in both classical Chinese and Japanese. His deep interest in the *Man'yōshū* and in the Buddhist poetry of the Chinese mystic Han Shan may be seen in his profound and deceptively simple verse.

KAYA SHIRAO (?1738–1791) A poet and critic who attempted to purify haikai by a return to an emphasis on nature and the expression of directly felt emotion.

KOBAYASHI ISSA, commonly known as ISSA (1763–1827) The finest haikai poet of the late Tokugawa period. The eldest son of a poor farmer, he led a difficult life, traveling between Edo (present-day Tokyo) and the mountains of Nagano. His humanity and compassion make his poetry unique. Although not well appreciated in his time, his work is now ranked with that of BASHŌ and BUSON.

NATSUME SEIBI (1749–1816) An Edo businessman, Seibi was a benefactor and mentor of ISSA and a self-taught man of letters, who believed that studying the poetry of the past was the best means to mastery. His poor health forced him to retire from the family business, but that also permitted him to devote most of his time to writing.

RAI SAN'YŌ (1781–1832) Confucian scholar, historian, and poet in classical Chinese, he represents the last flowering in the Tokugawa period of the composition of kanshi. His *Nihon gaishi* (Unofficial History of Japan), written in Chinese, was the most popular text of its kind in nineteenth-century Japan.

TACHIBANA AKEMI (1812–1868) A scholar of Japanese and Chinese literature in the late Tokugawa period. An admirer of the *Man'yōshū*, he tried to bring alive some of the earlier poetic virtues in his own tanka and often drew his subject matter from his daily life.

MASAOKA SHIKI (1867–1902) Born at the very beginning of the Meiji period, he became the first significant modern poet, polemist, and historian of haiku—the term to which he gave currency—and tanka. Ill much of his life, he nevertheless commanded an enormous reputation as a poet, editor, and teacher.

SHIMAZAKI TŌSON (1872–1943) One of the great novelists of modern Japan, he wrote a considerable amount of poetry as a young man and did much to introduce to his readers modern poetic forms that derived from Western models. His first book of poems, *Wakana shū* (Young Herbs), published in 1896, and subsequent volumes legitimatized modern poetry for a whole generation of poets.

YOSANO AKIKO (1878–1942) One of the first tanka poets to be profoundly affected by new currents in modern psychology and Western poetry. Her first collection of tanka, *Midaregami* (Tangled Hair), published in 1901, was unabashedly romantic and brought wholly different possibilities to one of the oldest poetic forms. She remained a pacifist and a champion of women's rights all her life and made excellent translations into modern Japanese of such classical works as *Genji monogatari* (The Tale of Genji).

KITAHARA HAKUSHŪ (1885–1942) Interested in estheticism, symbolism, and technique, he was a crucial figure in the development of modern Japanese poetry. His choice of colors and rhythms in verse made him unique. He was at ease with a great variety of poetic forms and even created some. Many of his poems that were set to music are still sung.

WAKAYAMA BOKUSUI (1885–1928) One of the most popular tanka poets of his period, he loved to travel and to drink. In much of his later poetry he expressed his mystic conviction in the powers of nature.

ISHIKAWA TAKUBOKU (1886–1912) From a modest background, he suffered terrible vicissitudes, financial and professional, even after establishing himself in Tokyo as a poet of tanka written in a fresh and highly personal style. He also experimented with "modern style" poems, some of which were quite successful. His growing interest in socialism might have radically changed his art, but he died of an illness at twenty-six.

SAITŌ MOKICHI (1882–1953) Psychologist by profession, he was inspired by reading MASAOKA SHIKI, became a tanka poet, and succeeded in harmonizing his contemporary sensibility with the traditional requirements of the form. He extolled the Man'yōshū and wrote a famous work on KAKINOMOTO NO HITOMARO.

TAKAMURA KŌTARŌ (1883–1956) Sculptor and poet, Takamura studied in France and elsewhere before World War I and returned to Japan determined to make what he had learned of Western art part of his own. He wrote on Western esthetics and was particularly interested in Rodin. The group of poems he wrote about his wife, Chieko, who became insane, probably makes him the most widely read poet of his generation.

HAGIWARA SAKUTARŌ (1886–1942) Considered by many as the first truly modern poet, because his first book of poems, Tsuki ni hoeru (Howling at the Moon), published in 1917, shows a masterful handling of colloquial language and effectively conveys his neurotic sensibility. In his later work he reverted to "literary" language.

OZAKI HŌSAI (1885–1926) An insurance executive with a law degree from Tokyo University, he could not hold his job and finally became a Buddhist sexton two years before his death. An eccentric and a heavy drinker, he seemed to find himself in his free-form haiku, in which he abandoned the traditional rules in order to concentrate on recording his perceptions of his spare existence.

MIYAZAWA KENJI (1896–1933) A devout Buddhist and school teacher, he wrote poetry and children's stories while attempting to alleviate the difficult life, physical and spiritual, of the villagers in Iwate Prefecture, where he was born. Little acknowledged in his time, his poetry is now widely appreciated for its beauty of imagery and insight.

NISHIWAKI JUNZABURŌ (born 1894) A brilliant scholar and linguist, he first wrote in English, French, and Latin during his stay in Europe from 1922 to 1925. Reading HAGIWARA SAKUTARŌ, he became convinced that a genuine contemporary poetry could be written in the Japanese language, and from the time of his first book of poems in Japanese, *Ambarvalia*, published in 1935, he has remained in the forefront of those who experimented with surrealist and other avant-garde techniques. He is the great cosmopolitan of modern Japanese poets and identifies Ezra Pound, T. S. Eliot, and the French surrealists as his spiritual contemporaries.

KANEKO MITSUHARU (1895–1975) A wanderer in Europe and Asia, a lover of Whitman and Baudelaire, he began to write in the 1930s in a fashion highly critical of the militarist politics of the day. During the war he lived in obscurity but later emerged as a major figure in postwar literature, his satire as biting as ever.

TAKIGUCHI SHŪZŌ (1903–1979) An associate of NISHIWAKI JUNZABURŌ in editing an early Surrealist journal, he introduced a number of André Breton's ideas through his translations. His experiments with surrealist verse were written before the war but not collected and published until 1967. He worked closely with many artists and wrote important art criticism.

ONO TŌZABURŌ (born 1903) A writer of avant-garde poetry since early in his career and a moderate anarchist, he wrote many poems describing the industrialized areas of Osaka. He was critical of Japanese militarism before the war, and his strong criticism of "tanka-esque lyricism," voiced after the war, has provoked as much controversy as Kuwabara Takeo's judgment that haiku is a "secondary art."

MARUYAMA KAORU (1899–1974) He failed in his desire to become a sailor for reasons of health, but wrote many poems about the sea. He was also active in editing and publishing contemporary poetry.

TACHIHARA MICHIZŌ (1914–1939) An architect by training and a lyric poet, he said he was strongly influenced by HAGIWARA SAKUTARŌ, Rilke, and the *Shinkokinshū*. He wished, he said, to write poems "like Chopin nocturnes." He died too soon to fulfill his enormous promise.

TAMURA RYŪICHI (born 1923) An important member of the postwar "Wasteland School," much influenced by the poetry and poetics of T. S. Eliot, Tamura has maintained his primacy among postwar poets. His literary criticism is also widely appreciated.

TANIKAWA SHUNTARŌ (born 1931) Son of a distinguished professor of esthetics, he gave up his education after high school to begin a career as a professional writer and since 1952 has steadily published poetry anthologies and other books. Because of his frequent contributions to weeklies and other mass-market publications, he is probably the best-known poet in Japan today.

ISHIGAKI RIN (born 1920) A bank employee since 1934 until her recent retirement, she has maintained the attitude that her poetry should derive from her experience as a working woman, rather than from a devotion to any of the intellectual movements that have characterized modern poetry in Japan and elsewhere. An "ordinary conservative person," she draws on her responses to a life that was mostly difficult.

ANZAI HITOSHI (born 1919) A newspaper reporter who began publishing poetry at thirty-six, he shows a strong interest in old Japanese poetry and poets, both in his essays—some sixty on the *Man'yōshū* alone—and in his poems. His sensibilities and language are, however, thoroughly of this age.

YOSHIOKA MINORU (born 1919) A self-taught poet, he was first drawn to the tanka of KITAHARA HAKUSHŪ and wrote in that form in his teens. But the poems in his first book, *Ekitai* (Liquid), published in 1941, were in non-tanka form and used a technique that has made him famous: accumulation of sharp images. He remains unique among postwar poets.

ISHIHARA YOSHIRŌ (1915–1977) A student of German and a Christian convert, he began to write poetry seriously after his experience as a prisoner of war: captured by the Soviet Army in Manchuria, he spent eight years in Siberia, released only by the general amnesty given at Stalin's death. He began to write at that time, he said, because he wanted to examine what it means to be a human being.

TOMIOKA TAEKO (born 1935) She published her first book of poems, *Henrei* (Courtesy in Return), in 1957, when she was a student at Osaka Women's University. In 1973 her *Collected Poems* was published. Toward the end of the 1960s she began to concentrate on prose and has since published many novels, collections of short stories, plays, and essays. The effect of her writings has been compared to that of the films of René Clair, because of her ability to bring freshness and fantasy to the simplest of verbal and psychological situations.

TAKAHASHI MUTSUO (born 1937) Since publishing his first book of poems, *Mino, atashi no oushi* (Mino, My Bull), in 1957, he has pursued homosexual themes both in poetry and fiction. His subject matter and his ability to blend the erotic and the spiritual make him unusual among the poets writing today.

A SELECT BIBLIOGRAPHY ON JAPANESE POETRY

It has not been possible to include here items from a number of small journals and little magazines. Most of the items listed are easily available and will serve as a good starting point for those wishing to explore the ever greater amount of material available in translation.

I. General Bibliographies

Rimer, J. Thomas, and Morrell, Robert, eds. *Guide to Japanese Poetry*. Boston: G. K. Hall, 1975.
Staff of the International House of Japan Library, eds., *Modern Japanese Literature in Translation: A Bibliography*. Tokyo and New York: Kodansha International, 1979.

II. General Anthologies

A. GENERAL ANTHOLOGIES

Blyth, R. H. *Edo Satirical Verse Anthologies*. Tokyo: Hokuseido Press, 1961.
———. *Haiku*. 4 vols. Tokyo: Hokuseido Press, 1949–1952.
———. *Japanese Life and Characters in Senryū*. Tokyo: Hokuseido Press, 1961.
Bownas, Geoffrey, and Thwaite, Anthony. *The Penguin Book of Japanese Verse*. Harmondsworth and Baltimore: Penguin Books, 1964.
Keene, Donald. *Anthology of Japanese Literature, from the Earliest Era to the Mid-nineteenth Century*. New York: Grove Press, 1955.
Rexroth, Kenneth. *One Hundred Poems from the Japanese*. New York: New Directions, 1956.
———. *One Hundred More Poems from the Japanese*. New York: New Directions, 1976.

——, and Atsumi Ikuko. *The Burning Heart: Women Poets of Japan*. New York: Seabury Press, 1977.

Ury, Marian. *Poems of the Five Mountains. An Introduction to the Literature of the Zen Monasteries*. Tokyo: Mushinsha, 1977.

Watson, Burton. *Japanese Literature in Chinese*. Vol. 1, *Poetry and Prose in Chinese by Japanese Writers in the Early Period*. Vol. 2, *Poetry and Prose in Chinese by Japanese Writers of the Later Period*. New York: Columbia University Press, 1975, 1976.

B. ANTHOLOGIES OF MODERN POETRY

Fitzsimmons, Thomas. *Japanese Poetry Now*. London: Rapp and Whiting, 1972.

Guest, Harry, Guest, Lynn, and Kajima Shōzō. *Postwar Japanese Poetry*. Baltimore: Penguin Books, 1972.

Keene, Donald. *Modern Japanese Literature*. New York: Grove Press, 1956.

Kijima Hajime. *The Poetry of Postwar Japan*. Iowa City: University of Iowa Press, 1975.

Kirkup, James. *Modern Japanese Poetry*. Queensland, Australia: University of Queensland Press, 1978.

Kōno Ichiro and Fukuda Rikutarō. *An Anthology of Modern Japanese Poetry*. Tokyo: Kenkyusha, 1957.

Ninomiya Takamichi and Enright, D. J. *The Poetry of Living Japan*. London: John Murray, 1957.

Sato, Hiroaki. *Anthology of Modern Japanese Poets. Chicago Review*, 25, 2 (1973).

——. *Ten Japanese Poets*. Hanover, N.H.: Granite Publications, 1973.

Shiffert, Edith, and Sawa Yuki. *Anthology of Modern Japanese Poetry*. Rutland and Tokyo: Tuttle, 1972.

Ueda Makoto. *Modern Japanese Haiku, An Anthology*. Toronto and Buffalo: University of Toronto Press, 1976.

Wilson, Graeme, and Atsumi Ikuko. *Three Contemporary Japanese Poets*. London: London Magazine Editions, 1972. (Includes translations of poems by Anzai Hitoshi, Shiraishi Kazuko, and Tanikawa Shuntarō.)

C. FOLK POETRY AND OTHER

Crihfield, Liza. *Ko-Uta: "Little Songs" of the Geisha World*. Rutland and Tokyo: Tuttle, 1979.

Hoff, Frank. *The Genial Seed: A Japanese Song Cycle.* Tokyo and New York: Mushinsha/Grossman, 1971.

——. *Song, Dance, Storytelling: Aspects of the Performing Arts in Japan.* Cornell: Cornell University East Asia Papers No. 15, 1978.

Philippi, Donald L. *Songs of Gods, Songs of Humans: The Epic Tradition of the Ainu.* Princeton: Princeton University Press, 1979.

Sackheim, Eric. *The Silent Firefly: Japanese Songs of Love and Other Things.* Tokyo: Kodansha, 1963.

III. Background and Genre Studies

A. Books

Blyth, R. H. *A History of Haiku.* 2 vols. Tokyo: Hokuseido Press, 1964.

Brower, Robert H., and Miner, Earl. *Japanese Court Poetry.* Stanford: Stanford University Press, 1961.

Harich-Schneider, Eta. *Rōei: The Medieval Court Songs of Japan.* Tokyo: Sophia University Press, 1965.

Henderson, Harold G. *An Introduction to Haiku.* Garden City, N.Y.: Doubleday, 1958.

Hisamatsu Sen'ichi. *Biographical Dictionary of Japanese Literature.* Tokyo and New York: Kodansha International, 1976.

Keene, Donald. *Japanese Literature: An Introduction for Western Readers.* New York: Grove Press, 1955.

——. *Landscapes and Portraits: Appreciations of Japanese Culture.* Palo Alto and Tokyo: Kodansha International, 1971.

——. *World within Walls: Japanese Literature of the Pre-Modern Era 1600–1868.* New York: Holt, Rinehart and Winston, 1976.

Miner, Earl. *An Introduction to Japanese Court Poetry.* Stanford: Stanford University Press, 1968.

——. *Japanese Linked Poetry.* Princeton: Princeton University Press, 1979.

——. *Japanese Poetic Diaries.* Berkeley and Los Angeles: University of California Press, 1969.

Nippon Gakujutsu Shinkōkai. *Haikai and Haiku.* Tokyo: Nippon Gakujutsu Shinkōkai, 1958.

Okazaki Yoshie. *Japanese Literature in the Meiji Era.* Tr. V. H. Viglielmo. Tokyo: Tokyo Bunko, 1955.

Putzar, Edward. *Japanese Literature: A Historical Outline.* Tucson: University of Arizona Press, 1973.

Reischauer, Edwin O., and Yamagiwa, Joseph K. *Translations from Early Japanese Literature.* Cambridge: Harvard University Press, 1951.

Ueda Makoto. *Literary and Art Theories in Japan.* Cleveland: Press of Case Western Reserve University, 1967.

————. *Matsuo Bashō.* New York: Twayne, 1970.

————. *Zeami, Bashō, Yeats, Pound: A Study in Japanese and English Poetics.* The Hague: Mouton, 1965.

Waley, Arthur. *Japanese Poetry: the 'Uta.'* (1919) Honolulu: University Press of Hawaii, 1976.

Yasuda, Kenneth. *The Japanese Haiku.* Rutland and Tokyo: Tuttle, 1957.

B. Articles

Brower, Robert H. "Ex-Emperor Go-Toba's Secret Teachings: *Go-Toba no in gokuden.*" *Harvard Journal of Asiatic Studies,* 32 (1972), pp. 5–70.

————. "Japanese." In W. K. Wimsatt, ed., *Versification: Major Language Types.* New York: New York University Press, 1972, pp. 38–51.

————. "Masaoka Shiki and Tanka Reform." In Donald Shively, ed., *Tradition and Modernization in Japanese Culture.* Princeton: Princeton University Press, 1971, pp. 379–418.

Ceadel, E. B. "The Two Prefaces to the *Kokinshū.*" *Asia Major,* new series 7, pt. 1–2 (December 1957), pp. 40–51.

Hibbett, Howard S. "The Japanese Comic Linked Verse Tradition." *Harvard Journal of Asiatic Studies,* 23 (1960–61), pp. 76–92.

Katō, Hilda, tr. "The Mumyōshō of Kamo no Chōmei and Its Significance in Japanese Literature." *Monumenta Nipponica* 23, 3–4 (1968), pp. 321–430.

Keene, Donald. "The Comic Tradition in Renga." In John W. Hall and Toyoda Takeshi, ed., *Japan in the Muromachi Age.* Berkeley: University of California Press, 1977, pp. 241–277.

Konishi Jin'ichi. "The Art of Renga." Tr. Karen Brazell. *Journal of Japanese Studies,* 2, 1 (autumn 1975), pp. 33–61.

————, Brower, Robert, and Miner, Earl. "Association and Progression: Principles of Integration in Anthologies and Sequences of Japanese Court Poetry, A.D. 900–1350." *Harvard Journal of Asiatic Studies,* 21 (1958), pp. 67–127.

Morrell, Robert. "The Buddhist Poetry in the Goshūishū." *Monumenta Nipponica* 28, 1 (spring 1977), pp. 87–100.

Sugiyama Yoko, "*The Wasteland* and Contemporary Japanese Poetry." *Comparative Literature* 13, 3 (summer 1961), pp. 264–278.

"Toward a Modern Japanese Poetry," a collection of articles on the development of new-style Japanese poetry during the Meiji period, including contributions by Tamie Kamiyama, William Matheson, Robert Morrell, J. Thomas Rimer, and Eugene Soviak. *Literature East and West*, 19, 1–4 (January–December 1975).

IV. *Translations of Poetry from Particular Periods and Individual Poets*

A. EARLY POETRY

Aston, W. G. *Nihongi: Chronicles of Japan from the Earliest Times to A.D. 597*. London: George Allen & Unwin, 1956; 1896 in two volumes.

Brannen, Noah, and Elliott, William W. *Festive Wine: Ancient Japanese Poems from the Kinkafu*. New York and Tokyo: Walker/Weatherhill, 1969.

Miller, Roy Andrew. *The Footprints of the Buddha, an Eighth-Century Old Japanese Poetic Sequence*. New Haven: American Oriental Society, 1975.

Nippon Gakujutsu Shinkōkai, ed. *The Man'yōshū: One Thousand Poems Selected and Translated from the Japanese*. Tokyo: Iwanami Shoten, 1940; New York: Columbia University Press, 1968.

Philippi, Donald L. *Kojiki*. Princeton: Princeton University Press, 1968; Tokyo: Tokyo University Press, 1965.

——. *This Wine of Peace, This Wine of Laughter: A Complete Anthology of Japan's Earliest Songs*. New York: Mushinsha/Grossman, 1968.

Wright, Harold. *Ten Thousand Leaves: Love Poems from the Man'yōshū*. Boulder, Colo.: Shambala, 1979.

Yasuda, Kenneth. *Land of the Reed Plains: Ancient Japanese Lyrics from the Man'yōshū*. Rutland and Tokyo: Tuttle, 1960.

B. Tanka

Ariwara no Narihira. *Tales of Ise: Lyrical Episodes from Tenth Century Japan.* Tr. Helen Craig McCullough. Stanford: Stanford University Press, 1967. See also H. J. Harris, Jr., tr. *The Tales of Ise.* Rutland and Tokyo: Tuttle, 1972.

Fujiwara no Teika. *Fujiwara Teika's Hundred Poem Sequence of the Shōji Era 1200.* Tr. Robert H. Brower. Tokyo: Sophia University Press, 1978.

———. *Fujiwara Teika's Superior Poems of Our Time: A Thirteenth-Century Poetic Treatise and Sequence.* Tr. Robert H. Brower and Earl Miner. Stanford: Stanford University Press, 1967.

Izumi Shikibu. *The Izumi Shikibu Diary: A Romance of the Heian Court.* Tr. Edwin R. Cranston. Cambridge: Harvard University Press, 1969.

Ōkuma Kotomichi. *A Grass Path: Selected Poems from the Sōkeishū.* Tr. Uyehara Yukuo and Marjorie Sinclair. Honolulu: University of Hawaii Press, 1955.

Saigyō. *Mirror for the Moon: A Selection of Poems by Saigyō* (1118–1190). Tr. William LaFleur. New York: New Directions, 1978.

Princess Shikishi. *Poems of Princess Shikishi.* Tr. Hiroaki Sato. Hanover, N.H.: Granite Publications, 1973.

C. Kanshi

Natsume Sōseki. "Sixteen Chinese Poems by Natsume Sōseki." Tr. Burton Watson. *Essays on Natsume Sōseki,* edited by the Japanese National Commission for UNESCO. Tokyo: Japan Society for the Promotion of Science, 1970.

Ryōkan. *Ryōkan: Zen Monk-Poet of Japan.* Tr. Burton Watson. New York: Columbia University Press, 1977.

———. *One Robe, One Bowl: The Zen Poetry of Ryōkan.* Tr. John Stephens. Tokyo and New York: John Weatherhill, Inc., 1977.

D. Nō

Fenollosa, Ernest, and Pound, Ezra. *The Classical Noh Theatre of Japan.* New York: New Directions, 1959.

Keene, Donald. *Twenty Plays of the Nō Theatre.* New York: Columbia University Press, 1970.

Nippon Gakujutsu Shinkōkai, ed. *Japanese Noh Drama.* 3 vols. Tokyo: Maruzen, 1955–1960.
Tyler, Royall. *Pining Wind: A Cycle of Nō Plays.* Cornell: Cornell University Press, 1970.
——. *Granny Mountains: A Second Cycle of Nō Plays.* Cornell: Cornell University East Asia Papers No. 18, 1978.

E. RENGA

Carter, Stephen D. "Three Poets at Yuyama: Sōgi and *Yuyama Sangin Hyakuin,* 1491." *Monumenta Nipponica,* 33, 2 (119–149) and 3 (241–283), 1978.
Hare, Thomas W. "Linked Verse at Imashinmei Shrine, *Anegakōji Imashinmei Hyakuin* 1447." *Monumenta Nipponica,* 34, 2 (summer 1979), pp. 169–208.

F. HAIKAI AND HAIKU

Kobayashi Issa. *The Autumn Wind.* Tr. Lewis MacKenzie. London: John Murray, 1957.
——. *The Year of My Life.* Tr. Nobuyuki Yuasa. Berkeley: University of California Press, 1972.
Matsuo Bashō. *Back Roads to Far Towns.* Tr. Cid Corman and Kamaike Susumu. New York: Mushinsha/Grossman, 1968.
——. *Monkey's Raincoat.* Tr. Maeda Cana. New York: Mushinsha/Grossman, 1973.
——. *The Narrow Road to the Deep North and Other Travel Sketches.* Tr. Nobuyuki Yuasa. Baltimore: Penguin Classics, 1966.
——. "The Saga Diary." Tr. Terasaki Etusuko. *Literature East and West,* 15, 4 (December 1971) and 16, 1, 2 (March and June 1972).
Santōka. Abrahms, James, "Hail in the Begging Bowl: The Odyssey and Poetry of Santōka." *Monumenta Nipponica,* 32, 3 (autumn 1977), pp. 270–302.
Yosa Buson. Sawa Yuki and Shiffert, Edith M. *Haiku Master Buson.* San Francisco: Heian International, 1978.

G. POETRY AFTER 1900

Hagiwara Sakutarō. *Face at the Bottom of the World and Other Poems.* Tr. Graeme Wilson. Tokyo and Rutland: Tuttle, 1969.

——. *Howling at the Moon: Poems of Hagiwara Sakutarō.* Tr. Hiroaki Sato. Tokyo: University of Tokyo Press, 1978.

Ishikawa Takuboku. *Poems to Eat.* Tr. Carl Sesar. Tokyo and Palo Alto: Kodansha International, 1966.

——. *Sad Toys.* Tr. Sanford Goldstein and Seishi Shinoda. West Lafayette: Purdue University Press, 1977.

Kusano Shimpei. *Frogs and Others.* Tr. Cid Corman and Kamaike Susumu. Tokyo: Mushinsha/Grossman, 1969.

Miyazawa Kenji. Poems translated by Gary Snyder in his collection *The Back Country.* New York: New Directions, 1968.

——. *Spring & Asura.* Tr. Hiroaki Sato. Chicago: Chicago Review Press, 1973.

Nakatsuka Ippekirō. *Cape Jasmine and Pomegranates.* Tr. Soichi Furuta. New York: Mushinsha/Grossman, 1974.

Ozaki Hōsai. " 'Free Verse Haiku' from *Big Sky.*" Tr. Hiroaki Sato. *Partisan Review,* 1979/1, pp. 92–101.

Shiraishi Kazuko. *Seasons of Sacred Lust.* Ed. Kenneth Rexroth. New York: New Directions, 1978.

Takahashi Mutsuo. *Poems of a Penisist.* Tr. Hiroaki Sato. Chicago: Chicago Review Press, 1975.

Takahashi Shinkichi. *Afterimages: Zen Poems.* Tr. Lucien Stryk and Takashi Ikemoto. Garden City, N.Y.: Doubleday, 1972.

Takamura Kōtarō. *Chieko and Other Poems.* Tr. Hiroaki Sato. Honolulu: University Press of Hawaii, 1980.

——. *Chieko's Sky.* Tr. Furuta Soichi. Tokyo and New York: Kodansha International, 1978.

Tanikawa Shuntarō. *Shuntarō Tanikawa.* Tr. William I. Elliott and Kazuo Kawamura. Portland: Prescot Street Press, 1979.

——. *With Silence My Companion.* Tr. William I. Elliott and Kazuo Kawamura. Portland: Prescot Street Press, 1975.

Tomioka Taeko. *See You Soon.* Tr. Hiroaki Sato. Chicago: Chicago Review Press, 1979.

Yosano Akiko. *Tangled Hair: Tanka from "Midaregami."* Tr. Sanford Goldstein and Shinoda Seishi. Lafayette: Purdue University Studies, 1971.

Yoshioka Minoru. *Lilac Garden.* Tr. Hiroaki Sato. Chicago: Chicago Review Press, 1976.

INDEX OF POETS

(Limited to those who appear in the Table of Contents)